PSYCHODRAMA

PSYCHODRAMA

Theory and Therapy

Edited by

Ira A. Greenberg

Camarillo State Hospital
and
California School of Professional Psychology
at Los Angeles

Behavioral Publications
New York
1974

Library of Congress Catalog Number 73-20227
ISBN: 0-87705-110-0
Copyright ©1974 by Behavioral Publications

BEHAVIORAL PUBLICATIONS
72 Fifth Avenue
New York, New York 10011

Printed in the United States of America
456789 987654321

Library of Congress Cataloging in Publication Data

Greenberg, Ira A   1924-
  Psychodrama: theory and therapy.

  1. Psychodrama. I. Title. [DNLM: 1. Psychodrama.
WH430 G798pa 1974]
RC489.P7G72   616.8'915   73-20227

This book is dedicated to the memory of the late F. Theodore Perkins, Ph.D., Professor of Psychology at Claremont Graduate School and an inspiration to his students.

CONTENTS

About the Contributors*

WALT ANDERSON, Ph.D., is a political scientist and social psychologist who lives in Berkeley, Ca., and leads psychodrama and encounter groups; his books are *The Age of Protest, Campaigns: Cases in Political Conflict, Politics and Environment, Politics and the New Humanism,* and (with Joe Allman)*Evaluating Democracy: an Introduction to Political Science.*

MAX ACKERMAN, D.O., is a psychiatrist in New York City and an inspector for residency programs for the American Osteopathic Association.

SYLVIA ACKERMAN, M.A., is executive director for the Central Queens (N.Y.) Psychotherapy Center.

SIMONE BLAJAN-MARCUS, M.D., is a psychiatrist in Paris.

THOMAS EDWARD BRATTER, Ed. M., is director of treatment, City Island Methadone Clinic, Bronx, N.Y.

ANNA BRIND, Ph. D., deceased, was a psychologist in Los Angeles.

NAM BRIND, Ph.D., practices psychology in Los Angeles.

IRENE E. CLEPPER is a free-lance writer in Minneapolis.

RAYMOND J. CORSINI, Ph.D., a diplomate in clinical psychology, is in private practice in Honolulu; his books

*The Editor was unable to obtain recent information on Sam Osherson of Harvard University, Robert J. Simon of New York University, and Lawrence A. Wolfe of California State University at Northridge.

include *Methods of Group Psychotherapy* and *Role Playing in Psychotherapy.*

JAMES M. ENNEIS, M.A., is both a psychologist and social worker and heads the psychodrama training and treatment program at St. Elizabeth's Hospital, Washington, D.C.; he also does community, police, and management consulting as a psychodramatist and sociometrist.

DOUGLAS GOSNELL, M.A., is a New York sociologist.

IRA A. GREENBERG, Ph.D., founder and executive director of the Psychodrama Center for Los Angeles, Inc., is author of *Psychodrama and Audience Attitude Chance,* and is on the staff of Camarillo State Hospital and on the faculty of the California School of Professional Psychology (Los Angeles campus).

MARTIN R. HASKELL, Ll.B., Ph.D., is founder and head of the California Institute of Socioanalysis in Long Beach and is a sociology professor at California State University at Long Beach; his books are *An Introduction to Socioanalysis, Psychodramatic Method,* and (with Lewis Yablonsky) *Crime and Delinquency* and *Criminology: Crime and Criminology.*

The Rev. PAUL E. JOHNSON, Ph.D., is a retired professor of pastoral counseling at Boston University who now lives in Centerville, Mass.

ALEXANDER KING, deceased, was a prominent New York City author.

JOHN KOBLER is a free-lance writer in New York City and the author of several books and numerous articles for national magazines.

JOSEPH MEIERS, M.D., is a psychiatrist in private practice in New York City.

ADOLF MEYER, M.D., deceased, was professor of psychiatry at Johns Hopkins University.

J. L. MORENO, M.D., is the creator of psychodrama, group psychotherapy, and sociometry.

ZERKA T. MORENO is director of training, World Center for Psychodrama Group Psychotherapy, and Sociometry, Beacon, N.Y.

GARDNER MURPHY, Ph.D., is the dean of American psychologists, author of numerous books on psychology, and is now, after distinguished careers at Columbia University and the Menninger Foundation, a professor at George Washington University.

HERBERT A. OTTO, Ph.D., is chairman of the National Center for the Exploration of Human Potential, San Diego, and author of numerous books and articles on humanistic psychology.

JAMES M. SACKS, Ph.D., a diplomate in clinical psychology, is in private practice and is a director at the Moreno Institute in New York City; he is also co-editor (with Valerie J. Greer, M.A.) of *Bibliography of Psychodrama.*

LEONARD K. SUPPLE, M.D., deceased, had practiced psychiatry in New York City.

EDGAR C. TRAUTMAN, M.D., is a psychiatrist in New York City.

HANNAH B. WEINER, M.A., sociologist and psychodramatist, is director of the Center for Experiential Learning, New York City, and psychodrama director of the South Oaks Hospital, Long Island, N.Y.

PETER WOLSON, Ph.D., is a clinical psychologist at St. John's Hospital in Santa Monica and in private practice.

LEWIS YABLONSKY, Ph.D., is a sociology professor at California State University at Northridge and is author of *The Violent Gang. Synanon: the Tunnel Back, The Hippie Trip, Robopaths,* and (with Martin R. Haskell) *Crime and Delinquency* and *Criminology: Crime and Criminology.*

1. MORENO
Psychodrama and the Group Process

Ira A. Greenberg

J.L. Moreno, the father of psychodrama, sociometry, and modern group psychotherapy,* is neither a neo-Freudian nor a behaviorist, but rather a psychological explorer whose postulates and the system he has derived from them place him somewhere between the two orientations. Unlike social inter-actionists as Adler and Sullivan, Moreno's is a tension-reduction type psychology. His theory is based on the dynamic forces of spontaneity and creativity, as well as on the concept of psychic configurations which includes insight through perceptual restructuring.

Moreno's personality theory, like his particular extroverted personality, is action-oriented. Pragmatic in its approach, its purpose is aimed more toward bringing about changes that would affect cures and solve problems, rather than breaching the boundaries of behavioral knowledge. Thus, as is the case with most theories derived from therapy, Moreno's is the end-product of his early psychiatric training, his clinical experience,

* In 1908, at the age of 16, Moreno published two papers, "Homo Juvenis" and "Das Kinderreich," on group activity with children in Vienna, two years after Joseph H. Pratt of Boston published a report on his group work treating consumptives (8, p. 265 and p. 282), but it was Moreno who, according to William Alanson White, coined the term, "group psychotherapy." (8, p. 19.)

and the genius of the unique insights that he brought to bear on the situations confronting him.

The key concepts upon which Moreno's theory of personality (and psychotherapy) is based are (1) *spontaneity and creativity*, (2) *situation*, (3) *tele*, (4) *catharsis*, and (5) *insight*. All of these are inter-related in such a manner that when properly focused in an individual or group therapeutic endeavor, a change invariably takes place through expression of suppressed or repressed material, through understanding of past problems, and through re-education for future behavior. Stated simply, "spontaneity . . . refers to the creative, uninhibited action that occurs on the stage (in a psychodramatic or sociodramatic session); tele refers to the interaction between two or more persons in a manner that transcends the Freudian concept of *transference*, and catharsis may be thought [of] in the Aristotelian sense of an emotional purgation, except that not only the audience (or other participants) but also the actor (or patient) experiences it" (5, p. 105). Situation, or *in situ*, refers to the event itself in the " *hic et nunc*" or the "here and now," (10, p. XII) meaning that no matter when or where an actual dream or fantasy involvement occurred, under Moreno's direction it would be an event dealt with in the "here and now" of the therapy session. Insight occurs as the result of the successful restructuring of the perceptual field to form a new gestalt.

Moreno, who legend has it was born in 1892 on a boat in the Black Sea (15, p. 7) and who was reared in Vienna, first discovered the "acting out" technique that is basic to his therapy in 1908. He developed this by having the children who played in the parks of his city enact their fantasies and by observing the creativity and catharsis this brought about. Five years after receiving his M.D. degree in 1917 from the University of Vienna, he founded the Theater of Spontaneity in that city and developed his psychodramatic techniques. Three years later, in 1925, he came to the United States, and here he perfected his theory of psychodrama and developed many of the techniques of psychodrama. At the same time, in the late 1920's and early 1930's, he formulated his theories of sociometry and group interaction therapy (including sociodrama) by working with public school children, reformatory school girls, and inmates at Sing Sing Prison in New York. An important result of this work was Moreno's development of the sociogram. Today this tool is widely used for determining the relationships of individuals in groups. In 1934, he published his famous sociometric study, *Who Shall Survive?*, and two years later he established the Moreno Sanitarium in Beacon, N.Y. In that same year, at Beacon, he built the nation's first psychodramatic stage. It was, and is today, a three-level series of concentric platforms, above which is a balcony (useful in fantasy depictions), in an 85-seat theater. The theater contains a multicolored lighting panel which is employed to help set the mood of the various therapeutic enactments taking place.

Moreno's theory of personality, which in its application to groups is as much sociological as psychological, will be presented in the theoretical and operational context of psychodrama, since this seems to be the most feasible means of reviewing in brief the results of his wideranging interests.

PERSONALITY THEORY THROUGH PSYCHODRAMA

Basically, psychodrama is nothing more than a grand extension of the clinical interview. The main difference between them is that instead of the patient being in a one-to-one relationship with the psychotherapist, he finds himself removed from the privacy of the consulting room and placed in a position where he is given opportunity to act out and thus experience various aspects of his problems in a larger-than-life dimension. In this process, the patient becomes the *protagonist* of the drama that he creates and may, while under the direction of the psychotherapist (the "producer" of this private drama), interact with other "actors." These "actors" play the roles of the "important others:" people who in normal life make up the environment of the patient's own world and are a part of the particular problem he brings to the therapy session. There may or may not be an audience (usually, other patients), but if there is, both patient and audience are expected to interact with each other and benefit therapeutically from the interaction.

So far as theory and techniques are concerned, psychodrama and sociodrama have much in common. The principal difference between them is not so much one of degree as of purpose. The goal of psychodrama is the accomplishment of individual therapy or problem solving for each person participating in the session, whether he is the patient-protagonist, the actor who serves as auxiliary ego by portraying a person important to the patient on the stage, or an individual in the audience. Each in his own way not only helps the patient work through the problem of the particular situation being enacted, but also through either active or passive participation is able to experience catharsis and insight by sharing and experiencing various aspects of the problem that may have bearings on his own problems.

Sociodrama, on the other hand, does not deal with the personal problems of the individuals concerned but instead with societal problems. These problems of society might involve racial or religious prejudice as seen by the individual sociodrama participants, or they might involve roles and functions, such as attitudes toward a policeman in the performance of his duty, toward a candidate for political office, or toward occupational groups such as lawyers, plumbers, ministers, or taxicab drivers, or population groups such as children, elderly people or women drivers. Thus, unlike psychodrama where the situation acted out concerns the patient-protagonist and specific real or imaginary people, sociodrama concerns itself with the individual's (patient-protagonist's) attitude toward symbolic or stereotyped representatives of groups that bring forth emotion-laden reactions from him.

In both psychodrama and sociodrama, role-playing and acting out are important to the patient, but in the former the protagonist reacts to the persons in the roles of individuals who are meaningful to him, while in the latter, he reacts to persons in roles of group symbols or stereotypes. In each case there must be a "working out" that brings about emotional catharsis through the action and some insight brought about by the action, the emotion, and the group discussion or sharing afterward. In the employment of psychodrama as the simplest approach to Moreno's system of psychology, fairly detailed definitions of his concepts will be presented, after which the operational aspects involved in psychodramatic psychotherapy will be defined, and from these elements the general theory should be expected to reveal itself as a unified system.

Spontaneity

Moreno defines spontaneity as the response a person makes that contains "some degree of adequacy to a new situation or a degree of novelty to an old situation." (10, p. XII). The amount of spontaneity displayed in various situations is useful in the assessment of a person's state of mental health, social competence, or situational involvement. The spontaneity-level of an individual may be raised either through psychodramatic therapy or through a sociodramatic type of education. Definite techniques of spontaneity training and spontaneity testing have been developed by Moreno and his associates (10, pp. 122-145). Spontaneity training, paradoxical though it may seem, has two purposes, namely, to help the individual to "liberate himself from the script," and "from the cliches of part stereotyped /or stimulus-response/ behavior and to help him gain new personality dimensions through his ability to perceive and respond to new situations " (10, p. 101.).

As seen from Moreno's cosmic point of view, spontaneity training is the means for man making the great leap into the future. "It is almost as if by means of spontaneity training Moreno sees an evolutionary avenue toward man's surpassing the heights of the Nietzschean Zarathustra, becoming a new kind of being, one who is free from his anxieties, unconstrained in his thinking, uninhibited in his actions—in short, a spontaneous being within a society of spontaneous beings, one who is in complete control of himself and his environment" (5, p. 109).

Moreno concludes his much acclaimed work, *Who Shall Survive?* by noting man's historic failure to live at peace with himself and others in a well integrated society and wonders if this failure does not carry within itself the question of "not only the survival or passing of the present form of human society but the destiny of man." He thereupon states that "man has a resource which is inherent in his own organism and in the organization of human society which he has never used beyond the rudimentary stage—his spontaneability " (14, p. 367.). Thus, as Moreno saw it as far back as 1934 when these words were published, man's survival is not to be found in bomb shelters or by his breaking out of his earthbound existence through space-age explorations, but rather by his breaking out of his own rigid personality molds, and by breaking the chains that constrict his psyche. This he can accomplish through spontaneity.

Situation

Man can develop his spontaneity most effectively in the psychodramatic *situation* (or in situations employing psychodramatic techniques, such as in spontaneity training), where the natural barriers of time, space, and states of existence are obliterated so that everything on the psychodramatic stage occurs in the present or *in situ,* in the "here and the now." There is no past or future in the psychodramatic situation, and geographical distance has no meaning. All occurs in the patient's present: past problems or future fears are brought to life in the "here and now" of the psychodramatic confrontation. The patient works out his problems by relating to "actors" who play the roles of absent people involved in his problems and fears. Whether or not these absent people are alive or dead—or not yet born—they can be easily incorporated in the psychodramatic situation. (If an "important other," such as a spouse or parent is present, this person may [often toward the end of the session] portray himself on the stage in order to help work out the patient's problem or help to solve the mutual difficulty; otherwise, this spouse or parent may remain in the audience and observe an "actor *[auxiliary ego]* portraying his role.) Just as distance can be obliterated on the psychodramatic stage (as on the ordinary theatrical stage), so also are the barriers of death done away with. Where the director feels it is necessary, the deceased may also be brought back into the "here and now" by being portrayed by auxiliary egos. This enables the patient to resolve a problem he was incapable of handling while the person was alive. Thus, it is the *situation* and the psychodramatic confrontation in the "here and the now" that is essential to the therapy, and to the development of its ultimate goal of spontaneity in reality.

Tele

Tele takes place as a part of the spontaneity-involvement of two or more people in a psychodramatic situation, and it is derived from the Greek word for "far" or "influence into distance" (10, p. XI). Moreno calls it a "feeling of individuals into one another, the cement which holds groups together," *[Ibid.]* and, referring to a definition he gave for *tele* more than forty years ago, calls it "therapeutic love" (11, p. 7). Thus, tele is:

> A meeting of two: eye to eye, face to face. And when you are near I will tear your eyes out and place them instead of mine, and you will tear my eyes out and will place them instead of yours, and then I will look at you with your eyes and you will look at me with mine.

In other words, tele is a "mutual exchange of empathy and appreciation," (5, p. 110) which, though essential to the psychotherapeutic situation, may at its best be considered a part of all human relationships, whether between husband and wife, parent and son, employer and employee, and among groups of more than two friends, though it is strongest when only two persons are involved in the telic communication.

Catharsis

Catharsis and *insight* are the end-products of the inter-relationship of *spontaneity* and *tele* that take place in the situation, and are the achievements of the patient-protagonist, the auxiliary egos, and the audience members following the successful conclusion of a psychodramatic session. Moreno employs the term *catharsis* in the Aristotelean sense of an emotional purging, but Moreno adds that "there is an element common to all sources which operates in the production of catharsis /and that/ I discovered the common principle producing catharsis in spontaneity, spontaneous dramatic action." (10, p. 18).

Insight

Insight may occur simultaneously with catharsis or following the experience of catharsis (which occurs at the end of an enactment) when the actors and the audience discuss what occurred on the psychodramatic stage and the audience members share some of their own problems as they may relate to those presented by the protagonist. This insight that Moreno deals with may be thought of in terms of sudden perceptions, such as the comic exclamation, "Eureka! I've got it!" that cartoon characters exclaim.

Psychologically speaking, insight is the result of perceptual or configurational learning that brings about an immediate solution to a problem. For example, when an ape uses a stick as an extension of his arm in order to reach a basket of fruit outside his cage (as in the famous Kohler experiments), the sudden solution to the problem when it occurs for the first time is an example of insight gained through changing two discrete fields of perception (the basket of fruit and the stick) into one perceptual field that encompasses both.

Thus it is also with psychodramatic insight. "The sensory stimulations of the psychodramas, together with the emotional catharsis brought on by spontaneity and tele can and do, according to Moreno, cause a restructuring of the protagonist's perceptual field (whether he is on the stage or in the audience) and bring insight or understanding to his problems by means of configurational learning" (6, p. 95).

OPERATIONAL ASPECTS OF PSYCHODRAMA

Terms and Techniques

Director

The psychodramatic *director* is the *chief therapist*, the *producer* of the psychodramatic event, and the *social analyst* at one and the same time. The first two identifications are self-explanatory, while as a social analyst he uses the "auxiliary egos as extensions of himself to draw information from the subjects on the stage, to test them, and to carry influence to them." (10, p. 252.) Besides having the training, skill, and sensitivity of all good therapists, the director "must be able to function effectively in a highly volatile state, and yet keep control at all times," (5, p. 113.) or, at least, be "on top of the situation at all times." The good psychodramatic director must, like Moreno himself, have certain charismatic qualities that enable him to *warm* up both the actors and the audience in order "to open up channels of communication among the entire group of participants to bring forth a sense of emotional excitement and intellectual interest, and to determine the purpose or goals of the group." (5, p. 114). The director may accomplish the *warm up* in many ways. He may start a general discussion at the beginning of the session; he may "fish" for topics by using a free association method in the group; he may designate specifically that a certain problem be dealt with; or he may determine what is happening in the participants' lives and how they feel at the moment. By questioning an individual beforehand, often in the presence of the audience, the director accomplishes Moreno's concept of the psychiatric interview in psychodrama as a part of the warm up process. The warm up is then followed by the director having the patient-protagonist set the scene and select the auxiliary egos who will take part in it with him and then begins the enactment. The director is responsible throughout the session for everything that takes place on the stage, and may call for such manipulations as bring about an increase or decrease of emotional involvement by the actors, changing the scenes as new insights are gained, and protecting the protagonist by seeing to it that he does not generate more emotion than he is able to deal with at the time. Also, the director must keep himself aware of the audience mood in order that it too may benefit from the stage action. Finally, at the conclusion of the stage event, the director must be able to effectively lead the subsequent group discussion and sharing so that a maximum of insight is gained by all. Thus, the therapist-director must be an outgoing person who possesses keen insight, quick imagination, warm sensitivity, and abundant energy. In other words, he must have a high degree of spontaneity.

Protagonist

The *protagonist* or patient in a psychodramatic production has as his purpose "not to act in the theatrical sense but simply to portray scenes and incidents from his own private world, which for each person is a unique world." (5, pp. 115-116.) The protagonist, brought to a state of spontaneity through the warm up and aided by the auxiliary egos, usually is ready to give free experession to his emotions as the scene gets under way and he begins to interact with the auxiliary egos. He is also aided by special techniques, among them are (as presented in the book, *Psychodrama and Audience Attitude Change*) *role reversal, the soliloquy, double, mirror, behind-the-back, high chair, empty chair, magic shop,* and the *"ideal other."*

Role reversal is one of the most effective techniques for generating the *tele* phenomenon on the psychodramatic stage. Here, "the patient-protagonist and one of the auxiliary egos (an actor-therapist helping the patient create his world on the stage) play each other's role; thus, the auxiliary ego acts in the role of the patient and the patient assumes the role portrayed by the auxiliary ego. In this way the patient is not only involved in a telic relationship with the auxiliary ego, in which he sees himself through the other's eyes, but he also is enabled to experience himself from the point of view of the person represented by the auxiliary ego (i.e., the patient's parent, spouse, employer, or any "important other "). (6, p. 90.)

In soliloquy, the patient-protagonist is enabled to work his way through emotional difficulties and states of high tension by airing his innermost feelings and thoughts, either in staccato-like outbursts of anger or disgust (similar to the theatrical "aside"), or in more lengthy verbalizations, somewhat like the famous Hamlet soliloquy, except that for the patient it would be a spontaneous expression, rather than the declamation of a memorized speech (*cultural conserve*). The technique of the *double* is a useful supportive device and is called for when the director sees that the patient is having a difficult time "holding his own" against other actors, whether they are assistant therapists or persons who are actually involved with the patient, such as a spouse, a parent, or a friend. The director simply designates another person (auxiliary ego), or several other people, to stand with or behind the patient and to act with him so that there are two individuals (or more) having the same identity, the identity of the patient. The double, who will seek to express the same body movements as the patient, may remain silent or speak out, in the role of the patient, on the basis of the double's perception of what the psychodramatic situation seems to call for. He will help the patient question his own thoughts by the double's speaking what he perceives or "feels" are the patient's thoughts, and in general will help the patient try to deal effectively with whatever occurs on the stage.

The *mirror* technique, like role reversal, is used to help the patient gain an understanding of how others see and tend to react to him. When the director feels this technique is required, the patient stands aside or seats himself in the audience and observes an auxiliary ego assume his role and interact with other auxiliary egos in a psychodramatic enactment of how they see his situation or behavior. Thus, the patient is able to see something of himself from a new point of view, from the point of view of how others may see him or how others see him as seeing himself. This is in an entirely different light, as mirrored by another, and has been found effective with regressed or withdrawn patients. In the *behind-the-back* technique, the patient sits on a chair on the stage with his back to the audience, and the director leads the audience in a discussion about the patient, giving the patient an opportunity to in this way gain knowledge about how others see him.

Like that of the double, the *high chair* and the *empty chair* techniques are useful as means of providing the patient with additional support, should he or his situation so require it. To employ the high chair technique, either an ordinary chair is placed on a box, so that when the patient sits on it he is higher than anyone else seated, or the patient stands on an ordinary chair, so that he is standing taller than anybody else on stage. This is very useful in providing the patient-protagonist with the power or feeling of power he might need in order to deal effectively with enemies or other persons who are important in his life but who tend to overwhelm him in the world of reality. The experience of the high chair may help the patient cope more effectively with some of the world's threats to him. In the *empty chair* technique, the patient acts out problems by imagining his antagonist seated in an empty chair on the stage, and the patient interacts with this "phantom" being, even to the extent of reversing roles with the phantom in the empty chair, and, in the phantom role, interacts with the imaginary other person in the role of the patient (himself). In other words, the patient, from the position of the absent person and in the role of the one who is absent, interacts with a phantom person assumed to have taken on the patient's identity after the patient and the absent or phantom being have reversed roles. This technique has been adopted by the gestalt therapists, many of whom are unaware that it was invented by Moreno and then utilized by Perls.

The use of the "*ideal other*" is helpful in reducing the

patient's tension at the close of a psychodramatic presentation, as well as in enabling him to experience a much desired relationship that might not otherwise be possible in real life. The "other," as employed here, refers to a spouse, parent, or friend, while the ideal "other" is this person portrayed by an auxiliary ego who in the enactment becomes the ideal type of person the patient might wish that this "other" was in real life. This has often been described as a very rewarding experience by those who have undergone it.*

Another means of experiencing a fantasy in psychodrama is through the technique of the *magic shop*, which is helpful in providing a person with some insights into what his real goals and desires in life are. In this situation, the person is confronted by the "proprietor" of the magic shop, who is often an auxiliary ego, but who can be portrayed by the director, just as some other roles might be enacted by the director, who thereby serves for short periods of time in a dual capacity. In this confrontation, the proprietor offers the patient anything in the world he might want, such as wealth, success, happiness, or genius-level intelligence. At the same time, however, the proprietor demands as payment something that the person may also value, such as health, love, or honor. This places the person in a dilemma and usually brings about much immediate introspection on the part of the person as to what it is he really wants out of life. The result of this confrontation is an acceptance or rejection of the "bargain" or, as occurs in many cases, the inability of the "customer" to make up his mind. Whatever the person's decision, the result invariably is that he has learned something new about himself.

*The author can confirm this on the basis of his personal experience, which, while of short duration, proved to be one of the most rewarding of his life. It took place in a psychodrama directed by Mrs. Zerka T. Moreno during August 1964, while the author was a student at the Morenos' World Academy of Psychodrama and Group Psychotherapy at Beacon, New York. (See "The Growth of a Psychodramatist," by Zerka T. Moreno, in 6, pp. XXVII-XXXI.)

Auxiliary Ego

Auxiliary egos are "actors who represent absentee persons as they appear in the private world of the patient," according.to Moreno, (10, p. XVII), with auxiliary egos functioning in dual capacities in that they are simultaneously an extension of the director in his interactions with the patient, as well as an extension of the patient in that they help portray the patient's inner attitudes toward the "important others" in his life. The patient usually selects those who will be the auxiliary egos in his enactment, and these individuals may be other patients, trained therapists, or audience members (though often the other patients are the audience members). Though the patient generally selects an auxiliary ego who resembles a particular person in his life, the actual physical resemblance in many instances is not important, nor is it necessary for the age or sex of the auxiliary ego to correspond with that of the person who is to be portrayed. For example, a patient who throughout his life has been overwhelmed by his mother might select a hulking man to play the part of his mother, though in actuality the mother might be of very small stature; the important thing in this instance is that the patient had always perceived his mother as a giant and so must have a large person to represent her. The auxiliary ego must involve himself in the stage situation as deeply as he is able, but at the same time "he must be alert to adapt his behavior in accordance with the verbal and body signals he receives from the director, as well as to a variety of cues he picks up from the protagonist." (5, p. 118.)

Audience

The responsibility of the *audience* is twofold: "It serves the protagonist when it reacts critically or supportively to what is occuring on the stage, and it serves itself through experiencing what is taking place on the stage and thereby gaining insight into its own motivations and conflicts, both as a collective whole and in its individual parts." (5, p. 119.) When the stage action is concluded, the audience members are in a position to help the protagonist gain insight into his problem, not by analyzing the protagonist in the manner of the stereotyped psychologist diagnosing a case but by sharing incidents from their own experiences that may in part resemble those of the protagonist. By doing this they are aiding the protagonist in another way, through providing him with the support of knowing that he is not alone with his problems, that others have like problems, and because of this mutuality are able to empathize with him and understand his situation.

CONCLUSION

Moreno's theory of personality, particularly as seen through the medium of psychodrama, appears at first glance little more than an action-technique that is effective in bringing about a positive change in individual and group behavior. Critics might assume that Moreno's approach to personality is more technique than theory, but they would be guilty of underestimating the importance of his findings, specifically as regards his concept of spontaneity. It is around this concept that his system is built and it is in this concept that it finds its strength.

REFERENCES

1. Anastasi, Anne. *Psychological Testing.* New York: The Macmillan Company, 1961.
2. Bischof, Ledford J. *Interpreting Personality Theories.* New York: Harper & Row, Publishers, 1964.
3. Bromberg, Walter. *The Mind of Man: A History of Psychotherapy and Psychoanalysis.* New York: Harper Colophon Books. 1963.

4. Enneis, James M. "The Dynamics of Group Action Process," in *Group Psychotherapy*. 1951. 4:17-22.

5. Greenberg, Ira A. "Audience in Action Through Psychodrama," *Group Psychotherapy*. June-September, 1964. Vol XVII, No. 2-3:104-122.

6. —————. *Psychodrama and Audience Attitude Change* Beverly Hills, Calif.: Behavioral Studies Press, 1968.

7. Hass, Robert Bartlett, and Moreno, J.L. "Psychodrama as a Projective Technique," Chapter 23 in Anderson, Harold H., and Anderson, Gladys L. *An Introduction to Projective Techniques*. Englewood Cliffs, N.J.: Prentice-Hall, Inc. 1961.

8. Johnson, V. Abstract of "The Function of an Audience Analyst" in Psychodrama, by Gerard Schauer. *Psychological Abstracts*. Vol. 26. Lancaster, Pa.: American Psychological Association. 1952. No. 7040.

9. Klapman, J.W. *Group Psychotherapy: Theory and Practice*. New York: Grune & Stratton. 1959.

10. Moreno, J.L. (Ed.) *Group Psychotherapy: A Symposium*. Beacon, N.Y.: Beacon House, 1945.

11. —————. *Psychodrama, Vo. I (Revised.)*, Beacon, N.Y.: Beacon House, Inc. 1964.

12. —————. *Psychodrama Vol. II*. Beacon, N.Y.: Beacon House, Inc. 1959.

13. —————. "Psychodrama and Group Psychotherapy." A paper read at the American Psychiatric Association meeting, May 30, 1946, Chicago.

14. —————. (Ed.) *Sociometry and the Science of Man*. Beacon, N.Y.: Beacon House. 1956.

15. —————. *Who Shall Survive?* Washington, D.C.: Nervous and Mental Publishing Co. 1934.

16. —————, Moreno, Zerka, T., and Moreno, Jonothan. The *First Psychodramatic Family*. Beacon, N.Y.: Beacon House, Inc. 1964.

17. Torrance, E. Paul. "Psychodramatic Methods in the College." Chapter 22 in *Psychodrama and Sociodrama in American Education*. (Ed.) Hass, Robert Bartlett. Beacon, N.Y.: Beacon House, Inc. 1949.

18. Vogeler, E. J., Jr., and Greenberg, Ira. A., "Psychodrama and Audience with Emphasis on Closed-Circuit Television," *Group Psychotherapy*, 1968. Vol. XXI, No. 1:4-11.
19. Walker, Nigel. *A Short History of Psychotherapy in Theory and Practice.* New York: The Noonday Press. 1960.

2. A MINNEAPOLIS CHURCH BRINGS PROBLEMS INTO FOCUS THROUGH THE THEATRE OF PSYCHODRAMA

Irene E. Clepper

"And if I don't get my job back, this town will burn!" Are those familiar words?

Yes, but not so familiar coming from a WASP (White-Anglo-Saxon-Protestant)... and shouted at a Negro.

Yet this strange scene took place on a Sunday afternoon in the Wesley Methodist Church Theatre of Psychodrama in Minneapolis Minn.

Called a "sociodrama," the impromptu performance was titled "Rioting in American Cities," and it included in the cast of characters anyone in the audience of more than 100 who wanted to join.

Negroes alternately portrayed Negro and white roles, and whites found themselves in equally unfamiliar situations—prejudiced, nonprojudiced and defending their right to hold a job, occupy an apartment or gain an education.

The Theatre of Psychodrama was started in the fall of 1966 when Wesley's minister, the Rev. John B. Oman, felt that it would serve as a valuable adjunct to the church's program of

Reprinted with the permission of the publishers from *Methodist Story* (June, 1968), pp. 34-35.

group counseling. He explains that there are troubled people who find great difficulty in stating their problems.

There are also many people who cannot see their problems clearly because—naturally enough—they are so involved in them as participants.

The answer to the question of how to present the problem and how to gain an objective view of it, is psychodrama. It is, simply, presenting the problem as a play.

The troubled person may play himself, his own son or wife or foreman. On the other hand, he might simply watch while others play the parts in his own life drama.

Dr. Oman sums up the psychodrama technique in terms of the biblical exhortation to "sit where they sit."

Psychodrama came into being in Vienna in the '20s when Jacob L. Moreno, a psychotherapist, found that actors could solve some of their problems after they had "acted them out."

Dr. Oman has used the technique in some of his classes at the University of Minnesota. By setting up actual job situations, he finds that the students learn thoroughly and unforgettably how to cope with some of the problems they will have after graduation. They play themselves, as they will be professionally. Then they may take the part of a typical customer, client or other person whom they would be likely to encounter.

The Theatre of Psychodrama is simply arranged. In one large room the stage is raised to about chair-seat level and carpeted. A lounge and several chairs constitute the only scenery. It is ringed by folding chairs and audiences of more than 100— capacity for the room—have been crowding into the theater every first and third Sunday, from 5 to 6:30 p.m.

Some of the "plays" presented have included themes of juvenile delinquency, marital difficulties, family feuds and hypochondria. The director of the play (and these vary) begins by asking the troubled person to describe a typical situation involving the problem.

Mary W. may begin by saying that she is unable to control

her teen-age daughter. "Only last night she simply left the house. Didn't tell me where she was going or when she would be back. . . ."

"Let's act it out," the director will suggest and will ask for a volunteer to enact the daughter's role. "Who else was there?" he inquires and fills in, with other volunteers, the role of father and grandmother and younger brother. As the play progresses, the troubled mother finds herself playing the part of her own daughter, then the father in the scene.

At one point, the mother is assigned a "double"—this is a person who stands or sits beside her during the enactment and speaks "what isn't spoken." This includes what the mother may be thinking or speculation on what others are thinking. It may be questions, in the form of possible solutions to the problem.

The charisma of psychodrama is that each participant truly becomes for that time the person whose role he plays. Two strangers playing roles as half-brothers, arguing over where their mother should be buried, became so involved that they were actually shouting furiously at each other. At this point, "role reversal" was instituted, and they had to take up the argument from the opposite point of view.

The August session on race riots was the first "sociodrama" which the theater had tried. Picking an explosive theme almost guaranteed complete audience involvement with the roles.

The afternoon's director, Charles Brin, asked the audience for any experiences concerning the matter of race relations, minority repression or riot incitement.

A young white man, who had had a summer job at a local manufacturing plant, reported a rumor he had heard that "they" were going to stage a riot at the plant. Asked to be more explicit, he said that he had heard, quite reliably, that if layoffs of Negroes took place, a Negro organization would put on a demonstration.

A Negro present jumped to his feet and said that he had firsthand information that the jobs were only 90-day jobs, given to help ease the city through last summer's riot threat. Asked if he felt that city officials had not acted in good faith in offering the jobs, he responded that they had not. Negroes apparently were submitted to stringent tests—physical and mental—for jobs which did not require particularly high standards and were disqualified in a number of places after the 90-day period.

The white boy was given the role of a young Negro. The Negro portrayed the role of a city official. From merely reporting a rumor, the white youth actually became a Negro fighting for his job. The bureaucratic double talk from the white official (Negro) infuriated him to the point where he was shouting threats of burning the town down.

A Negro mother in the audience volunteered to join in an enactment of what a Negro goes through trying to rent and occupy an apartment in a white neighborhood. She makes the first approach by telephone and is welcomed by the white real estate agent. In person, she is subjected to cliche evasions.

The mother appears at a second interview, accompanied by her attorney, and succeeds in renting the apartment. Other enactments involve meeting the new neighbors—among the group is a policeman (rankling from charges of "police brutality") and his wife, and a man from the deep South and his wife (he's sure that the "Negro" family will be more comfortable "among yoah own kahnd").

Roles are reversed frequently, and there are "doubles" to muse "why are they being so sweetly polite—why don't they say what they are really thinking?" "I'm uncomfortable. How can I get out of this without unpleasantness or compromising what I believe and should say?"

From the audience come queries of:

> "Sure, you'll accept the 'right kind' of Negro, but what if the wrong kind comes and, well—sits on the front porch eating watermelon?"
>
> "If a Negro woman moves into the neighborhood, should the white woman invite her over, call on her or wait for the Negro

woman to make the first overture?"

"When I got this invitation to attend a psychodrama on race riots, I wondered why I had never received an invitation to anything here before?"

There were moments of humor. The Negro mother, inspecting an apartment which is obviously in a dilapidated condition, comments, "Well, I was really interested in something a little more substantial." The agent asks what she means. She steps gingerly across the stage, "A little more substantial . . . maybe with a *floor,* you know!"

The cliches of "some of my best friends are . . ." and "I'm not prejudiced, but my neighbors . . ." brought wry laughter from both Negroes and whites.

The sociodrama ran over the allotted time and finally had to be arbitrarily ended by Dr. Oman. He made a few concluding summations and announced that the afternoon's presentation had been so successful in broadening and deepening understanding of the problems behind race riots that the next sociodrama on this question would be held at a later date in North Minneapolis, once the scene of racial troubles.

Three television stations covered the entire afternoon's proceedings, and the Minneapolis metropolitan newspaper bannered the story of the Theatre of Psychodrama across the entire eight columns of the section page.

It was felt by those who explored "Rioting in American Cities" one Sunday afternoon in August that, with sociodrama, Wesley Church has made an important step in taking religious principles into the marketplace.

3.. THE THEATER THAT HEALS MEN'S MINDS

John Kobler

Stranger dramas were never staged than those that continuously unfold in a small private theater at Beacon, New York, beside the high, green banks of the Hudson River. The actors are unrehearsed, their words and gestures spontaneous, and the plots they improvise may take months to reach a denouement. They wander about as fancy dictates on a three-level circular platform or on the balcony overhanging it. A projector floodlights them with colors symbolizing their prevailing mood—yellow for sorrow, blue for introspection, red for violence. There is no curtain, scenery or props except a table and chairs. The theater seats eighty-five, and on occasion, by invitation, specially qualified outsiders attend. Otherwise the audience is limited to the extraordinary old man who founded the theater, Dr. Jacob Levy Moreno, and his staff.

People privileged to watch Moreno's unpredictable amateurs find themselves powerfully moved in a way no professional performance moves the spectator. For the tears these actors shed, the cries they utter, arise from real anguish. They are mental patients, acting out, as a form of group therapy that Moreno invented, their own desires, hatreds, terrors. He named it psychodrama, and its object is to teach the sufferer to resolve his conflicts by reliving them in a miniature society, free of conventional restraints.

Reprinted with the permission of the publishers from *The Saturday Evening Post*, Vol. 235 (Oct. 27, 1962), pp. 70-73, and with the permission of the author.

MAJOR ADVANCE IN THERAPY

Conceived forty years ago in Vienna, where Moreno began his medical career, psychodrama remains among the most substantial advances in mental therapy since Freud introduced psychoanalysis. Although many leading psychiatrists challenge his theories, more than 100 American mental hospitals apply his method, along with other therapies, to cases ranging from alcoholism to schizophrenia.

I recently spent five days at the Moreno Institute. Sprawling over thirty hilly acres, it consists, in addition to the theater, of four buildings which can lodge thirty-nine patients and a staff of twelve. Moreno, who turned seventy last May, occupies a modest frame house with his tall, dark, Dutch-born wife Zerka, twenty-five years his junior, and their son Jonathan, aged ten. Mrs. Moreno is the institute's executive director as well as a therapist.

The doctor's personality combines the verve and flamboyance of a master showman, which indeed he is, with the roguish charm of a Viennese *bon vivant*, which he once was. Massive and broad-browed, he wears his sandy hair in the Bohemian artist's style of yesteryear, longish and curling over the ears. His blue eyes are heavy-lidded, giving him an expression at once somnolent and watchful. His language, embellished by a lilting Austrian accent, tends to be epigrammatic, poetic, paradoxical.

"My work," he observed during our first talk, "is the psychotherapy of fallen gods. We are all fallen gods. As infants we have a godlike sense of power, what I call normal megalomania. Because everybody around the infant responds to his needs, he feels at one with the whole world. Every event seems the result of his own spontaneous creation. But as society makes its demands, our once boundless horizons shrink, we feel diminished, and our frustrations can produce mental disorders. Psychodrama helps the patient recover something of his primary self, his lost godhead."

Spontaneity, he elaborated, is the essence of psychodrama. The most effective people are those who can readily adjust to new situations. Such adjustments require flexible, spontaneous reactions. The man incapable of revising his outlook when confronted by a new situation is the likeliest to develop mental illness. Thus psychodrama above all seeks to stimulate spontaneous behavior.

A patient suffering from hallucinations will at first be encouraged to enact scenes which reflect those hallucinations. Later, through interactions with other characters of the drama—patients themselves, therapists, members of his own family—he grows to realize the inadequacy of his responses and tries to substitute better ones. "If he can learn to do that on the stage," Moreno said, "he can do it outside."

He put it another way. The pathological failure yearns to play certain roles in life which his inflexibility has denied him. He may not consciously know what those roles are. Psychodrama enables him to experiment with various roles until his hidden urges and latent capacities emerge. It then becomes possible to redirect him into channels that can better accommodate his valid needs. For example:

Ralph Coplan (a fictitious name) is a manic-depressive, nineteen years old, the only child of rich parents. His father, a lawyer, has always been indifferent to him, his mother suffocatingly possessive. At college Ralph had shown brilliance as an art major until he fell prey to acute melancholia. He was committed to the institute after he attempted suicide. He had been under psychodramatic treatment for two months.

When we entered the theater, he was sitting slumped in a back-row seat beside a male nurse. He kept twisting a letter. Moreno gently touched his hand. "News from home, Ralph?"

"Make mother stop writing to me," the boy pleaded. "Make her leave me alone. I wish—"

"Show us, Ralph," Moreno broke in. "Show us what you wish."

VIOLENT EXCHANGE ON STAGE

Ralph took up a position on the lowest level of the stage and never left it. The choice, Moreno pointed out to me, typifies the withdrawn psychotic, whereas the superegos with delusions of grandeur gravitate to the balcony, high above everybody.

At a nod from her husband, Zerka Moreno mounted the stage. The doctor whispered to me, "She will function as what we turn an auxiliary ego, assuming roles according to the demands of the situation. Now she is Mrs. Coplan."

"Can I have the car today, please, mother?" Ralph began.

"No," said Mrs. Moreno. "You're staying home with me. Your father's off on another trip. I'm always left alone."

"I don't blame him. I'd do anything to get away from you."

The exchange grew violent. The projector turned the stage red. At the climax of the quarrel Moreno shouted, "Reverse roles!" whereupon Ralph portrayed his mother while Mrs. Moreno portrayed Ralph.

"You may be in college," the boy said, expressing what he believed his mother felt, "but you're still a helpless baby."

"And you're a selfish old woman!" rejoined Mrs. Moreno.

An application of the precept, "Put yourself in her place," this role reversal is a device Moreno employs to bring out and correct the patient's distorted view of others.

In the next scene, resuming his own identity, Ralph cried, "Why don't you just die and leave me alone!"

"Wait," Moreno commanded. "Your mother *is* dead. She's lying there before you." Mrs. Moreno pulled two chairs together and stretched out on them. "How do you react?"

"I'm glad. Now I'm free."

"Is that all? Try a different version. She's your mother, after all. Look, here's your father. What do you tell him?"

The male nurse stepped up on the stage. The red floodlight changed to yellow. Ralph stared at the "body." Then: "I suppose she meant well. I feel a little guilty."

"Nothing else?" said Moreno. "Come, try again."

"If she were alive—" The boy faltered. "If she were alive, I wouldn't say such terrible things to her anymore. I guess I really cared." He was weeping.

A miraculous change of heart? No. But Ralph had at least glimpsed the possibility of a maturer relationship, a more constructive role he might play in real life.

TREATMENT FOR THE FAMILY

I asked Moreno how he estimated the chances of curing Ralph. "'Cure' is a word I avoid," he replied. "Say rather a transformation of personality. In time no doubt we can restore Ralph to society, and he will function usefully. But such problems as Ralph's do not concern the patient alone. They are interpersonal, involving as well the problems of his family. For psychodrama to produce lasting effects, they, too, must undergo certain transformation. That is why, as treatment progresses, we try to bring all of them willing to cooperate into the play instead of relying entirely on auxiliary egos. We expect to have Ralph's parents here soon, acting out their domestic situation with him. Otherwise, although the patient may attain a degree of social recovery, the roots of his conflicts, being interwoven with innumerable factors outside himself, remain obscure and make it difficult to prevent relapse. Psychodrama treats not simply the individual but also the group."

I witnessed several startling instances of this interpersonal action, and in Moreno's files I read case histories that included many more. He once brought together on a stage a pathologically jealous husband, his wife and the friend he falsely imagined to be her lover. After a dozen psychodramatic encounters the husband came to understand that the "triangle" existed only in his mind. The hidden conflicts, of which his suspicions were symptomatic, could then be explored. The marriage was saved.

A paranoiac believed he was Jesus. In Moreno's theory a patient so disoriented must first be dealt with by the people around him exactly as he sees himself, must be encouraged to carry his delusion to completion and thus objectify his inner urges. Accordingly the doctor persuaded the paranoiac's relatives, twenty-seven of them all together, to help. That many people could not, with convenience, be repeatedly assembled in the theater. So the psychodrama was staged in the patient's home. Moreno and the relatives gathering there at frequent intervals. The latter played prophets, saints and apostles to the patient's Messiah. They addressed him as "Lord," listened reverently to his sermons, pretended to be healed by him. The intensely emotional scenes also exposed and helped to amend psychological flaws in the attitudes of many of the actors toward one another as well as toward the patient. The masquerade lasted two years before he had fully externalized his fantasy and could view it with some perspective. At that point, under Moreno's direction, the supporting characters began reverting to their own identities. The patient gradually accepted the new situation as more valid than his illusory Biblical world and followed family and friends back to reality.

It is seldom easy for patients to lose their self-consciousness and spontaneously act. To get them started, Moreno uses various "warming up" techniques. The mirror technique, for example. A therapist familiar with the patient's history will impersonate him in some highly emotional dilemma while the patient watches.

What chiefly distinguishes Moreno's ideas from psychoanalysis is its emphasis on the patient's acts and feelings as opposed to mere verbalization. Psychodrama, moreover, investigates conflict in its immediate form, whereas much of the psychoanalyst's data stems from the patient's earliest recollections, dreams and fantasies.

BROADWAY OUTPATIENT CLINIC

But psychodrama is by no means confined to the treatment of psychoses. In New York, near the corner of Broadway and 78th Street, stands a three-story building, each story containing a circular stage and about 100 seats, which Moreno operates as a kind of outpatient clinic for investigating ordinary problems in human relations. Conducted almost daily by either Moreno himself or his associates, the sessions are open to the public, a fee of $2.50 being charged to cover running expenses.

I watched married couples acting out before other married couples the frictions threatening their marriages. I watched a girl and her fiance dramatizing the religious and social disparities between them and, discovering them to be irreconcilable, agreeing to part. I watched freshmen from a segregated southern college portraying Negro students in order to assess their own racial feelings.

Moreno considers his methods applicable to almost every human dilemma, a view from which other psychiatrists sharply dissent. Says an eminent New York practitioner: "Group therapy, of which psychodrama is only one aspect, undeniably has advantages that individual therapy lacks. Someday they may be combined with profit. But the idea that psychodrama is quicker, easier or more effective is nonsense."

Moreno's image of man as a fallen god stems from a memory of his own infancy. He was four years old, the youngest of six children born to a well-to-do Romanian exporter living in Vienna. His parents went visiting one Sunday, leaving him to play at home with some neighborhood boys. "Let's play God and His angels," proposed little Jacob. "I'll be God." He designated the ceiling as Heaven. To reach it, they made a tower of chairs and, while the others held the chairs steady, he climbed up. "Why don't you fly?" an angel asked. Jacob flapped his arms. The angels let go of the chairs. He crashed and broke his right arm. "It may have been my fall," he speculates, "which taught me that even the highest being depends on others, on auxiliary egos, and that the patient-actor requires them to act adequately. I later learned that other children like to play God too."

SPINNING CHILDREN'S TALES

Children were his first psychodramatic subjects. Strolling through the city parks, while a medical student at the University of Vienna, seeing children rebel against their parents, nurses and authority in general, he felt they needed a special sort of teacher, and he so appointed himself. Gathering groups of them around him under a tree, he would spin wondrous, supernatural tales that lifted them out of themselves. Soon they were spontaneously enacting myths of their own invention and in the process getting rid of some of their hostility.

A child Moreno particularly remembers was a freckled reddish-haired girl of nine nicknamed Liesl, whose father, a tailor, complained that she never stopped fibbing. Moreno assured him she was no compulsive liar, but a naturally gifted creator of imaginary situations more real to her than reality. At his suggestion the tailor sent Liesl to drama school. As Elizabeth Bergner she came to rank among Europe's finest actresses.

The concept of drama as therapy evolved from a theatrical experiment Moreno launched in Vienna after World War I, while practicing both general medicine and psychiatry. He called it the Theater of Spontaneity, and he intended it to be simply a new form of entertainment. Professional performers, taking their cues from the audience and later from current events, would improvise plot, action and dialogue. Among the first actors hired was a footloose former bank clerk named Peter Lorre.

Moreno's Theater of Spontaneity became his theater of

psychodrama following the marriage of an actress, Barbara (as Moreno's records identify her), to a young playwright, George. Barbara always portrayed gentle, wistful ingenues. But according to what George confided in desperation to Moreno, at home she was a hellcat who cursed and kicked him when he tried to make love to her. The day of the next performance the newspapers reported the murder of a streetwalker by her pimp. Convincing Barbara she would broaden her range, Moreno cast her as the streetwalker. She played the part with such ferocity, rousing the actor who played the pimp to such a frenzied response, that at the climactic murder scene the audience stood up, screaming "Stop!"

At home after the show, temporarily purged of her aggressions, Barbara was all tenderness. Moreno kept her playing violent characters, and she grew tractable away from the theater. He then put George on the stage opposite her to duplicate episodes of their private life. "Some months later," he recounts, "they sat with me in the theater, full of gratitude. They had found themselves and each other."

Barbara's case embodied an element which remains basic to psychodrama, an element Moreno derived from the ancient Greek dramatists. They believed tragedy should serve as a catharsis for the spectator, purging him of overpowering emotions by depicting them. "In psychodrama," Moreno explains, "the catharsis takes place in the actor, in the victim of the tragedy."

By 1923 he had expounded his theories in nine books. As we have seen, they are the antithesis of psychoanalysis, and he once seized the opportunity to tell Freud so. "You reduce people's dreams," he said to the great man after hearing him lecture at Vienna's famed Neuropsychiatric Institute. "I expand them."

"Good," replied Freud. "I wish you well."

Moreno moved to the U.S. in 1925 because he felt it offered the widest scope for the growth of new ideas. In New York he continued to combine private practice with public psychodramas, staged primarily to entertain. "I had to do both to promote my theories," he says. Acceptance was slow. The influential Freudians deplored his theories as well as his showmanship. But the American Psychiatric Association elected him a member, and mental hospitals throughout the country began looking into psychodrama.

DEMONSTRATION IN A PRISON

My visit to Beacon coincided with a unique event in the history of nearby Matteawan State Hospital, one of the world's most famous institutions for the criminal insane. Its fourteen-man psychiatric staff, struggling with the formidable task of treating more than 2000 inmates, many of them violent, had asked Moreno what benefits psychodrama might confer. "Probably no complete recoveries," he told them. "We would have to work with their families for that. But it could make their lives and yours a little easier," and he offered to demonstrate his methods. I accompanied him and Mrs. Moreno to Matteawan.

In the visitors' room, which had been cleared for the demonstration, Moreno drew an imaginary circle as a stage and seated the psychiatrists around its periphery. The inmate chosen was an unmarried middle-aged Negro merchant seaman whom we shall call Joe. Before his guard brought him in, the psychiatrists reviewed his caae. One night last summer, in a Harlem bar, Joe picked up a colored prostitute and took her to his one-room tenement flat. After finishing a quart of whisky, they fell to quarreling over the price she wanted to stay all night. According to what Joe later told the police, there was a knife on his dresser and she grabbed it. He wrested it from her, shoved her through the door and locked it. He swore that was all he remembered.

JOE'S PARANOID DELUSIONS

Next morning the landlady found the woman's body outside Joe's door, stabbed through the heart. Joe lay fully clothed on his bed, still dead drunk. Protesting that the woman had left his room alive and unhurt, he was arraigned for murder. A psychiatric examination, however, showed him to be suffering from paranoid delusions. The judge therefore committed him to Matteawan until such time as he might be competent to stand trial. His mental state having since improved, it seemed likely Joe would shortly be released to face a jury and perhaps long imprisonment.

He came in, a small, grizzled man, bewildered, but plainly eager to please. Moreno patted him on the back and thanked him for his cooperation. "I'm here to help you," he said. As he plied him with sympathetic questions about his family, his friends, his life at sea, Joe visibly warmed to him. At length Moreno asked him to arrange a table and chairs to represent the layout of his flat.

Mrs. Moreno entered the circle. "Let's suppose this is the woman you met that night," said Moreno.

"But she's white," said Joe.

"It doesn't matter. This is only make-believe."

Under Moreno's deft prodding, Joe soon lost himself in the reenactment of the fatal events. He sprang at Mrs. Moreno, gripped her wrist so tightly he left a red mark, snatched an imaginary knife from her, fell back, advanced again, now holding the knife blade foremost. After two hours of reexperiencing not only his physical actions but also his emotions, reversing roles at Moreno's command, he suddenly stopped dead, as if struck on the head by a mallet.

"I must of done it," he said. "It couldn't of been no other way. I'm responsible, and I got to pay for it."

"And how do you feel about that?" Moreno asked.

Joe's eyes flooded. "So relieved, I never felt so relieved. I can face things now."

"Yes," said Moreno, turning to the fascinated psychiatrists who never knew Joe to admit the possibility of his guilt, "truth is the beginning."

4. PSYCHODRAMA AND ITS DIVERSE USES

Simone Blajan-Marcus, M.D.

Psychodrama is not only a method of group or individual psychotherapy. Not unlike psychoanalysis, it goes further, being, as its creator J. L. Moreno said, a "Revolution." The fact that it involves the body makes it already the most universal of all ways of communication. Going above any language barrier, it widens the spread of links between races, countries, social or intellectual levels. Psychologically, it involves the deepest language, one antedating verbal communication in the infant's development, the body language.

So it is not surprising that it can be of help to all categories of people, from educators to psychotics, from actors to ministers, from cultural to deeply hallucinated schizophrenic groups.

We shall attempt to classify the diverse utilizations of the psychodramatic method, group or individual, in five large sections: Psychodrama in therapy, as a means of training, as a social therapy (sociodrama), as a means of education, and recreation.

Reprinted with the permission of the publishers from International Mental Health Research Newsletter, Vol. X, No. 2 (Summer, 1968), pp. 70-71, 73.

PSYCHODRAMA AS THERAPY

The mentally sick person is primarily alone, and desocialized because of his troubles. But this, in turn, makes him even sicker, and it becomes a dangerous and vicious circle.

As group therapy, psychodrama is a potent way of de-isolation. This is the minimum a group can do. Even catatonic or very regressed patients often become interested in something that is expressed, not in words, but in gestures, and they begin to imitate or even to react with original emotions.

But this is not the only effect. A group situation in itself stimulates expressions of fear, hatred, love, need of approval, etc. By that token, it helps the mute or repressed patient to go from inner, organic language, such as somatization or impulsive acting out, into an outward, voluntary expression, mimic, gestures, and psychodramatic play. In a later progress, he will, through this, eventually become capable of talking as well as playing, and to attain a fuller, more mature way of communication.

From his primitive relation to others, the schizoid protection, the wall of silence or the "introjection" of more or less distorted images, he will gradually confront them, discover his own autonomy, his identity, experience jealousy and rivalry, and beyond it, find a new "progressive" kind of identification.

This will take place through the group dynamic, in which the director takes an attitude that is:

a) non-directive of the theme and its expression, so that it would become as spontaneous as possible;

b) directive of the means of expression, that is the psychodramatic play, to help the best, most direct and active way of communication as well as insight to take place.

Practically, there is little or no interpretation by the leader, as the group is encouraged to associate and comment during, and especially, after the play. Interpretations take place mostly when there is tension or disorder between the members of the group, if it cannot be worked out through a play.

But it is directive for the play itself. The director helps the protagonists set the place for the drama to be played, which is a part of the "warming-up process." Everything is focussed on helping the "star" to express as fully and as spontaneously as possible his problems and conflicts, on "actualizing" them in the "here and now" of the session, thus enabling the group and auxiliary egos (who play with him) to partake, as much as they can, in his emotions. The group is then never a public, but fulfills more the function of the ancient Greek "chorus."

TRAINING

The minimum of training for a future specialist in psychodrama is through playing auxiliary ego. But it goes further than that: even to observe a group from behind a screen may be therapeutic and much more so, if he becomes a member of a group. We call that "didactic psychodrama," by analogy to the way most analysts are trained by using the couch like a patient. This permits experiencing more fully the problems of inhibitions, impulsions and in general, of human interrelations. The future therapist or auxiliary ego is thus enabled to relive his childhood conflicts, solve them as much as possible, and in any case, not use them against his therapeutic freedom and efficiency.

Psychodrama is used on at least three levels for trainees:

a) Spontaneity tests can be operated to select more gifted subjects. Some people can be good therapists but will not be good directors or auxiliary egos if they don't know how to express themselves freely, using body language;

b) Attending sessions as part of the staff, playing auxiliary ego to patients, and discussing afterwards;

c) "Didactic" psychodrama. In our groups trainees stay as long as it is necessary for them to open up, become aware, not only intellectually, but emotionally, of their difficulties, to become more mature on all levels. When this change has been judged sufficient, they go into a "Technical Perfecting Group," in which the only difference from the ordinary training group is the autonomy in technique given the members. The directors observe, but do not "direct," except on very rare occasions. When there is something that needs to be played, a member of the group will be chosen to animate, or volunteer and be accepted.

After the play is completed and comments concluded the group is invited to: discuss and criticize the way the session was directed, also to try to discover the themes, roles, etc. that went on during this time. This "mental gymnastic," consisting of being as subjective as possible for one hour, then objective in the next half-hour, is not easy but very rewarding.

SOCIODRAMA

As a whole, sociodrama is psychodrama in which "I" is replaced by "We." For example, it can happen in an ordinary training or patient group that a conflict arises between Jews and non-Jews, men and women, or that the "haves" feel guilty towards the "have-nots." A group can split in two, for instance, new members on one side, older ones on the other. The director may name a "herald" for each "party" and make them discuss, others join them by spontaneous "doubling" or entering the debate directly. Reversing roles is always very important, so that each group can understand and identify with the other.

Some groups are entirely based on sociodrama as a means of clarifying and reducing prejudices and tensions between ethnic groups such as Arabs and French, Jews and non-Jews, Negro and Whites, or various society layers, who "do not speak the same language." Of course, such prejudices, psychosociologists know, are often covered up by reaction-formations, guilt, denial.

On the other hand, they themselves are mostly defenses against more personal conflicts. One such group discovered that "positive prejudices" existed too, and were linked with hastily generalized experiences, as well as negative ones. Playing, reversing roles, make psychodrama reachable not only by people who talk and think easily but also by those who react impulsively provided they are willing to be sincere, and, above all, those who cannot speak fluently, whether out of inhibitions, ignorance or being a foreigner. One can see there the tremendous interest such groups present, to give only one example, for newly implanted immigrants. It would have none of the "brainwashing" or coercive persuasion of well-intentioned courses of any such organizations. Moreover, our experience shows that a language is learned more easily and quickly through emotional working through and human contacts than with grammars, however perfect and vividly illustrated.

EDUCATION

Moreno, as early as in 1933, experimented with girls in an institution. This was based on sociometric study, that is a study of interrelation between the inmates. But he saw, as well, how the learning process was blocked or stimulated by mimicry, free expression, working through the roots of emotional inhibitions.

In our psychodrama groups, where we have university students, they very often present and play their examination problems. The simple fact of having them play their tests beforehand in the way they dread most, sometimes with several different types of "professors," helps them pass with success.

Learning is also often a problem. Psychodrama has again and again helped students to clarify the causes of their difficulties, and often to overcome them, by playing their fights, conflicts, fears, but also their future possible success, to make them experience the pleasure, but also the guilt and anxieties attached to it of which they were totally unaware. Stage fright is also often quickly cured by psychodrama, whereas hypnosis or psychoanalysis might have failed or seems too long a process.

Another way of developing culture and taste is what we have called the "Psychodramatic Club." Inspired by the numerous and popular "Cine-Clubs," in which members see and then discuss a film chosen in order to stimulate intellectual exchanges, our Club meets once a month, not only to discuss, but to play parts or sequences of a film, a play or even a book chosen the month before by the majority of the members. Sometimes a sequence, most stimulating for the group, will be played two, even three times, by two or three different sets of protagonists who react in a variety of ways to the parts or the scene. Any difference or departure from the scenario will be accepted as an interesting distortion coming from the personality of the participant. We do not encourage people to criticize the actors or to discuss the authors but to be spontaneous and subjective. Exchange can be very vivid, and is always rewarding.

It mostly helps people not to stay passive, which is unfortunately too often the case in our modern spectacles, to react, "emote," work through. We believe it promotes a real culture, not only a knowledge of classic or contemporary creations. "Choredrama," can complete it, such as when after having seen and played sequences of "Zorba the Greek," our Club members spontaneously asked for the music to be played, and improvised dances on it. Some members, who had never been participants before, began really to open up, starting with this dance session.

RECREATION

Psychodrama is also a means of relaxing. Traditions, mores, collective and individual imperatives make a more or less narrow frame for our freedom. Anxiety arises if any "excess or unknown kind of emotion or expression occurs in us or in others. So, sometimes, the need for a wider horizon, a free "vital space" is felt, without the need for any deeper aim of therapy.

To play a role we never could play in our life, to encounter a person or a group of beings we are sure never to meet, and perfectly safely as to consequences, is an experience. Of course, children do it spontaneously, but this is very quickly curbed, along with agreement of social rules and the oedipal interdiction interiorized.

The Club that was mentioned in paragraph V can fulfill this task. One participant who had come to a session grumpy and tired said she came back relaxed and feeling as fresh "as if she had taken a ten days' vacation." She had wanted to play a sequence from a film which is very poetic and takes place on a seashore, surrounded by beautiful dunes, with soft sand under her body. The whole group spontaneously played, some the sea gently stroking her feet, some sailboats gliding in the sun, and therefore, she had felt the sympathy of the others for her untold troubles. This alleviated her fatigue.

The Spontaneity Group whose aim is more directly re-creation can accomplish this even more. Re-creation expresses best that people need to re-build themselves, to find and expand their distorted, contracted beings again, more than to distract or futilely amuse themselves. The very proof is that, if, as in our Spontaneity groups, the themes of role-playing come from the audience (they are not encouraged to be too personal), they are likely to lead gradually or directly to serious themes, and most invariably evoke death. The only exception, in one session, came from a very frivolous little group of three who decided to "have fun," but could not, either take the rest of the audience with them, or go along with the majority. One whole session which turned out to be a riotous "psycho-comedy" was based on a crime that had just been published in the papers: two grand-mothers assassinated by the moron of the family, with the unanimous planning or agreement of their relatives and descendants.

The relief arising from freedom of imagination, the right to wish and "act" anything, even the most forbidden deeds, without legal or reality consequences, is tremendous. It can, of course, arouse anxiety in people who have trouble distinguishing between imagination and reality. But this very anxiety can be a revelation to the subject and show him his symptoms, his need eventually to undergo treatment. And, as such, any psychodrama, whatever form it takes, is bound to be, at the minimum, a revelation of one's personality and problems, but more often, a therapy in itself.

CONCLUSIONS

If anything is therapeutic, then like a drug, it can be dangerous if ill-used. Some people, talking about group-dynamics, humorously call it *"group-dynamite."* Psychodrama is not a "symptom-killer," like many drugs, but real therapy, meaning it goes into the roots of the ailment, helping the patient to help himself, to actively undergo a deep modification of his inner being. Even people who are not aware of their troubles, who would not even think of making an appointment with a psychiatrist, become aware of their "problems," when confronted with others, and with whatever impulsive action or talking might break through their guard against spontaneous reactions.

What is the real difference, then between all these forms of psychodrama? It is in the conscious motivation of the individuals who form the group. A group of Arabs wishing to understand and dialogue with, say, Negroes, cannot be directly encouraged to play their family problems. They would not understand, or would not even want to do it. Also, it would be false to reduce all symptoms and conflicts to individual frictions, however deep and ancient they can have been. Cultural, collective imperatives are strong factors of security, therefore of pressure on the individual against his need for freedom.

But, throughout all these varied aspects, there is only *one* psychodrama. The genius of its inventor is primarily the fact that he understood that human relations are the core of our psyche, from the mother (or substitute) infant link to the most elaborate, collective ones. And also the use of *spontaneity* as the fundamental, royal way towards truth and harmony between people as well as in themselves.

In expert hands, psychodrama could and should be the answer to most (if not all) problems in human conflicts, whether personal or collective, along with training, education or recreation.

As a quiet, bloodless revolution, it can be a potent auxiliary to progress and peace throughout the world.

5. SELF-ACCEPTANCE THROUGH PSYCHODRAMA

Sam Osherson

I want to describe in this paper a recently conducted psychodrama in which I was the protagonist. The director was a psychodrama instructor* and the audience consisted of the first year graduate students in clinical psychology at Harvard University. The students in the first year class were from various parts of the country and had degrees from highly dissimilar universities and colleges. Although no one knew anyone else in the class before the semester began, we became a closely-knit group, for we all seemed to share common views and interests on many matters. We had often discussed personal problems freely among ourselves and I considered everyone present a close personal friend of mine. In the course of my psychodrama I was able to disclose a long-standing emotional problem which I had never before been able to admit publicly. In this paper I will attempt to describe the psychodramatic situations and their particular resolutions which enabled me to overcome my fears. Dialogue will be quoted whenever essential to an understanding of the situation.

The psychodrama took place in one of the rooms of the Department of Social Relations, equipped with a psychodrama

Reprinted with the permission of the original publishers from *Group Psychotherapy*, Vol. XX, No. 1 (March, 1968), pp. 12-19.

* Trained at the Moreno Institute, Beacon, N.Y.

stage, in the late evening. This was the first of a series of "psychodrama workshops" by which the graduate students hoped to familiarize themselves with its uses and methods. None of the students knew very much about psychodrama, and most, including myself, had never participated in one. The particular psychodrama to be described was the second to take place that evening, so that everyone had the advantage of a long "warm-up" period.

After the finish of the first psychodrama, I volunteered to be a protagonist, for I was interested in seeing what—if anything—I would be able to do with psychodrama. I had read that people were often able to express their deepest troubles in the accompanying torrents of emotion. This is what I hoped would happen to me—that I would lose both my self-consciousness and my inhibitations and would, finally, be able to speak of something that had been torturing me for years. I had made many attempts in the past to discuss my problem with people towards whom I felt close but had failed to such an extent that no one even suspected its existence. My behavior always followed the same pattern—I would want very much to talk with someone about my secret but my fear and shame would be too strong and I would not be able to bring it into the open. Since coming to Harvard, however, events had taken a new turn. I had long been angry with myself for not being able to disclose this secret to my closest friends. Now I found myself among fourteen people towards whom I felt the highest regard and affection and who obviously had the same feelings for me. As a result my anger towards myself was intensified and I felt almost a need to confess the problem to them. I realized that I could no longer, in effect, lie to the group—for every day that I kept this problem to myself I was denying its existence to them. Thus, at the psychodrama that evening I felt two forces within me—a strong motivation to tell everyone what was plagueing me, and the familiar, powerful inhibitions to prevent me from disclosing anything.

After volunteering, I was asked which of the three psychodrama instructors I would like to have direct me. I immediately picked the same one who had directed the first psychodrama. I did this because I perceived him as a very compassionate and understanding individual who was, at the same time, quite directive and forceful; thus, one part of me was rallying all its strength to avoid any meaningful disclosure, while the other part hoped desperately that this person had the skill and courage to prevent me from escaping the situation.

We started by recreating a meeting I had had during the summer with a professor. The director told me to begin by walking around the long oblong table at which everyone in the room was seated, while describing my feelings and emotions just before I had arrived at the professor's office:

> I feel pretty good. . . . I am going to discuss some research plans with Dr. T. . . . I feel no different than usual. . . . I have just come from my apartment, and want to discuss an experiment we are designing together. . . .

One of the audience assumed the role of Dr. T and I entered his "office" on the psychodrama stage. The director asked for my thoughts regarding Dr. T. This was a subject to which I had given much thought for I liked Dr. T very much, yet also perceived him as a vulnerable person who was somewhat unsure of himself. I immediately replied that "he is a lot like me. I see a nervousness underneath his outer show of self-confidence. I guess I identify with him. I think he is basically insecure."

The director then told me to tell this to Dr. T. After I did, "Dr. T" replied: "Gee, Sam, what makes you think that? I don't understand how you got that impression." The other graduate student and myself reversed roles; he was now Sam Osherson while I was "Dr. T." My response to "Sam's statement was:

> Well, Sam, I appreciate your mentioning your impression to me, for I see you mean it in good faith. But I don't think you're

correct—after all, my behavior has not shown me to be insecure
or anxious. I don't see why you should have that opinion of me.

After this answer, the director asked me where I could
remember experiencing a nervousness similar to that which I
now felt in myself and thought to be present in Dr. T. My
response was; "in high school." This was not a difficult answer,
for my high school years—due to an interaction of familial
turmoil and unfortunate school experiences—are a source of
many of the areas of my greatest emotional sensitivity. In
response to query, I specified high school English classes as a
source of particular anxiety to me.

With the aid of another graduate student who assumed the role
of a high school chum, I attempted to recreate the emotions of a
typical high school English class. However, now I felt myself
closing up. Before mentioning my high school days to the
audience it had been easy for me to disclose whatever emotion or
thought came into my mind. The imparting of my current
feelings of anxiety came as a surprise to the audience—for I was
felt to be one of the calmer and more secure members of the
group. Yet I had wanted this disclosure to occur, for I resented
the assumption by the others of my imperturbability, when in
reality I was facing a deeply felt, although not outwardly
shown, anxiety. Any more than this, however, I was not
prepared to reveal, and by reconstructing my high school days
we were approaching an area of myself that I was determined
not to let the others see—namely, my strong feelings of inferiority and inability to compete socially with my peers. As a
result of this resistance, the conversation in English class with
my "high school friend" felt very artificial to me and never went
past my asking if he had done his homework. Again we reversed
roles, the other graduate student playing Sam Osherson and I
portraying "his friend." After another attempt to begin a
conversation the director asked me, as "Sam's friend," what I
thought of Sam. The answer hurt, but I said it anyway: "Well

... Sam's O.K. ... But, well ... there isn't very much to him."
Again I switched roles with the other student, and the director
asked me: "Sam, what is your opinion of your friends?" My
answer was simple: "I don't think very much of them. We just
use each other. That's the way it is in Westchester County—
kids associate with each other because they're the only ones
around, not because they particularly want to."

The suddenness and simplicity of the director's interpretation
startled me: "So, Sam, you felt inadequate in high school."
Through the director's probing, it was drawn out of me that
while my feelings of inadequacy were especially strong in my
relations with girls, they were also present in my interactions
with other boys. It was mainly a feeling of social, rather than
intellectual inadequacy. The director then asked for one person,
out of everyone I ever knew, with whom I would have liked to
discuss these feelings. I immediately had two associations:
Dr. A, a psychotherapist whom I had seen while a senior in
high school, and who is still a close friend—and Dr. B, a young
English instructor, whom I had felt quite close to while a
sophomore at the University of Vermont. For some reason this
English instructor had been on my mind for several days prior
to the psychodrama, and I picked him for the talk. I described
to the audience a particular day on which he had invited me to
his office for a friendly chat. During the course of our talk I had
wanted very much to tell him about the anxiety and inferiority
feelings I felt, both in and out of class, but had been unable to,
and the conversation had stayed on a superficial level. I never
forgot my frustration at the instructor's warmth and interest
towards me, and my inability to be open and honest with him.

After describing this man's office I sat down and the director
told me to tell the instructor how I felt. Furthermore, I was to
play both roles—speak as myself, and reply as Dr. B. Again I
could feel my resistance to further disclosure increasing. The
psychodrama had already gone farther than I originally wanted
and I found myself becoming increasingly fearful of the

direction in which it might proceed. But, amazingly enough, I did not think of the alternative of stopping the psychodrama altogether. I told the director that nothing more was going to come out and I doubted whether I could play both roles, but was told to go ahead anyway. I sat on one of the chairs in the "office," and said:

> Dr. B, there's something I've been wanting to tell you for a long time. I know you consider me to be quite self-confident, and outstanding in class—but actually I feel quite inadequate. . . . I don't feel at all like the person you probably think I am. I'm actually quite a scared person. . . .

At this point, I could not do anything but look straight ahead, at the chair in which Dr. B was supposed to be sitting. I felt a great aching inside, similar to the feeling I usually experience in a highly tense situation with direct reference to myself. I looked toward the director and told him that I did not know what Dr. B would, or should, have said to me. The director then came on stage and said he would play Dr. B.

> But, Sam, you're one of the brightest guys in the class. How can you say you're inferior? Most of the kids are not half the student you are.

I replied:

> It's not an intellectual inferiority I feel. I don't feel up to the others socially. I don't seem able to relate to any of the girls. I feel incapable in that area.

A few moments passed during which I became increasingly numb. I mean this literally, for this is a reaction I frequently experienced when a situation was very threatening to the one area of my personality that I wanted no one, ever, to see or to know. The director told me to turn my back to the audience.

Then he turned off the lights and explained that we were going to engage in "behind-the-back" technique:

> Now let's share with Sam. Sam feels inadequate socially. He feels that he was a failure with girls in his early college years. Does anybody have anything he would like to say?

My first reaction to the director's statement was that nobody else would have anything to add, that I was the only one present with this problem, and that I must really look like a fool. Then I thought that anything anyone said would probably be false and merely an attempt to make me feel better by saying that they had similar experiences. Suddenly I heard a friend's voice, easily recognized in the dark:

> When I was in high school I always wanted girls to like me. I couldn't see why they wouldn't, but I didn't have the confidence to see why they would. So I built up handles which people could touch and be attracted to. I became intelligent—"Oh, he's very smart," the girls would have to say. I became a good athlete, worked with weights, and so on, forever. But whenever I was with a girl, I would give her these handles to magnetize her onto me. I was too afraid to give her myself for I thought I wasn't good enough for her to want. And, of course, this only brought defeat; no one wants handles to a person. It took me a long time before I met someone I was able to give myself to, and still, with people I often feel so inadequate that when I shake hands with them, I hold myself back.

Another easily recognized voice said:

> When I was in high school I was very lonely. I didn't think anybody cared to look for what I was really like. I was an academic hero in my class, but it was more important to me that I felt I lacked all the things that I thought were attractive to other people. I felt I just showed up at school to be bright, and went home, and no one thought about me. Now I realize how much all the others lacked—that none of them were the kind of

person I would want for a friend—and that I was incapable of seeing it because I was so concerned with being acceptable.

Finally, a third voice said:

I want very much to say something to you, Sam, but I can't.

Although I started to check myself I found myself replying: "That's strange, L, because I've always felt very close to you." The director cut in sharply: "Don't talk, Sam, just *listen*."

There was a prolonged silence. I was so touched by what had just been said that my earlier numbness had left me. From the tone of the voices and the feelings they contained—in some cases there was almost much quavering—I did not doubt their sincerity and honesty. I realized then that I had to tell this particular audience what I had been holding inside for the last nine years. No sooner had I resolved to tell the audience this than I felt a tremendous constriction in my throat. I ignored the enormous fear I felt—I could not lie any more to these people. Feelings of inadequacy may have been the cause of what I was now going to tell those present, but it was far easier for me to speak of that then to reveal this "hideous secret" of mine. What would they think of me when they heard of this weakness? I realized, now that it might be withdrawn, how much the deep bond I had formed with these people meant to me.

I heard the director say from the other side of the room:

Sam, you've been carrying a weight on your back for years. Come, take it off, share it with us. . . . What is it?

I replied that "I have something to tell everyone but I won't do it with my back to them." I turned around while the director quietly turned the lights on. No room ever seemed as silent as this one when I said, in a low voice:

Never before, except once, have I ever admitted to anyone what I am going to tell you. . . . You should feel proud of yourselves—

although I'll probably regret it in the morning, when I wake up from this dream. . . . As a result of the feelings of inadequacy I experienced through junior and senior high school, I . . . developed a fear . . . this fear . . . that I . . . that I . . . well . . . that I stuttered. . . . And ever since junior high school I have been terribly afraid of stuttering in front of people. Now, I know that I don't stutter. . . . Oh, I stutter a little sometimes, but there is *no* anatomical reason why I should . . . but all these years I have had a fear of speaking in front of people. . . . And if ever anyone carried a weight on their shoulders, this was one.

I couldn't say any more. I literally felt as if I had been purged of some inner devil. I stared blankly ahead, half slumped over in my chair. I could see the audience, but as far as I was concerned it was as if they were so many statues. My secret had finally come out. The feelings of inadequacy spoken of earlier in the psychodrama had given rise to a belief—beginning when I was in the seventh grade—that I stuttered. As a result of my shame at the thought that I might stutter, I often found myself very hesitant to speak in front of groups or among friends. The fact that I was scared of stuttering was a secret I had kept to myself since then.

The director stood up and asked me if I wanted to assume his role while he played mine. He went on stage, sat down, and said in a weak voice:

I'm scared. I feel inadequate and unable to speak to people. What can I do? I don't know what to do.

I answered harshly:

I don't *know* what to do. If I knew, I would tell you.

The director said to me: "Play the director's role. Sam is asking for your help. Give him an answer." He repeated his statement. I said:

Don't be so goddamn weak. Be honest. What else can you do?

"Sam" said:

> I don't know what to do.

My anger toward myself was aroused:

> Don't whine! It's hard to be honest, but you have to try. Oh,
> God, how many people have you been false with! Two girl friends
> last year—for how long did you lie to them? The only thing to do
> is be completely honest with other people.

My anger and hostility towards the "Sam" on the stage was
quite great, but this opportunity for expression had alleviated it
somewhat.

The psychodrama ended when we returned to the first
situation which had been created—myself and Dr. T, discussing
research plans several months before. I no longer felt much
tension, and in fact, felt elated at all that had passed. "Is there
anything you want to tell Dr. T?" asked the director. I smiled at
the student playing the role, shook his hand, and said:

> Thank you very much, Dr. T. I hope you work things out,
> because I sure have.

I sat down at the table, emotionally drained. I saw everyone
smiling at me and knew nothing had changed in anyone's view
of me as a person. I said: "I can see that no one thinks any
differently of me."

The director smiled even more and said: "I'm scared that if
we say anything we will lose the beauty of what just happened."
Everyone laughed. Then came a flood of comments and
questions:

> —"I never heard you stutter!"
> —"Oh, I heard you stutter a few times, but I never thought
> anything of it. We all do it."
> —"Sam, who is the person to whom you did tell your fear." (I
> explained that I once told it to Dr. A, the psychotherapist I
> mentioned earlier.)

I thanked everyone at the table and told them that the

emotional catharsis I had experienced in telling them of this fear was—as I had been slowly realizing over the past few months—the one thing I needed most. Intellectually I had always known that my fear was irrational and without any basis in reality. But I could not get my emotions to follow my intellect.

Finally, the director asked: "If you all wanted to express your feelings toward Sam non-verbally right now, how would you do it?" Three people immediately rose and shook my hand vigorously. The others came over and embraced me. I doubt if I ever before have been affected in the same way as, one after the other, both men and women came over and put their arms around me—we were human beings trying in the clearest way to show how close together we felt.

As it was after midnight—we had started the workshop at eight o'clock that evening—we broke up and went home. I felt elated. It was a fresh, free feeling. By the time I got back to my apartment I was quite excited and spent at least an hour making notes on all that had happened.

The next day, everyone in the class seemed especially warm to me. I could see that they thought I might be ashamed of what had passed the evening before, and I did my best to show them that I was not. This was soon evidenced by my hearty response to their greetings—their knowledge of my fear of stuttering became something that brought us even closer together.

I have, of course, stuttered a few times since the psychodrama evening, both among my friends and among strangers. But it no longer affects me as before. To others stuttering is another form of speech; to me it had always been a shameful stigma. Self-acceptance came through psychodrama.

REFERENCES

Moreno, J. L., *Psychodrama,* Vol. I, Beacon House, 1945.

Moreno, Zerka T., Psychodramatic Rules, Techniques and Adjunctive Methods, Beacon House, 1967.

Part II
THEORY: SPECIFICS

Introduction

Creativity and spontaneity, two of the most important concepts in the Morenean philosophic system, are dealt with in the article that opens this section wherein Moreno discusses their role in enabling man to fulfill his potentialities. In this article, besides defining the specific terms, he draws upon a few of the models he had developed in the 1930's and 1940's to illustrate some of his points, specifically those of the *cultural conserve* and the *robot*. These he sees as the antithesis of spontaneity-creativity. Moreno makes no predictions as to *how* man may develop but explores two of the diverse ways in which he *can* develop. Moreno's article is followed by two technical type articles, Zerka T. Moreno's "Survey of Psychodramatic Techniques," and Bratter's "Dynamics of Role Reversal," both of which consider some of the important theoretical subtleties that are found in psychodrama. Mrs. Moreno describes and provides a case-illustration on role reversal. Bratter's brief paper on the same subject turns into a delightful philosophical exercise as the author explains one of Moreno's major technical contributions. Other major psychodramatic contributions by Moreno, which Mrs. Moreno also explores in her survey include the soliloquy, the double, and the mirror, which are among the essentials of her paper. She also deals briefly with such other techniques as the multiple double, self-presentation, symbolic realization, analytic psychodrama, the auxiliary world, and dream re-enactment. Following these is a short article by Enneis, "The Dynamics of Group and Action Process in Therapy," that concerns itself primarily with some simple but useful warm-up techniques.

Concluding this fairly brief section is an article by Greenberg that presents the key theoretical concepts of the Morenean system as seen by Ledford J. Bischof, author of an important theories-of-personality book, and by Moreno, according to statements he made to the editor of this volume more than two years ago. A principal strength of this article is that most of the definitions and explanations are presented in the words of the two authors, including Moreno's own definitions of such esoteric concepts as the *co-conscious, co-unconscious,* and *surplus reality.* Bischof presents 10 major principles while Moreno deals with nine major concepts and defines a 10th.

6. THE CREATIVITY THEORY OF PERSONALITY
Spontaneity, Creativity and Human Potentialities

J.L. Moreno, M.D.

HUMAN POTENTIALITIES IN THE SETTING OF THE TWENTIETH CENTURY

Since the end of World War II, a growing interest in the concepts of spontaneity and creativity has emerged. Creativity and spontaneity research, tests, and their application to practical objectives have become the vogue in current education. They are also the focal points in all the arts—poetry, music, dance, painting, drama, and psychodrama.

In our world of change, transitory and restless, we crave for reliable points of anchorage. Before we go into actually naming and defining creativity, spontaneity, and their correlated concepts, it may be elucidating to survey the leading thoughtwaves that preceded the present creativity explosion.

Two philosophers particularly were the major forerunners in shaping this development, Henri Bergson and Charles S. Peirce.

Reprinted with permission of the publisher from *New York University Bulletin, Arts and Sciences, Vol. LXVI, No. 4* (January 24, 1966), pp. 19-24. In part from J. L. Moreno's "Spontaneity, Creativity and Human Potentialities" in the forthcoming Symposium *Explorations in Human Potentialities* by Herbert A. Otto (Editor), Publisher Charles C. Thomas, 1966.

To Bergson goes the honor of having brought the principle of spontaneity into philosophy at a time when the leading scientists were adamant that there was no such thing in objective science. His *donnees immediates,* his *elan vital* and *duree* were metaphors for the one experience which permeated his life's work—spontaneity—but which he vainly tried to define. It remained a biological mystique.

Soon after, almost on his heels but independent of Bergson, the American, Charles Sanders Peirce, founder of pragmatism, made astonishing references to spontaneity which remained unpublished until long after his death. "What is spontaneity? It is the character of not resulting by law from something antecedent. I don't know what you can make out of the meaning of spontaneity but newness, freshness and diversity."[1] Throughout Peirce's posthumously published work run scattered references to spontaneity. But his speculations had a weak point. Chance and spontaneity appeared to him as the same thing. However, as long as they remained undifferentiated, no progress could be made in spontaneity research. Bergson and Peirce failed therefore to provide us with clear definitions of creativity and spontaneity that could be used as an anchorage point for the current developments. It was my privilege to attempt to bridge this void in a number of books and articles since 1914.

WHAT IS CREATIVITY?

It is not sufficient to define creativity by its semantics, as for instance: "Cause to be or to come into existence; or to make a new form out of pre-existing substance." Creativity can only be defined by its inner dynamics. It requires that we enter into its dialectic opposites so as to make clear what it means. One way

[1] Charles Sanders Peirce, *Collected Papers,* Vol. I., Harvard University Press, 1931.

of defining creativity is by its maximum condition, maximum creativity—the fullest penetration of the universe by creativity, a world that has been creative from beginning to end and that never ceases to be creative. The opposite condition of creativity would be then zero creativity—a world that is entirely uncreative, automatic, that has no past or future, no evolution or purpose, absolutely changeless and meaningless.

Creativity manifests itself in a series of creative states or creative acts. An example is the creation of new organisms capable of surviving on land at the time when animal life was confined to the sea. A new animal organism would arise when it would undergo, through the evolutionary process, anatomical and physical changes. This may be called biological creativity.

A second example is the Sermon on the Mount as it emerged, however unformed, for the first time from the mind of Jesus. This is a form of religious creativity.

A third illustration is musical creativity, *e.g.,* the music of the *Ninth Symphony,* at the moment it was being created by Beethoven, in contrast to the same music as a work of art—a finished product—separated from the composer himself. On the surface, it may appear as if the creative units that went into the *Ninth Symphony* —its musical themes, its climaxes, its harmonies, etc.—must also have been in its original matrix, and that no difference exists between the one in Beethoven's mind and the other in its conserved state—except only that of locus.

Closer inspection, however, will show that this is not true. As Beethoven was walking through his garden, trying intensively to warm up to his musical ideas, his whole personality was in an uproar. He made use of every possible physical and mental starter he could muster in order to get going in the right direction. These visions, images, thoughts, and action patterns—both musical and nonmusical inspirations—were the indispensable background out of which the music of the *Ninth Symphony* grew. But all this background—which cannot truth-fully be divorced from the state in which Beethoven was when he was truly being a creator—is not to be found in the finished product, the musical score or its performance by a noted orchestra. Only the result of the artistic creativity of Beethoven is there.

Creativity belongs to the category of substance; it is the arch substance, the elementary X without any specialized connotation, the X which may be recognized by its acts.

WHAT IS SPONTANEITY?

Creativity is a sleeping beauty that, in order to become effective, needs a catalyzer. The arch catalyzer of creativity is spontaneity, by definition from the Latin *sua sponte* which means coming from within. But what is spontaneity? Is it a form of energy? It is energy but unconservable. It emerges and is spent in a moment; it must emerge to be spent and must be spent to make place for new emergence like the life of some animals which are born and die in the love act. It is a truism to say that the universe cannot exist without physical and mental energy which can be conserved. But it is more important to realize that without the other kind of energy, the unconservable one—or spontaneity—the creativity of the universe could not start and could not run; it would come to a standstill. Spontaneity operates in the present, *hic et nunc*. It propels the individual towards an adequate response to a new situation or a new response to an old situation. Thus, while creativity is related to the act itself, spontaneity is related to the warming up, to the *readiness* of the act.

Here follow three types of spontaneity: The first type is a novel response to a situation but a response not adequate to the situation. Psychotics, for example, may state that two times two equals five, certainly a novel response but hardly adequate. Children are another group of people who are bursting with spontaneity and who have a wide range of novel experiences, but the creative value of their responses is often doubtful from the point of view of an adult world, just as the creative value of the novel responses of psychotics is doubtful from the point of view of normal individuals. This form of spontaneity is the pathological variety, entailing novelty, but very little adequacy.

The second type of spontaneity is a stereotype variety. It consists of a spontaneous response which is adequate to the situation, but which lacks sufficient novelty or significant creativity to be fruitful to the situation. The comedian's repetitive reaction to a situation soon loses its novelty, and although it may continue to provoke some laughter, it soon ceases to be a spontaneous response.

The third type of spontaneity is the high-grade creativity variety of genius. In this type there is an adequate response accompanied by characteristics that are both novel and creative. The resulting phenomenon may be in the form of an act, or a substantive article such as a poem, story, art object, or piece of machinery. To be truly spontaneous, the results must be in some way new and useful for some purpose.

WHAT IS THE CULTURAL CONSERVE?

The finished product of the creative process is the cultural conserve, which comes from *conservare*. It is anything that preserves the values of a particular culture. It may take the form of a material object such as a book, film, building, or musical composition, or it may appear as a highly set pattern of behavior such as a religious ceremony, a theatrical performance of a prewritten play, a fraternity initiation, or the inaugural ceremonies for the President of the United States. As a repository of the past, cultural conserves preserve and continue man's creative ego. Without them man would be reduced to creating spontaneously the same forms to meet the same situations day after day. For example a cultural conserve such as the dictionary makes it unnecessary for men to redefine words every time they wish to communicate. In addition to providing continuity to the heritage of human existence, *the cultural conserve plays an even more significant role as the springboard for enticing new spontaneity toward creativity*.

However, there lies a danger in the over-reliance of mankind on the cultural conserve. This danger is inherent both in the conserve's state of finality and in its abuse by mankind. For spontaneous creativity—however supreme it may be in itself— once conserved is, by definition, no longer spontaneity; it has lost its actuality in the universe. There are two forms of creativity—the freely emerging flowing creativity and conserved creativity. The latter fills the world in the form of cultural conserves that contains creativity in a dormant frozen state. These conserves wait for "Prince Charming Spontaneity" to awaken them from their sleep. Left to themselves, nothing "new" would ever happen. But conserves represent the greatest cultural capital, a form of property and power, a means of expressing superiority when the superiority of immediate spontaneous creativity is not available.

CATEGORIES OF CREATOR

The realization or fulfillment of creativity in man takes many forms. Among them are two outstanding categories of creator: (1) the devotee of the truly perfect; (2) the devotee of the truly imperfect, the lover of spontaneity.

The devotee of the truly perfect upholds the conserve as the ultimate value and is skeptical of spontaneity. He is a devotee of theory and a master of words. That is why he is compulsive, authoritarian, and critical of those who act. He loves to develop magnificent theoretical systems, physical, social, and cultural projects. He sponsors theories of religion, of altruism, of love, and preferably on the theoretical reflective level. He shrinks from experimenting existentially with religious or theoretical creativity. He does not strive for the embodiment of sainthood in his own life.

The improvising creator, in contrast, is devoted to experimentation of all forms—religious, therapeutic, scientific. He is the improvisor in art, science, and religion. Rather than writing books and formulating systems he loves to act and create. Whereas the "truly perfect" is loved by an elite, the improvisor is loved by the multitude. It is a profound contrast between the aristocrat and the people's leader.

Thus, there is a profound contrast between the theoreticians of religion, sainthood, and altruism such as St. John, St. Augustine, Plato, Plotin, Spinoza, Kant, and Hegel, and the experimenters, producers, and practitioners of religion and sainthood such as Jesus, Buddha, St. Francis, and Baal Schem. These experimenters and lesser luminaries such as Sabbatai Zwi, Savonarola, Pascal, and Kierkegaard often look inadequate, imperfect, overbearing, eccentric, ebullient, stupid, even pathological, but they were trying to live a life of truth and preferred an imperfect existence to a perfect theory.

The future of a culture is finally decided by the creativity of its carriers. If a disease of the creative functions, a "creativity neurosis," has afflicted the most primary group, the creative men of the human race, then it is of supreme importance that the principle of creativity be redefined and that its perverted forms be compared with creativity in its original states. There are higher and lower forms of creativity. The highest forms of human creativity are manifest in the lives of prophets, poets, saints, and scientists; the lower forms are operating in every humble existence, day by day.

HUMAN POTENTIALITY

Man and Spontaneity

There is apparently little spontaneity in the universe, or, at least, if there is any abundance of it, only a small particle is available to man, hardly enough to keep him surviving. In the past he has done everything to discourage its development. He could not rely upon the instability and insecurity of the moment with an organism that was not ready to deal with it adequately; he encouraged the development of devices such as intelligence, memory, social and cultural conserves which would give him the needed support with the result that he gradually became the slave of his own crutches. If there is a neurological localization of the spontaneity-creativity process, it is the least developed function of man's nervous system. The difficulty is that one cannot store spontaneity, one either is spontaneous at a given moment or one is not.

If the spontaneity function is such an important factor for man's world, why is it so poorly developed? The answer may be that man *fears* spontaneity and the uncertainty of it just as his ancestor in the jungle feared fire; he feared fire until he learned how to make it. Man will fear spontaneity until he learns how to unleash it, train and control it. A great deal of man's psycho- and sociopathology can be ascribed to the insufficient development of spontaneity and therefore the inability to mobilize the potential sources of creativity. Spontaneity "training" is therefore the most auspicious skill to be taught to scientists, educators, and therapists in all our institutions of learning and it is their task to teach students or clients how to be more spontaneous without becoming pathological.

To do this, we have to first recognize the fact that spontaneity and creativity can operate in our mental universe and evoke levels of organized expression that are *not* fully traceable to preceding determinants. This fact causes us to question the validity of many current psychological and sociological theories openly or tacitly based upon psychoanalytic doctrine. These levels of expression suggest a "creative theory of personality" to replace the doctrine of psychoanalysis.

Man and the Robot

One can visualize that the course of the universe has been and may continue to be moving indefinitely in the same principal direction, however much the constellation of cultures may change in volume, intensity, and in depth.

However, if one surveys the long history of the human cosmos, this process of unfolding in one direction seems gradually to be called to a temporary halt and uprooted by the phenomenon of the robot, from the Slavic root "robota," which means to work. It has emerged in manifold varieties, from the book to the high-speed electronic computer to the spaceship. They represent forms of existence that are utterly different from the other processes of creativity with which man has identified himself. The robot evolved in many of its applications not to confirm man's existence and creativity, but to supplant, destroy, and deny it. It worked like the dissonance in a symphony which the conductor tries desperately to bring into synchronization with the total composition itself.

What is a robot? It is one of these mysterious paradoxes in the development of man, following the lines of the cultural conserve, emerging out of his greatest loss of spontaneity and creativity. The robot is lifeless. It is neutral. It is the same at every instant; it does not grow, it does not change. A human infant results from the conjugation of a man and a woman. A robot results from the conjugation of man with nature itself. In both cases, the offspring takes over some features from both parents. In the robot, for instance, there is some feature of the man-producer and some feature of natural energy modified by him.

Once upon a time we envisioned God as the one who could destroy us anytime he wanted to. This power has been passed over to man; by means of robots he, too, can give a single individual the power to rule and perhaps to destroy the universe instantly. But the robots can not produce an ounce of spontaneity.

The control of the robot is complicated for two reasons. One, the robot is man's own creation. He does not meet it face to face as he did the beasts of the jungle, measuring his strength, intelligence, and spontaneity with theirs. The robot comes from within man's mind; he gives birth to it. He is confounded by it like every parent is by his own child. Rational and irrational factors are mixed, therefore, in his relationship to robots. In the excitement of creating them, man is unaware of the poison which they carry, threatening to kill their own parent. Second, in using robots, man unleashes forms of energy and perhaps touches on properties that far surpass his own little world and that belong to the larger, unexplored, and perhaps uncontrollable universe. His task of becoming a master on such a scale becomes a dubious one as he may well find himself more and more in the position of Goethe's Sorcerer's Apprentice, who could unleash the robots but who could not stop them. The apprentice had forgotten the master's formula, how to stop the robot. We have the formula to make them but not to stop them.

The fate of man threatens to become that of the dinosaur in reverse. The dinosaur perished because he extended the power of his organism in excess of its usefulness. Man may perish because of reducing the power of his organism by fabricating robots in excess of his control.

Man had to create the robot in order to survive. If there had been an abundance of spontaneity in man's world, the world of the robot may never have come into being. It may have been a part of the creator rather than a thing apart from him.

Man's Future

The future of man is surrounded with perplexing question marks and tragic conflicts. The process of evolution and natural selection may not allow for harmonization. Man may be at the crossroads. He may be forced to live and survive in two different environments: one, the natural environment in which his freedom as a biological being, the function of the creator, is the most supreme criterion; and the other, a technological, automatic, or, better said, a conserved and conserving environment in which his freedom and his creative function are restrained and forced to flow between the bedrock of mechanical evolution. Races of men fit for the one may be unfit for the other. The criteria of unfitness are different in both environments. One line of evolution may lead inescapably to societies of men similar to societies of insects, harmonious and 100 percent efficient but unindividualistic. The other line of evolution may lead inescapably to a new race of men who tacitly will follow the direction of their ascendance up to date, modified and enhanced by the triumph over the robot. There will be then two possibilities of survival for man: one, as a zootechnical animal, a robot; the other, as a creator. The notion of Darwin of the survival of the fittest gains herewith a new slant. Both environments may guarantee survival to man en masse, but the same type of man who survives in one environment may not survive in the other. The criteria for fitness are different for each environment. In an environment in which the machine and the technical conserve dominate, the fittest will be the servant of the machine, the machine addict. And, by the same token, the type of man who is supreme in a creator environment will be doomed to perish in the other. The future may well see two independent evolutions flourishing side by side and breeding two different races of man, leading consequently to the most important division since man arose from certain genera of the ape man to our own genus Homo.

But if man is fortunate in the development of the future cosmos, the robot may well attain greater significance still and become the link between the human cosmos and the cosmos at large. It is like the two-faced god, Janus. For if properly manipulated in the hands of creative man, the robot world may be the forerunner of a new kind of universe, one in which man is the propelling and ruling force—creating a new universe which may replace the old one, even transforming man himself. But this transformation of himself and the universe may be the greatest expression of his potentialities; for man's creativity may become continuously necessary to feed and propel the robot world. Thus the robot similar to the cultural conserve may become the agent to activate, mobilize, and constantly stimulate and renew the creative potential of man.

REFERENCES

1. Bischof, Ledford J. *Interpreting Personality Theories.* New York, N.Y.: Harper & Row, 1964.
2. Moreno, J.L. *Sociometry and the Science of Man.* Beacon, N.Y.: Beacon House, 1956.
3. ————. "The Future of Man's World," *Group Psychotherapy, A Symposium,* Beacon, N.Y.: Beacon House, 1945.
4. ————. "Creativity and Cultural Conserves," *Sociometry,* Vol. II, Beacon, N.Y.: Beacon House, 1939.
5. ————. *The Words of the Father.* Berlin: Gustav Kiepenheuer Verlag, first German edition 1920; Beacon, N.Y.: Beacon House, American edition, 1941.
6. ————. *Who Shall Survive?* Washington, D.C.: Nervous and Mental Disease Publishing Co., 1934.
7. ————. *Psychodrama Volume I.* Beacon, N.Y.: Beacon House, 1946.
8. Peirce, Charles Sanders. *Collected Papers,* Vol. I, Cambridge: Harvard University Press, 1931.

7. A SURVEY OF PSYCHODRAMATIC TECHNIQUES

Zerka T. Moreno

The psychodrama is not a single technique, it is a methodology, a synthetic method in which many dimensions of experience are mobilized in behalf of the patient. We will enumerate a few of them, adding some brief illustrations. These are by no means all of them, directors are frequently forced to invent new techniques or to modify old ones on the spot so as to meet a challenging situation presented by the patient.

SOLILOQUY TECHNIQUE

This is a "monologue" of the protagonist "in situ." The patient enacts a scene in which he is on his way home from work, for instance. He is walking from the subway station to his apartment. In life itself his thoughts would not be verbalized as he is alone, but he is thinking about himself. The psychodramatic therapist-director instructs him to use the soliloquy technique, to talk out loud as he walks, what he is thinking and feeling at this moment, here and now. The patient uses the large, bottom level of the psychodrama stage. He walks and walks, shaking his head, warming up to this situation, one which he encounters daily. His face is frowned, his head tucked

Reprinted with the permission of the publishers from *Group Psychotherapy, XII, 1 [March, 1959], pp. 5-14.*

between his shoulders, dropping halfway on his chest, he is very despondent. His voice is low, barely audible as he speaks: "I am sick and tired of my life. I enjoy my work, it is true, but oh, how I hate to go home at night. I know just what is going to happen when I get there. There is my old mother with her complaints, an endless series of aches and pains which no doctor is able to cure. And then there is my sister Jane, a sour, unhappy old maid who resents having to dedicate her life to mother because life is passing her by. But she does not have the get-up-and-go to change the situation and find another life for herself. And here am I, her male counterpart, resenting both of them because I have to support them."

THERAPEUTIC SOLILOQUY TECHNIQUE

This is the portrayal by side-dialogues and side-actions of hidden thoughts and feelings, parallel with overt thoughts and overt actions, the private reactions of the protagonist to his role. It is particularly useful in highlighting the distance between the patient's perceptions and the actual events in an interpersonal relationship; it permits the patient and his life partner to bridge the gap between them, to share experiences which they feared to bring to expression or failed to perceive in all their aspects. The following illustration shows this very concretely: The patient and his wife are both present; they portray the scene which, according to him, propelled him to propose to her two years earlier. They are in a boat, he is holding the line while she is baiting the hooks for him. His expression is one of complete bliss, he is quite obviously happy. He cannot see her facial expression, for she is seated at the very end, half turned away from him, looking completely miserable. The patient takes a deep breath, says out loud: "Oh what a beautiful day. Weren't we lucky the weather held out for this trip, Marlene?" Marlene responds non-committally: "Hm, hm." The director instructs each one to soliloquize at this point. The patient: "I'm so glad I thought of taking her fishing. It's a good thing for us to do things together, to share each other's pleasures. I wonder if I will have the courage to ask her to marry me this evening? I do love her and we get along so well. We have similar goals and interests. I hope she will say yes. Now's a good time to ask her, after such a peaceful, blissful day." Marlene: "My God," she blurts out, "this is a revolting job to give me. I should have refused to do it when he asked me. It's my first experience at fishing, and it's going to be my last, too. Imagine his nerve to make me do this!" At the sound of her words—to which he is not permitted to respond in the soliloquy situation—the patient looks up astounded and falling out of the role, he states "Good Lord, if I had known she felt that way about it, I'd never have dared to propose to her that evening."

TECHNIQUE OF SELF-PRESENTATION

The patient presents himself, his mother, his father, his sister, his minister, his employer, his girlfriend, and so forth. The patient, a fourteen year old boy, a runaway problem, takes the role of his father in a typical home situation, an auxiliary ego takes the role of his mother. Bill has informed the auxiliary ego how his mother acts in relation to his father. Bill, as his father, from offstage (representing where his office is located) shouts to his wife in an angry voice: "Stella, for heaven's sake, stop crying. It drives me crazy. I can't work here." Mother: "I'm so desperate about Bill (weeps, wails louder and louder), you just don't care, you have no heart, you never had and you never will. Much of the way Bill is today is your fault! My mother always says . . . (weeps again)." Bill (as father): "Your mother! For crying out loud! Why do you always have to bring her into everything?" (Slams door)

TECHNIQUE OF SELF-REALIZATION

The protagonist enacts the plan of his life, with the aid of a number of auxiliary egos. Because the description of this would take more space than can be used here, we will merely describe how this technique is put into operation. The patient believes himself to be Adolf Hitler. His former identity has dropped away and the psychotic structure has replaced it. In order for him to free himself from his psychotic production, he needs helpers who embody for him the personages who interact with him as his new self. The patient is unable to complete this self-realization alone in the world of reality, but at the same time he is convinced that his psychotic world is the real one, indeed, it has become the only real world for him. The auxiliary egos who during the therapeutic sessions take the roles of Hess, Goering and Goebbels, among others, become midwives, assistants in the birth of his psychodrama. They make it possible for him to bring his psychodramatic pregnancy to fulfillment and, once the psychotic baby has been completed, to be delivered of it.

HALLUCINATORY PSYCHODRAMA

The patient puts his delusions and hallucinations to a reality test. Hallucinations do not follow the law of physical gravity, they may rise into space or come down from above. They disregard the laws of sensory perception, they may speak to and touch the patient. In the following scene the patient is sitting at the dining room table. The director decided to have the psychodrama session deal with his everyday situation because it was a stressful one for the patient as well as her table partners, most of whom were present and taking their own roles. One of the patient's neighbors speaks to her, "Linda, please pass me the salt." Linda does not move. Another one addresses her: "Linda, please give Mr. Stone this glass of milk." Again, Linda remains frozen, she is physically present but otherwise absent from the reality of the scene. She gazes fixedly into space. Director: "What are you looking at, Linda?" Linda: (in a hushed and fearful voice) "Don't you see them?" Director: "Yes, I do, but how many are there?" Linda: "Three of them."

Director: "How are they dressed?" Linda: "They are dressed in black, cloaked like members of the Ku Klux Klan." Director: "Can you see their faces?" Linda: "No, they are completely hooded." Director: "Just where are they?" Linda: "Hovering on the ceiling." Director: "Do they represent anything?" Linda: "Yes, they are the spirit of hate, fear and death." Director: "Hate, fear and death. Are they alone?" Linda: "No, each one is standing in front of a coffin." Director: "Are the coffins empty?" Linda: "No." (Throughout this interchange she does not stir, her answers are given in concise form; it is evident that she perceives all this very clearly.) Director: "Are there figures in them?" Linda: "Yes." Director: "Get up, Linda, let us pick from among the people the spirit of hate, fear and death."

Director takes Linda by the hand; she assists in the choice of the auxiliary egos—all patients who have experienced hallucinations—places them on the stage. Director: "And now, Linda, who is the first figure?" Linda: "I see my mother lying in the coffin of death." Director: "You go now and lie down in the coffin of death." Linda does so, representing the figure which is under the spell of this particular spirit, that of death. Her actions and use of the coffin correspond with the feeling-tone emanated by the spirit. Here she lies with her eyes closed, arms relaxed at her sides, the image of sweet repose. Director: (addressing Linda as her mother) "Mrs. Mann, I am sorry to see you here. What happened?" Linda: (in sepulchral tone) "I am better off dead. That daughter of mine, she killed me. That Linda, she used to upset me so, she gave me heart attacks. I am better off this way." Director: "I understand, but where is Linda now? What is she doing without you?" Linda: "She is dead, too." Director: "Is she in a coffin?" Linda: "Yes, she is a murderess and had to die too." Director: "You are Linda now, there in the coffin?" Linda: "Yes. This is me." Director: (turning to the spirit of death) "What do you feel about this, oh spirit of death? Do you have anything to say?" Patient: (a very regressed schizophrenic who was rarely able to warm up to any role other than his own fragmentations) "She is too young and pretty to die." Director: "Shall we forgive her her sins and let her live?" Spirit of death: "Yes." Director; "And will you restore her mother to life also?" Patient: "Yes." Director: "Linda, come with me, the spirit of death will relinquish his claims on you. Leave the stage, spirit of death." Patient does so. Director and Linda now turn to the next coffin. Director: "Linda, which coffin is this?" Linda: "The spirit of fear." Director: "Get in the coffin and show us how it is in his coffin." Linda crouches on the floor, like a frightened animal, her back arched over her knees, her arms crossed over her head. Director: "Who are you?" Linda: "I am all the patients in mental hospitals, especially state hospitals." Director: (turning to the spirit of fear) "What do you think of this, spirit of fear? Spirit: (another very disturbed patient) "I can only show her the fears she creates for herself." Director: "Is this true, Linda?" Linda: "Partly, I can't help it and the others don't help me." Director: (signalling to all those present to join in speaking to Linda, as in a chorus) "We promise to help you, Linda, please have no more fear." (The chorus speech is repeated several times, more loudly and insistently.) Director: "Come out of that coffin now, Linda, for we will do our best to help you. And therefore, the spirit of fear may depart." Spirit leaves the stage. Director, taking Linda to the third coffin: "And here is the final one, Linda." Linda: "The spirit of hate." Director: "Get into the coffin and show us how hate feels." Linda lies down, her arms and legs twining around her body, like self-imprisoning bands of hate. Director: "And who is this?" Linda: "This is me when I don't get what I want." Director: "What, for instance?" Linda: "When I want them to stop using electric shock on me." Director: "Spirit of hate, how do you feel about this?" Patient, as spirit of hate: "They use electric shock when it is necessary, it is supposed to help patients." Director: "Has it helped Linda?" Spirit: "I suppose so, or else they would not have given it to her." Director: "What do you think about that, Linda?" Linda: "It's too dreadful a treatment." Director: "Did you ever have it here?" Linda: "No." Director: "How long ago is it since you had it?" Linda: "I think about one year ago." Director: "We all promise you will not get it as long as you are here, Linda, so you may rise and the spirit of hate will depart."

DOUBLE TECHNIQUE

This is used in the penetration of the subject's conflicts on the ego level. An auxiliary ego is placed side by side with the patient, interacting with him "as himself," physically duplicating him in space and assisting him in the assessment of his problems. The patient is in her bedroom, reviewing the happenings of the day just ended. Both she and the auxiliary ego are going through the motions of preparation for bed. The patient is very evasive until the auxilary ego as her double, sensing her unhappiness, bursts into tears, crying, "Why do I go on lying to myself! I can lie to others but I can't fool myself." Maureen, the patient, now commences to cry also, retorting, "What's the use of crying myself to sleep *again*. I've done that too often."

MULTIPLE DOUBLE TECHNIQUE

The patient is on the stage with several doubles of himself. Each portrays part of the patient. One auxiliary ego acts as he is now, while the patient acts himself as he was when he was little, and as he was soon after his father's death, another auxiliary ego how he may be thirty years hence. The masks of the patient are simultaneously present and each acts in turn. With psychotic patients the multiple double technique has been usefully employed when the patient suffered from numerous delusions involving parts of the body; each of the auxiliary egos then represented a different organ, responding to the delusional stimuli produced by the patient.

MIRROR TECHNIQUE

This is used when the patient is unable to represent himself in word and action as, for instance, in catatonia, or after psychotic episodes or shock therapy which produced residual or pseudo-amnestic states. An auxiliary ego is placed on the action portion of the psychodramatic space, the patient or group of patients remaining seated in the audience or group portion. The auxiliary ego proceeds to represent the patient, assuming his identity, is addressed by the director by the patient's name, and re-producing the patient's behavior and interaction with others, either real or delusionary—all as seen through the eyes of the patient. The patient sees himself "as in a mirror" how other people experience him.

ROLE REVERSAL TECHNIQUE

In this technique the patient, in an interpersonal situation, takes the role of the other person involved. Distortions of perception of "the other" in interaction may thus be brought to the surface, explored and corrected in action, in the fold of the group. Role reversal has been used effectively with infants and children as a technique of socialization and self integration. An illustration is the role reversal between a mother and a three year old child, the child assuming the role of authority. Jonathan was fearful of a very large black dog which used to appear on the grounds as if out of nowhere. The dog would make attempts at being friendly with the child, tried to come close, to lick his hand, jumping around him. Jonathan became so fearful of him that he would cling to his mother's skirt even when the dog remained at a considerable distance. Verbal assurance was unable to assuage this fear. It was decided to work it out in the following manner:

Mother: "Jonathan, there is the big black dog again." (The dog was nowhere in sight.)

Jonathan: (Runs to his mother, hides his face in her skirt, exclaims) "I'm afraid of him, Mummy, I'm afraid."

Mother: "But honey, there is nothing to be afraid of. First of all I'm here and I wouldn't let him hurt you. Besides, he really wants to be friends with you and play with you. Wouldn't you like to pat him on his back?"

Jonathan: "Will he bite me?"

Mother: "Of course not. If you are nice to him he will be nice to you and besides I'm here with you." (Takes Jonathan's hand who reluctantly allows her to use his hand to pat the back of the dog.)

Mother: "Now, you will be me and I will be Jonathan."

Jonathan: (as mother; his voice taking on notable strength, his posture becoming far more erect) "Jonathan, here is that black dog. Now, don't be afraid of him."

Mother: (as Jonathan, crouching low on the ground, clinging to his mother) "Mummy, I'm afraid, I'm afraid, I'm afraid."

Jonathan: (as mother) "Honey, there is nothing to be afraid of." (Puts his hands tenderly around his baby) "Don't forget, Mummy is here with you and she wouldn't let you get hurt."

FUTURE PROJECTION TECHNIQUE

Joyce, the protagonist is in love with Emmett, but she is postponing marriage until he has completed his college education. In order to test the strength of their relationship and to assess how much of her image of the future is involved with Emmett, the director asks her to project herself into the future ten years hence.

Director: "Describe the situation to us. Where are you?"

Joyce: "At home in a house in Montclair. It has six rooms.

We are married and have two children, both girls, one is four and the other one is two."

Director: "What are their names?"

Joyce: "Mary Ann and Judy. Judy is the eldest."

Director: "What are you doing when the scene begins?"

Joyce (to Director) "We are sitting in the livingroom reading; the children are in bed."

Joyce: (to Emmett) "The children were very noisy today. I'll be glad when Judy goes to school."

Emmett: "What were they noisy about?"

Joyce: "They pick on each other. I guess I will have to take them for a walk and let them meet some new children. Those two little kids across the street are so spoiled they are always fighting with one another. They are spoiling my children."

Emmett: "Might as well learn how to get along with them. We are going to have to live here."

Joyce: "I know, I'll have to try a little bit more, but I think that woman across the street doesn't discipline her children enough. If she did, mine would behave better because they play with them. After all, you are conditioned by your environment."

Emmett: "I heard that word environment ten years ago. I told you we are going to have to live here for a little while."

Joyce: "I know dear, I'll try to do better."

DREAM TECHNIQUE

Instead of telling the dream, the patient re-enacts it. He takes his position in bed, warming up to the sieep situation. When he is able to reconstruct the dream, he rises from the bed and represents the dream in action, using auxiliary egos to enact the role of the dream characters. This technique further makes use of retraining the patient, giving him an opportunity to "change" his dream and redirect his dream pattern. This is the unique contribution of psychodrama to dream therapy, for other types of dream therapy rely on analysis and interpretation.

SYMBOLIC REALIZATION TECHNIQUE

Enactment of symbolic process by the protagonist using soliloquy, double, reversal or mirror for their clarification.

ANALYTIC PSYCHODRAMA

An analytic hypothesis, for instance, that of the Oedipus complex, is tested out on the stage in order to verify its validity. The patient takes the role of his mother in a situation with his father (coming home, fired from his job because of a heart ailment). The analyst sits in the audience and watches. Analysis of the material is made immediately after the scene.

AUXILIARY WORLD TECHNIQUE

The entire world of the patient is restructured around him "in situ" by the aid of auxiliary egos. William has been classified as a dementia praecox. He calls himself Christ and has written a proclamation to the world which he wants to save. The auxiliary egos around him live in his world and are completely guided by his needs. One auxiliary ego becomes the apostle John. Christ asks him to kneel in a corner of the room with his head bowed. He does not want him to kneel in any other room or in any other corner. Another auxiliary ego becomes the apostle Paul with whom he prays together. A third is the apostle Peter who is the only one he permits to bathe him once a month. He does not permit members of his family to come to visit him. The only persons he accepts are those who people the world of his psychosis, according to his instructions.

TREATMENT AT A DISTANCE

The patient is treated in absentia, usually without his knowledge; he is replaced by an auxiliary ego who is in daily contact with him and is the go-between patient and therapist. He acts out in the clinic all crucial episodes in which the patient is involved. Other members of the immediate environment are drawn into the action, for instance, the parents of the patient.

WARMING UP TECHNIQUES

These are used to induce spontaneous states.

TECHNIQUES OF SPONTANEOUS IMPROVISATIONS

The protagonist acts out fictitious roles and tries to keep his personal character uninvolved from his fictitious characters.

THERAPEUTIC COMMUNITY

This is defined as a community in which the disputes between individuals and groups are settled under the rule of therapy instead of the rule of law.

MIRROR TECHNIQUES—BEHIND YOUR BACK

Many mirror techniques are so constructed that the individual can "see" and "hear" himself through other people's perceptions of him.

In the classic mirror technique described above, the protagonist is physically present, but psychologically absent. The auxiliary ego acts "as if" the patient were not present, so as to challenge the patient when he realizes that the person portrayed on the stage is a radically truthful exposition of himself. But there are other forms which are used by Moreno and his associates at the New York Institute:

Behind Your Back Audience Technique:

The entire audience is instructed to leave the theatre but

actually they are permitted to remain seated, pretending that they are not present, so as to give the protagonist full freedom of expression. The patient tells each member of the group how he feels towards them; the audience members are not permitted to respond, no matter how much he provokes them. The members of the group are now put on the spot, they see themselves in the mirror of the protagonist's world. This is frequently the starting point, the warming up period preceding a psychodrama. It is often effective if the members of the group *actually* turn their back.

The Turn Your Back Technique.

Protagonists are frequently embarrassed to present a particular episode face to face before the group. They are then permitted, if unavoidable for the warm up, to turn their back to the group and to act as if they would be alone, in their home, or wherever the episode takes place. The director, too, may turn his back to the audience so as to observe the protagonist or protagonists. Once the protagonists, for instance in the case of a matrimonial couple, have reached a high degree of involvement, they become ready to face the audience.

The Black-out Technique

The entire theatre is blacked out although all actions continue as if there would be full daylight. This is done so that the protagonist may go through a painful experience unobserved, to retain for the protagonist the experience of solitude.

IMPROVISATION OF FANTASY

Since the early days of psychodrama, improvisation of fantasies have been usefully applied in order to attain therapeutic aims (see Bulletin of Psychodrama and Group Psychotherapy, *Sociometry*, Vol. VI, 1943, p. 349). A popular technique was and still is the *Magic Shop Technique.* The director sets up on the stage a "Dream or Magic Shop." Either he himself, or a member of the group selected by him, takes the part of the Shopkeeper. The shop is filled with imaginary items, values of a non-physical nature. These are not for sale, but they can be obtained in barter, in exchange for other values to be surrendered by the members of the group, either individually or as a group. One after another, the members of the group volunteer to come upon the stage, entering the shop in quest of an idea, a dream, a hope, an ambition. They are expected to come only if they feel a strong desire to obtain a value which they cherish highly or without which their life seems worthless. An illustration follows: A depressive patient who was admitted after a suicidal attempt, came to the Magic Shop requesting "Peace of Mind." The shopkeeper, a sensitive young therapist, asked her "What do you want to give in return? You know we cannot give you anything without your willingness to sacrifice something else." "What do you want?" the patient asked. "There is something for which many people who come to this shop long," he replied, "fertility, the ability and willingness to bear children. Do you want to give this up?" "No, that is too high a price to pay, then I do not want peace of mind." With this she walked off the stage and returned to her seat. The shopkeeper had hit on a sensitive spot. Maria, the protagonist, was engaged but she refused to get married because of deep-seated fear of sex and childbirth. Her fancy preoccupations involved images of violent suffering, torture, death, etc. in the act of childbirth.

This illustration indicates the diagnostic value of the dream shop technique. The crux of the technique is for the shopkeeper to demand of the client what he wants to give in return, what price he is willing to pay.

Another fantasy technique is the dramatization of fairy tales as described in Moreno's *Stegreiftheater,* pp. 35-37. The tale remains entirely unstructured so that the protagonists are required to fill in with their own fantasies around the theme.

Still another fantasy technique is improvisation of early childhood experiences. In the process of acting them out the protagonists go far beyond that which they actually remember.

Many psychodramatic experiences—there are more than three hundred of them—however odd and fantastic they seem, can be traced back to the rituals and customs of ancient cultures and are found in the classic writings of world literature. Moreno has merely rediscovered and adapted them to psychotherapeutic objectives. *Their real inventors are the mental patients of all times.* The number of applications of the psychodrama method is practically unlimited, although the core of the method remains unchanged.

8. DYNAMICS OF ROLE REVERSAL

Thomas Edward Bratter

Undoubtedly the most singular aspect in the spectra of man is his capacity for growth; to be alive, a thing must grow; when it ceases to grow, it ceases to live. Life is essentially development and growth; conversely, to develop and grow is to live.

"The self, as that which can be an object to itself, is essentially a social structure, and arises in social experience," wrote G.H. Mead [1] In order to engage in this self-aware process of social interaction, the individual can never be a mass-man, he must think first. Mead perceived thinking as preceding the act in an intelligent relationship where the mode of action is based on the individual's total picture of the social process. Thinking was "inner conversation" to Mead and formed the basis for significant "social intercourse." [2]

Mead defined the "I" and the "me" in relation to the social community because he continually stressed that people do or act and are simultaneously aware of themselves. The "I" then is the responsive self; the "I" reacts to the attitudes of others while the "me" is the organized set of attitudes which the "I" accepts as the social response. The "I" expresses itself through experience and action as the "me." The "I" is the individual's initiating, thinking, decision-making self which responds to the

Reprinted with the permission of the publishers from *Group Psychotherapy,* Vol. XX, Nos. 1-2. (March-June, 1967) pp. 88-94.

[1] G.H. Mead, *Mind, Self and Society,* Chicago University Press, 1934, p. 140.

[2] *Ibid,* pp. 141-142.

"me" of the community through acting. The human personality, Mead believed, needs an "I" to respond to a "me" which is social experience. Without an "I" there would be no communal "me," only irrational animals. Man has language which affords him the opportunity to discuss situations. He also has the capacity to utilize his "I" to reflect upon the social situation.

Social change occurs when the "I" reacts to the situation by initiating new ideas and concepts. Essential to Mead's contribution as a social behaviorist was his view that the self cannot be reconstituted without also altering the community and the social relations of the self to others within the community. Social progress is related to individual progress, growth, and attainment.

Abraham H. Maslow expresses the feeling that all basic needs can be categorized under the general heading of self-actualization, that is "everything that the person can become."[3] Maslow listed ten characteristics of the healthy, most fully human individual.

1. Clearer, more efficient perception of reality.
2. More openness to experience.
3. Increased integration, wholeness, and unity of the person.
4. Increased spontaneity, expressiveness, full functioning; aliveness.
5. A real self; a firm identity, autonomy; uniqueness.
6. Increased objectivity, detachment, transcendence of self.
7. Recovery of creativity.
8. Ability to fuse concreteness and abstractness, primary and secondary process cognition.
9. Democratic character structure.

[3] Abraham H. Maslow, "Psychological Data and Value Theory," *New Knowledge in Human Values*, edited by Maslow, Harper & Brothers, 1959, p. 123.

10. Ability to love. [4]

As Maslow wrote: "The human being is simultaneously that which he is and that which he yearns to be."[5]

J.L. Moreno finds a parallel between the problem dealt with by behaviorists, existentialists and psychoanalysts and attempts a synthesis. Moreno's constructs, socio- and psychodrama, both utilize and are concerned with "spontaneity theory of learning." In a letter to *The American Journal of Psychiatry*, Dr. Moreno condenses his theory into two tenets:

1. The principle of a-historical treatment, and here-and-now.[6] "Both Freud and Jung have studied man as an historical development; and the one from the biological, and other from the cultural aspects. On the other hand, our approch has been that of direct experiment: man in action; man thrown into action, the moment not part of history but history part of the moment—sub species momenti." (1932)

2. Behavior is a very abused term with multiple meanings. It is preferable to focus on acts, action and specific situations which manifest the behavior of the patient concretely. According to the spontaneity theory of learning, whenever spontaneous remission takes place, it is through the autonomous experience and learnings of the patient (mental role reversal, mirroring, etc.), that the neurotic symptoms from which he ails are overcome or corrected *in situ.* Gradually the neurotic residua begin to vanish. The patient "learns primarily through self-discovery. He has a better chance to learn if his responses are not inhibited by interpretative, analytical comments

4 *Ibid,* p. 127

5 *Ibid,* p. 130.

6 Jacob L. Moreno, *The First Book on Group Psychotherapy.* Beacon House, 1932. Also: Robert B. Haas, Editor, *Psychodrama and Sociodrama Education,* Beacon House, 1948.

which stifle the possibilities for self experimentation."[7,8,9]

There is a feeling of need, of insecurity, and frustration, which leads men to seek for some authoritative source of wisdom and direction. To meet the demands that modern life makes upon the individual, however, each person must in the end discover the way for himself. At best, he can find in the experience and ideas of others suggestion and instruction, but the final decisions in this undertaking must be his own. Every human being must have a set of guiding principles by which he can govern his existence—there are moments in the life of each person which reveal with clarity the deeper needs of human spirit and which stimulate with greater urgency the search for a satisfying philosophy. Actually the issue is not whether the individual desires a philosophy by which to live; it is a question rather of adopting a vague, inconsistent, a half-conscious, blindly accepted, and probably foolish philosophy or having one that is carefully conceived and based upon the best available information about the individual and of his world. Gradually, unconsciously, but surely, every person absorbs from parents, from friends, from the texture of early life, those attitudes and convictions which provide the framework of the individual's working philosophy of living. What a person accepts uncritically as right or wrong, what a person feels most deeply concerned about, what a person spends time and effort in securing for himself—these values shape a person's view of life as naturally and inevitably as the things an individual has to eat and wear influence preferences for food and clothing. It is of

[7] Gordon, Allport, *In Psychodrama*, Vol. II, Beacon House, 1959.

[8] W.S. Shaw, *Spontaneity Training, in Role Playing in Business and Industry.* Free Press, 1960.

[9] Jacob L. Moreno, "Behaviour Therapy," *The American Journal of Psychiatry*, Vol. 129, No. 2, August, 1963, p. 195.

such deeply rooted, unreasoned conviction and values as these that a working philosophy consists, even as a person begins to examine life more critically and objectively for himself. Indeed, the very process of reasoning, by which a person conducts a more mature self-examination, is itself shaped by these underlying convictions. There is no such thing as complete objectivity in philosophy; a person cannot construct a philosophy of living for himself as a person might plan to erect a new home and occupy it at his convenience. All the individual can hope to do is to reexamine in some larger and more mature perspective the actual convictions to which he gives allegiance, seeking to identify obvious limitations in his outlook and inconsistencies in his conduct. Gradually, if he is determined, he may perhaps reshape his underlying attitudes and convictions into a fairly consistent whole somewhat more nearly in line with the facts of experience and the enduring values of life. His task, then, is comparable not to the building of a new house but to the reconstruction of the home in which the individual is living and in which he must continue to live while the re-building is in progress. A philosophy of living which evolves from an inner calmness of spirit which comes in turn from knowing what the individual believes and why—and that outer strength of purpose which comes with a sense of inner peace and security.

It is in this domain that Moreno's psychodrama not only stimulates the person to think for himself, but develops an instrument of greater inclusiveness. "Existential theorists have contributed much to our comprehension of the central position of the experience of time in human existence"[10] They have demonstrated the future's precedence over the past. They have accentuated the need for including the future in any conceptualization of human existence. "Personality can be understood only as we see it on a trajectory towards its future,"[11]

[10] Henri Ellenberger, *Existence,* "A Clinical Introduction to Psychiatric Phenomenology and Existential Analysis," p. 39.

[11] Rollo May, *Existence,* Basic Books, 1958, p. 69.

wrote Rollo May. Much earlier Gordon Allport reminded us that "People, it seems, are busy leading their lives into the future, whereas psychology for the most part is busy tracing them into the past."[12] Existential theorists have proposed that the future and past meet in the present to form the movement of action.

By "re-living," through the vehicle of Moreno's psychodrama, a person forces the future and past to merge together in the recreated spontaneous present. Initially, the individual encounters great hesitancy to enter into the real situation,[13] to reveal a "naked intensity of spirit,"[14] or to relive the agonizing situation. The reluctance to become personally involved diminishes with the aid of the director and auxiliary ego, enabling the protagonist to ventilate his anguish, hostilities, irrationalities and/or hatred. At the zenith of this involvement—when the emotionally charged vendetta has been re-experienced—the director of the psychodrama suggests a "role reversal" of the protagonist to the role of the other person involved.

To further illustrate the role reversal is, indeed, difficult. The driver of an automobile, for example, accelerates his car slowly and, after the lapse of several seconds, attains the arbitrary speed of fifty miles per hour. At this juncture, to reverse roles would entail having the driver shift to "reverse" immediately and go backwards over the same road travelled. According to physics, however, this cannot be accomplished because of an intermediate phase of inertia that must occur prior to going into "reverse." Even this instantaneous deceleration, assuming it is possible, would lurch the person forward and disturb the existing heretofore equilibrium. The impact upon the driver, in

12 Gordon Allport, *Becoming*, Yale University Press, 1955, p. 51.

13 Carl R. Rogers, *On Becoming a Person*, Houghton Mifflin Company, 1961, p. 109-110.

14 Thomas Wolfe, *The Story of a Novel*, Charles Scribner's Sons, 1960, p. 17.

brief, would be tremendous. To attain a corresponding rate of propulsion backwards would scientifically require, the same process of going from +50 miles per hour to 0 to—50—a total speed difference of 100 miles per hour. No technological analogy, however, should be overemphasized because human behavior is more complex.

It is this spontaneous transition, suspended in eternity, immediately preceding the shifting from "drive" to "reverse" that interests me: the moment of impact, of explosion, of transition. It is this point when the individual is furthest, it seems, from reconciliation from either any objective (or subjective) solution that he must enter into that diametrically opposed world of the antagonist. (In comparison to the car analogy, the human personality is more flexible.) The hostility, hatred, nihilism the protagonist experienced is now viewed from the perspective of the other, the sweat, the blood, the guts, the agony. And it is precisely by creating this dialectic of the thesis and antithesis that produces a synthesis which, ultimately, may be only tangentially related to the former components. It is this creative process of merging two polar concepts and/or sentiments that creates not only anxiety but also provides insight. Individuals must be free to exercise their creativity and their imaginations. Gardner Murphy wrote, "The impulse to perceive, to understand, to imagine is just as much part of human nature as are the specific adjustment processes which we describe in terms of visceral drives."[15] The human being must be permitted and encouraged to explore the unknown heights and react toward "the potentials for becoming a human being."[16] Goethe has said "A young man must dare to be happy." In the final analysis, it may be a matter of courage—of advancing beyond the confronting but restricting frontiers of

[15] Gardner Murphy, *Human Potentialities*, Basic Books, Inc. 1958, p. 23.

[16] *Ibid.*, p. 32

knowledge and experience acquired at twenty and penetrating the darker but maturing areas of the unknown. The goals of psychodrama, I believe, are to enable the protagonist to reach a stage of independent action and control; to gain success according to his own interests, abilities, and needs; to gain increased confidence in and an understanding of himself and others, and to take his rightful place in interpersonal relationships.[17]

Rollo May suggested a person is subjectively equipped to confront unavoidable anxiety when he is convinced (consciously or unconsciously) that the values gained in progressing are greater than those created by escape.[18] The connotation of "escape" possesses great significance because the protagonist will probably avoid maximum effort, maximum involvement by attempting to escape.

But being able to evaluate oneself realistically (objecively) requires an inner courage and sensitivity in order to promote a self-trust which makes it unnecessary for an individual to prove his prowess (to himself and/or others) and enables him to ascertain reality with productive energy.[19] Men who are aware of their strengths and weaknesses are seldom haughty because knowledge of self, combined with experience and education, has a humbling effect of recognizing a person's limitations.

Anxiety, often confused with guilt, as is May's error, is a destructive, negative emotion that impairs self-awareness and growth. In this context, anxiety assumes the form of shame, and differs from guilt in that the former involves not the exposure of a wrong doing; but the exposure of the individual's self which is accomplished through psychodrama. Shame can

17 Katherine D'Evelyn, *Meeting Children's Emotional Needs*, p. 31.

18 Rollo May. *The Meaning of Anxiety*, The Ronald Press Company, 1950, p. 229.

19 Bonaro Overstreet, *Understanding Fears in Ourselves and Others*, Harper Brothers, 1951, p. 95.

accompany socially acceptable behavior and cannot readily be that which, in turn, threatens the person's being. Shame manifests itself. The shameful person tends to conceal his shame, becomes more ashamed for covering it which results in a negative cycle. If dealt with, however, according to Helen Lynd: "Shame can become not primarily something to be covered, but a positive experience of revelation."[20] Lynd believed it is the conquest of shame resulting in pride and self-respect that creates and fosters a genuine humility.[21] Guilt, a by-product of psychodrama, if it is to be constructive to man, must be based on self awareness and a commitment to a value system. Guilt, a rational and positive factor, assists the individual in his interpersonal relations and with himself.

These feelings of anxiety, guilt, shame, revelation, occur when it is possible for the person to re-examine the various components of his irrationality or experience a nuance of feeling without the paralyzing or blinding passion—to stand away from and view within.

To tell a mother, for example, that she is overly aggressive and should not regulate her child's life as much as she does will not and cannot produce significant behavioral change. She will only alter her behavior when she perceives herself to be wrong— when she gains *"action insight."* J.L. Moreno believes the quickest, most effective method to obtain action insight is through psychodrama. If she is forced to live under her dictates, if only for a few moments, while she role reverses with her child, it may be sufficient to produce significant change.

Each person has a variety of ways of reacting to a familiar situation, differing because of a multitude of complex personality factors. Any conflict—conscious or unconscious— consumes psychic energy which otherwise would have been utilized to cope with the problem. In order to cope with the

[20] Helen Merrill Lynd, *On Shame and the Search for Identity,* Harcourt, Brace and Company, 1958, p. 20.

[21] *Ibid.,* p. 258.

problem, it may be beneficial to construct a microcosm (a stage) which is indicative of the more complex macrocosm. To exist with conflicts, to view them before they can be solved—herein is the essence of the existence of the delicate psyche.

9. THE DYNAMICS OF GROUP AND ACTION PROCESSES IN THERAPY
An Analysis of the Warm-up in Psychodrama

James M. Enneis

One of the primary problems facing any therapist is the establishment of channels of communication. In group psychodrama this is done through the warm-up. This is a process by which the group focuses. By the merging of varied interests, it centers on a problem area with which it is willing to be concerned during a particular session. There is an exclusion of peripheral concerns, and a crystallization of the more basic areas with which the group will deal.

Thus far we have found three major types of warm-up: (1) the Cluster Warm-up, (2) the Chain of Association Warm-up, (3) the Directed Warm-up.

In the *Cluster Warm-up* the group comes in, takes their seats, and begins discussing various topics. Each topic or discussant draws a cluster of people. These clusters of people begin to interact and there is a merger of the interests through

Reprinted with the permission of the publishers from *Group Psychotherapy*, Vol. IV, Nos. 1-2 (April-August, 1951), pp. 17-22. Read at the annual meeting of the American Psychiatric Association (Symposium on group-psychotherapy), May 11th, 1951, Cincinnati, Ohio.

which one topic becomes predominant. During interaction the group may arrive at a new area which has not been the topic of any one cluster. Thus the group selects the area with which it is willing to be concerned. This merging, focusing, and exclusion process may take place with a great deal of constructive discussion, joking, bantering, or extreme hostility between the clusters.

For example, the group comes in, is seated, and is silent. The director maintains the silence and the tension grows within the group. Finally, one man begins talking about his relationships to one of the girls present. How he would like to date her, but he feels that this would be being unfaithful to his wife. He begins to draw a cluster around him which discusses the degree to which one should maintain faithfulness to one's spouse and the meaning of this. Another group discusses the relationship of alcohol and love. The starter or instigator for this group being a man who says that when he goes out of the hospital he will get really drunk and make love to everyone that he meets. The first cluster is discussing the disappointments of love, letters from their wives and mothers which have been discouraging to them. A new cluster begins to form around a student, a Catholic priest, who comes in. They begin talking of love and the resurrection. This moves into areas of relationships to fathers, and to dreams which have been occuring with several of them about their family relationships. These three clusters draw together on the subjects of dreams and begin describing dreams of rejection and anxiety types, dealing mostly with parental figures. Resurrection keeps coming back in as a part of this warm-up and results in a discussion of the love of fellow man. A new cluster begins to form which includes the people who have been, thus far, left out of the discussion. They talk of being wallflowers, how one feels when one is a wallflower, and what might be the underlying cause of this.

The whole group draws together on the subject of being afraid of people, then moves to expressions of love to people, saying that this is the basic difficulty. They are not able to express love or to make adequate relationships with others. The "Star" is spot-lighted by the group and with their support comes forward; this is the person in whose personality this problem area is most clearly crystalized. This person moves into action using members of the group to help him portray his psychodrama. Action serves as a further focusing mechanism which maintains the warm-up, allowing the session to contribute specifically to the group's understanding and handling of the problem.

An example in the *Chain of Association Warm-up:* The group comes in in high spirits, joking and laughing with each other. One patient is chewing grass and says to the director, "I hope you don't mind if I chew grass." The director says, no he doesn't mind. One of the patients says, "Humans are not supposed to be herbivorous." Another member of the group says, "If you keep chewing that grass you are liable to give milk." Another one says, "If you do, come over and squirt on me." Another one brings up the subject of masturbation and they begin chattering about masturbation and their feelings about it. Then one says, "The trouble with that is that I beat my meat too much. I used to go away from home and stay away to get away from my mother and father and play with myself. I was really a son-of-a-bitch. My mother didn't like me a bit. She caught me playing with myself and that is why she didn't like me." This person becomes the "Star" of the group. The group is willing to be concerned with his problem, and with this area of the development of the personality.

The *Directed Warm-up* may be directed by the leader of the group, by some one person within the group or by the group as a whole. This type of warm-up is commonly used in training psychodrama. Here the leader has specific information with which this particular session must deal, and therefore he warms up the group to this area, and action takes place within its limits. The patient directed warm-up, is likely to begin by a patient saying, from the group, that he has something which he wishes to do today and asking the group to allow him to be the star and to portray his particular problem. He will warm the group up to himself and perhaps to the problem area as well. There are also group directed warm-ups in which the group pushes a particular patient who has not been able to participate in action before, or one toward whom it has strong emotional feelings. The group directed warm-up usually has further integration of the group as its goal.

Once the group has selected the area with which it will be concerned, and the therapeutic person, that is, the people in whose personality the problem area is most clearly shown, action is begun. We have established, essentially, channels of communication through which the action on stage and the feelings of the group can merge into beneficial processes of catharsis, the development of insight, and relearning. Vicariously the entire group benefits from the action process through catharsis and the expansion of perceptual fields.

As the star is warmed up to the roles which he is to play in relationship to the people who are causing difficulty in his current or past life, other members of the group are selected to portray the roles of people in his environment, or social atom. These auxiliaries are selected on the basis of their need, or opportunities inherent in the situation for developing insight themselves. In other words, the auxiliary egos chosen will be people for whom the experience of taking these particular roles will be a therapeutic one.

In the action the problem is usually shown in its present status, its development, how it is affecting current relationships, and possible solutions and insights regarding this type of behavior. After this has been done on stage, the problem and the star, or the therapeutic personae, are returned to the discussion level with the group. The star and the problem come from the group and are returned to the group. Thus the problem area is worked through to a meaningful conclusion giving a sense of closure in each session.

The teles and transferences are controlled and are built primarily between the members of the group with a minimum directed toward the leader as therapist. The transference-telepolarity is a vital part of psychodramatic therapy.* The psychodramatic therapist can be more objective and realistic in handling these phenomena, as they are set up between members of the group rather than being wholly directed toward him.

In order to facilitate the development of a climate which affords an optimum opportunity for these warm-up processes to take place, sociometry is used in selecting groups. Sociometry is a choice procedure. All potential members of the group are asked to list in the order of their preference, the people with whom they would like to work in a therapeutic setting, and to list in the order of their displeasure, the people with whom they would not want to work in such a group. This data is used to form groupings in which inhibitory influence is minimal and freedom for creative production is maximal. There is a minimum of personal threat involved in the relationships between members of the group. Therefore a maximum of productivity is achieved in a relatively short period of time. The extent to which any individual can contribute to the therapy process is limited only by his relationship to other members of the group. If he is able to feel free with them he may contribute and receive. However, if he feels a paralyzing threat from his relationship to

*Freud restricts the term transference to displacement of mental components taking place during therapeutic psychoanalysis. It is basically concerned with the displacement of matters of infantile sexuality upon the physician. (See Hinsie-Schatzky, Psychiatric Dictionary, p. 168.)

Moreno's "Tele" is a far broader term and concept. It explores and tests the degree of reality in interpersonal and intergroup relations; it is applied to therapeutic as well as to non-therapeutic situations (See Hinsie-Schatzky, p. 167, also J.L. Moreno, Interpersonal Therapy and The Psychopathology of Interpersonal Relations, Sociometry, Vol. I, 1937.)

one or more members of the group, his gain will be correspondingly limited.

Once the group has become productive, jelled, and entered a stage in which communication is possible, we find that potential members who have been excluded before, now become acceptable. Whatever threat was involved has been resolved through catharsis, relearning, and greater objectification which has been taking place on the part of the group.

Even though the group is selected sociometrically, it is not a cohesive unit when it first meets. The process through which the group forms itself into a cohesive unit may be roughly outlined as follows:

1. First, the members of the group begin testing each other and the leader in order to learn the extremes and limits of behavior for themselves. They also test to obtain information regarding the limits or extremes to which other members of the group may go. This is a getting acquainted phase.

2. Next they begin to do what they feel is expected by the other members of the group and by the leader. This is actually a further testing procedure—a sort of feeling out of the therapy setting to ascertain further delineation of purpose and goal.

3. The group continues to function in this way until the process moves towards an interest in relationships to authority figures. At this point it enters a power struggle with itself and with the leader or director. Each individual wants to do the thing his way and be the center of attention. There is a personal transference through which each desires to express himself without regard for the group. The group, in a sense, has partially disintegrated into a number of individuals who are struggling one with another for the position which they feel will help them most. Here there is a sharing of anxiety experience and the beginning of the recognition of the group as a force.

4. The fourth phase comes about when there is a recognition of the group process and the importance of the relationships within the group for therapy. This necessitates the

modification of the behavior to fit the demands of each member of the group and of the group as a whole. The result is a jelling of the group and interpersonal communication becomes possible.

The length of time involved in this process, varies considerably and depends upon the skill of direction, frequency of meetings, size of groups, and the environment from which the group's population is drawn. Patients from the prison section of the hospital spend much more time in the testing phases than do acute and chronic patients from other sections of the hospital. Groups whose membership is constant show less fluctuation than do those in which there is a rapid turnover. Those which meet three times a week, jell in fewer meetings than do those having two meetings per week. They also hold the jell better.

It is the purpose in group psychodrama to create a climate in which there can be a maximum of catharsis, of relearning and insight gained, to stimulate therapeutic potentials within the group, and to make each patient something of a therapist in his relationship to other patients.

If we are to achieve anything approximating adequate therapeutic coverage of current patient loads, the group approach affords the only hope. Of these the action methods seem to offer more in economy of time and adequacy of achievement. Personality growth is facilitated through the closure of tension systems, development of insights and the expansion of the concept of self. There is a continual assessment of relationships, perceptions, and motivations, which stimulate personality growth. The treatment is carried out in situations, which are as close as possible to those in which the problems have arisen. This results in a more speedy transfer of the benefits of therapy to the patient's extra-therapeutic living.

10. OTHER THEORETICAL SPECIFICS
Bischof and Moreno

Ira A. Greenberg

There are many ways of organizing the concepts of J.L. Moreno so that they may be presented in a meaningful and systematic manner, and two important methods are briefly detailed here. The first approach to forming some sort of *schema* out of Moreno's many contributions is that of Ledford J. Bischof, who Moreno has informed me (while discussing the preparation of this volume on May 10, 1970, in San Francisco, and on Sept. 6, 1970, in Miami Beach) is one of the foremost interpreters of his system today. The second approach is by Moreno himself.

In his excellent book, *Interpreting Personality Theories* (1964, revised 1970), Bischof lists the following as the most important parts of the Morenean system: (1) *Social atom principle*, (2) *tele principle*, (3) *warming up principle*, (4) *role playing principle*, (5) *spontaneity principle*, (6) *creativity principle*, (7) *cultural conserve principle*, (8) *group development principle*, (9) *sociogenetic law principle*, and (10) *measurement principle*. Of the principles listed, those dealing with tele, warming up, role playing, and spontaneity have been discussed to some substantial degree in a number of places throughout this volume, while most of the remaining principles have been described to a small extent elsewhere in this volume; nevertheless, these latter principles will be dealt with once more here.

Moreno defines the *social atom* as the smallest living social unit, the cement that binds society together. Unlike tele, it has neither positive nor negative characteristics but is a reciprocal relationship between two people, each of whom is important to the social atom's existence. Thus, in the causal relationship between the sales clerk and the customer no further reduction is possible without destroying the relationship. Bischof gives various examples of the social atoms as a means of defining it and its place in explaining human interactions. This procedure is followed for each of the 10 principles that he presents and then delineates in exquisite detail. For the *creativity principle*, he quotes Moreno, who stated, "Creativity is a separate entity from spontaneity and a separate entity from cultural conserve but strategically linked to both." (Bischof, 1970, p. 257.) In this regard, Moreno sees spontaneity as the catalyst for the three types of creativity—chance creativity, spontaneous creativity, and conservable creativity—and as a catalyst it remains unchanged by the action of creation it had brought about. To put it another way, one might say that spontaneity may be thought of as the energy, creativity as the act of the moment, and the cultural conserve as the result. Bischof thus ties the *cultural conserve principle* to the other two entities while explaining creativity. He writes: "Creativity may produce a new way of behaving for the individual, a new way of behaving for the group, or a new building, poem, story, oil painting, industry, or form of government [and] the product of the spontaneity-creativity continuum is called a *cultural conserve*." (*Ibid.*, p. 256.)

Discussing the *group development principle*, Bischof has abstracted from Moreno's works the concept that "the principle of group development is an extension of the psychosocial network," which emerged out of the many combinations of social atoms inter-relating (Ibid., p. 262), as well as out of the concept that groups, like the individuals composing them, have developmental stages. Groups also are structural and dynamic, and Bischof notes that Moreno's investigation of groups revealed that each group contains three types of formations: "organic isolates, horizontal and homogeneous groupings, and a vertical structure running from the strongest to the weakest, with the strongest exerting powerful influences on the behavior of the weaker members of the group." (Ibid., p. 265). From his studies of various groups in different settings, Moreno formulated the *sociogenetic law principle,* which states that higher group organizations develop out of lower ones, as is the case in biogenetic law, in which man's past is traced back through the subhuman primates, the lower (in evolutionary development) mammals, the reptiles, the sea creatures, all the way down to one-celled amoeba. As Bischof says, "Essentially the sociogenetic law states that ontogenetically all groups go through some modifications of form, as did ancient and primeval societies in the historic evolution of man. That is, there is a law of developmental sequence from simple to complex in the formation of every group." (Ibid.)

The *measurement principle* simply concerns the fact that what exists can be measured and through such measurement greater understanding may be achieved. Consequently, it should come as no surprise that the man who could derive basic principles of individual and group interactions as elements in the structure of society would also be capable of devising ways to measure the interactions as a means of furthering his study and validating his findings concerning man, groups, and society. Moreno's investigations in grammar schools, reformatory schools, and prisons during his early years in the United States led to his development of the science of sociometry. This measures intragroup and inter-group dynamics, both horizontally among those with equivalent status and vertically from the most influential to the least, and its principal tool is the sociogram. Later, out of his ongoing refinement of psychodrama and sociodrama, Moreno developed the various tests for individual spontaneity as an adjunct to his training program to develop increased spontaneity-creativity in individuals. This then is a brief version of one interpreter's approach to some of the key concepts in the Morenean system, many of which are integral parts of psychodrama while the remainder are indirectly involved with psychodrama.

Moreno himself lists nine principal concepts of psychodrama, which he has stated (in a letter to me, dated June 17, 1970) are just as current today as in the early days of psychodrama almost 50 years ago. These concepts are (1) *warming up principle*, (2) *creativity*, (3) *spontaneity*, (4) *encounter*, (5) *tele*, (6) *co-conscious and co-unconscious*, (7) *role*, (8) *role vs. ego*, and (9) *role-reversal*. The first three concepts, as well as the fifth, have already been dealt with elsewhere, and so the next few paragraphs will concern the concepts of encounter, the co-conscious and co-unconscious, and the role concepts, with all of the material quoted being taken from the introductory part of Moreno's *Psychodrama, Vol. I* (1964).

The *encounter*, of course, is what occurs when an individual immediately and meaningfully confronts himself and important people in his life (as portrayed by auxiliary egos) on the psychodramatic stage. The encounter always occurs in the "here and now" of the enactment, whether its roots are somewhere in the past or in future anticipation. As Moreno would say, what happens must happen *in situ*, with the barriers of time, space, and states of existence (alive or dead, real or fictional) transcended by the needs of the psychodramatic encounter. The most striking depiction of an encounter relates to the concept of tele, and this is the oft-quoted "eye-to-eye" statement Moreno first published in 1914 and which appears at the front of *Psychodrama, Vol. I.*

"Role," states Moreno (p. IV) "is the functioning form the individual assumes in the specific moment he reacts to a specific situation in which other persons or objects are involved." Therefore, *role* must be seen in many forms, changing from moment to moment, redefining itself according to its needs or manner of growth and development, and from these many roles emerges the *self* or the *ego*. Moreno states:

> Every individual—just as he has at all times a set of friends and a set of enemies—has a range of roles in which he sees himself and faces a range of counter-roles in which he sees others around him. They are in various stages of development. The tangible aspects of what is known as "ego" are the roles in which he operates, with the pattern of the role-relations around an individual as their focus. We consider roles and relationships between roles as the most significant development within any specific culture.
>
> Role is the unit of culture; ego and role are in continuous interaction. (Pp. V-VI.)

Role reversal, which has been much discussed elsewhere in this book because it is such an important part of psychodrama and Morenean theory, is the direct route to the *co-conscious* and the *co-unconscious,* and in psychodrama can get to pre-conscious and unconscious material within a period of a single one-hour or half-hour psychodrama session, something that may require many hours in Freudian or Jungian therapy. The concepts are best presented in Moreno's own words, taken from the short section, entitled, "Co-Unconscious States and the 'Inter-Psyche.'" Moreno's statement follows:

> By means of "role reversing" one actor tries to identify with another, but reversal of roles can not take place in a vacuum. Individuals who are intimately acquainted reverse roles more easily than individuals who are separated by a wide psychological or ethnic distance. The cause for these great variations are the developments of co-conscious and co-unconscious states. Neither the concept of the individual unconscious (Freud) nor that of the collective unconscious (Jung) can be easily applied to these problems without stretching the meaning of the terms. The free associations of A may be a path to the unconscious states of A; the free associations of B may be a path to the unconscious states of B; but can the unconscious material of A link naturally and directly with the unconscious

material of B unless they share in unconscious states? The concept of individual unconscious states becomes unsatisfactory for explaining both movements, from the present situation of A, and in reverse to the present situation of B. We must look for a concept which is so constructed that the objective indication for the existence of this two-way process does not come from a single psyche but a still deeper reality in which the unconscious states of two or several individuals are interlocked with a system of co-unconscious states. They play a great role in the life of people who live in intimate ensembles like father and son, husband and wife, mother and daughter, siblings and twins, but also in other intimate ensembles as in work teams, combat teams in war and revolution, in concentration camps or charismatic [sic] religious groups. Marriage and family therapy, for instance, has to be so conducted that the "interpsyche" of the entire group is re-enacted so that all their tele-relations, their co-conscious and co-unconscious states are brought to life. Co-conscious and co-unconscious states are, by definition, such states which the partners have experienced and produced jointly and which can, therefore, be only jointly reproduced or re-enacted. A co-conscious or a co-unconscious state can not be the property of one individual only. It is always *common* property and cannot be reproduced but by a combined effort. If a re-enactment of such co-conscious or co-unconscious state is desired or necessary, that re-enactment has to take place with the help of all partners involved in the episode. The logical method of such re-enactment *a deux* is psychodrama. However, great a genius of perception one partner of the ensemble might have, he can not produce that episode alone because they have in common their co-conscious and co-unconscious states which are the matrix from which they drew their inspiration and knowledge. (pp. VI-VII.)

It may therefore be seen that although Moreno does not postulate such Freudian hypothetical constructs as conscious, preconscious, and unconscious, nor such Jungian constructs as individual and collective unconscious, he does have constructs which deal in their own way with material that is similar in part to what Freud and Jung respectively deal with. Which of the series of hypothetical constructs that go into the formulation of a theory of personality or a theory of psychotherapy is the best of the three giants named here is difficult to say. Each theory reads well and is logically presented in the writings of the three, and each does an excellent job explaining human behavior, and, therefore, an attempt to predict here which theory will predominate in the future would be somewhat presumptuous.

Every well produced psychodrama will take a moment or an event in the life of an individual and expand it in various dimensions, including those of time, space, and emotion. In this way, the protagonist gets the opportunity to re-experience the event or to experience it in a new way. As a result, he is in a position to gain insight from the actions he has undergone on the stage. For example, a simple verbal exchange that may in actuality have lasted no more than two minutes may in a psychodrama be expanded to fill a half-hour period of exploration and may be spread over the range of a large stage, while the emotional involvement, through the spontaneity generated by the stage-action, can be many times more intense than what was experienced in real life. Such is what is involved in what Moreno calls *surplus reality.*

In an article, entitled, "Therapeutic Vehicles and the Concept of Surplus Reality" *Group Psychotherapy,* Vol. XVIII, No. 4, 1965, pp. 211-216), Moreno states the following:

> Psychodrama consists not merely of the enactment of episodes, past, present and future, which are experienced and conceivable within the framework of reality—a frequent misunderstanding. There is in psychodrama a mode of experience which goes beyond reality, which "provides the subject with a new and more extensive experience of reality, a *surplus reality.*
>
> I was influenced to coin the term "surplus reality" by Marx's

concept of "surplus value." Surplus value is part of the earnings of the worker of which he is robbed by capitalistic employers. But surplus reality, is in contrast, not a loss but an enrichment of reality by the investments and extensive use of imagination. This expansion of experience is made possible in psychodrama by methods not used in life—auxiliary egos, auxiliary chair, double, role reversal, mirror, magic shop, the high chair . . . . (*Ibid.*, pp. 212-213.)

REFERENCES

1. Bischof, Ledford J. *Interpreting Personality Theories.* New York: Harper & Row, Publishers. 1964. Revised 1970.

2. Greaves, William. "100 Madison Avenues Will Be of No Help," The New York Times, Sunday, August 9, 1970.

3. Greenberg, Ira A. "Audience in Action Through Psychodrama," *Group Psychotherapy,* Vol. XVII, Nos. 2 & 3 (June & Sept., 1964), pp. 104-122.

4. ————. *Psychodrama and Audience Attitude Change.* Beverly Hills, Calif.: Behavioral Studies Press. 1968.

5. Moreno, J.L. *Who Shall Survive?* Washington, D.C.: Nervous and Mental Disease Publishing Co. 1934. Revised and enlarged in 1953 (Beacon, N.Y.: Beacon House, Inc.).

6. ————. "Spontaneity Procedures in Television Broadcasting," *Sociometry,* Vol. V. (1942), p. 7.

7. ————. (Ed.) *Group Psychotherapy: a Symposium.* Beacon, N.Y.: Beacon House, Inc. 1945.

8. ————. *Psychodrama, Vol. I.* Beacon, N.Y.: Beacon House, Inc. 1946. Revised and enlarged in 1964.

9. ————. (Ed.) *Sociometry and the Science of Man.* Beacon, N.Y.: Beacon House, Inc. 1956.

10. ————. *Psychodrama, Vol. II.* Beacon, N.Y.: Beacon House, Inc. 1959.

11. ————. *Psychodrama, Vol. III.* Beacon, N.Y.: Beacon House, Inc. 1969.

Part III
THEORY: GENERAL

Introduction

Two of this book's most important papers, from the point of view of theory and philosophy, make up this section. The first is an essay, "Spontaneity," by Adolf Meyer (1886-1950) who at the time of its publication was America's most revered psychiatrist. The second is Moreno's lengthy and very meaningful monograph, "Mental Catharsis and the Psychodrama," published in 1940 as a major statement of position. Meyer discourses enthusiastically about what many consider the most important of the Morenean concepts and is the very model of a modern humanist when he declares: "Spontaneity, responsiveness and initiative and not only imagination and sense or acquired unassimilated habit or chance, that is what we have to respect, *[for]* we are not losing ourselves in metaphysics but include biological human reality, and with it a vision and idealism guided and chastened by experience and a consciousness including conscience, and a spontaneity with responsibility."

Meyer would substitute spontaneity and idealism for the approach of experimental psychology "with its demands for mathematical accuracy," in the study of man and in the attempts to solve his problems and in this many might think that Moreno, the humanist who had discovered the spontaneity-creativity in man, would give his wholehearted support, but here they would be mistaken. Moreno, whose own thinking has throughout his life leaped unconstrainedly from one intellectual peak to another, nevertheless has accepted the discipline of scientific quantification, not only in sociometry, which is to be expected, but also in the areas of spontaneity-training and measurement. His procedures are clearly explained in

Psychodrama,vol. I (1946, 1964), and call for simple assessment of observed behavior under conditions of novelty and stress; and they require the use of statistical procedures to compare an individual's score against a group average or to compare groups. In any event, this is a minor point compared to the overall importance of Meyer's essay, and the essay says enough things, and says them well enough to make it an enjoyable experience for both the "fuzzy-headed" humanist and the "hard-nosed" experimentalist.

The editor finds himself particularly pleased to be able to include Moreno's monograph in this section for two reasons. The first of course concerns its being a significant contribution to the literature of psychodrama but the second reason is of a personal nature. The editor had occasion to read it somewhat early in his career in psychology, during the spring of 1963 while completing a master's program. He found himself so excited by the contents of this work that he literally could not sleep from thinking about it. It was this work of Moreno's, more than any other, that made the editor decide he had to know more about psychodrama and that caused him to play with the possibility of doing his doctoral dissertation in the area of psychodrama, which he subsequently did. (Greenberg, 1968.)

Early in "Mental Catharsis and the Psychodrama," Moreno examines the concept of the *cultural conserve*, which is simply anything of cultural value that lasts, i.e., a book, a statue, or a poem that is memorized. In examining this concept he found himself required to deal with its exact opposite, the concept of *the moment*, which became and still remains a foundation block of the Morenean philosophical edifice. In this same section of the work, entitled, "General Theory of Spontaneity and the Cultural Conserve," Moreno explains how he sought to get beyond the cultural conserve:

My first step was to re-examine the factors of spontaneity and creativity, and to determine their place in our universe. Although it was evident that a spontaneous creative process is the matrix and the initial stage of any cultural conserve . . . the mere confirmation of such a fact was barren of any kind of progress. It simply brought to the fore the relationship between the moment, immediate action, spontaneity and creativity, in contrast to the customary link between spontaneity and automatic response. This first step led to a dead end.

The way out of the "dead end" was for a theory of spontaneity to grow from a theory of action, and this Moreno thereupon demonstrates in the monograph and in "action-therapy" itself, which is synonymous with the name Moreno. This is a part of the prelude to Moreno's concept of *mental catharsis,* which he explores throughout the remainder of the exposition within the framework of psychodramatic theory and application. The important implications for large-group therapy is self-evident.

> The discovery of a spectator-catharsis in mental patients opened up a prospect of treating them at the same time as the patient on the stage. The latter became more and more a prototype of pathological mental processes for the entire group of patients in the audience. Patients who suffered from similar complaints or who had similar patterns of delusion or hallucination were selected to sit together in the audience. They then had the similar cathartic experiences when a patient with a problem resembling their own was being treated on the stage.

Little more need be said about this lengthy work, except to point out the obvious, that it is as valid today as it was more than thirty years ago when Moreno published it.

REFERENCES

1. Greenberg, Ira A. *Psychodrama and Audience Attitude Change.* Beverly Hills, Calif.: Behavioral Studies Press, 1968.
2. Moreno, J.L. *Psychodrama, Vol. I.* Beacon, N.Y.: Beacon House, Inc., 1946 and (revised) 1964.

11. SPONTANEITY

Adolf Meyer, M.D.

ELEMENTALISM AND HOLISM

In the face of a mood that has led science to seek progress largely in the direction of elementalism, the sense for units or totalities through integration has not made equal progress. The sense for totalities has been exaggerated before in philosophic and religious and animistic thinking. It had to undergo and face a deflation. Today it is at an unnecessarily low ebb in scientific concern, and has not as yet absorbed as much of the concept of integration as it well might. And among people who are not specifically scientific, comprehensive concepts are side-stepped or at least are inactive and rarely cultivated. For long periods in historically accessible time the larger units accredited with initiation and spontaneity were shaped in terms of gods or spirits; and St. Thomas Aquinas began his description of the spontaneous forces of the universe with a discussion of God and then in the second place proceeded to discuss the nature of the angels in terms of eternity, and only in the third place the

Reprinted with the permission of the original publishers from *Sociometry*, Vol. IV, No. 2 (May, 1941), pp. 150-167. Dr. Meyer presented this paper in the form of an address as part of the program of the Mental Hygiene Division of the Illinois Conference on Public Welfare at Chicago, October, 1933, and it was published by the Program Committee of the Conference in a pamphlet entitled: "A Contribution of Mental Hygiene to Education."

readily accessible nature of man. The big forces among mankind figured as dynasties *dei gratia* and in more humanized Greece as oligarchies and tyrannies. With the rise of the individual as a real concern and not a mere chattel (i.e., chief or capital "movable belonging"), there came rearrangements of integration, with unit formation, biologically and socially regulated by heredity and inheritance, or by appointment (selection) or election or usurpation, with concentration of power in the hands of a despot, the dictator of modern times, or the boss or the political party; with centralization or decentralization; in short, there is a problem of the human dynamo— the centers of spontaneity and origination. In the principle of government and governed, of power, of law, of rule, or the freedom from rule in anarchy, in the principle of individualism, class rule or a variously general rule in democracy—we always find as the center the individual or group with spontaneity. Since the days of the great army, we have been too apt to think in terms of intelligence tests; but most of us have learned, I hope, to value spontaneity as especially vital in human evaluations, since we may see some bright persons with high I.Q. flounder and many with low I.Q., although slower and limited, prove fully as worthwhile as their apparently more gifted fellows when dependability and final result are considered. Similarly, in the same individuals, we see moods and attitudes of inactivity or of arousal and freedom and what we call and feel as spontaneity, as the very condition and foundation of spirits, readiness and action.

I therefore feel it is worthwhile for us to direct our attention to this question of spontaneity, variously disciplined and balanced, which leads us to a further point, viz., that of the regulating factors in spontaneity.

In these days when the teacher, the social worker, the psychiatrist are so eager to get the dependable and telling facts about a person, and when one speaks freely of instincts and hormones, of intelligence quotients, and the social setting and economics (for both consumers and producers) and earnings and employment and jobs, *the degree and the kind of spontaneity* become one of the most important items in the case—a commodity that differs widely from person to person and from time to time in most persons.

By the *person's spontaneity*, I mean that which the person may be expected to rise to and to rise with on his own, "sua sponte," with his "spons" and "response" and finally "responsibility." It is more than "muscle twitch" or reflex, an incorporation and integration of wider relationships. Certainly both in our practical and our scientific habits of dealing with persons—with one's own self and with the many others—we like to express the needs and possibilities in terms of what the person has and does and what can be expressed as resources and possessions. The individual cannot profitably come to be largely an abstract center treated like a mathematical point, for, as a matter of fact, it is the way the personality sums up as relatively active or inactive with its type of spontaneity that determines the probable success or failure according to adaptation. We want to know what we may expect of a person at any moment, and in the course of time, on his or her own initiative and integrated organization; this expectation may be relatively or largely unpredictable but surely does not result from "casual chance."

The type and the degree of emergent initiative and spontaneity become a most vital concern, in view of the fact that in the nature of the individual and group life there is always a setting, a past and a future, there are always the leaders and the led, and the fate of large numbers and of the various ranges of communities is usually largely dependent on a limited number of individuals and the working of their spontaneities and the morale of the rest. The history of the last twenty years has been full of disciplined and undisciplined centers of spontaneity. We have to choose between spontaneity of a revolutionary type and spontaneity of an evolutionary type. So much of human life and nature is influenced by specific contingencies and combinations of events that much depends finally on the individual's *disciplined spontaneity*.

SCIENCE, THE ADAPTATION OF DEPENDABLE METHODS AND CONCEPTS ADJUSTED TO THE TASK

The whole development of psychobiological integration is a growth and differentiation of structure and functions within the bonds of heredity and mutation but with organization and integration of spontaneity. More than ever we realize that every mother has to face a new entity in her baby with its own and specific range of spontaneity. There shapes itself an organism for action, guided by meaning functions in a plastic flow of more or less grasp and inclusion of the realities with consciousness, and subject function or personality function. What we call mind or, better, mentation is the specifically integrated action itself and not merely action as the servant to an abstract self. To treat the action and integration facts as if they could be a special superentity is anthropomorphism. Each person proves to work as if with a constitutional government, a bundle of forces to be won for cooperative action or turned off into an army of revolt, with its energy and spontaneity in harmony or out of harmony with itself, in more or less biographic unity, and at the same time a not altogether predictable agency for success or failure in the familial, social, communal and national units—with a capacity or inadequacy of foresight and with biological and sociological conscience and conscientiousness as well as consciousness.

It is spontaneity that I want to study and inquire into and cultivate and respect as the all important characteristic quality of a person. It is the range of spontaneity, with its range of dependability and the capacity to rise to the various ranges of occasions and demands and opportunities of life. Call it psychology or behavior-study or, as one of my pupils suggests, ergasiology (using ergasia as the term for mentally intergrated function)—organized common-sense allows us to reduce it all to terms of "experiments of nature." Whether we study the units or the group or the part, the questions are always the same simple questions of critical inquiring common-sense:

What is the fact?

The conditions under which it occurs and shows?

What are the factors entering and at work?

How do they work?

With what results?

With what modifiability?

This is a formula which does justice to the factors of both elementalism and integration, to hindsight as well as foresight, and to the spontaneity of chance and purpose, individual and social.

If spontaneity is not an absolutely fixed quantity—only relatively constant—that is evidently the nature of this kind of fact and we must find the methods to do it justice.

Spontaneity covers the range of performance to which the individual is able to rise in the continual status nascendi with the endless or at least ever available "credits of time," within at least the range of expectancy of life, be it in mere waking up or in meeting any specific task or situation or opportunity.

In psychobiological study and work I should look for the capacity to see the problems and opportunities and to meet them constructively.

Our intelligence tests bring out "the spontaneity in the face of a multiplicity of questions."

An intelligence test of life is much more a real spontaneity test than would be the case with any absolutely planned experiment; it is an experiment of nature with its mixture of necessity or determinism, chance and contingency with law and order of growth, and choice under the evolution of ever accumulating and self-maintaining experience, i.e., etymologically and factually "*that which one is* from having gone through" (=ens, peritus, ex) function and performance in changing and yet more or less balancing processes.

VERBAL, CONCEPTUAL, AND
FACTUAL IMPLICATIONS

Somehow we cannot afford to let the case rest with a science of mere "happening."

There was a time when the person's will power and energy and naturalness were perhaps too glibly spoken of and treated as if they were the function and activity of a kind of superagency in the person, a capacity more like verbal magic than reality. If we used these concepts as those do who speak of "memory" as that which remembers, and of "volition" as that which "wills," we obviously would be indulging in mere verbal tautology. Spontaneity is not the generator, but evidence of generation. It refers to the dependencies as well as the independencies of the agent's rising to performance and attainment. It points to a quality of the agent very much as "consciousness" points to a state of specific functional relatedness, and "concensus" refers to a common intelligibility and goal—a condition to be treated as a question of fact, with a question whether it is or is not present in any case under consideration. The obligatory center is always as far as we know a living person or group of living persons with their spheres of varying implications and belonging and feeling and working together, and not simply a dried up abstract reduced to a mere mathematical intellectualistic point or a ghost made up in the image of our fancy.

Unfortunately to speak of spontaneity sounds almost like heresy, like expecting something out of nothing. The term can readily be taken amiss as belonging to the category of free will, of spontaneous generation and the like. Even if in our childhood we were taught to hitch our wagon to a star of naive absolutism and omnipotence of the personified infinite, we need not go from one extreme to another with equally naive blindness to facts.

My thought is not of the ultimate of everything. It turns directly to the obvious fact that some things or persons have to be moved in order to move, while others show spontaneity.

The wisdom or natural sense for discrimination and creative thought shows some interesting facts in the evolution of the pertinent terms and what they draw upon of necessity in keeping with human nature.

Root Sources for 'Spontaneity'

The word as such is of interest. When we see someone do things spontaneously, *sua sponte,* and (evidently using the same root *spons*) responsibly, without extraneous suggestions or duress, but of one's own accord and nature, there is something involved which seems to have played an important role which cannot be left out of consideration—leading also to the kindred and suggestive word and concept of "spendere." The Greek root "spendo" with its dominant sense of pledging oneself to an allegiance through the rites of a libation throws an interesting light on the nature of will and determination, as "pledging." There lies in this a groping in a direction inherent in the nature and capacity and range of integration of cause and purpose, an intelligible if not inevitable emergence in a *balanced and disciplined* spontaneity.

The fundamental sense I imply in spontaneity is one of naturalness; no matter how attained, whether grown by integration or by special creation and miracle as assumed by some, it certainly is inherent in life and in personality function. The "sua sponte" points to an inclusion of voluntariness and will, and I cannot help wondering about the hanging together of the roots and concepts inherent in the words play, pleasure, the German "pflegen" and "Pflicht," when I follow the root of "spouse" to our response and the inevitable concept of responsibility.

There inheres in the nature of all our action combinations of chance, coincidence and creation by growth and creation by anticipation and purpose, by potency and will, by cause and by reason, and by knowledge, of the senses and finally also of *sense* —that sense which with the French expresses itself in the progression from mere connaitre to savoir—and the ken which goes closely with what one "can" and what the German includes in können. From "sua sponte" and its well of capacity and ability we come naturally to responsibility, as we come from consciousness to conscience and from a passive materialism to an active progressive creative spontaneity integrating both idealism and objectivity. I see in this progression of terms and concepts a fact-determined and not merely wish-determined realization of relations and potentialities and necessities of comprehensiveness.

How can I, on the other hand, save this concept of spontaneity from any hasty charge of "vagueness" by those who fail to turn to the nature of the fact and want to limit the meaning of a word and concept, when we should sense also the direction, not only the limited but the open character of a time-binding process with its open definitions and specifications?

In actual work with specific persons, there is a strong tendency to belittle what cannot be brought to a sampling and bottling in a test tube with an experimental stab at performance. Yet, thinking in terms of the extent of spontaneity inherent in a person or human performance is perhaps more important than any show of superaccuracy in a field of so many relativities and such a wealth of potential inclusiveness as is inherent in the nature of man. Spontaneity comes closest to the verbal description of that actual functioning and resourcefulness which the teacher and the social worker and the physician and the subject should look to and cultivate—and which we can accept as a reality, provided that in spontaneity, as in the concept of "life," we eliminate mere magic.

Seeking a 'Science of Life'

Spontaneity, responsiveness and initiative and not only imagination and sense or acquired unassimilated habit or chance, that is what we have to respect. We are not losing ourselves in metaphysics but include biological human reality, and with it a vision and idealism guided and chastened by experience and a consciousness including conscience, and a spontaneity with responsibility.

Experimental psychology with its demands for mathematical accuracy has done much to make us neglect or underrate what needs also other methods of demonstration, analysis and understanding and evaluation. One longs for direction of attention to what might revitalize the interests in man and bring them closer to what assures attention to the person and not largely some formulas favoring cut-and-dried or dogmatic conceptions of mechanization.

A "science of life" without full respect for life where it lives and as it lives is not true science. There is a real place for life only in a conception of the universe which does respect (i.e., consider again) its type of progress and march in time as well as in space. A view of reality that does not include and respect the multiplicity and interpenetration of relations in a way that holds for the individual, and also for the groups that have to pull together, is not broad and inclusive and dynamic enough for our task. A philosophy based only on the physics of the inanimate and trying to legislate a conception of the whole without respect for biology and psychobiology where they operate, is not an adequate guide for man. (See H.S. Jennings, The Universe and Life. Yale Univ. Press, 1933). Whoever treats human life without respect for the inclusiveness and creativeness of the individual and group (i.e., entities with fluctuating "fields" of implication) is not a safe leader nor a safe follower. There is no need of suspecting at once a claim of a detached "vital force," or an assumption of a tapping of ultra-biological reservoirs of knowledge. We might rather speak of a vital and biographic organization and integration held up to us in an attitude guided by the question: "How are we to *be* and to *grow*, and to yield in time to the next generation?" Any fact inherent in the conception of life and of person must be alive and anything that makes claim to more than immediate significance must be sharable. Spontaneity is in line with the fact of a far-reaching privacy of implicit function and fancy consistent with the capacity for communicable function and teaming. The social fact of belonging and reciprocity is deeply rooted and related to the fact that man cannot even persist and perpetuate himself alone, and that there has to be a reasonably elastic but truly elastic linking together of groups and clearly sensed and clearly felt and clearly practiced common social principles, not merely sexual love or only possession and being possessed.

SPONTANEITY SEEN AS 'STABILITY IN MOTION'

It is naturally preferable to large numbers and groups of "humans" to keep aloof from the complexities and to think in terms of statics, or to think of persons as lasting entities and of minds, where the more functionally trained speak of mentation, allowing it to rise and subside geyser-fashion in a continuity carried by the organism in an order and integration of function and of dynamics. The essential principle will tend to express itself in philosophies and religions and absolutistic or pragmatic special ways and yet with the more or less of a general common-sense core, in spite of the widely differing historical and contemporary garbs. There is bound to be much individual spontaneity, but also a growth of spontaneity that includes a maturing common-sense, an appreciation of the best consensus and consideration. The most critical period of spontaneity is no doubt that of adolescence, today in a turmoil because the traditional relations of the young and the elder and the oldest and the youngest of the coexisting contemporary generations

are not easily grasped and adapted to mankind on an ac-
celerated move. We must be able to sense stability in motion.
Even inertia is not a standstill but maintenance of the existing
pace; growth is not static physics and chemistry but the
physics and chemistry working in lifetimes and in orderly
successions. In life, there are laws of chance as much as laws of
order. Passing from a philosophy of absolutism to one of relativities creates a specially difficult period. Yet relativity does
not demand a sweeping negation of the absolute where one
actually does deal with detachable realities, but it calls for
respect for relations wherever and however they exist. Since the
speed of average man ceased to be only 4 miles an hour, since
roads and vehicles have made it possible to go from start to
destination more quickly and with fewer changes of loading
than is provided by the present types of street cars and
railroads, and since time and space have become a vital and not
merely extraneous factor in the life of many, we have had to
meet and shall have to meet new demands with new capacities
and comprehensions. When "the air" carries words and even
pictures it becomes urgent to have a morality of "news" in
words and pictures quite different from the days when
questionable indulgences could be peddled among the few with
limited danger of reaching those apt to be harmed. And it also
becomes essential that we should teach not only eternity but
also the now and here, not under a logic or either-or, but of both-
"and," with a "side by side" of young and old, and a capacity of
leaders who also know and respect the led.

Not Beginning, but
'Being on the Way'

   In order to keep on safe and controllable ground, I like to
emphasize the not particularly fashionable start from the actual, immediate data ("donnees immediates") in contrast to the
reaching out for a something behind it all; I look for a middle
ground between the two exclusively and naively mechanized

reality of much of modern science (and also specifically of too immediate and obligatory a use of over standardized and over mechanized types of a hypothetical "unconscious"), and, on the other hand, the elasticity of the wish and uncontrolled and undisciplined vision, intuition and revelation. I like to think of the tried and critically controlled realities and the principles of well-planned visions and projects and uses, and the concrete reports of the actual emergent attainment and performance (which seems to be the vital principle of what the Russian workers and planners call "dialectic materialism"; a vision obligatorily thought out and tried out, and progressing to the next vision to be tried out, the very antithesis to Nietzsche's eternal recurrence); not an eternal beginning at the first beginning (for there still are serious gaps between the successive sets of integration) but a recognition of one's being on the way, and unable ever to begin again quite at the same place, with any such smug contentment as that of the Boston lady who does not need to travel because she basks herself in the fact that she is "already there." I am thinking—if I read it correctly, for it does not seem simply stated—of G. Mead's Philosophy of the Present or of "the ever-new" of growth and integration. Our flights of fancy come from off the earth, and they have to be brought to earth again in a practical thought of practice and of education ready to start with the ever-newly arranged material in hand, with all the sobriety of concrete experience, doing now and here at least what plain sense and a knowledge of history tell us, with plenty of room for ventures; not mere venture, but we might say earned and seasoned venture.

We may summarize our preliminary general considerations as follows: Both science and the theory and practice of education and of social problems have occupied themselves very much with the rather theoretical problem of nature and nurture and the plasticity of the human being. I propose to suggest as of equal if not greater importance attention to the problem of spontaneity as the issue that deals directly with the use of the available capacities.

Of Interest Is What Man Does
That Arises Out of His 'Own Nature'

It is spontaneity that concerns us vitally in practical life—
that which we may expect as the person's own—with or without
the help of others, and at any time, irrespective of conditions. A
mere enumeration of isolated capacities does not bring that to
us. We are interested in what man does "sua sponte," as a
natural rise "of his own nature"—be it in action or rest, effort or
restraint, it is spontaneity as long as it is the individual's or
group's own nature, as part of a course of behavior and performance in action or planning or in fancy, or contemplation of
the doings of others, with action, rest, recuperation and again
action, with specific temperament, disposition, inhibition or
release.

Respect for spontaneity and its cultivation (in harmony with
what man learns from the "astronomy" of the universe and also
from modern micro-physics, and from the chemical affinities,
but biologically conditioned in us) is absolutely essential for
actual life and especially for educator, social worker and
physician. Spontaneity is not unscientific just because it may be
too susceptible to misinterpretation by those biologically poorly
trained. It is not just a concern of metaphysical reasoning and
religious dogmatism, but the natural upshot of psychobiological
integration or behavior open to critical obligatory observation
and active planning in our work with human beings (including
ourselves). It leads us far into social and political life, with the
leaders and the led. It is that which we want to cultivate in its
best disciplined and adjustable form.

Spontaneity, if it is to constitute any smoothly running
performance or adjustment, depends on a fitness and congruity
of setting or environment which can never be anywhere near
absolute. It requires proportion and plasticity and security of
background and perspective of possibilities. It requires a certain
morale and stability and continuity, which today are very
seriously shaken up through surrender of false props, often

without corresponding readjustments in the guidance and natural conditioning of the growing person or the one facing life, and a sense of a respected career with a balance of stimulus and contentment. One is staggered by the ease with which dictatorships can get a hold and the extent to which democracy is surrendered. This is explained only by the serious malorientation under the pressure of ruthless propagation of patterns which are difficult to fit into the scheme of actual production and consumption and something like a code. One realizes the need of a simultaneous cultivation of culture, self-dependence and a balance of budget and its burdens, and of satisfactions from socialized life. The conditions affecting the balance of spontaneity and allegiance to the State and to law have to bring together the individual and the group in a reasonable and intelligible reciprocity of helpfulness. It should be obvious that adequate creative and planned attention should be given to the psychobiological needs and the balancing of the individual and group participants in the family, community, business and legal and political life. We need not only vocational advice but a morale and clearness of orientation and a place for the vocations; we need education of the individual and the groups, not merely as formal entities to be perpetuated but as time-bound personalities to live our span of life in our place in the procession of generations. We need our contact with actuality, but also with the spontaneities laid down in the human atmosphere.

Need to Arrive at
New Concepts of Democracy

Somehow the history of language shows that there was and is a natural groping in a general direction more inclusive than is generally needed today. Does it not look as if even the root underlying the words pleasure and play (also back of pflegen, i.e., cultivate, and Pflicht or duty) and the word-complex including prayer had also sensed as "precarious" too much dependence on prayer or begging for favor? And can we adequately appraise the spontaneities of art of music, of creations in word and picture and drama and even the modest charade?

All these possibilities reach into very complex relations. We have to go seriously and actively into the business of learning to know, and to guide, and to provide for, our human spontaneities. We cannot afford always to go back in religion to Adam and Eve and the reiteration of their sad story, and to a seven-day creation by the Creator, or to a picture of absolute perfection which gives the appearance of insignificance to the actualities of real life. Nor can we afford in science to begin always with the atom of physics and chemistry or, today, with the electron and proton as the only concern of progress, or with an astronomical cosmos, where our actual life is a differentiation and maturing of a biological order. We must be willing and able to rise to common-sense or a consensus of today. We cannot leave out or just allow to drift the human capacities, attitudes and needs and achievements or blunderings as slaves of machine and of credit booms. That can easily get out of control. We cannot have blind and fitful experimentation either in education or in government, in civics and in economics, in fits of despair of a real democracy or group order and dreams of revolutions. Rebellions when necessary; but destruction? We may need reconsideration of the Constitution from time to time as demands occur, not as mere patchwork but in reply to a healthy and constructively spirited referendum; there is no need of revolution or sweeping landslides of hate and false enthusiasm born of mere remonstrance. We have to rise to new concepts of democracy recognizing that men are *not* all born equal but born to be fair and to be treated with fairness. We need a constitution that is not merely a bill of rights but a formulation of individual and civic code within which we can also see our obligations. We want laws for guidance so as to avoid compulsion and revulsions. There should be no legislation without an expose of the facts from which a demand for legislation and a goal can be accessible and clear to every citizen. We want a closer relation between civil rights and obligations and criminal law; we need a clearer knowledge of the range of consensus on property and trade and credit so that we may understand where reprehensible operations begin and must be avoided. We want legal interests to have constructive obligations and not largely an interest in ways of getting around the stipulations of consensus, politics with definition of obligation and pledge in contrast to the implication of feeding private interests on the res publica. It is ludicrous to be asked whether you actually have had a fire when you seek legal help to get a road to your house so as to be accessible to the fire-protection. It is humiliating to sense that politics, the occupation with public interests, has come to denote largely the exploitation of public interests and machinery for private interests, with an apparent incapacity to agree on an organization accessible and acceptable to the rank and file of adults and not a bewildering spectacle to the adolescent. In the midst of resulting frustrations, Miss Schlotter's account of the Development of Recreation in a State School and Colony is a tremendously heartening and stimulating demonstration of the cultivation of the meaning of all that which we call spontaneity. It represents not mere wishing and dreaming and an adding together of casual items, but solid experience to be taught and fostered and applied not only in an institution with its concentrated necessities. To maintain the achievement and to give it a normal setting, the methods of education for the rank and file must be kept free from jeopardy through injudicious blunder of public administration.

When economics are forced on us, the school budget is apt to be pounced upon. Yet the school system is the practical expression of the hope of an advancing civilization. We should pledge ourselves to go without luxurious and conspicuous waste before touching the none too well supported provisions for the young who have to accept also the consequences of adult social and political and economic blundering.

Today we certainly have to look out for what is happening when frequently untrained though well meaning boards of estimates and boards of education invade the basic understructure of education for sound democracy to hand over its much needed funds to patch up the sins of mismanagement of credit and taxation. Nothing of this kind should be tolerated until the members of these boards have themselves begun to suffer from pangs of uncertainties and even from pangs of hunger one or two days a week. There is obviously a demand for interrelations which can be maintained only with sound foundations for spontaneity.

Civilized Institutions Are Products and States of Order

When we want to maintain or rather to create a modern democracy, a democracy adapted to modern needs and demands and opportunities, we have to see that the chosen leaders work at least with what can be intelligible to the rank and file, who then can be expected to operate at least with the sense they were born with.

Democracy and civilization do not just happen. They are products as well as states of order, and conditions that require a progressive self-maintenance and self-development.

In such growth, laws have to be principles of guidance and not only a privilege to enforce and to prohibit and to punish. Every law must be an education and not only an arbitrary order. The sooner legislators begin to understand this, the smaller will be the number of laws and the greater their nearness to human nature and needs and benefit. In Swiss legislation every voter receives a statement of the basic data and discussions, and there is a definite limitation to the number of proposals that can be submitted to the voters and thereby a self-regulating principle. Can we leave the promulgation of facts for civic organization and discussion of policies to a press that is supporting itself by the sale of advertisements? Can administration be at its best when it is drawn into the rivalry of competing parties as the spoils of the victor? Without a basic stability even the best spontaneity is apt to miscarry. The same holds for economics, where personal and civic budgeting is well-nigh impossible.

Experimentation is a privilege. H.G. Wells speaks of the English as muddling through. What word can we use and what developments can we expect when whole social strata have the stock market as their main interest and center of their philosophy? And, instead of balanced thrift a credit system so useful within its limits, yet so apt to get out of hand, and, like the machine, apt to pass from being a tool into becoming a ruler in insufficiently organized humanity?

These become momentous history-making issues in the management of our spontaneities, which are our most distinctive human fate and nature. Man is a maker of tools and also a maker of history including himself. It is our historian Robinson that writes for us of "Mind in the Making." To understand and regulate himself, man must know himself as a machine and also as a center of relative spontaneity, growth and action and imagination. The physicist is apt to show us and to force upon us either the clutches of non-humanized rule chance and experimentation or then a divinity of astronomy too far from life. It has taken several generations to bring forth and train a small group of students of man working on the beginnings of a science of man and his conduct and functioning—already, prematurely, making of themselves a new practicing profession. What we need is the huminization of science generally and the influence of the regulating lawful procedure of science to digest man's human tendencies. We need balance; we need common-sense, a natural way of looking for what we can accept as common, in spite of all our individualism, and therefore respect for both individualism and social law and order: We need time for judgment and yet preparadness to act when the moment is at hand and decision is wanted. In the continual change and development of new conditions we need a balance of venture and consistency, and concentration and comprehensiveness, a capacity to use history and imagination for foresight. We need a balanced resourcefulness, a balanced spontaneity, the cherished good of humanly integrated life. When the spontaneity of leaders fails, there comes waves of undisciplined spontaneity and the upshot yields the curves of dependency of our civilizations.

Resignation Seen as 'Forced Patience and Tolerance'

All this calls for a capacity in balancing education and medical work and economics and politics which is not everybody's capacity, but is sharable in spite of individual differences.

The universities bring together armies of people with tremendous vigor but still without the experience to be derived from the lickings one gets out of mature life, especially in these days in which parents are too busy in the stock market and in costly and time-consuming competition in what Veblen called conspicuous waste, in a life running on, or eager for, wheels and aircraft, or eager for thrills of life as compensation for their boredom with themselves and their contemporaries. Shall we resign ourselves to an inability to be satisfied with a sound middle ground of steady and basic attainment and an attitude capable of accepting and cultivating reality as a matter of more than forced patience and tolerance? The biological as well as sociological unit, the family, is apt to be maligned and correspondingly mismanaged as a school for discontent and divorce, with hardly a word for its ever returning potentialities and the call for resuscitation in a period of change.

There are no doubt inevitable contradictions in the scheme of life. In our hospitals we may be retarding the weeding out of the unfit and may create new cripples and what might even be called public burdens because we want to save those who are worth while. We accept this as a side product of really saving the many that need it and are needed. And we turn it to the good of human experience. Today, we arrest such diseases as paresis after the harm has gone far enough for a diagnosis. In two generations we could destroy the disease if we could or would heed our knowledge, as foresight about spirochaetes and their hosts and not as mere hindsight. In the meantime we do as well as we can and turn to the use of more experience that which is not wholly ideal. Perhaps alcohol as a renewed problem will again give us cause for thinking and acting creatively rather than for making a mere reputation in different kinds of crusading. Perhaps, a little more conscience, and keener sense of responsibility for health for oneself and for the group will do better than prohibition legislation. Perhaps the American Legion promises to be our army for peace rather than as a school for exploitations and a "will to group power" destructive of state or democracy.

Work and leisure, employment and unemployment, earning and spending, credits and debts, they all have to be balanced and leaders are to be trained also to be led, at least by their own best judgment. They are products and problems of human spontaneity.

Instead of expecting magic and revelation by magic, we are learning to use facts, the data and the lessons and experiments of success as well as failure; and it is here that this conference of social workers has valuable experience to enrich our resources. The short-lived but widespread enthusiasm concerning technocracy showed how eagerly humanity is looking for help. If it can make itself intelligible and if the basic principles are near enough to actual life, there is no danger of indifference in these days of threat and fear of trouble.

Man Needs Balance In a State of Flux

The live human being needs his balance of pleasure and

seriousness, his play and work, his variety as well as order, his outlook as well as performed history whether old or in the making.

He must have his joys in fancy, in contemplation and rest as well as in the satisfactions of achievement.

He needs approval and evidence of security and not only the mere possibilities and promises of hope and charity.

He needs his emotional ritual tradition of religions and popular customs as well as reasoned principles of intellectual and inventive progress.

He needs balanced spontaneity. Free will? and will to power only? Tantrums and revolutions for the sake of attainment at all cost? Will is free when in reasonable harmony with sound tendencies and not making for destructive conflict. A reasonably moderate progress beginning "at home" before one wants to enforce or prohibit, and project one's hopes and one's rules on others, should go a long way to make for evolution rather than revolution.

The remarkable attainments in educational experiments promise to make unnecessary much unhappiness and unhappy ways of attempt at remedy. More and more remedy comes from the joy of health and less wallowing in display of pathology and public thrills from exhibits of confession, and thrills from crime and misdemeanor.

A great question naturally is that of the modifications of undesirable trends formed by human spontaneity. Forcible education with punishment has been so misused that the pendulum has swung in the direction of total non-interference. That is certainly as much an error as the Dalton and complete non-interference scheme in technical education. But the trend today is one of wanting to work out the methods on ground of respect for spontaneity, instead of guidance merely by the mood of the trainer. Preventive management and correction of minor beginnings presuppose foreknowledge and a keen sense for order even in plasticity. We may learn to prevent in childhood the tantrums that play havoc in adolescence.

What will our government do for those who labor for the improvement of resources and vision of providing also nonremunerative opportunities enriching actual life with new types of leisure? This one thing is certain. The support of the system of education has to be kept out of the vacillations of budget and arbitrary disturbances of continuity of service. Separation of ethical and religious-ritual training, as I have already said, has perhaps been too radical and has left the interest in the vital spontaneity and attitude of the pupil, home and public too much out of consideration in the school, in the court, in the corrective agencies and in the physician's domain. More knowledge and more tact will have to make collaboration more acceptable. The conscience of today should not be adding pain to what cannot be changed but should make us forward-looking and constructive in matters of demeanor and in matters of health and of business. For this we need investigation and agencies that can bring the resources of better knowledge to those who need it.

Extreme Polarizations
Not the Answer

We cannot afford to indulge in extremes. Russia has gone boldly ahead. But she still has the secret police with its terror. She has "class" hatred as a dynamo. She has her hunger and restrictions of liberty mixed in with a new balance of freedom. She has a long history of hard struggles to rise from. We are in the habit of calling her a laboratory of experimentation. She shows us new groupings at work; dearly paid for but active, tolerable only in a setting that would spell dire hardship to us. We, in turn, must remember that we are spoiled conquerors, still ruthlessly exploiting the spoils of a continent; we should not forget that that our supposed freedom is marred by boss-and-racket ridden organizations which might seem terrible to unprejudiced or differently prejudiced onlookers.

It would almost seem as if it took misery, a Chicago fire, or some other disaster, to give chances for progress and to make unnecessary the willful disasters of rebellion—or do we want to rise to and muster our spontaneity? Have your choice!

The remedies lie in a sense for balance which we are striving to attain.

What we need is a mixture of stability and plasticity, possible where there is enough clearness and chance for understanding and using one's understanding at home and at large, beginning at the self but also including the very real entity called the state. The state, we should remember, has to live with a sense for all that which is implied in vital spontaneity instead of serving as an ever-ready victim to be plundered, and has to maintain a government which also should not be tempted to bribe the individual by bonuses or party benefit from legislation.

Thinking and working with and for man is thinking and working with and for a set of relations and realities nearest to us. But we also need perspective. There is not a boon that cannot also become a poison. Religion means to be the greatest aid to happiness and yet it has bred the most cruel inquisitions and still entails endless retardation of general progress by the holding back of its own adjustments. Law has been used by tyranny and through its hopeless obstinacy has made some turn to anarchy. Education has to be balanced or it creates a hotbed of discontent and armies of discontented learned fools and parasites. Modern life demands sense for work and sense for leisure.

Moreno's 'Here and Now' Approach and
Mead's 'Philosophy as the Present'

With a growing sense for human spontaneity and its good and bad features, we need the philosophy of the here and now illuminated by history and by a cultivation of outlook and creative fancy. Mead's "Philosophy of the Present" needs rewriting and further development for the many that should have it. We must learn to realize that life is history in the making and that it is the status nascendi that constitutes Mead's present, operated under the guidance not of unattainable eternity, but of a vision of the passing and still active and coming generations at hand, and a use of historical time and the centuries within reach of our knowledge and imagination.

To sum up, spontaneity is a quality that we have reason to pay special attention to in order to get out of the purely static habit of disregarding the active and forceful features of our subjects, the human individuals and groups. Scientific objectivity does not imply disregard of human differences and especially that difference which we call spontaneity, and among the spontaneities those that pull together play, pleasure and what one does sua sponte, as one's nature, response and responsibility. In other words, we must treat man with and for the spontaneity that spells also responsibility as made up of ever recurrent and disciplined spontaneity.

12. MENTAL CATHARSIS
AND THE PSYCHODRAMA[1]

J. L. Moreno, M.D.

Catharsis, as a concept, was introduced by Aristotle. He used this term to express the peculiar effect of the Greek drama upon its spectators. In his "Poetics" he maintains that drama tends to purify the *spectators* by artistically exciting certain emotions which act as a kind of homeopathic relief from their own selfish passions.

This concept of catharsis has undergone a revolutionary change since systematic psychodramatic work began in Vienna in 1920. This change has been exemplified by the movement away from the written (conserved) drama and toward the *spontaneous* (psycho) drama, with the emphasis shifted from the spectators to the actors.

In my treatise: "The Spontaneity Theatre" (Das Stegreiftheater), published in 1923, the new definition of catharsis was: "It (the psychodrama) produces a healing effect—not in the spectator (secondary catharsis) but in the producer-actors who produce the drama and, at the same time, liberate themselves from it." To gain a full comprehension of the developments

[1] Reprinted with the permission of the publishers from *Sociometry,* Vol. III, No. 1 (January, 1940), pp. 209-244. Presented as a course of lectures during the 1940 Summer Session of the Psychodramatic Institute, Beacon Hill, Beacon, New York.

since the time of Aristotle and the present-day meaning of catharsis, the historical background which led up to the spontaneity experiments in Vienna, the concept of the moment and the theories of spontaneity and creativity—all these must be reviewed.

THE HISTORICAL BACKGROUND

One of the most important concepts in all human thought, the concept of the moment—the moment of being, living and creating—has been the step-child of all universally known philosophical systems. The reasons for this are that the moment is difficult to define; that it has appeared to most philosophers as but a fleeting transition between past and future, without real substance; that it is intangible and unstable and therefore an unsatisfactory basis for a system of theoretical and practical philosophy. Some phenomenon on a different plan than that presented by the moment, itself, had to be found which was tangible and capable of clear definition, but to which the moment was *integrally* related. I believe that I accomplished this more than twenty years ago when, in analyzing cultural conserves, I found a concept in the light of which the dynamic meaning of the moment could be reflected and evaluated and thus become a frame of reference. Up to this time the moment had been formulated as a particle of time and space, or as a mathematical abstraction; hence it had been pragmatically useless and theoretically sterile. If the concept of the moment could be constructed against a more adequate background, the way would be open for a modern theory of the moment and a theory, perhaps, of spontaneity and creativity as well.

As I look back on my own writings on the subject, I can see that it was with my three dialogues, "The Godhead as an Author", "The Godhead as a Speaker" and "The Godhead as an Actor", that my swing in the direction of a new philosophy of spontaneity and creativity began. The theme of the three dialogues was an analysis of how the Godhead, himself,—

considering him as the highest possible value of spontaneity and creativity, the top-value on any axiological scale—would perform in the roles of author, speaker and actor. This brought about the analysis of three types of cultural conserve: the book, the memorized speech and the conventional drama of today. This second analysis, in turn, led to the postulation of a frame of reference for every type of action, work, or performance, each with two opposite poles: the maximum of spontaneity at one pole and zero spontaneity at the other, with many degrees of spontaneity in between the two, every degree representing a different quotient of spontaneity. This was an axiological scale; the ideal exponent of the one pole was a totally spontaneous creator, and the ideal exponent of the other, the total cultural conserve (the book, the motion picture, etc.). In two later publications, the "Discourse on the Moment" and my treatise, "The Spontaneity Theatre," these new concepts were put to a concrete test in their application to inter-personal and inter-social relationships.

The lack of an adequate concept of the moment has spoiled any attempt at forming a theory of creativity and spontaneity. This is shown in the confusion in the works of Nietzsche and Bergson, for instance, whenever they had to deal with related problems.

The gods and heroes who became the basis for Nietzsche's value-theory were, like Beethoven, Bach, Wagner and others, persons who lived in the service of the cultural conserve. Since their achievements were "works," i.e., high-grade cultural conserves, these became the frame of reference for Nietzsche's valuations. From the point of view of the creative matrix, however, *all* conserves, whether high-grade or low-grade, were on the same plane. In spite of his recommendations, therefore, to be a "creator," to be "creative," his evaluation was virtually based on "works" or finished products. Similarly, his higher evaluation of the superman (Napoleon, Cesare Borgia, etc.) over the holy man (Christ, St. Francis, etc.) was merely a shift from one inflexible set of precepts to another. Nietzsche did not perceive that, whereas, on one occasion, love and charity may be the strongest responses to a situation, on another occasion their direct opposites, harshness and selfishness, may be the requisite answers. The old precept: "Love thy neighbor" became its opposite, a higher value, but as long as both thesis and antithesis led to rigid patterns of conduct we know that there was no gain made, since both were related to the cultural conserve. The exchange of new conserves for old does not change the position of man in his struggle with the realities of the world around him and cannot aid in the development of a human society of which man is to be the true master.

Bergson came closer to the problem than any of the modern philosophers. He was sufficiently sensitive to the dynamics of creativity to postulate time, itself, as being ceaseless change—as being totally creative. In such a scheme there was no place, however, for the moment as a revolutionary category since every particle of time ("duration," as he called it) was creative in every one of its instants, in any case. One had only to plunge into immediate experience in order to participate in that stream of creativity, in that "elan vital" and "durée." But he, Bergson, did not build a bridge between that creative absolute and the man-made time and space in which we live. The result is, then, that even if these immediate experiences were to have the quality of final reality he claimed for them, they have an irrational status and hence are useless to methodology and scientific progress.

During the last few decades, spontaneity and its collateral terms—"spontaneous" and "extemporaneous", in English, "spontanéité" and "immediat" in French, "Stegreif", "spontan" and "unmittelbar" in German—have been in increasing use. This has brought about a growing clarification of the actual meaning of the whole concept. We watch various terms have their origins, their ascendencies and their falls from use and we know that they often pass through many changes in the course of their careers. Ultimately their finite meanings may crystalize and they may become permanent parts of scientific and, even, everyday language. Spontaneity and its collaterals have reached a climax in our time, and in the course of my studies it has become clear what their meaning is and what complexes of ideas they represent. "Spontaneity" and "spontaneous" have finally come to mean a value—a human value. Spontaneity has become a biological as well as a social value. It is today a frame of reference for the scientist as well as for the politician, for the artist as well as the educator.

Here is an example: politicians, newspaper men and commentators often refer to a certain development in public opinion as a "spontaneous" movement. When they do this they really mean to say that the development in question is a genuine, sincere and truthful expression of the thoughts and wishes of the people. This term they apply to nominations, elections, political and cultural ideas, acts of revolution and acts of war. The consideration of spontaneity as a barometer of that high value, the will of the people, has become an axiom in politics. The theory behind this phenomenon is that if spontaneity is an expression of what the people think, then the man who can draw the spontaneity of the people to himself and his ideas should - also have the right to exercise the greatest power over them. The desirability of even the label "spontaneous" is shown in the shrewd politician's use of propaganda to distort public opinion in his favor. Of course, after a change favorable to his plans has taken place, he will deny that propaganda or anything of the sort has been used. He will hasten to hail the new trend in public opinion as a "spontaneous" one.

Spontaneity is also used as a standard for cultural values. It is not so long ago, for instance, that an orator who came before his audience unprepared was considered arrogant and superficial, largely because the generally accepted standard of values was that a man should prepare a speech in advance in every detail and come before his public with a well-polished, finished product. During the last few years we have heard increasingly often—and with overtones of praise—that this or that address was an "impromptu" or "extemporaneous" one, with the clear implication that because it was spontaneous it must have contained the speaker's innermost and sincerest views on the subject. All this suggests that a far-reaching change in the evaluation of spontaneity is now taking place and that this change is receiving wide public recognition. This is probably one reason why my theories of spontaneity and creativity, which received little attention twenty years ago, are now more timely. A change in attitude all over the world has stimulated many other researchers to think along similar lines. A sympathetic trend towards spontaneity can be observed in cultural endeavors of all sorts—in the arts (the drama, for instance) in music and many others.

GENERAL THEORY OF SPONTANEITY AND THE CULTURAL CONSERVE

The book is the archetype of all cultural conserves—the cultural conserve par excellence. In essence it existed long before the printing press in the hand written volumes of the monasteries and the memno-technical conserves of the Buddhist monks. The book has been perhaps the most important single factor in the formation of our culture. The cultural conserve aims at being the finished product and, as such, has assumed an almost sacred quality. This is the result of a generally-accepted theory of values. Processes brought to an end, acts finished and works perfected seem to have satisfied our theory of values better than processes and things which remain unfinished and in an imperfect state. These perfection-ideas were associated with the God-idea, itself. It is significant to note, in this connection, that many of God's quasi-conserve qualities may have been overemphasized (his "works," his "universe," his "all-might," his "righteousness" and his "wisdom"), whereas his function as a spontaneous creator—the most revolutionary concept of a god's function—is nearly always a neglected one. The cultural conserve became the highest value it was possible to produce (the books of the Bible, the works of Shakespeare, Beethoven's symphonies, etc.). It is a successful mixture of spontaneous and creative material molded into a permanent form. As such it becomes the property of the general public— something which everyone can share. Due to its permanent form it is a rallying-point to which one can return at will and upon which cultural tradition can be based. The cultural conserve is thus a consoling and a reassusing category. It is not surprising, therefore, that the category of the moment has had a poor opportunity to develop in a culture such as ours, saturated as it is with conserves, and relatively satisfied with them.

We may well assume that it must have been difficult for the primitive minds of a primitive, inferior culture—or the early stages of our own culture—to evolve the idea of the moment and to maintain it before cultural conserves ever existed, or when they were at best weakly developed and thinly distributed. It must have appeared to our ancestors much more useful and valuable to put all their energy into the development of cultural conserves and not to rely upon momentary improvisations in individual and social emergencies. Cultural conserves served two purposes; they were of assistance in threatening situations and they made secure the continuity of a cultural heritage. But the more developed the cultural conserve became—the more widely they were distributed, the greater their influence became and the more attention there was given to their completion and perfection—the more rarely did the people feel the need for momentary inspiration. Thus the spontaneous components of the cultural conserves, themselves, were weakened at the core and the development of the cultural conserve—although it owed its very birth to the operation of spontaneous processes—began to threaten and extinguish the spark which lay at its origin. This situation called forth, as if to its rescue, the diametric opposite of the cultural conserve: the category of the moment.

This event could only have occurred in our time, when cultural conserves have reached such a point of masterful development and distribution en masse that they have become a challenge and a threat to the sensitivity of man's creative patterns.

Just as an analysis and a reevaluation of the cultural conserve was forced upon me by the apparent decay of man's creative function when faced with the problems of our time, I was, in turn, forced to focus my attention from a new point of view upon the factors of spontaneity and creativity. The problem was to replace an outworn, antiquated system of values, the cultural conserve, with a new system of values in better accord with the emergencies of our time—the spontaneity-creativity complex.

My first step was to reexamine the factors of spontaneity and creativity, and to determine their place in our universe. Although it was evident that a spontaneous creative process is the matrix and the initial stage of any cultural conserve— whether a technological invention, a work of art or a form of religion—the mere confirmation of such a fact was barren of any kind of progress. It simply brought to the fore the relationship between the moment, immediate action, spontaneity and creativity, in contrast to the customary link between spontaneity and automatic response. This first step led to a dead end.

The second step was far more rewarding. I started with the idea that the spontaneous creative matrix could be made the central focus of man's world not only as the underlying source but on the very surface of his actual living; that the flow of the matrix into the cultural conserve—however indispensable this may appear to be—is only one of the many routes open to the historical development of creativity; and that a different route is perhaps more desirable, a route which will carry the spontaneous creative matrix to the periphery of man's actuality—his daily life.

At this juncture numerous questions arose which could not be answered by intellectual means, such as, for instance: is it the fate of the spontaneous creative matrix always to end in a cultural conserve because of the fallibility of human nature? To this and other questions there was only one answer possible: systematic experiments which would permit a theory of spontaneity to grow as a theory of action.

Numerous theoretical preparations were made and many precautions were taken. All dogmatic assumptions were discarded except those immediately needed to provide satisfactory conditions for the experiment. Some of the dogmas which were set aside may be worth discussion here since they indicate the atmosphere from which we had to free ourselves. One dogma, for instance, was the consideration of spontaneity as a sort of psychological energy—a quantity distributing itself within a field—which, if it cannot find actualization in one direction, flows in some other direction in order to maintain "equilibrium". Take, for instance, the concept of the libido in psychoanalytic theory. In accordance with this theory, Freud thought that, if the sexual impulse does not find satisfaction in its direct aim it must displace its unapplied energy elsewhere. It must, he thought, attach itself to a pathological locus or find a way out in sublimation. He could not even for a moment conceive of this unapplied affect vanishing because he was biassed by the physical idea of the conservation of energy. [2]

If we, too, were to follow this precept of the energy-pattern when we consider spontaneity, we should have to believe that a person has a certain amount of spontaneity stored up to which he adds as he goes on living—but in smaller and smaller quantities the more he is dominated by cultural conserves. As he performs actions, he draws from this reservoir; if he is not careful he may use it all up—or even overdraw! The following

[2] A sterling illustration of the fact that physical concepts such as energy cannot be transferred onto a social or a psychological plane is the process of catharsis, which brings about fundamental changes in a situation without effecting any alteration in the energy-pattern of the situation.

alternative seemed to us to be just as plausible as the foregoing. This person is trained not to rely upon any reservoir of spontaneity; he has no alternative but to produce the amount of emotion, thought and action a novel situation demands from him. At times he may have to produce more of this, say, spontaneity, and at others, less—in accord with what the situation or task requires. If he is well-trained, he will not produce less than the exact amount of spontaneity needed (for if this were to happen he would need a reservoir from which to draw) and he will likewise not produce more than the situation calls for (because the surplus might tempt him to store it, thus completing a vicious circle which ends in a cultural conserve).

Another dogma whose acceptance we succeeded in avoiding— for we believed it to be only a half-truth—was that the climax of intensity of experience is at the moment of birth and that the intensity is de-sensitized as living goes on and recedes to its lowest ebb towards the end of life. To a person who is comparatively passive, this may seem a plausible point of view, but for a person who acts on the spur of the moment and who has no reservoir from which to draw energy—not consciously, at least—and at the same time is faced with a novel situation, such a situation is for him very similar to that of birth. He has been trained to put himself (by means of the "warming-up" process[3]) into motion in order to summon as much spontaneity as the emergency with which he is faced requires. This whole process is repeated again and again, no matter with what rapidity one novel situation follows another. At every such moment his training enables him to respond to a situation with the appropriate spontaneity.

This theoretical preparation led to several experimental methods in spontaneity. In one, the subject throws himself into a state—into an emotion, a role or a relationship with another

[3] See "Normal and Abnormal Characteristics of Performance Patterns," Sociometry, Vol. II, No. 4, p. 41.

subject, any of these operating as a stimulus—or, as we say, he "warms up" to it in a fashion as free as possible from previous patterns. This does not mean that the units comprising the state are expected to be absolutely new and without precedent for the subject; it means that the experiment is so intended as to bring the subject, as a totality, to bear upon his act, to increase the number of possible combinations and variations, and—last but not least—to bring about such a flexibility of the subject that he can summon any amount of spontaneity necessary for any situation with which he can be faced. It is clear, therefore, that the factor (spontaneity) which enables the subject to warm up to such states is not, in itself, a feeling or an emotion, a thought or an act which attaches itself to a chain of improvisations as the warming-up process proceeds. Spontaneity is a readiness of the subject to respond as required. It is a condition—a conditioning—of the subject; a preparation of the subject for free action. Thus, freedom of a subject cannot be attained by an act of will. It grows by degrees as the result of training in spontaneity. It seems certain, therefore, that through spontaneity training a subject becomes relatively freer from conserves—past or future—than he was previous to the training, which demonstrates that spontaneity is a biological value as well as a social value.

Another experimental method arose from the fact that the subject in action was often found to be controlled by remnants of roles which he had assumed at one time or another in the past, and these conserves interfered with or distorted the spontaneous flow of his action; or the subject, after having been liberated from old cliches in the course of spontaneity work, may have shown an inclination to conserve the best of the thoughts and speeches which he had extemporized and thus to repeat himself. In order to overcome such handicaps to untrammeled spontaneity and in order to keep him as unconserved as possible by the influence of conserves, he had to be deconserved from time to time. These and many other steps were taken before we could be sure that our subjects had reached the point at which they might begin to operate in a truly spontaneous fashion.

The term "spontaneous" is often used to describe subjects whose control of their actions is diminished. This is, however, a usage of the term "spontaneous" which is not in accord with the etymology of the word, which shows it to be derived from the Latin *sponte*, "of free will".[4] Since we have shown the relationship of spontaneous states to creative functions, it is clear that the warming-up to a spontaneous state leads up to and is aimed at more or less highly-organized patterns of conduct. Disorderly conduct and emotionalisms resulting from impulsive action are far from being desiderata of spontaneity work. Instead, they belong more in the realm of the pathology of spontaneity.

Spontaneity is often erroneously thought of as being more closely allied to emotion and action than to thought and rest. This bias probably developed because of the assumption that a person cannot really feel something without at the same time being spontaneous and that a person who is thinking can have a genuine experience without spontaneity, but this is not the case. There seems to be a similar misconception that a person in action needs continuous spontaneity in order to keep going, but that no spontaneity is required by a person at rest. As we know now, these are fallacies. Spontaneity can be present in a person when he is thinking just as well as when he is feeling, when he is at rest just as well as when he is in action.

Another confusion—the difference between a cultural conserve and the spontaneous creative matrix of this conserve at the moment when it is springing into existence—should be cleared up. An example may help to clarify this difference. Let us imagine the music of the Ninth Symphony at the moment it was being created by Beethoven, and let us also imagine the

[4] Funk & Wagnalls New Standard Dictionary of the English Language, New York and London, 1935, I. 858

same music as a work of art—a finished product—separated from the composer himself. On the surface it may appear as if the creative units which went into the Ninth Symphony—its musical themes, its climaxes, its harmonies, etc.—must also have been in its original matrix, and that no difference exists between the one in its state in Beethoven's mind and the other in its conserved state—except only that of locus. It might seem as if it were merely a transposition of the same material—the same sum total of creative units—from one locus in time (the mind of Beethoven) to another, (the musical score). Closer inspection, however, will show that this is not true. As Beethoven was walking through his garden trying intensively to warm up to his musical ideas, his whole personality was in an uproar. He made use of every possible physical and mental starter he could muster in order to get going in the right direction. These visions, images, thoughts and action-patterns—both musical and non-musical inspirations—were the indispensable background out of which the music of the Ninth Symphony grew. But all this background (which cannot truth-fully be divorced from the state in which Beethoven was when he was truly being a creator) is not to be found in the finished product—the musical score or its performance by a noted or-chestra. Only the result is there. The fact that this background has been deleted from our present-day idea of Beethoven is the result of an intellectual trick which is played upon us by cen-turies of being indoctrinated by the cultural conserves. If we look upon the initial spontaneous creative phase in Beethoven's composition of the Ninth Symphony as a positive phase and not as a transition in the direction of an end-product, we can see in Beethoven's musical compositions, his concepts of God, the universe and the destiny of humanity, in the loves, joys and griefs of his private life and—especially—in the gestures and movements of his body a united pattern from which a surface layer (the cultural conserve) can be lifted to satisfy certain pragmatic demands.

At the moment of composition, Beethoven's mind experienced these concepts, visions and images in conjunction with the developing symphony. They were integral parts of a creative act—of a series of creative acts. He made a cross-section through them in such a way that only the material which could be fitted into the prospective conserve was included; the direction of the cross-section was determined by its frame. In this particular instance, the frame was that of musical notation; in another case it might have been the frame of language notation; at still another, it might have been a mechanical invention.

It is exactly at this point that our theory of spontaneous creativity is able to take a stand against what Beethoven, himself, did—and probably was trying to do. If we imagine a Beethoven who would remain permanently in that initial, creative state—or, at least, as long as the state lasted—and who would refuse to give birth to musical conserves, a Beethoven, however, who would be just as determined as ever in his efforts to create new musical worlds, then we can grasp the psychological meaning of pure spontaneous creativity on the psychodramatic stage.

SPONTANEITY TRAINING AND SPONTANEITY SCALES

Experiments on the psychodramatic stage have confirmed by hundreds of tests the validity of the above conjectural analysis of the inner, initial processes experienced by creative geniuses. It was confirmed that "spontaneous states are of short duration, extremely eventful and sometimes crowded with inspiration".[5]

These spontaneity tests opened up two avenues of experimentation. In the one case, spontaneity testing became the

5 See "Inter-Personal Therapy and the Psychopathology of Inter-Personal Relations," Sociometry, Vol. I, Nos. 1 & 2, p. 69.

means whereby we could study the structure of spontaneity states and creative acts; in the other case, spontaneity tests enabled us to examine the readiness of any given subject to respond to new situations. When it was discovered that a certain subject lacked in readiness—that his organism was unequal to the demands put upon it—spontaneity training was applied. "The difficulty encountered by the subject is that a motive may arise in him a fraction of a second earlier than the gesture which corresponds to it; hence the component portions of an act are diffused. Therefore, the organism of the subject must become like a reservoir of free spontaneity in order to have in constant readiness the ability to perform the greatest possible number of varied, swift and practicable movements and acts."[6]

From the point of view of systematic research in spontaneity, perhaps the most significant phase consisted in the measurement of spontaneity and the development of spontaneity scales. The earliest study in spontaneity scales concerned itself with calculating the quotient of spontaneity for any cultural conserve. For example, a motion picture at the moment of presentation has a zero spontaneity quotient; a puppet show has a certain small degree of spontaneity in a moment of presentation because the factor of spontaneity enters via the personality of the persons who activate the strings; a theatrical performance has a quotient still higher than the puppet show because the actors are there in the flesh.

Another spontaneity scale attempted the reverse: it tried to determine the relative conserve quotient in various quasi-

6 ". . . die Schwierigkeit des Stegreifspielers besteht darin, dass ihm die Idee ein Nu früher eingefallen kann als die zugehorige Gebarde, wodurch die im Akt zusammengehörigen Teile leicht auseinander geraten. Der Körper des Spielers muss wie ein Reservoir von Freiheid die Ansätze zu einer möglichst grossen Anzahl verschiedener, rapid und sicher ausführbarer Bewegungen bereit haben." "Das Stegreiftheater," p. 40.

spontaneous patterns—the commedia dell' arte, for instance. Underlying its improvisatory character, this form had strong conserve components, types like "Harlequin", "Columbine" and "Pantaloon", and a dialogue which was, to a great extent, repeated at every performance, a high conserve quotient.

Other spontaneity scales are based on the degree of readiness shown by various subjects in different impromptu situations or on their deviation from a statistically established normal response in standard life-situations.

THE VITALIZING EFFECT OF SPONTANEITY TECHNIQUES ON CULTURAL CONSERVES

The first significant consequence of spontaneity work is a deeper view and a vitalization of the cultural conserves. One illustration of this effect comes from religion, prayer.

A prayer consists of four components: speech, thought content, feeling and the pattern of action. The essence of prayer is true repetition; it would be sacrilegious to change the speech, thought and gestures prescribed in the prayer. But when it comes to the feeling the subject can transcend the conserve, actually nullifying its repetitiousness by introducing a spontaneous factor. Feeling is the wedge by which spontaneity training can enter a religious experience. By the introjection of a spontaneous factor, the variation and intensification of feeling with which the subject accompanies a prayer may bring a depth into a stereotype—literally the same for millions of others— which may differentiate him from all other people praying at that time.

Another illustration is the drama. The dialogue and the thoughts of the playwright are sacred and inviolate, but the actor trained along spontaneity lines becomes able to turn out a new play at every performance. Feeling and, often, gestures are here the vehicles for reinvigoration.

For still another illustration let us turn to the performance of musical compositions. Numerous techniques can be used in order to stimulate the phantasy of the players in an orchestra, for instance, as they play one of Beethoven's symphonies, so that they may attain a semblance of the spontaneity which was the composer's at the moment when he created the symphony. As a prelude to their performance, the musicians can be trained to undergo auxiliary experiences similar to those Beethoven underwent when he was creating.[7]

The more a cultural conserve is—in the moment of presentation—a total recapitulation of the same process, and the more a subject is conditioned to respond to it with the same feeling (in essence, the same feeling today as, let us say, ten years ago), the more the question arises as to what value the conserve has for the subject. It cannot be denied that the recall of a conserve is accompanied by great satisfaction and even joy. The periodic recapitulation seems to whisper into the subject's ear that all is the same, all is well—the world has not changed. The cultural conserve renders to the individual a service similar to that which it renders as a historical category to culture at large—continuity of heritage—securing for him the preservation and the continuity of his ego. This provision is of aid as long as the individual lives in a comparatively still world; but what is he to do when the world around him is in a revolutionary change and when the quality of change is becoming more and more a permanent characteristic of the world in which he participates?

MENTAL CATHARSIS

A change may take place at any time in the life-situation of an individual. A person may leave or a new person may enter his social atom, or he may be compelled to leave all members of his social atom behind and develop new relationships because he has

[7] See "Creativity and the Cultural Conserve," Sociometry, Vol. 11, No. 2, p. 31.

migrated to a new country. A change may take place in his life-situation because of certain developments in his cultural atom. He may, for instance, aspire to a new role—that of an aviator—which brings him, among other things, face to face with the problem of mastering a new machine. Or he is taken by surprise by new roles in his son or his wife which did not seem to exist in them before. Illustrations of changes which might press upon him could easily be multiplied. Influences might threaten him from the economic, psychological and social networks around him. It can well be said that, with the magnitude of change, the magnitude of spontaneity which an individual must summon in order to meet the change must increase in proportion. If the supply (the amount of spontaneity) can meet the demand (the amount of change) the individual's own relative equilibrium within his social and cultural atoms will be maintained. As long, however, as he is unable to summon the spontaneity necessary to meet the change, a disequilibrium will manifest itself which will find its greatest expression in his inter-personal and inter-role relationships. This disequilibrium will increase in proportion to the falling-off of spontaneity and will reach a relative maximum when his spontaneity has reached its maximum point. It is a peculiarity of these disequilibria that they have their reciprocal effects. They throw out of equilibrium other persons at the same time. The wider the range of disequilibrium, the greater becomes the need for catharsis. Numerous methods—therapeutic situations—have been developed in the course of time which produce some degree of purification—catharsis. It may be interesting to review some of these catharsis-producing media from the point of view of our spontaneity theory.

CATHARSIS IN THE CONVENTIONAL DRAMA

Let us consider, first, the situation with which Aristotle introduced the concept of catharsis—spectators witnessing a

Greek tragedy. What is it that makes the drama catharsis-producing—in the spectator? Aristotle explained it by a brilliant analysis of the emotions in the spectators, and he was correct as far as he went. But from the point of view of the spontaneity theory, however, he omitted the salient point: the spectator is witnessing and experiencing this human tragedy *for the first time;* these emotions, these roles, these conflicts and this outcome are in this constellation a novelty for him. For the actors on the stage, however, the novelty has diminished more and more with each repetition. Their need for and their possibilities of mental catharsis were consummated equally in the course of their inspirational readings and rehearsals. The more the drama became a conserve for them, the less catharsis could they obtain from it.

It is different with the spectator, however. The effect upon him of the performance of the spectacle he happens to witness resembles the effect of the first reading upon the actor. The events in the drama may arouse in the spectator emotions which may have disquieted the spectator privately, but which are now magnified before him on the stage. However, it is the *spontaneous factor* of the first time which, on the one hand, arouses his disequilibrium to a high degree of articulation—a degree of which he would not have been capable, by himself—and, on the other hand, makes him a wide-open target for the purge of his impure emotions—in other words, his mental catharsis.

A spectator, just as he may read a book a second or a third time, may be anxious to see a drama or a motion picture more than once. Every time he sees it he may experience portions of the spectacle which he overlooked earlier and which will act on him as another "first time", so to speak, operating as an irritating and a catharsis-producing agent. But as soon as he is well acquainted with the entire spectacle, he will react to it as a conserve. By that time, moreover, his possibilities of and his need for catharsis will have become almost nil.

The spectators, as private persons, have no experience and no knowledge of the trials and pains through which the playwright, the director and the actors have had to go in order to make possible a performance on the stage or in a film, or of the anxieties and strains the actors go through at the time the spectators are watching them. Comparatively speaking, the spectators are in a state of mind free of pain and fear. They are in an aesthetic situation, entirely inactive and quite willing to let their feelings follow the impressions which they receive from the stage, and to allow their ideas to develop in such a way that they may fit in with the pattern of the play. It is, in other words, the warming-up process of the inactive subject. The more the spectator is able to accept the emotions, the roles and the developments on the stage as corresponding to his own private feelings, private roles and private developments, the more thoroughly will his attention and his phantasy be carried away by the performance. The paradox is, however, that he is identifying himself with something with which he is not identical: the hero on the stage is not he, himself. The spectator can sympathize with acts which take place on the stage just as if they were his own acts, but they are not his; he can experience with the actors all the pain and the torture, all the misery and joy which they go through—and still be free of them. The degree to which the spectator can enter into the life upon the stage, adjusting his own feelings to what is portrayed there, is the measure of the catharsis he is able to obtain on this occasion.

The written drama of today is the organized mental product of one particular person, the playwright. For him, the creative states and the roles which he has introjected into his drama may correspond, in some degree, to certain of his private notions and unactualized roles. From this point of view we may say that the process of writing the drama may have been accompanied by a catharsis—at least during the time of writing.

But for the actors, to whom this man's ideas are foreign, the situation is entirely different. If it should happen that an actor has a certain affinity for the part which is assigned to him—if the playwright has managed to express certain of his private emotions better than he, himself, could have expressed them— we may expect some degree of catharsis to take place in the private person of the actor. But one must not forget the effect made upon the actor by the great number of times he has to repeat his performance of this role in the course of rehearsing the role and, later, playing it night after night on the stage before an audience.

There are actors who give their best performances at their first reading of a role and their performances grow more and more conserved from this point on. Apparently they are more spontaneous at the first reading, and if there is a tele-relation between their own emotions and life-roles and those expressed by the part to which they have been assigned, they are spontaneous in proportion to the novelty of the experience of acquaintance. The more often they have to rehearse and play a part, the more will they lose in spontaneity and sincerity—and in private interest—in the part. The amount of private interest an actor has in a part is a measure of the spontaneity he is able to display in it. The amount of spontaneity, in turn, is a measure of the amount of catharsis which the private personality of the actor will gain from the process of acting this part.

Aristotle and, with him, most later theorists of the drama like Diderot, Lessing and Goethe, were apparently influenced in their judgment of what mental catharsis[8] is by their common

---

[8] Breuer and Freud called their early hypnotic treatment of hysteria a "cathartic" procedure. Later, Freud replaced hypnosis with free association and the idea of cathartic procedure was abandoned. Their concept referred to the patient's discharge of memories in a state of hypnosis. Obviously, their cathartic procedure had no relationship to the drama.

frame of reference, the drama-conserve. Their views would have been vastly different if they had approached the problem from the point of view discussed in this paper, the point of view of the spontaneous drama.

CATHARSIS IN THE PSYCHODRAMA

Historically there have been two avenues which led to the psychodramatic view of mental catharsis. The one avenue led from the Greek drama to the conventional drama of today and with it went the universal acceptance of the Aristotelian concept of catharsis. The other avenue led from the religions of the East and the Near East. These religions held that a saint, in order to become a savior, had to make an effort; he had, first, to save himself. In other words, in the Greek situation the process of mental catharsis was conceived as being localized in the spectator—a passive catharsis. In the religious situation the process of catharsis was localized in the individual, himself,—in the actor, so to speak, his actual life becoming his stage. This was an active catharsis. In the Greek concept the process of realization of a role took place in an object, in a symbolic person on the stage. In the religious concept the process of realization took place in the subject—the living person who was seeking the catharsis. One might say that passive catharsis is here face to face with active catharsis; aesthetic catharsis with ethical catharsis.

These two developments which heretofore have moved along independent paths have been brought to a synthesis by the psycho-dramatic concept of catharsis. From the ancient Greeks we have retained the drama and the stage, and we have accepted the Near East's view of catharsis; the actor has been made the locus for the catharsis. The old locus (the spectator) has become secondary. Furthermore, as actors on our stage we now have private persons with private tragedies, instead of the old Greek tragedians with their masks, their make-up and their detachment from the theme of the drama.

These private tragedies may be caused by various disequilibrating experiences, one source of which may be the body. They may be caused by the relationship of the body to the mind or by that of the mind to the body, and result in an inadequacy of performance at the moment. They may also be caused by an individual's thoughts and actions toward others, and by their thoughts and actions toward him. Again, they may be caused by a design of living which is too complicated for the amount of spontaneity the individual is able to summon. Practically speaking, there is no sphere of the universe imaginable, whether physical, mental, social or cultural, from which there may not emerge, at one time or another, some cause of disequilibrium in a person's life. It is almost a miracle that an individual can achieve and maintain any degree of balance, and man has continually been in search of devices which will enable to attain or increase his equilibrium.

One of the most powerful media which can produce this effect is mental catharsis. It can take place and bring relief from grief or fear without any change being necessary in the external situation. Large amounts of energy are thus retained which otherwise would go into efforts to change reality. Every disequilibrium, however, has its matrix and its locus, and the catharsis-producing agent—in order to achieve the effect intended—has to be applied at the seat of the ailment.

Mental catharsis cannot be reproduced wholesale and on a symbolic plane to meet all the situations and relationships in which there may exist some cause for disequilibrium within a person. It has to be applied concretely and specifically. The problem has been, therefore, to find a medium which can take care of the disequilibrating phenomena in the most realistic fashion, but still outside of reality; a medium which includes a realization as well as a catharsis for the body; a medium which makes catharsis as possible on the level of actions and gestures as it is on the level of speech; a medium which prepares the way for catharsis not only within an individual but also between two, three or as many individuals as are interlocked in a life-situation; a medium which opens up for catharsis the world of phantasies and unreal roles and relationships. To all these and many other problems an answer has been found in one of the oldest inventions of man's creative mind—the drama.

THE PHENOMENA OF REDUCTION AND EXPANSION ON THE PSYCHODRAMA STAGE

One of the problematic characteristics of human relations—as we live through them—is their quality of looseness. A love-relationship, for instance, takes time to develop. All worthwhile experiences in life take a long time to come to fruition. From the point of view of common sense, life appears full of tensions, disillusions and dissatisfactions.

There is a pathological aspect to all life-situations as they exist in our culture today—regardless of the mental conditions, normal or abnormal, of their constituents. Very few relation-ships are continuous and permanent, and even these few are often prematurely ended by the death of one of the partners. Most relationships are fragmentary and end in a most un-satisfactory fashion. In one case a life-situation is distorted because the two people who compose it spend too much time together; in another case because they spend too little time together. In one case, their life-situation is distorted because they have to exist side by side in one narrow room; in the other because they have too much freedom from any one locality. Such phenomena are not consequences of the economic structure of our society but, as we know from studies of such phenomena as the sociodynamic effect[9], they are inherent in the psychological currents which underlie all inter-human rela-tionships.

9 See "Statistics of Social Configurations," Sociometry, Vol. I, Nos. 3 & 4, p. 359.

Excepting rare instances, therefore, but few undertakings of any of us ever get so much as started. Every one of us has ideas—"dreams"—of himself in a variety of situations. These we call "roles". Most of our roles remain in the "dream" stage— they are never attempted or begun, and any attempts at actualizing our roles (rare as they are) remain, like most of our relationships, fragmentary, inconclusive, loose ends.

The number of major and minor disequilibria rising from instances such as these is so large that even someone with superhuman moral resources might well be confused and at a loss. These phenomena have become associated in the mind of sociometric and psychodramatic workers with the concepts of the social and cultural atoms. It is these concepts which illustrate systematically and in the most dramatic fashion how impermanent and uncertain the organization and the trend of human lives can be.

In the course of studying the cultural atoms of individuals, we have most often encountered two groups of people in particular. In one group, the demands made upon them by the roles and role-relationships of the group in which they live is so much greater than their resources or their interests that they would prefer being transferred, if possible, to a society whose total design is simpler and in which the number of roles in which they would have to function is reduced. A trend like this should not be compared with infantile behavior; the reason for this desire to live in fewer roles and relations may be that these people wish to live more thoroughly in a few roles, rather than less so in a greater number of them. The other group desires to develop and realize many more roles than the pattern of the society in which they live can afford them. They would prefer an expansion of their society and not a reduction—an enrichment of design and not a simplification. In between these two extremes there fall groups of people who would prefer a reduction of some phases of life but an expansion of some others.

It is important to present, from this point of view, an illustration of how the principle of reduction operates in a psychotherapeutic device—the monastery. The cultural atom of a monk—after he has joined a monastery—in comparison with his cultural atom during the time he lived in society, must show a drastic, well-nigh revolutionary, change. As long as he was in the world outside, he acted, for instance, in the role of husband to his wife, in the role of father to his children, in the role of supporter to his parents and in the role of employer to the hands on his farm. If he had desires for women other than his wife, then he may have acted in the role of a Don Juan; he may have been an adventurer, a gambler, a drinker, etc. In other words, he acted in a number of roles which were suited to the pattern of society in which he lived. By entering the monastery he moved into a society which reduced the number of his roles to a minimum; the roles of husband, father, employer, etc., were cut off at one stroke. The greater the number of roles in which an individual operates in any society, the greater will be the number of conflicts in which he can become involved. The monastic community, by contrast, offers to the newcomer a culture of the simplest possible design. By reducing the number of roles, disequilibrium arising from suffering is also reduced— catharsis by reduction.

If we consider the monastery as a purely psycho-therapeutic device, divorced from its religious trappings, it can be said that it takes its "patients" out of the society in which they have been living (and to which they are never to return) and places them in a society modelled after different principles but in better accord with the requirements of the "patients". The psychodramatic situation, based on a different philosophy and aimed at different ends, has utilized in modern form a similar point of view. It takes the patient away from the world in which he lives and places him in the center of a *new* world, separated from the rest of his experiences. This new world is a dramatic stage, equipped with all the devices which can throw him into a new pattern of society—a miniature society—in which living is different and much easier. At times it is simpler and at others it is much richer than the society from which the patient has come, but to him it is just as real as—sometimes more real than—the world outside. On the stage he continues to live his own life, but it is more compact because it has been reduced to its essentials. Husband and wife, after twenty-five years of marriage, go onto the psychodramatic stage and in a few hours exchange experiences of a depth which they have never before known. On the psychodramatic stage things are accomplished so much more quickly than in real life; time is so intensified. It is characteristic for the design of the psychodrama that, in it, things begin and end within the time and space allotted to them.

The subject (or patient) is allowed in psychodramatic work to omit many scenes and details of his life—at least to begin with. This gives him at the start a freedom from the complexities and intricacies of his everyday life at home. Sometimes he is also allowed to emphasize certain key moments and situations of his life and to leave unmentioned what seems to him monotonous and insignificant. This, also, brings him relief.

A subject is put on the psychodramatic stage and given the opportunity to live his life just as he would wish to live it. A lifetime is condensed into an hour or two, and the fragmentary quality of existence outside the theatre is reduced to proportions in which we are able to express the essential experiences of our existence. Thus the psychodramatic stage is able to give one's own life a unity and completeness which a great dramatist presents to his public on a symbolic level only.

Some mental patients exhibit a strong trend towards a simplification of their life-designs and a reduction of the number of roles they are called upon to play. As an illustration let us take the case of a woman who was suffering from a progressive form of manic-depressive psychosis. She showed a one-role pattern[10] for, although she expressed agreement when asked to

[10] Trends in psychotic patients and patterns of society towards reduction should not be taken as "regression" to an infantile level in the psychoanalytic sense.

play the role of a princess on the psychodramatic stage, she did not act out the role when it came to the actual playing of the scene, but began to voice to her "suitor" in the scene her delusionary plaint which involved her desire to die and a compulsion to work and save money to send to her husband who was in South America. Placed in the role of a salesgirl, a housewife, a nurse or a school teacher, although it apparently was her intention to act out these roles according to the proposed design, she did not make an attempt at any illusion but always acted her delusionary role.

Accordingly, we tried to reduce the dimensions of the world around her and on the stage, as well, in order to be more in accord with her own spontaneity. When we had, to some degree, accomplished this we perceived that an open catharsis took place in the patient, an increase in the coherence of her action on the stage at times when her behavior outside the theatre showed a high degree of incoherence and confusion. As she began to improve it still was characteristic of her performance on the psycho-dramatic stage that she mixed a certain number of private elements with the roles, but in lucid intervals which approached the normal she was finally able to carry out a symbolic role without too obvious reference to her private problems.

Many patients have come to my attention who, in the course of a paranoid form of dementia praecox, have brought to near-extinction one after another of the roles which normal life demanded of them but not, apparently, because of any trend towards reduction. On the contrary, they seemed to have a frantic desire to make room for numerous other role-aspirations which were impossible of expression within the bounds of their normal existence.

An illustration of this phenomenon of expansion is the case of a mental patient whose conduct showed the presence of the seeds, at least, of many roles. At breakfast he claimed to be an aviator; at lunchtime he said he was a member of the British royal house; he spent the afternoon as a cowboy and at the supper-table he was a Chinese citizen. In a normal group these roles remained almost entirely on a verbal level since they received no support from the reality around him[11]; he confused the people around him and he became more confused, himself, by their lack of response. To the growing vagueness and subjectivity of his paranoid conduct a stop was put when psychodramatic treatment was undertaken. The stage work showed that the action-pattern of his delusionary roles had a greater coherence than had been apparent in real life and that there was often more organization to them than mere verbal symbols. When the patient was supported by appropriate partners it was seen that these roles—unlivable in the outside world—could be given a semblance of reality for him on the psycho-dramatic stage. Since these roles were short-lived he could live through many of them within a two-hour session in the theatre and derive satisfaction from the realization of all of them. For these completely hallucinatory roles and relations the psychodramatic stage was, indeed, the only possible vehicle. His optical and acoustic hallucinations found not only an expression through the aid of his partners but, in the audience in the theatre, they found a world which could give them a social reality—a world whose flexibility was able to accomodate the patient's trend towards expansion of his constellation of roles.

PERSONAL AND INTER-PERSONAL CATHARSIS

It has become an accepted fact in psychodramatic therapy

[11] It has been a significant finding in the course of psychodramatic work that schizophrenic patients experience complicated patterns of emotion, thought and inter-personal relations. This is contrary to the general view of Freud and Bleuler that the experiences of schzophrenics are almost entirely confined to the verbal level and that verbal suggestion of an event is just as satisfactory to them as the actualization of an event would be.

that action-patterns have a definite value in the process of catharsis. The climax in a patient's treatment usually takes place in the course of psychodramatic work on the stage and not during the interview preceding it or the analysis which comes after each scene. Interview, psychodrama and post-dramatic analysis form a continuous pattern, often so intertwined that it is difficult to tell where one leaves off and the other begins. But however relieving an analysis of situations may be for the patient, for a final test he must go back onto the stage in a real-life situation. There it may rapidly become clear that the equilibrium he had thought to have gained from the analysis is not adequate. What seems lacking is a "binder" between whatever analysis can give him in the way of equilibrium and the action in the moment of living. This binder is the spontaneity which the patient must be able to summon with split-second swiftness when a life-situation calls for it. Re-test after re-test must be made in order to assure the patient that the necessary catharsis has been attained within him. It is spontaneity in its various expressions which at last crowns the efforts of the psychodrama and gives the patient the final certainty of an established equilibrium.

Theoretically speaking, the subject should be able rapidly to summon the spontaneity required for any given situation. Nevertheless, we often see a patient who puts up great resistance when asked to act out his problem. It may also happen that his mind is willing and he is able to make a start on the verbal level but the body lags behind; or, the body is brought into incomplete action which results in cramped gestures and movements and a disequilibrium of the function of speech, as well; or undue haste and impulsiveness may throw the body into overheated action. In situations like these, the spontaneity associated with verbal and mental images does not have the power to carry the body along with it. Analysis does not help; action is required. The method is to warm the subject up by means of mental and physical starters, calling in another person to assist, if necessary. If this method is applied again and again, the subject learns through self-activation to get his organism ready for spontaneous action. It is a training in summoning spontaneity. In the course of overcoming the disequilibrium between the somatic and the mental processes, larger and larger portions of the organism are brought into play, pathological tensions and barriers are swept away and a catharsis takes place.

Disequilibrating experiences are often found between two or more persons in the roles and situations in which they are compelled to live. When they are placed upon the psychodramatic stage they seem to lack sufficient spontaneity in respect to one another to operate together in a common task. Psychodramatic methods can bring them to a point where they can reach one another at a depth-level which has been missing from their relationship. At this depth-level they can exchange thoughts and express emotions which will go far toward clarifying and erasing the causes of their conflict.

Two persons may carry on a relationship for an indefinite time in harmony. All of a sudden they find themselves enemies—they do not know why. In the treatment of our interview with a single person it is impossible to find the true seat of the disequilibrium; both people are necessary, and they must be brought together in a situation which is crucial for them and in which they can act spontaneously. On the psychodramatic stage in one of these situations they will find themselves discarding evasions, reticences and equivocations, and revealing their true, naked emotions and feelings. They remain essentially the same two individuals who, a moment ago, stepped upon the stage, but facets of their natures are revealed which each had forgotten in the other person—if, indeed they had ever been apparent before. It is here, on this level, that the true point of conflict is revealed. The basic features of their inter-personal clash can be gradually brought to visualization and, finally to their co-experience. If this depth-level had been ignored—if the essential core of their conflict had remained undiscovered and unexplored—no sound and permanent solution for their difficulty could have been reached. It required the stimulus of one personality upon the other in a spontaneous interaction to bring it to light.

SPECTATOR AND GROUP CATHARSIS

We have found that persons who witness a psychodramatic performance often become greatly disturbed. Sometimes, however, they leave the theatre very much relieved, almost as if it had been their own problems which they had just seen worked out upon the stage. Experiences such as these brought us back to the Aristotelian view of catharsis—as taking place in the spectator—but from a different angle and with a different perspective.

The audience in a therapeutic theatre was originally limited to persons necessary to accomplish the treatment. This is still considered the classic approach. At first we concerned ourselves with what this group meant to the actor-patients on the stage. It was soon discovered that they represented the world—public opinion. The amount and the kind of influence which the group exerted upon the conduct of a patient on the stage became an object of research, but in the course of time we made another discovery—the effect of psychodramatic work upon a spectator. This effect is bound to have important consequences for the psychodramatic treatment of groups.

By its own momentum the psychodramatic situation arouses people to act their problems out on a level on which the most intimate inter-individual and inter-role relationships find expression. This momentum is a dynamic factor which drives the subjects—once they have started—to act and talk things out in a way which takes them (and the spectators) by surprise.

There is a significant difference between the catharsis experienced by the spectator of a conventional drama and that experienced by the spectator of a psychodramatic performance. The question has been asked again and again: what factor produces this difference and in what does this difference consist? The persons on the psychodramatic stage do not really act, in the conventional sense. They are presenting themselves, their own problems and conflicts and—this must be emphasized— they make no attempt to make plays out of their problems. They are in dead earnest; they have been hounded by a conflict and they have come up against a blank wall in trying to escape. The spectator in the conventional theatre and the spectator of a psychodramatic preformance can be compared to a man who sees the motion picture of a volcano in eruption and a man who watches the eruption from the foot of the mountain itself. It is the drama of life, in primary form, which, through the vehicle of the therapeutic theatre, comes to view. It never does, otherwise. Man protects such intimate relationships and situations from inspection with every possible means of concealment.

The ultimate, private—yet anonymous—character of the psychodrama makes every spectator in the audience a silent accomplice of those on the stage, no matter what may be revealed there. More and more the whole meaning of his function as a spectator vanishes and he becomes a part of and a silent partner in the psychodrama. This may explain the different character of the catharsis experienced by an onlooker in the therapeutic theatre compared with that which he attains from a conventional theatrical performance.

We are now about to consider the still deeper effect of psychodramatic work upon mental patients when they are spectators. It has been noticed here at Beacon Hill—and I have referred to this phenomenon before—that mental patients show a remarkable sensitivity for one another in daily life, a tele-relation for one another's actions and words which is often surprising to the staff, and which amounts to a high appreciation of their various ideological and emotional patterns. This heightened sensitivity was brought to a true test when we began to permit mental patients to witness a delusionary or a hallucinatory, a depressive or a paranoid experience of another patient, reproduced on the psychodramatic stage.

From a psychodramatic point of view the behavior of mental patients can be divided into three categories: refusal to enter the theatre, willingness to enter the theatre but only as a spectator and, finally, willingness to take part in what is going on upon the stage. The gap between the first two categories is relatively wide, but sooner or later every patient can be persuaded to become a spectator and once he has reached this phase, a therapeutic approach to his disorder is possible, even if he never goes onto the stage. The mental patient who, from his safe seat in the audience, witnesses a psychodrama—especially if the central person in it is a patient with whom he is acquainted—will show an interest and a curiosity far surpassing the normal and will reveal profound repercussions afterwards. The explanation of this effect is that the dramatization of psychiatric phenomena brings into three-dimensional expression for the spectator-patients patterns of experience which have not been permitted validity in the world outside the theatre. The mental patient in the audience thus comes into contact with the delusionary or hallucinatory portion of another patient's world; he sees it worked out before his own eyes as if it were reality. There are hidden correspondences between the delusionary portion of the scene he has seen acted out and his own delusions, many of which he has refrained from verbalizing. In addition, the after-reactions of mental patients to what some other mental patient has acted out on the stage reveal relationships between his own delusions and those he has seen worked out which are suggestive both of his relations outside the theatre on the psychotic level with this particular patient and of the kind of catharsis he experienced in the theatre.

The discovery of a spectator-catharsis in mental patients opened up a prospect of treating them at the same time as the patient on the stage. The latter became more and more a prototype of pathological mental processes for the entire group of patients in the audience. Patients who suffered from similar complaints or who had similar patterns of delusion and hallucination were selected to sit together in the audience. They then had similar cathartic experiences when a patient with a problem resembling their own was being treated on the stage.

The importance of this approach as a method of group psychotherapy is evident. At times, instead of using the mental patient as a prototype, specially-trained psychodramatic assistants—so-called "auxiliary egos"—have been used with equally beneficial results. Methodically, the use of the auxiliary ego was an advantage because of the frequent difficulty of influencing more or less non-cooperative mental patients to choose situations or plots which were fruitful for the whole group and not merely for themselves. The employment of auxiliary egos who were under our own control and sufficiently sensitive to the experiences of the psychotic, marked an important step forward in the technique of "group catharsis".

The return via the psychodrama to the Aristotelian view of catharsis has vitalized the original conception. Large mental hospitals, mental hygiene clinics, child guidance bureaus and community theatres may be able to make use of the following scheme which has the obvious goal of treating large numbers of people at the same time. It is, of course, a special experiment within the psychodramatic sphere. It has to be tried out under the direction of someone who is highly skilled along psychiatric, psychodramatic and theatrical lines. It does not exclude the methods and techniques outlined in this paper and will never be able to replace them, but it may become an important auxiliary technique where individual or inter-personal treatment is practically impossible and where group catharsis is the method of choice.

The playwright of the conventional drama is, in this scheme, replaced by a more complicated mechanism. The community in which the subjects live—they may be mental patients or normal people—is explored, and by direct interviews or other means the dominating ideologies, emotions or illusions of the community are determined. The more thorough this preliminary investigation is, the better. In addition, many of the subjects may already have acted on the psychodramatic stage and thus may have been able to supply pertinent material about themselves. All this material is then studied carefully by the auxiliary egos, and the design of one or more psychodramas is worked out. These psychodramas are so constructed that they may reach the depth-levels of as large a proportion of the subjects as possible. They may even be assisted in this process by some of the subjects themselves. The resultant psychodrama is preferably spontaneous, but a conserve drama can be visualized as possible in this situation.

The actors of the conventional drama are replaced for this psychodrama by auxiliary egos. If the objective is to be the treatment of mental patients, the auxiliary egos will have been trained to portray delusions or hallucinations—or any psychotic processes which suit the purpose.

In contradistinction to the conventional theatre, the spectators of this psychodrama are then witnessing a performance which is expressly intended to relate (and which, in fact, does relate) to their specific individual problems. The reactions of the spectators during and immediately following the performance can be made the basis for individual psychodramatic treatments. Thus is Aristotle's concept of catharsis brought to its rightful, logical culmination.

The therapeutic aspect of the psychodrama cannot be divorced from its aesthetic aspect nor, ultimately, from its ethical character. What the aesthetic drama has done for deities like Dionysus, Brahma and Jehova and the representative characters like Hamlet, Macbeth or Oedipus, the psychodrama can do for every man. In the therapeutic theatre an anonymous, average man becomes something approaching a work of art—not only for others but for himself. A tiny, insignificant existence is here elevated to a level of dignity and respect. Its private problems are projected on a high plane of action before a special public—a small world, perhaps, but *the* world of the therapeutic theatre. The world in which we all live is imperfect, unjust and amoral, but in the therapeutic theatre a little person can rise above our everyday world. Here his ego becomes an aesthetic prototype—he becomes representative of mankind. On the psychodramatic stage he is put into a state of inspiration— he is the dramatist of himself.

COMMENTS AND CONCLUSIONS

At this juncture it is logical to consider what processes in other types of psychotherapy are used to attain mental catharsis. Throughout this paper it has been my purpose to demonstrate the close relationship between spontaneity and mental catharsis, the material being largely drawn from actual psychodramatic experiments and studies. It can readily be assumed that any other genuine psychotherapeutic approach to the same problems must disclose similar basic conditions and that catharsis will be attained by similar devices.

An interested investigator can observe a plain relationship between other types of psychotherapy (such as hypnosis, suggestion or psychoanalysis) and the psychodrama. All of these might be viewed as variously undeveloped stages of a complete psychodramatic pattern of treatment. The spontaneous factor operates in all psychotherapies up to certain limits. It operates in the "free association" technique used in psychoanalysis, in suggestion therapy or during a hypnotic session. On the basis of the conclusions reached in this paper, there must be a relationship between the spontaneity quotient of any type of psychotherapy and the extent of mental catharsis it achieves. Similarly, the other principles discussed, such as the patterns of roles and role-relationships which are given so much prominence in psychodramatic work, can be discerned as operating—even if only in a fragmentary fashion—in every psychotherapeutic technique.

Students of psychotherapy—especially those who practice psychoanalysis or use such psychoanalytic terms as "transference," "regression," "libido," "unconscious" and many others—may well wonder what usefulness remains for these concepts. These psychoanalytic concepts can be superseded by more inclusive ones which originated as the result of psychodramatic and sociometric findings. An illustration is the concept of "transference," considered by Freud the cornerstone of all psychoanalytic therapy. The stimulating value of a concept must come to an end when new findings and dynamic factors demand a re-orientation of the whole field in which they are applied. Any new concepts should show the limitations of previous concepts in this sense: Bernheim's concept of "suggestion" was discarded by Freud in favor of what he called "transference", a larger concept which also included "suggestion". Within the last twenty years, studies of inter-individual relationships and of attraction-repulsion patterns in large groups have led me to develop a new concept, "tele", which is inclusive of "transference" (which, in turn, includes "suggestion") and, in addition, is able to take in its stride processes as widely separated as the "narcissistic" psychoses on the one hand, and psychosocial "networks" on the other.

TERMINOLOGICAL COMMENTS

Psychodrama is a form of the drama in which the plots, situations and roles—whether real or symbolic—reflect the actual problems of the persons acting and are not the work of a playwright. It has been found that psychodramatic procedure is accompanied by profound forms of mental catharsis. The psychodrama, as originally conceived, is carried out in a quasi-theatrical setting, with a stage and a selected audience.

Psychodrama, in the wider sense in which the word is used today, is an exploratory approach to the conserved and the improvised forms of the drama, reevaluated on the basis of psychodramatic concepts.

The psychodrama developed out of the impromptu play. The impromptu play, as a principle in psychotherapy, was first used by me in the treatment of children, and later in the treatment of mental patients. From the year 1911 to the year 1930 I was practically alone in using this principle—at least in a systematic fashion, but in the last few years the number of educators and psychiatrists to take up the use of this principle has been increasing. In educational and psychiatric literature terms like 'play-techniques', 'release therapy', 'play therapy', 'projection methods' and others, which suggest the use of the impromptu-play principle, have begun to be current. Although it had its inception in the idea of the impromptu play, the psychodrama of today is vastly different from it and should not become confused with it. In order to show how the psychodrama developed out of the impromptu play and to indicate wherein the courses of the two have diverged, I shall here describe the process which resulted in this differentation.

I began my work with children at a time when there was only one alternative to allowing children to play spontaneously by themselves: an imitation, on the children's level, of the conventional, conserved drama. A therapist could either watch the children at their games and interpret their behavior in terms of some ideology, like psychoanalysis, for instance, or he could teach them to rehearse and act out, like adults, a play made from, shall we say, the story of 'Little Red Riding-Hood'. I initiated a technique which was considered, at the time, something of a novelty: I assisted the children in putting together a plot which they were to act out, spontaneously, with the expectation that this impromptu play would, in itself, produce in its participants a mental catharsis.

The greater the number of situations and roles involved and the more complex they became, the more difficult it grew to use the word 'playing' in this connection—in fact, its use became rather absurd. When I began to use the impromptu-play principle with adults, as applied to their actual, intimate problems, the reality of the situations, the earnestness of the participants and the consequences implied for them in the procedure were so great that the suggestion that they were playing a game was abandoned; the word 'drama' seemed much closer to the factual experiences. But the word 'drama' still seemed to imply a poetic, fictional product and therefore the qualifying prefix 'psycho-' was added.

ROLES AND THE CULTURAL ATOM

Every individual—just as he has at all times a set of friends and a set of enemies—has a range of roles in which he sees himself and faces a range of counter-roles in which he sees others around him. They are in various stages of development. The tangible aspects of what is known as 'ego' are the roles in which he operates; the pattern of role-relations around an individual as their focus is called his 'cultural atom'.

The use here of the word 'atom' can be justified if we consider a cultural atom as the smallest functional unit within a cultural pattern. The adjective 'cultural' can be justified when we consider roles and relationships between roles as the most significant development within any specific culture (regardless of what definition is given to the word 'culture' by any school of thought). Just as sociometric procedures are able to investigate the configuration of social atoms, spontaneity tests and psychodramatic procedures are the means of studying cultural atoms.

REFERENCES

1. Bergson, Henri, "Creative Evolution," Henry Holt & Co., New York, 1911.
2. Borden, Ruth, "The Use of the Psychodrama in an Institution for Delinquent Girls," *Sociometry*, Vol. III, No. 1, pp. 81-90.

3. Butcher, S.H., "Aristotle's Poetics: a Treatise," New York and London, 1902.

4. Dewey, John, "Art as Experience," Milton, Balch & Co., New York, 1934.

5 Franz, J.G., "The Place of the Psychodrama in Research," *Sociometry*, Vol. III, No. 1, pp. 49-61.

6. Freud, Sigmund, Collected Papers, Vols. I-IV, International Psychoanalytic Library.

7. Moreno, J. L., "Die Gottheit als Autor," Verlag Gustav Klepenheuer, Berlin, 1918.

8. — — — — — — "Die Gotthelt als Redner," Verlag Gustav Klepenheuer, Berlin, 1919.

9. — — — — — — "Rede Ueber den Augenblick," Verlag Gustav Klepenheuer, Berlin, 1922.

10. — — — — — — "Das Stegreiftheater," Verlag Gustav Klepenheuer, Berlin, 1912.

11. — — — — — — "Who Shall Survive?", Nervous and Mental Disease Publishing Co., New York and Washington, D.C., 1934.

12. — — — — — — "Inter-Personal Therapy and the Psychopathology of Human Relations," *Sociometry*, Vol. I, Nos. 1 & 2, pp. 9-80.

13. — — — — — — "Psychodramatic Shock Therapy," *Sociometry*, Vol. II, No. 1, pp. 1-30.

14. — — — — — — "Creativity and the Cultural Conserve," *Sociometry*, Vol. II, No. 2, pp. 1-36.

15. — — — — — — "Psychodramatic Treatment of Marriage Problems," *Sociometry*, Vol. III, No. 1, pp. 1-23.

16. — — — — — — "Psychodramatic Treatment of Psychoses," Vol. III, No. 2, pp. 115-132.

17. — — — — — — In collaboration with Joseph Sargent and Anita M. Uhl, "Normal and Abnormal Characteristics of Performance Patterns," *Sociometry*, Vol. II, No. 4, pp. 38-57.

18. Murphy, Gardner, "The Mind Is a Stage," *Forum Magazine*, May, 1937.

19. Nietzsche, Friederich, "Authorized Translation of Nietzsche's Works." (Oscar Levy), 1909-13.

20. Sullivan, Harry Stack, "Concepts of Modern Psychiatry," *Psychiatry*, Vol. III, No. 1, (1940), published by the William Alanson White Psychiatric Foundation, Washington, D.C.

21. White, William Alanson, "Foundations of Psychiatry," Nervous and Mental Disease Publishing Co., New York and Washington, D.C., 1921.

Part IV
DEVELOPMENT:
HISTORY AND BIOGRAPHY

Introduction

Although several specific years have at various times been designated as *the* year in which psychodrama was born, it is more appropriate to say that psychodrama was not born suddenly and at once but rather that it developed out of an accumulation of experiences and insights that were a part of the childhood, youth, and early manhood of Jacob Levi Moreno. Some say that the first psychodramatic session occurred during Moreno's fourth year when he and several other children played a game involving God and his angels. It is needless to speculate as to which of the children assumed the role of the deity. Others say that psychodrama found its beginnings in 1908 when Moreno, a 16-year-old philosophy student at the University of Vienna, began meeting with children in the parks of his city to tell them stories and to encourage them to act out their fantasies. Still others see psychodrama, and group psychotheraphy as well, as being born a few years later when Moreno, a medical student, began organizing groups of prostitutes in Vienna for discussions aimed at promoting their personal growth and seeking to prevent their exploitation by others.

And there are those who argue that psychodrama found its beginnings in 1921 when Moreno, a young psychiatrist, organized his Theatre of Spontaneity in Vienna. So it can continue, with individuals selecting various episodes in Moreno's long, active, and highly creative life to say that "It is at this point that psychodrama began." Of course, they are all correct and at the same time they are all mistaken, as Walt

201

Anderson says in the opening article, "J.L. Moreno and the Origins of Psychodrama: a Biographcal Sketch," since psychodrama had no one point of origin but emerged out of the life and endeavors of a man who was very much involved with the world about him. But Moreno is much more than psychodrama, sociometry, group psychotherapy and his other creations. He is and always has been a man in touch with his times, as much in tune with tomorrow as he is aware of yesterday, and very much a part of today. Moreno is as much a man of religion as he is a man of medicine, as much the philosopher as he is the scientist, and this is what Anderson brings out, capturing the full flavor of the man while presenting the facts of his contributions. This article is followed by the very moving article, "Is God a Single Person?" in which Moreno recounts his first meeting with the woman who is now his wife. Since it appeared shortly after he was interviewed by Anderson, it may account for the connection between the concluding comment in the biographical sketch and Moreno's recalling of that event.

These initial articles are, however, merely the beginning of what this section of the book seeks to accomplish, namely, to show how psychodrama became what it is today. And, as seems obvious, depiction of the development of psychodrama must deal with what might be called the flavor of the man Moreno, and this is done in the articles that follow the first two. In the short articles that follow after Lew Yablonsky's warm reminiscences of Moreno in the 1950's, Gardner Murphy and Alexander King detail some of their experiences of Moreno and psychodrama in the preceding decades. In "Legend of Moreno in Hudson," Murphy recounts observing Moreno directing a psychodrama of an adolescent girl in 1935 and subsequently compares Moreno with E.L. Thorndike and John Dewey. The other article, King's "Psychiatry on Trial—1948," is the personal statement of a man in anguish and, at the same time, a delightful glimpse of what Moreno's sanitarium at Beacon,

N.Y., was like a quarter-of-a-century ago. This in turn leads to an exciting climax that concerns the therapeutic breakthrough made by another patient at the sanitarium.

In the sixth selection in this part, "History of Sociometric Movement in Headlines," Zerka T. Moreno pins down the important points in the development of the Morenean movement and brings the reader from the beginnings of psychodrama to 1949, the year the article was published and, incidentally, the year Zerka Toeman became Mrs. J.L. Moreno. It is obviously about time for a second piece of this sort to cover the Morenean movement's progress during the past 20 or more years. The next article, "Moreneans, the Heretics of Yesterday Are the Orthodoxy of Today," also by Mrs. Moreno, contains a further historical approach to Moreno's contributions. It begins with introductory paragraphs dealing with Freudianism, behaviorism, existentialism, eclecticism, and then goes into Moreneanism and Moreno's cosmic approach and its demand for a "therapeutic world order." This was given voice in some of his early writings and has remained, throughout his life, a central theme of his view of man and of man's responsibility to others. Mrs. Moreno's article is followed by one by Moreno, "The Viennese Origins of the Encounter Movement, Paving the Way for Existentialism, Group Psychotherapy and Psychodrama," which further explores Moreno's philosophy and the development of his work. Divided into three parts—Moreno's early existentialism, his contributions in America, and his early days in Vienna—the article opens with his famous "eyes-for-eyes exchange" statement of 1914 and then delineates the viewpoint that not only its Viennese origins but also the work that emerged after he moved to the United States had an important influence on today's encounter movement. Among some of the lesser known of Moreno's contributions mentioned in the article is the "Choice-of-Parents" event or "happening" that Moreno periodically practiced while working with children in the parks and woods of Vienna.

A very important article, "Scandinavian Myth About the Psychodrama: a Counter-Statement to S. R. Slavson's 'Preliminary Report'," concerns the true information about who invented psychodrama. In the article, Joseph Meiers reports on his investigation of Slavson's declaration that a Danish psychiatrist was the inventor. The psychiatrist in question states in the report that not only did he not invent psychodrama in 1915 or at any other time but that he himself has never been interested in this form of therapy. Why Slavson should credit someone other than Moreno as being the creator of psychodrama is difficult to understand, but Moreno himself makes an attempt to explain Slavson's unusual behavior in a short account of his first meeting with Slavson and of what had emerged from this meeting. Moreno calls this speculative report, "Psychodrama of Sam Slavson." The final article in Part IV is a report by two friends of the Morenos dealing with how Mrs. Moreno responded in part to the loss of her arm. In "Group Psychotherapy and Psychodrama, a Footnote to Their History," the late Dr. Anna Brind and her husband Nah Brind, also a psychologist, very briefly describe a psychodramatic *tour de force* by Zerka Moreno as she role-reverses with her then five-year-old son (not present during that enactment) and experiences his reactions, as she perceived them, to her loss of an arm following its amputation because of bone cancer.

13. J.L. MORENO AND THE ORIGINS OF PSYCHODRAMA
A Biographical Sketch

Walt Anderson

A favorite story of Moreno's, often recounted, places the birth of psychodrama back into the last century. Moreno, four years old at the time, was playing with a group of children in the basement of his parents' home. He organized the group into an impromptu play in which he took the role of God and the other children were angels. They piled chairs upward toward the ceiling and Moreno sat on the top of the structure while the children circled about it, flapping their arms like wings and singing. He reports that he found the whole production satisfactory until one of the children suggested that he fly. He tried it—no doubt well warmed-up to the role—and found himself on the floor with a broken arm. The incident was a long way from formal psychodrama, but it contained most of the basic elements: creativity, spontaneity, catharsis, and, it is safe to assume, insight. Moreno was launched on the road which he has followed for over 70 years, weaving together his own idiosyncratic pattern out of the main currents of 20th-century science and existential philosophy, with a strong influence from Judeo-Christian religious tradition.

Jacob Levi Moreno was born in Bucharest, Rumania, on May 20, 1892, the son of Nissim Moreno and Pauline Wolf Moreno, who had married her husband at the age of 15. The family was of the sephardic Jewish community, but Moreno had received little formal religious training beyond the traditional rituals of circumcision and Bar-Mitzvah. He recalls having gone to a Bible school when he was four, which may have influenced the Godplaying incident. At any rate, religion has been an important part of Moreno's thinking throughout his life, particularly during his years in Austria, and it was influential in his group psychotherapy work. As early as 1908 he founded, with a small group of friends, a society called the "religion of the encounter."[1]

The family moved to Vienna when Moreno was four, and by the time he was 12 he had decided to become a doctor. He studied mathematics and philosophy at the University of Vienna from 1910 until 1912, when he entered that university's Medical School. He recalls that among the philosophers who particularly interested him in those years were Spinoza, Kant, Nietzsche, Hegel, and Kierkegaard.

While a medical student in Vienna, Moreno began to formulate the ideas which would in time lead to the development of his therapeutic system. Those were the years when he often spent his afternoons in the gardens of Vienna, telling improvised stories to groups of children—and observing the natural form which evolved in the process, as his listeners arranged themselves in concentric circles. He has related this experience to the Godplaying theme, as well as to his personal reaction against the Freudian emphasis on the neurotic characteristics of heroes and geniuses. "I wanted to show," he wrote in *Who Shall Survive?*, "that here is a man who has all

[1] The society's motto was the poetic statement quoted in the front of *Psychodrama, Vol. I* (Moreno, 1964), which includes the following:

> A meeting of two: eye to eye, face to face.
> And when you are near I will tear your eyes out
>   and place them instead of mine,
>   and you will tear my eyes out
>   and will place them instead of yours,
>   then I will look at you with your eyes
>   and you will look at me with mine.

the signs of paranoia and megalomania, exhibitionism and social maladjustment and who can still be fairly well controlled and healthy, and indeed, of apparently greater productivity by acting them out than if he would have tried to constrain and resolve his symptoms—the living antithesis of psychoanalysis, foreboding the protagonist of psychodrama."[2]

Thus, some time before he was himself a practicing psychiatrist, Moreno had formulated ideas strongly opposed to the Freudian prohibition against the "acting out" of neurotic drives, and in general favoring expression over repression.

For a little over a year, Moreno was with the research staff of the Psychiatric Clinic of Vienna University, and during this time he had some personal contact with Freud, whose psychoanalytic theories at the time were just beginning to attain international recognition.

A year or two later, while still a medical student, Moreno became involved in the project which he considers to have been the real beginning of group psychotherapy: the organizing of weekly discussion meetings among small groups of prostitutes in the Am Spittelberg district of Vienna. He has written that in those meetings he was struck by four basic considerations which became the cornerstones of group psychotherapy: the autonomy of the group, the presence of group structure, the problem of collectivity, and the problem of anonymity.

Moreno received his M.D. degree in 1917, about a year before the end of World War I and the collapse of the Austro-Hungarian monarchy. The young doctor was made a superintendent of the children's hospital in the displaced persons' community of Mittendorf, established to handle the floods of Austrial refugees fleeing from the advancing Italian armies in the Tyrol. Moreno studied the changing social structures of this community during the three years of its existence, and during this time he began to think of the

[2] J.L. Moreno, *Who Shall Survive?* (Beacon, N.Y.: Beacon House, Inc., 1953), p. xix.

possibility of planning communities according to the social dynamics among its members. The science of sociometry, which would become the analytical underpinnings of Moreno's system of psychodrama and group psychotherapy, was beginning to develop.

Moreno practiced psychiatry in Vienna and the neighboring community of Voslau from 1919 until 1925, and also founded a monthly literary and philosophical publication, *Daimon*, to which Martin Buber became a contributing editor. During this period, nine books by Moreno were published anonymously. They were mostly of a religious nature; among them were *The Words of the Father* and the autobiographical novel *Der Koenigsroman*.

In *Der Koenigsroman*, Moreno recounts the first "official" psychodramatic session, an attempt in 1921, to channel some of the uncertainties and frustrations of a group of Austrians into a spontaneous production. The location was a theater, the Komedian Haus, and the only pieces of stage properties in use there were a large thronelike armchair and a gilded crown. Moreno describes the experiment as follows:

> It was an attempt to treat and purge the audience from a disease, a pathological cultural syndrome which the participants shared. Postwar Vienna was seething with revolt. It had no stable government, no emperor, no king, no leader . . . Austria was restless, in search of a new soul.
>
> But, psychodramatically speaking, I had a cast and I had a play. The audience was my cast. . . . The natural theme of the plot was the search of a new order of things, to test everyone in the audience who aspired to leadership, and perhaps to find a saviour. Each according to his role, politicians, ministers, writers, soldiers, physicians and lawyers, they all were invited by me to step upon the stage, to sit on the throne and to act like a king, unprepared and before an unprepared audience. The audience was the jury. But it must have been a very difficult test: nobody passed it. When the show came to an end none was found worthy of being a king, and the world remained leaderless.

The Viennese press the next morning was greatly disturbed about the incident.[3]

The next step in the evolution of psychodrama was the founding, in 1921, of *Das Stegreiftheater*, the Spontaneity Theater. For several years this theater group, a center for the creative activities of many radical young artists, entertained the Viennese with dramatic productions which were improvised spontaneously upon the stage. This kind of action took many forms; one was the Living Newspaper, in which recent happenings—sometimes local incidents, sometimes developments in world politics—were spontaneously dramatized. *Das Stegrieftheater* was significant not only as a laboratory for the development of psychodramatic techniques, but also as a forerunner of modern improvisational theater.

Moreno regards 1923 as the year when his main orientation turned from religious and philosophical to scientific in the modern sense. By this time he was working on an invention, a machine for the recording and playback of sound on steel discs, which he patented in 1924 and brought to America in 1925. His interest in this form of technology led to later experiments with the recording and playback of therapist-patient interview sessions.

He decided to remain in the United States, began medical practice in New York and was eventually naturalized as an American citizen. He immediately set out to introduce psychodrama into the mental health professions and into American culture in general. He began psychodramatic work with children at the Plymouth Institute in Brooklyn and also became involved with the Mental Hygiene Clinic at Mt. Sinai Hospital. In 1929 he began the first regular program of large-scale "open" psychodrama in America: the Impromptu Group Theatre in Carnegie Hall, where sessions were held three times a week. During this period there was also considerable progress in

[3] J.L. Moreno, *Der Koenigsroman*, quoted in *Psychodrama*, *Vol. I* (Moreno, 1964), pp. 1-2.

sociometry. Moreno made sociometric studies among prisoners at Sing Sing in 1931 and 1932, and from 1932 to 1938 he was engaged in the long-term sociometry project at the New York State Training School for Girls at Hudson, N.Y.

Moreno was now becoming well known, both to the general public as a result of newspaper reports on the Impromptu Theatre and Living Newspaper demonstrations, and also within the psychiatric community. Much of his publicity in the latter category had to do with controversies such as his celebrated exchange with Dr. A.A. Brill, a disciple of Freud's, over what Brill claimed were the neurotic characteristics of Abraham Lincoln. In this exchange, Moreno defended the former president against Brill's psychoanalytic assault during a meeting of the American Psychiatric Association.

Through the 1930's and 1940's the various institutions which were to become the framework for the development of psychodrama and sociometry were established. The Beacon Hill Sanitarium, site of the present Moreno Academy and of the World Center for Psychodrama, Sociometry, and Group Psychotherapy, was founded in 1934. In 1936 the first stage specifically designed for psychodrama was constructed at Beacon. A few years later, Moreno founded the scientific periodical, *Sociometry, a Journal of Interpersonal Relations,* with Gardner Murphy as its first editor; *Sociometry* later became an official publication of the American Sociological Association. Also, in the 1930's, Moreno gave the first university courses, on psychodrama at Teachers College of Columbia University and a course on sociometry at the New School for Social Research.

In 1941 a theater of psychodrama containing a special stage that was modeled on the one at Beacon, was constructed at St. Elizabeths Hospital in Washington, D.C.—the first such facility in a large mental hospital—and in 1942 the New York Institute of Psychodrama was opened in New York City. In that year the Society of Psychodrama and Group Psychotherapy (now the American Society for Group Psychotherapy and Psychodrama) was founded, with Moreno as its first president. The society's journal, *Sociatry* (now *Group Psychotherapy*) began publication in 1947.

If the period prior to 1925 was the time when most of the ideas of Moreno's system were beginning to take form, then the longer period stretching from the time of his arrival in the United States through the 1930's and 1940's was the time when psychodrama and sociometry developed into the forms in which we know them today and, also, it was the time when the greatest effort was expended on introducing them into the medical and academic communities.

A final note: when I was gathering information for this short biographical outline, I asked Dr. Moreno what he considered to be the single most important event in his creative life. He replied that it was his partnership with Zerka Toeman, who began to work with him in 1941 and became his wife in 1949. I also asked him if there was anything in his career he would like to change, or that he wished might have been different. The only thing he could think of was that he wished he had met her 15 years earlier.

14. IS GOD A SINGLE PERSON? MY FIRST ENCOUNTER WITH A MUSE OF HIGH ORDER, ZERKA

J. L. Moreno, M.D.

One of the difficulties in our mythologies of God is that he is usually pictured as a single person, either a God or Goddess. Loneliness was the penalty which we had to pay for monotheism. In the mythology of the Greeks, which was carried on a lower level of intensity, God married and produced off-spring, like Zeus and Juno. The stories about these marriages are full of disappointments but they are more real. Anyway, I was searching for an integrated partnership, for the Muse of Integration, so as to bring the Godplayer down to earth.

THE FIRST ENCOUNTER WITH ZERKA, I AND THOU

On a sunny summer afternoon, Anno Domini 1941, the door opens and a young woman steps into my office. (She was accompanied by three adults but I seemed only to notice her first, later the others began to emerge, one by one.) She has a little boy in her arms, about three years old. I look at her, she looks at me, and that was it. I say to myself (my double speaks): "Yes, yes, yes," and I stretch out my arms in a broad, all-embracing manner. I feel that she is already mine and that I am already

From J. L. Moreno's forthcoming book: *Fantastic Journey Through the Cosmos*, Beacon House, New York, 1971. Reprinted with the permission of the publishers from *Group Psychotherapy*, Vol. XXIII, Nos. 3 and 4 (1970), pp. 75-78.

hers. There she is; I don't know anything about her, but that is SHE. I can even feel what she is saying to herself, right this moment, here, now. Zerka: "I am very unhappy. My sister is ill. He may think that this is my child. I have no children, I am single. I came to find a doctor, a psychiatrist, for my sister." Then she makes a pause. I wait, until I hear her again. "This man is not a simple psychiatrist. He looks and acts more like an artist, a creative man." Now there is silence between us, but it comes into my mind: "If her sister is sick and her sister's husband is with her, why does she come along?" As if she hears my query, she replies in her own mind: "He doesn't understand, these people are European refugees, refugees from the Nazis. He doesn't know that they have just arrived here. I am with them not only to help them, but to protect the boy from further abuse. My sister is too confused to care for him; when left alone with him, she is so bewildered that she tries to kill herself and the child. I almost feel as if he were my child, not hers. I feel responsible. Besides, my brother-in-law speaks very little English. He needs an interpreter." And then it comes to her in a flash: "I did not expect to find such an enchanting, warm man. He greets us so warmly, as if he is glad to meet us. I expected a purely formal event between a doctor and a patient meeting for the first time. And he is so human, so charming, not just professional." I see tears in her eyes. "I like that. He is hand-some too, so masculine, in that white suit and blue shirt. The color of his shirt emphasizes his great, extraordinarily luminous, penetrating, deeply expressive eyes. What color are they? Oh, blue. I adore blue eyes in a man; somehow they always strike my heart. But why is he so lonely? I heard the nurse who greeted us say that he has a baby girl about the same age as my nephew. So he is or was married. It really doesn't matter. Yet, he is lonely, deeply lonely, possibly even unhappy, as unhappy as I am." Silence. Now I hear her again, or I imagine that I hear her: "I am lonely and unhappy, too, having just broken off a love relationship with a man I planned to marry." "So," I say to myself: "she was planning to get married. Then the child is not hers." Zerka again: "We were well along the way to setting the date and preparing the event itself. Now I have no one." A long silence, then: "It hurt badly for a while, but somehow I am glad to be free again. I'm getting ready for a new relationship, a more mature one. This doctor is old enough to be my father, although he doesn't look or act old. But he couldn't be interested in me personally; he obviously loves people, young and old, especially children. See how he smiles at the child and asks questions about him."

At this point the baby glides off her lap, walks towards the fireplace and starts playing with the brass fire irons. He drops one with a clatter and we all focus our attention upon him. Zerka goes over to see if he is hurt and gently brings him back to the chair, taking him once again on her lap.

The scene changes, she is back at her depth. Now she looks at me again and we smile at each other, assessing and confirming: "This has all happened before, hasn't it? But when? Where? Oh no, it has never happened before. Not like this. It is the first time, it is happening now." A pregnant pause here. Then another flash breaks in on her—she seems full of electricity which discharges itself in my direction, sparked off by my own; now it seems to me that I hear her voice very clearly: "He is not a simple man; this man is a great genius, perhaps the only true genius I will ever meet. Many men make believe, or try to, but this man is the genuine article. Oh, what could we possibly have in common? I am a rather inexperienced person, just starting to learn about life and its darkest corners. Yet, he looks at me with as much interest as he spends on my sick sister, his patient. What can he be thinking? Perhaps it is just that my sister and I are physically so different. People are always astounded at that. And now we are certainly also clearly very different emotionally. But I feel he can see that we are somehow deeply tied up, that I am very depressed at this new outbreak of her emotional illness." Silence. "I fear he will get the wrong information or no information at all about her emotional history. I will have to make sure to see him alone so I can help him to get to know her. She can't cooperate, she is too confused and doesn't recognize the nature of her condition." Side remark: "My brother-in-law is a poor refuge. He has had to borrow heavily to pay for her care here. He is not yet employed or working, having only arrived two days ago. We must make sure the treatment does not take too long or he will not be able to carry the burden of it all. Besides, we need money to place the child in a temporary foster home. All this is a terrible, crushing burden." More silence and searching out, then: "But why is the doctor so interested in me? What does he want from me?" And I am asking myself at the same time: "What do I want from her?" It comes to her sharply: "Why am I so interested in him? What do I want from him, besides help for my sister?" Now there is another voice; it is her mother's voice out of her childhood and adolescence: "Don't get in your sister's way! This is *her* friend now, *her* doctor. *She* is the one to get his whole-hearted attention. Make yourself be almost invisible, subservient to *her* needs. *Don't* inject yourself! Don't take his attention, the focus, the love away from her. You know you've managed to do this since you were little; the whole family loved you as their toy. You are the baby. Your sister is the eldest. Your father and brothers adored you. Now she needs all the love she can get, especially that of a good father; don't make trouble for her again." There are other voices, just as sharp, those of public opinion: "What could a *married* man want from a young, single girl? He is not supposed to be too interested in single girls unless they are his patients. Is this a purely professional interest he shows for you? Remember, he is also the father of another child, a baby girl. Whatever else his child needs, she needs her life undisturbed. Don't make waves. Don't get involved. Stay out of too close, too personal a contact between you. Only a professional relationship will do." Silence, her eyes are cast downwards, as if inward-looking, then, reasonably: "Oh, remember, they almost didn't make it to America. Your family was stuck, first in France, later in North Africa. They might all have succumbed to the Nazis, as have already untold hundreds of thousands. You have helped to *save* their lives. Are you now deliberately going to ruin or complicate it? No! They must have every possible consideration first. They need every kind of help desperately, their life is a shambles. The boy needs his own mother and father. However much you love him, he is not yours. You are but a temporary substitute. Don't ever get into any parent's way. It will pursue you till the end of time. Your conscience will not prmit it, just as it would not let you rest until you had snatched them away from the shores of dying, agonizing Europe. Now, you must show what kind of ingredients you are made of. Keep in the background. Don't think of yourself now."

They have all left the room to settle the patient into hers. I am sitting, waiting to see Zerka and the others before they depart for the city. Will I see her alone at all? As if in reply, there she is, back again, knocking at the door; she has come to ask me for an appointment at my office in the city where she wishes to talk to me alone.

15. A BRIEF VIEW OF MORENO

Lewis Yablonsky

I first met Moreno when I was a sociology graduate student at New York University. A man named Ed Borgatta, also a graduate student at that time, who was working with Dr. Moreno, went through the files of all graduate students in sociology and for some strange reason selected me for a scholarship with Moreno. This was in 1949. I went to the Moreno Institute in New York City, then located at 101 Park Avenue, and to the larger operation in Beacon. At the Institute in New York they had open (to the public) Friday night sessions—much like what we have now at the California Institute of Psychodrama in Los Angeles—including special closed groups, student groups, and others.

The thing I remembered most about Moreno at our first meeting were his eyes. I never had anyone look at me so directly, honestly and with such intensity. When I later read Moreno's "Concept of the Encounter," it put in words what I experienced. Without words, I immediately had a very direct and personal encounter with a man I felt had some mystical qualities. I really don't believe in those things, but with Moreno I had the feeling that if there was such a thing as mindreading he could do it. I later found out he could. In the hundreds of sessions I participated in with him, I saw him work many miracles of solving human dilemmas.

He had a very warm handshake at our first meeting, and we embraced. I was tremendously impressed with this unusual man before he had said a word to me. Then I began to go to psychodrama sessions, and it offered up an entirely new educational direction for me. I think what students are burning down universities for today, in the seventies, is in frustration over not getting what I was getting then from Moreno the Teacher. He provided a very personal and intellectual communication that was *relevant* to immediate life situations. I studied with him in what I can best describe as a sort of European apprenticeship.

I began to go to Beacon, N.Y. (World Center for Psychodrama, Sociometry, and Group Psychotherapy) for weekend workshops. Today we hear about marathons and other weekend type encounters, but Moreno was doing it in the early forties at Beacon. We had non-stop weekend workshops.

A dominant theme of Moreno is that he is a holy man, in the sense that he is whole or holistic. All of his work and all of his personal and familial relationships are part of his system. In Beacon in those days he had patients, he was writing, he was lecturing, he was learning. I had the rare opportunity to observe a brain, blood-and-guts intellectual in action.

There was no hypocrisy; so many people have role conflicts in the roles they play (husband, worker, son, etc.), and Moreno was all of these things at the same time. To me he was a highly significant intellectual role model, and I availed myself of the opportunity to work with him in his varied roles. He would at one moment be lecturing to a group of psychiatrists or students or working with patients in his Sanitarium at Beacon or writing his books, and all of these practices were integrated.

Another characteristic of my early days with Moreno was his realistic assessment of the social science view of him. Of course he had many colleagues and co-workers, but many of the members of the "helping professions" around at that time (1950's) were very threatened and hostile. One has to remember that therapy in those days was an individually oriented approach. Here was Moreno talking of the importance of the group in working to modify personality. He had already introduced sociometry, psychodrama and sociodrama, and these ideas were already beginning to stir up the minds and guts of all stripes of psychiatrists and psychologists.

Many of them felt threatened because most of their professional lives centered around the training and practice of individually oriented psychotherapy. Those who saw the validity of Moreno's social science system and the necessity of having to change their direction so dramatically were often distraught.

Now, of course, almost everyone's on the bandwagon, except a few remote and alienated holdouts practicing the old psychoanalysis, and one of the most important experiences of my life has been to witness Moreno's impact and in a modest way through my own involvement help change the orientation of so many people from the individual to the validity of the group viewpoint of society.

One of the striking things about Moreno is his integrity in practicing what he preaches. When he talks about the fountainhead or the godhead and beginning fresh and spontaneously with a relationship in a group of an idea, he follows through. Consequently, although I've seen his body age over these 20 years of our relationship, Moreno's intellectual acumen remains fresh, creative and alive. For example, in very recent years, with the advent of the hippie concept or life-style, Moreno, unlike most older people, relates very directly and immediately to their ideas. They talk about the "plastic society," but for most of Moreno's life he has opposed and written about his opposition to the robot-like tendencies of individuals in societies. His book, *Who Shall Survive?* is as penetrating and meaningful, if not more so, to our contemporary crisis, than it was in the thirties when he wrote it.

In brief, Moreno is an intellectual giant who has contributed more to the possible salvation of our civilization than any other man of his time. Moreno's enormous and powerful practice and writing is increasingly being utilized internationally to solve the vast problems of our ahuman societies. Who shall survive? Moreno.

16. LEGEND OF PSYCHODRAMA IN HUDSON

Gardner Murphy

I shall never forget the day I had the privilege of taking William Heard Kilpatrick out to see Moreno's demonstration of psychodrama at Hudson. Adolescent girls, mostly somewhat retarded intellectually, who had gotten into trouble with the law, were being given a normal schooling with vocational training and a rich social life by Fanny French Morse, and Moreno had come there to set free the personality potentials of the girls through free enactment of little scenes into which they could project themselves. We had learned beforehand only that the psychodrama gave each participating individual an opportunity to throw herself immediately and without preparation into any social role that had meaning for her. Twenty-five girls were waiting for us. "Now girls," Moreno said, "it's a hot afternoon in the summer. You, Pauline and Helen, are driving along the parkway and pull up to a roadhouse. You, Ruth, are Helen's little daughter. You, Hazel and Janet, are the waitresses. Mary, you are the proprietor. All right, go ahead girls." However remote this situation might be for urban lower-class girls, they threw themselves into this scene with imagination and energy. It was a great show. Then Moreno would say, "All right, you girls there, criticize this play." Eunice, Viola, and Grace had comments immediately. "Helen

Reprinted with the permission of the publishers from *Group Psychotherapy*, Vol. XVII, No. 1, (March, 1964) pp. 18-20.

didn't act like she was really hot and tired; anybody could see Hazel wasn't really waiting on tables; she got nervous; she talked too fast." These girls were learning social membership by enacting it, and this was a part of a vivid scheme of social education now being given a somewhat psychiatric coloration. There was no doubt whatever that the girls were learning in the sense in which John Dewey used the term.

On the way back in the car, Kilpatrick made a remark, suddenly pulling a world of uncertainty into a knot and posing a dilemma with clarity. "If Moreno," he said, "is as much as half right, Thorndike is more than half wrong!" He paused. I could not think of anything worthy to reply to such a remark. "If Moreno is as much as half right. Throndike is more than half wrong!" This was patently John Dewey speaking through the lips of Kilpatrick in an inspired utterance. That Sunday in 1935, when both Dewey and Throndike were still alive, epitomized the problem of the law of effect, or what we today would call reinforcement learning. Wait until you get what you want, then *reward* it. If something you don't want happens, *ignore* it, or in certain situations, *punish* it. But many of these girls had already been punished by life over and over again, and had gone on doing the punished thing. Moreno had hit upon the fact that social motivation and social reinforcement are often inseparable; or rather, if you know the motivation, you do not have to apply—cannot apply—external rewards and punishments. Moreover, if you know motivation, if you know where life is going, you know that reinforcement, when effective consists of allowing the motivation to pursue itself, as indeed all modern educators from Pestalozzi onwards have seen. There remains a place—but how limited a place—for the external reward-punishment treatment!

There is, however, another package rolled into Kilpatrick's statement. Moreno held in this case the teacher's role. When he has failed, as he sometimes has, I think it has been due to the authoritarianism of the teacher's role. When he succeeded, as he often has brilliantly (as in that day at Hudson), it came from the simple, natural, direct, fatherly handling of co-workers and co-learners in a situation which all could share. Note the ease with which the assignments were made, and especially the atmosphere in which the girls could criticize the work of their peers in a casual, matter-of-fact way. Note the way in which the Moreno program fitted into Fanny French Morse's emancipation program as a whole.

17. PSYCHIATRY ON TRIAL—1948

Alexander King

While I was shopping around for a more suitable retreat to park my disaster, a friend of mine told me about the Moreno Clinic out in the country. This place wasn't a drug-cleaning joint at all. It handled only genuine cuckoos, and it treated them with an entirely new method called psychodrama, a system of psychotherapy I'd never even heard about. My friend told me that the patients at this booby hatch acted out all their difficulties on a real stage, under the guidance of special clinical directors, and that some remarkable results had been achieved there. I liked the idea, so I phoned Dr. Moreno, and he told me to call at his New York office the next day, since he was coming into town anyway.

Let me tell you, I was much impressed with Moreno during that first interview. He proved to be an unusually intelligent person with wide human and cultural interests, and for any man who presumes to function in the capacity of a psychiatrist or psychoanalyst that is surely a basic requirement. Of course, that is still no guarantee of his having any special gifts for this highly exigent calling, but it is certainly an absolute must as a starter, isn't it?

Now, Dr. Moreno, who was also Viennese, which did him no

Reprinted with the permission of the publishers from *Group Psychotherapy*, Vol. XVII, No. 1, (March, 1964), pp. 18-20 and with the permission of the publishers from *Mine Enemy Grows Older*, by Alexander King, Simon and Schuster, New York, 1959, pp. 141-47.

harm with me, told me right off the bat that he didn't generally tackle dopeys. But I liked his manner and his looks, which were a cross between Rembrant and Diego Rivera—that is to say, plump, bright-eyed, curly-haired and alive—so I decided to persuade him. Not that I believed for a moment that any, or all, of his attributes were necessarily going to cure me of my addiction, since that, in the final analysis, was entirely up to me; all he could really provide for me were certain routine, clinical facilities and his own sympathetic medical and human perception. My liking for him had hardly any connection with my own malady at all; he just sounded like a gifted person who, in an emergency, could tie a package better, or more originally, than the next man. I asked him earnestly to take me on, and he finally agreed.

The following day I landed at his aviary, which was located in beautifully landscaped grounds on the left bank of the Hudson, opposite Newburgh, I think. They gave me a fine corner room but confiscated my radio and all my eleven tubes of tooth paste which showed that despite their inexperience with junkies they had a pretty cool idea of what such varmints were capable of. Otherwise I had the run of the place, and I was particularly invited to attend my first psychodrama session that afternoon.

Since I'd had my lunch on the train coming up, I had over an hour to kill until showtime, so I meandered into the doctor's library. He had a marvelous collection of books in many languages, and, to my delight, I found a few volumes of poetry that Moreno himself had written many years ago in Austria. Now, listen to this, this stuff of his was quite self-respecting. It was not the amateur ranting of some rhyme-crippled medic and I was delighted that he had lived up to my hunch, that he was a cool stud and really had something on the ball.

You may have surmised by now that I have deep prejudices against psychoalanysts and psychiatrists, and, believe me, I have. The majority of the practitioners I have personally known, and I have known about twenty-five during the last three decades, where a bunch of presumptuous pfooshers who shouldn't have been allowed to treat an introverted turtle. Of course, I *have* seen people who have been helped by psychotherapy, but I wouldn't go so far as to say I've seen them cured. The patients generally have to go back to their refueling stations for the rest of their lives. These psychotherapeutic udders became as indispensable to them as opium is to a drug addict; and I say, pfui! You might point out that that is still preferable to real drug addiction, and I will grant you that it is, but only because it isn't illegal. But that's about all I'll give it. I'm fully aware that there are dedicated, scholarly, and earnest workers abroad in the field, but I tell you that, at this moment, too much of the actual therapy is just a hit-or-miss proposition and has about as much relation to real science as alchemy has to modern chemistry. I'll tell you, further, that at the present stage of its growth too many of the operators who function in its ranks are dangerous ignoramuses, or out-and-out scoundrels who just like to make themselves a fast and easy buck. You might reasonably object that there are more fakers in the art world than in psychotherapy, and you would be quite right. I'd just like to point out that when a wretched artist makes a bum picture it just means a waste of paint and a ruined canvas, but when a blundering ass of a psychotherapist sticks his dirty fingers into an already infected mind it is liable to cause some unfortunate creature the permanent loss of his sanity. That, I think, is pretty obvious, and there you have the reason for my truculent and censorious attitude.

So you can imagine that it wasn't exactly a dreamy little boy who attended the psychodrama seance up at the sanitarium that afternoon. The sesson I witnessed took place in a tidy little theatre which had been especially constructed for these meetings, and when I arrived about twenty-five persons were already scattered about the auditorium. These people faced a slightly raised circular platform, which eventually proved the main stage of action. I can see now that this theatre was the forerunner of the playhouses that some well-healed off-Broadway producers have since constructed and utilized to present their much less interesting dramas.

Dr. Moreno opened the session by announcing that a visitor, a Mrs. Mehlmann, was expected to arrive the next day. Before he stepped down from the stage he asked whether Mr. Mehlmann cared to express himself, one way or another, about the impending reunion with his wife.

Mr. Mehlmann slowly rose from his seat in the audience and said, "I'm glad she's coming."

"You're glad?" said Dr. Moreno. "That's good. Not like a month ago when you refused to see her, eh?"

Mr. Mehlmann scratched his large nose and looked at the floor.

"What happened to change your mind about her? Would you care to tell us, Mr. Mehlmann? Suppose you step up here and tell us why you didn't want to see her on her last visit."

Dr. Moreno stepped down and Mr. Mehlmann dragged himself reluctantly onto the platform.

He was a short, pale, flabby man, almost bald, with colorless eyes and a long untidy Slovak mustache, like mine. He was around fifty and I judged him to be a hardware dealer. He had that unhealthy hardware-dealer's skin. When he got on stage he looked around for a moment, blinked in the direction of Dr. Moreno, pulled at a pretty substantial ear lobe, and smiled foolishly.

"It was your wife's birthday," said the doctor, "and she brought you a piece of her cake, didn't she?"

"Yeah, she did," said Mehlmann. "I watched her from upstairs, when she got out of the car with the packages."

"Where did you watch from?" asked the doctor.

"From Joe's room," said Mehlmann.

"Suppose," said the doctor, "you arrange the furniture on the stage as it looked up in Joe's room."

Mr. Mehlmann turned around and began to lug at some

characterless furniture that had been waiting in the shadows behind him. Still farther to the back, I noticed, was a child's blackboard on some wooden rollers.

It was plain to see that Mr. Mehlmann was an old trouper in psychodrama, and he was gaining authority and poise with every passing moment; as a matter of fact, he proceeded to crouch down, without self-consciousness, behind one of the chairs, to simulate his actions of the month before.

"Did your wife come up from the right side of the house?" asked Dr. Moreno.

"No, she came from the left," said Mehlmann. "She couldn't open the door with her hand account of the packages."

"Just a minute," said the doctor. "Would Miss Mathew please be good enough to take the part of Mrs. Mehlmann?"

A young woman, who, I later learned, was a trained practitioner in psychodrama, rose from the audience and approached the stage from the left side. She made believe that she was carrying some bulky packages in her arms, and, as she stepped onto the platform, she pretended to kick open an imaginary door.

"No!" said Mehlmann. "No! No! She kicked the door with her right foot! She don't use her left foot much, she has arthritis in the knee."

I discovered later that the woman assistant was instructed to make carefully calculated and prescribed mistakes, for the very purpose of rousing the patients' critical and corrective faculties.

I've bothered to tell you about this Mehlmann person not because he was particularly interesting; he was, as a matter of fact, just a mediocre paranoid performer, with the usual persecutionary overtones. But something happened during his turn that was really wonderfully exciting. While describing a breakfast he'd once had with his wife, he happened to mention the word "beigel."

No sooner was this word out of his mouth than a pretty dark-haired woman, called Millicent, jumped out of her seat and shouted, "Wrong!"

Mr. Mehlmann stopped and peered nearsightedly out into the audience. He finally spotted Millicent, who raised her arm and once more shouted, "Wrong!" Her arm slowly came down but she still trembled with excitement. I noticed that a nurse had suddenly materialized in back of her.

"You don't say 'beigel,'" said Millicent. "You're supposed to say 'bagel.'" She passed the back of her hand across her forehead and chuckled to herself. "You talk like a Galician," she said, as she sat down again.

Although I was quite a distance from her, I felt waves of excitement surging around Millicent, and I couldn't understand why Dr. Moreno had suddenly crossed the room and placed himself just a few feet from where she was sitting.

"Come, Millicent," said the doctor, "go up on the stage and show Mr. Mehlmann the correct way of pronouncing 'bagel.' Why don't you write it out for him on the blackboard?"

After a moment, Millicent got up again and slowly, in complete stillness, like a trance-walker, proceeded down the aisle toward the stage. She walked as one, who, after a long illness, is relearning how to properly balance her body's equilibrium. In passing Mr. Mehlmann on her way to the blackboard she stopped and smiled at him, and he good-naturedly smiled back at her and even pattered her on the shoulder. It was a perfectly commonplace tableau, in which a woman of Russian Jewish descent had corrected the pronounciation of a Polish Jew, and the correction had seemingly been accepted with kindly tolerance. So what?

Just this: Millicent had, for almost a year, been a totally uncommunicative un-co-operative patient and had, during all that time, failed to respond to any form of physical or psychological stimulus. It seems that a few days after childbirth she had encircled herself within a complete wall of silence, which had been breached for the first time only that afternoon, when she heard Mr. Mehlmann give his parochial twist to the word, "bagel."

I know that such small miracles happen every day in sessions of group therapy, but I'm maintaining that group therapy was only a twinkle in somebody's eye in those days, when nobody had as yet bothered to kibitz this valuable aspect of the Moreno technique. Incidentally, Dr. Moreno was not at all doctrinaire about psychodrama in the treatment of his patients. He freely utilized all established methods of psychotherapy at his clinic, but I've heard psychodrama scorned and belittled by practitioners who have shamessly plagiarized his most significant discoveries.

18. HISTORY OF THE SOCIOMETRIC MOVEMENT IN HEADLINES

Zerka T. Moreno

The history of the sociometric movement falls naturally into three periods: (a) the period during which Moreno lived in Europe and was the only writer on the subject, preparing the foundations for inter-personal theory and experimental study of small groups, from 1905-1925; (b) the period during which he lived in the United States and found here a growing number of collaborators and co-creators in the development of sociometric theory and practice, from 1925 to 1941; (c) the period during which sociometry and sub-disciplines came to be generally accepted and universally applied, from 1941 up to the present.

Moreno is the founder of sociometry, psychodrama and group psychotherapy. But it may well be that he will be longer remembered as the creator of social inventions without which these new disciplines might never have reached the scientific stage. He invented the *open, multidimensional, circular stage,* without being an architect. He invented the *living, dramatized newspaper,* without being a newspaper man; he brought it to the United States in 1925 and the idea reached, through the March of Time, the newsreel and W.P.A., wide popularity. Only a few scientific writers were aware that it was first introduced by Moreno in Vienna in 1924, as an aftermath of the Theatre of Spontaneity. He invented the electric *"psychorecording,"* the

Reprinted with the permission of the publishers from *Sociometry,* Vol. XII, Nos. 1-3 (February-August, 1949), pp. 255-259.

idea of transcribing and "playing back" sound phenomena for exploratory and therapeutic aims. Moreno proposed this idea since 1925, particularly in his "Application of the Group Method to Classification," 1931, and has been for years its persistent advocate. Psycho-recording is now universally applied and has become an almost indispensable tool in the hands of the psychotherapists. Non-directive counselors, psychoanalysts, group psychotherapists, and so forth, are using it, especially since 1941. He invented among other procedures the *sociogram, psychodrama, sociodrama,* and the *psychotherapeutic motion picture.* These inventions have one thing in common, their artistic character of conception, initiating a new era in the development of the social sciences, the arts coming to their rescue and aiding towards a synthesis.

FIRST PERIOD   1908-1925

1908-1912   Group psychotherapy applied to children, Vienna.

1911   Theatre of spontaneity for children, Vienna.

1913-1914   Group psychotherapy applied to deviates, Vienna.

1914-1924   Development of inter-personal theory.

1916   Letter to the Department of the Interior, Austro-Hungarian Monarchy, suggesting a sociometric scheme for reorganization of Mitterndorf, a resettlement community near Vienna. The term "sociometry" used for the first time.

1921   Psychodrama at the Komoedienhaus, Vienna, the first large scale public session.

1922   Opening of the Stegreiftheater (Theatre of Spontaneity) in Vienna. Invention of the inter-action diagram.

1923   "Das Stegreiftheater," a publication. It opened the way to sociometric study of group structure as a whole, spontaneity research, role-research, and action-research.

1924   Die Lebendige Zeitung (The Living Newspaper), Vienna.

1925   First exhibit of the multi-dimensional, circular stage at the Internationale Ausstellung Neuer Theatertechnik (International Exposition of New Theatre Technique) inaugurated by the city of Vienna.

1925   Invention of the electro-magnetic recording disk which led to the idea of psycho-recording.

SECOND PERIOD 1925-1941

1925   Plymouth Church, Brooklyn, N.Y. Psychodrama applied to a Sunday school; demonstration of psychodrama at Mount Sinai Hospital, Department of Pediatrics.

1929-1930   Impromptu Theatre, Carnegie Hall, combining group psychotherapy with psychodrama sessions. Among its visitors were many who later applied psychodrama and group psychotherapy to various social situations.

1931   The National Committee on Prisons and Prison Labor convenes during the meeting of the American Psychiatric Association in Troronto. Moreno suggests program on Group Psychotherapy for prisons, mental hospitals, and schools.
The Living Newspaper presented at the Theatre Guild.   Sociometric Study at Sing Sing Prison.   Invention of the sociogram.

1931   Publication of the "Application of the Group Method to Classification." Coining of "Group Therapy" and "Group Psychotherapy."

1932   First Round Table Conference on Group Psychotherapy during the meeting of the American Psychiatric Association in Philadelphia, with William A. White, M.D., as moderator, who had shown interest in Moreno's inter-personal theory since 1929. Group psychotherapy, sociometry, and role-playing are discussed.

1932-1938   Long range sociometric study at the New York State Training School for Girls, Hudson, New York, in collaboration with Helen H. Jennings. Sociometric study of a complete public school. P.S. 181, Brooklyn, N.Y., in collaboration with Helen H. Jennings.

1933   Exhibit of over 100 sociometric charts at the meeting of the Medical Society of the State of New York, held in New York City. "Psychological Organization of Groups in the Community," an experimental study of small groups, paper read by J.L. Moreno during a joint meeting of the American Association for Mental Deficiency and the American Psychiatric Association, at Boston.

1934   "Who Shall Survive? A New Approach to the Problem of Human Interrelations," by J.L. Moreno, with a Preface by William A. White. Covering dimensions of community organization, especially home and industrial relations.

1935-1936 U.S. Department of Agriculture and Department of Interior sponsor sociometric research related to subsistence homesteads. Showing of the therapeutic film, "Spontaneity Training," during the meeting of the American Psychiatric Association at Washington, D.C. Development of social microscopy and microsociology, dynamic sociometry, sociodynamics and role playing.

1936   Publication of the *Sociometric Review,* containing among other articles, Dr. Winifred Richmond's sociometric research at St. Elizabeths Hospital, Washington, D.C., and studies of laissez-faire, authoritarian, and sociometric structure of groups, initiating group atmosphere exploration—since then widely treated and discussed.

1936   First Theatre of Psychodrama, Beacon, N.Y.

1937   Founding of SOCIOMETRY: *A Journal of Inter-Personal Relations,* first scientific journal bearing this title; editor, Dr. Gardner Murphy.

   a) inter-personal influence and public opinion research (Moreno, Lazarsfeld)

   b) sociometry and socioeconomic status (Lundberg)

   c) sociometry and leadership (Jennings)

   d) sociometry of race cleavage (Criswell)

   e) sociometric analysis of resettlement (Davidson and Loomis)

1937   Round Table Conference on Sociometry held during the meeting of the American Sociological Society, at Atlantic City, N.J., moderator, Dr. George A. Lundberg.

1938   Sociometry in a Cooperative Community, Hightstown, N.J.

1941   Theatre of Psychodrama at St. Elizabeths Hospital, Washington, D.C. (Dr. Winfred Overholser, Margaret Hagan).

1941-1945   Recognition of group psychotherapy and psychodrama by the United States in War

Department, Technical Bulletin 103 and War Department Bulletin TBMED84.

1941   Founding of a publishing house, Beacon House, for sociometric books and monographs.

1942   Founding of Theatre of Psychodrama, Psychodramatic Institute, Sociometric Institute, New York City.
Introduction of *action* research methods, techniques, tests, and practice.

1942-1944   Sociometric selection methods in the British Army.

1944   Psychodrama applied to alcoholic problems.

1944   Audience research and role analysis (Toeman).

1944-1947   Psychodrama: Psychodramatic Institute, Denver University.

1945-1946   Founding of the American Sociometric Association.

1946-1948   Initiating of psychodrama and role-playing in Veterans Hospitals: West Brentwood, Los Angeles; Lyons, New Jersey; Winter General Hospital, Kansas; Little Rock, Arkansas, etc.

1947   Pastoral psychodrama, pastoral group psychotherapy: Department of Theology, University of Chicago, Church of the Brethren, Illinois.

1947   Psychodrama at New York University and U.C.L.A.

1947   Founding of *Sociatry: A Journal of Group and Inter-Group Therapy.*

1947   Psychodrama in France.

1948   Sociometric Institute, Paris.

1949   Sociometric anthropology (French Oceania).

1949   Psychodramatic anthropology (Eskimo, Alaska).

Convention of the American Sociometric Association, New York.

A.S.A., Member of the World Federation for Mental Health.

Spontaneity research in Parapsychology (C.C.N.Y.).

Psychodrama in Prisons (San Quentin, California).

Spontaneity Theatre and Psychodrama at Boston Psychopathic Hospital.

Theater of Psychodrama, Harvard University, Henry A. Murray, Director.

Psychodrama at the Mansfield Theater, New York City. Psychodramatic Directors: Anthony Brunse, M.D., James Enneis, Ernest Fantel, M.D., Robert B. Haas, Helen H. Jennings, Leona M. Kerstetter, J.L. Moreno, M.D., Justus F. Randolph, III, Zerka Toeman.

19. MORENEANS,* THE HERETICS OF YESTERDAY ARE THE ORTHODOXY OF TODAY

Zerka T. Moreno

We, the Moreneans, were the heretics between 1910 and 1950. Today, on the eve of 1970, the picture has changed. We are now respectable, almost orthodox; everybody under many flags, is doing what we started. Many of the concepts which we have introduced have become the "Mardi Gras" of psychiatrists, psychologists, educators, religionists and philosophers. We must protest therefore against uncritical use of our methods and techniques.

FREUDIANISM

It is not so long ago that Freudian concepts and methods were sacrosanct. "Id, ego, super-ego, subconscious and unconscious, cathexis, the couch and free association," were on all lips. Today, these terms and processes are used more and more critically or disregarded. For id, ego and super-ego, we have substituted creativity, spontaneity and the cultural conserves; for psychoanalysis, group psychotherapy; for free association, the role, for the couch, the stage or open action space; for in-

Reprinted with the permission of the publishers from *Group Psychotherapy*, Vol. XXII, Nos. 1-2 (April, 1970), pp. 1-6.

* Moreneans, practitioners following Moreno's principles. Morenism, related to J.L. Moreno's work and related developments.

terpretation, the warming up process and psychodrama and for verbal communication, the act.

BEHAVIORISM AND BEHAVIOR THERAPY

It is not so long ago that behavioristic concepts, borrowing their ideas from various schools of thought and diluting them, from Pavlov, Watson, Thorndike, Dollard, and others, were overhauled in the name of behavior therapy but the vogue for it is also beginning to lose in appeal, because behavior itself is only a symptom, which must be grounded in a meaningful philosophy of life.

EXISTENTIALISM AND EXISTENCE THERAPY

The third and more recent step in this evolution of programs is academic existentialism. But what is existence? Where is the existentialist? Where are the "Christs of our time?"

SUPER ECLECTISM AND THE "LINGUA PSYCHIATRICA"

At the end of a long chain emerged the present condition of psychology, psychiatry and sociology, unlimited numbers of pseudomodifications, hundreds of so-called "new" techniques, thousands of "new" terms and prescriptions, a super-anomia, an anomia "without end." A new lingua franca of mental hygiene has developed, a mixture of terms borrowed from all schools, the lingua psychiatrica.

MORENEAN POSITION

Moreno did not invent the methods and techniques as encounter groups, sensitivity training, role reversal and others, for their own sake. They are based on a theory of life; without their comprehension they are meaningless, even harmful. According to Moreno, the roots of life are simple. Let us quote from his oldest book, The Words of the Father, and other books which followed.

"The universe is infinite creativity.[1] It is not sufficient to define creativity by its semantics, as for instance: 'Cause to be or to come into existennce; or to make a new form out of preexisting substance.' Creativity can only be defined by its inner dynamics. It requires that we enter into its dialectic opposites so as to make clear what it means. One way of defining creativity is by its maximum condition, maximum creativity—the fullest penetration of the universe by creativity, a world that has been creative from beginning to end and that never ceases to be creative. The oppositve condition of creativity would be then zero creativity—a world that is entirely uncreative, automatic, that has no past or future, no evolution or purpose, absolutely changeless and meaningless."

"Spontaneity-creativity is the problem of psychology; indeed, it is *the* problem of the universe."[2] "Creativity is *the* problem of the universe; it is therefore, the problem of all existence, *the* problem of every religion, science, the problem of psychology, sociometry, and human relations. But creativity is not a *'separate'* mystic, aristocratic, asthetic or theological category; if it is on top, it is also on the bottom; it is everywhere; if it is in the macrocosmos, it is also in the microcosmos; if it is in the largest, it is also in the smallest; it is in the eternal and the most transitory forms of existence; it operates in the here-and-now, in this pencil and in this paper, as I am writing these words to the reader."

"When the nineteenth century came to an end and the final accounting was made, what emerged as its greatest contribution to the mental and social sciences was to many minds

[1] The Words of the Father, 1920 and 1922, 1941.
[2] Op. cit. page 126.

the idea of the unconscious and its cathexes. When the twentieth century will close its doors that which I believe will come out as the greatest achievement is the idea of spontaneity and creativity, and the significant, indelible link between them. It may be said that the efforts of the two centuries complement one another. *If the nineteenth century looked for the 'lowest' common denominator of mankind, the unconscious, the twentieth century discovered, or rediscovered its 'highest' common denominator—spontaneity and creativity.*" [3]

MORENO'S IDEAS OF A SCIENCE
OF HUMAN RELATIONS

An adequate science of human relations did not exist before the advent of sociometry. [4]

"Comte's Hierarchy of the Sciences, 1) mathematics, 2) astronomy, 3) physics, 4) chemistry, 5) biology, and 6) sociology, has become obsolete. His assumption that all sciences can be treated by the same basic methodology is an error. The social sciences need—at least in their crucial dimension— different methods of approach. The crux of the ontology of science is *the status of the 'research objects.'* Their status is not uniform in all sciences. There is a group of sciences like astronomy, physics, chemistry and biology in which the research objects are always mere 'objects.' Their actions speak for themselves and the generalizations concluded from them are not threatened by any metaphysical protest or social revolution of their kind.

Then there is another group of sciences, the social sciences. It is because of a chronic inertia in their development that sociometry has raised the question: *how are social sciences possible?* It has found that the social sciences like psychology, sociology, and anthropology require that its objects be given

3 J.L. Moreno, *Who Shall Survive?*, 1934 and 1953, p. 49.

4 Op. Cit., p. 63-64.

'research status' and a certain degree of scientific authority in order to raise their level from a pseudo objective discipline to a science which operates on the highest level of its material dynamics. It accomplishes this aim by considering the research objects not only as objects but also as *research actors*, not only as objects of observation and manipulation but as *co-scientists* and *co-producers* in the experimental design they are going to set up." Our two chief experimental designs are sociometry and psychodrama.

DIFFUSION, LACK OF UNITY

A large number of derivatives and outgrowths of Moreno's work have sprung up, as: body therapy, contact therapy, joy therapy, behavior therapy, sensitivity training, encounter groups, etc. It may be to the point, therefore, to bring some historic facts to the attention of the reader, dealing with their origins.

A long list of these ideas were originated, initiated and disseminated long before the birth of the present generation; the concept of the encounter and encounter groups, 1914; group therapy and group psychotherapy with its natural extensions as family therapy, conjoint therapy and community psychiatry, 1913, 1932 and 1934; the interaction diagram and sociogram, 1923; the concept of interpersonal sensitivity and sensitivity training, 1937; the concept of acting out and psychodrama, 1937; the permanently ongoing psychodrama, marathon, 1950's.

That psychologists are not entirely unaware of these roots is borne out by a letter from Dr. Abraham Maslow to the Editors of Life Magazine, issue for August 2, 1968: "Sirs: Jane Howard's article on Esalen and other new developments in education and psychology was excellent. I would however like to add one 'credit where credit is due' footnote. Many of the techniques set forth in the article were originally invented by

Dr. Jacob Moreno, who is still functioning vigoriously and probably still inventing new techniques and ideas."

Behind many breakthroughs in sociology, psychology, psychiatry, education, and theater, peers the cryptic image of Moreno. Think of the inspiration and influence of Moreno upon Buber's concepts of "encounter" and "I and Thou" (1914). Think of the influence and inspiration of Role Theory in the writings of T. Parsons and E. Goffman (1934). Think of the pervasive influence of the role concept and of spontaneity and creativity in the entire literature of modern education; the beginnings of play therapy in the early work of Moreno, directly or indirectly influencing Anna Freud and Melaine Klein (*Die Gottheit als Komödiant, 1919; Das Stegreiftheater,* 1923). Think of the concept of "playing for adults," or "Kindergarten for adults" which he postulated and now exemplified in the game theories and the games—formal or informal—people play.

THE LIVING THEATER
AND OPEN THEATER

Think of Moreno's influence upon the so-called Living Theater and Open Theater, participation of the audience, removal of barriers and differences between actors and audience members, the stress upon here-and-now which is neither here or now in these theaters. Think of the frequent misrepresentations of Shakespeare as a psychodramatist. True, Shakespeare described role-playing techniques within the context of a number of his plays. But it is one thing to use role-playing techniques as part of a finished script for a theatrical play, it is something very different to use role-playing in the here-and-now with real people. The role-playing of Hamlet or Falstaff as part of the script is a different phenomenon from a "live" psychodrama. Moreno has been the mighty exponent of the "Age of Ad Libbing," which is now current on radio, television, in the theater and films. Around 1920, f.i., film improvisation and spontaneity were taboo, and even today many actors state: "Security is knowing every word in the script." Many great theater and motion picture producers abjure the destruction of the script, plead for the restoration of classic structure and the complete submission of the actor to its directives; everything else stands for death to the theater in their opinion.

It is not so important that Moreno's school did these things first. That is merely one aspect of the problem. But we want to pierce the vanity and outrageous bravado of our many good friends and enemies who, under the broad mantle of science, have disowned and absorbed these ideas and are brazenly trying to get away with it. The problem is not "getting a bigger bag of better working tricks:" The problem is far more serious; the disowners undermine a system of thought, a view, a philosophy of the world, a synthesis of methods which hang together and whose break-up produces confusion instead of enlightenment, invite disaster instead of producing cohesion.

Freud's dilemma was holding his ideas tight to himself, therefore his rejection of everyone who did not recognize his priority and adhere to the dogma: Jung, Adler, Rank, Stekel, Ferenczi, among others.

Moreno did the opposite. He is tolerant and devoted to his students. His secret weapon was "giving away" his ideas; his strength lay in letting people use his ideas, encouraging them to try them out, making them their own. There was considerable risk in this; losing the priority claim was only one small part, the deeper conflict arose out of separating the methods from the philosophy. Substitute theories and philosophies are false and misleading, as they abrogate or abort the compnete execution of the methods, Moreno's position was therefore: "Take my ideas, my concepts, but do not separate them from their parent, the philosophy; do not split my children in half, like a Solomonic judgement. Love them in toto, support and respect the entire structure upon which they rest. Make them your own as completely as I do. Role reverse with me and put yourself entirely into my position."

Many have not done this; they have split the children and separated them from their true parent, like the false mother before Solomon intended. But an ever-growing number are becoming aware and the recognition gap is slowly narrowing. If Moreno continues to make his students aware of this gap, his way may yet prove to be the winner.

All the above listed concepts and ideas have a serious purpose, leading up to the philosophy of a world system, to the ethical prospect of a "therapeutic world order," a unity of mankind, as foreshadowed in 1934 in the opening sentence of *Who Shall Survive?* "A truly therapeutic procedure can not have less an objective than the whole of mankind." A therapeutic world order is mandatory, it is the next cosmic imperative if our world is to survive.

In view of the escalating anarchy of all values and ideas, it is paradoxical that Moreno is now beginning to be honored in many places, all over the world, but the most astonishing is that he has been honored in an unusual manner in Austria, his spiritual soil.

Moreno has been in contact with many of the great men of his time, shared and exchanged ideas with them: Trotzky, Freud, Adler, Buber, Stekel, John Dewey, William Alanson White, Gardner Murphy, Pitrim A. Sorokin, Henry A. Murray, among them. But academia was rarely approving of men of the caliber of Freud and in this respect the University of Vienna was no exception.

This can however, no longer be said in connection with Moreno, who saw a great change of attitude take place in his own lifetime. 1. Laboratoire d'Experimentation, Sociometrique et Psychologique, Sorbonne, Paris, 1951. 2. International Committee of Group Psychotherapy, 1950, Paris. 3. Sociometry becomes an official journal of the American Sociological Association, 1956. In 1964, the Faculty of Medicine of the University of Paris saw fit to sponsor the First International Congress of Psychodrama; the same occurred in 1968 when the

Fourth International Congress of Group Psychotherapy took place under the sponsorship of the Medical Faculty of the University of Vienna; in 1968 the Faculty of Medicine of the University of Barcelona extended a Doctor Honoris Causa to him; the Medical Society of the State of New York awarded him in 1967 a Citation for Fifty Years of Medical Service. In 1969, the Faculty of Medicine of the University of Buenos Aires made him their Guest of Honor and sponsored the Fourth International Congress of Psychodrama and Sociodrama; in 1970, the Medical Faculty of the University of Sao Paulo is doing the same thing in behalf of the Fifth International Congress of Psychodrama.

In May 1969, we undertook a pilgrimage to Austria which had as its primary purpose two events. The ceremony at the Medical Faculty of the University of Vienna. Moreno receiving the Golden Doctor Diploma. The ceremony in Voslau, the unveiling of the Plaque in Dr. Moreno's honor. Though modest in themselves, they may yet prove to be of considerable historic consequence.

20. THE VIENNESE ORIGINS OF THE ENCOUNTER MOVEMENT PAVING THE WAY FOR EXISTENTIALISM, GROUP PSYCHOTHERAPY AND PSYCHODRAMA

J. L. Moreno, M.D.

THE FORERUNNER OF AUSTRIAN EXISTENTIALISM

There are thousands of little groups today, spread over the American continent, especially in the U.S.A., practicing what is called "encounter groups," frequently not conducted by professionally trained leaders, but rather by laymen or "hippiephrenic" individuals. They have become part of our therapeutic culture in transition.

The question is: how did this happen? For the backward looking historian the answer is simple. Existentialism, group therapy, group dynamics, psychodrama and sociometry have at least one common origin, in the Austrian encounter group. It has taken almost sixty years to bring the original form to a vivid renewal. It was then, as it is now, a hodge-podge of discussion, analysis, evaluation, group and role-playing, role-testing and role-training, physical tenderness, joy of being and joy of life. There have been many efforts at formalizing under various names, different aspects of it, but in our time it has

Reprinted with the permission of the publishers from *Group Psychotherapy*, Vol. XXII, Nos. 1-2 (April, 1970) pp. 7-16.

come back to the meeting of people, eye to eye, the *encounter*, in the Here and Now. I have defined "encounter" numerous times, but the clearest definition is *Begegnung* (1) (1914). Professor Paul Johnson[1] described my effort in his book *Psychology of Religion* (2) as follows:

> In the spring of 1914 Moreno published in Vienna the first of a series of poetic writings entitled *Einladung zu einer Begegnung* (*Invitation to an Encounter*), which is evidently the first literary definition of encounter, the concept which has become central in the existentialist movement. To describe the encounter, he portrays two persons exchanging eyes to comprehend and know each other:
>
> 'A meeting of two: eye to eye, face to face. And when you are near I will tear your eyes out and place them instead of mine, and you will tear my eyes out and will place them instead of yours, and I will look at you with your eyes and you will look at me with mine.' (p. 42-43),

The literary magazine *Daimon,* (3) of which he was the editor, carried in the February issue, 1918, a dramatic dialogue by Moreno entitled 'Einladung zu einer Begegnung: Die Gottheit als Autor' (Invitation to an Encounter: The Godhead as Author). In this article (page 6) appears the term 'interpersonal communication' (zwisehenmenschlicher Vertehr). The term 'interpersonal relations,' which Robert MacDougall used in 1912 came to prominence in his book *Who Shall Survive?* (1934) (4) and in the journal he founded in 1937, *Sociometry:*

A Journal of Interpersonal Relations. [2] (5) During the years 1918-20, Martin Buber was a contributing editor of *Daimon,* and his articles appeared side by side with Moreno's, prophetic of the role each would have in the history of interpersonal theory. The I-Thou concept of God was the keystone of the interpersonal

[1] Dr. Paul Johnson, Professor Emeritus, Boston University and Visiting Professor at Christian Theological Seminary, Indianapolis, Ind.

[2] The first journal which has the phrase "interpersonal relations" in its title.

[3] By J. L. Moreno, anonymously published.

arch as documented in their publications, 1920-23. *Das Testament des Vaters*, 1920 [3] (*The Words of the Father*), (6) contains dialogues of direct address in the form of Ich und Du. It was the forerunner of Austrian existentialism, but also the creative moment of group psychotherapy and psychodrama. The meaning of the encounter definition indicates confrontation, a positive correlation between encounter and sensitivity; sociometry, psychodrama and group psychotherapy have served as instruments to facilitate them. Professor Hoff pointed to the crucial importance of the encounter concept in his opening address at the Fourth International Congress of Group Psychotherapy, Vienna, 1968: (7) "The theme of the encounter will occupy us not only in relation to the emergence of this phenomenon in psychodrama but we will have to discuss the basic rules of the encounter in the group altogether." [4]

A more comprehensive definition of encounter is contained in *Progess in Psychotherapy*, Vol. 1.[5] "Encounter, which derives from the French *rencontre,* is the nearest translation of *Begegnung.* The German *zwischenmenschlich* and the English 'interpersonal' or 'interactional' are anemic notions compared to the living concept of encounter. *Begegnung* conveys that two or more persons meet not only to face one another, but to live and experience one another—as actors, each in his own right. It is not only an emotional rapport, like the professional meeting of a physician or therapist and patient or, an intellectual rapport, like teacher and student, or a scientific rapport, like a participant observer with his subject. It is a meeting on the most intensive level of communication. The participants are not put there by any external authority; they are there because they

[4] Group Psychotherapy, Vol. 21 No. 2-3, 1968, pg. 93, Opening Address by the President of the Fourth International Congress of Group Psychotherapy, Vienna, Austria, September 16, 1968.

[5] J.L. Moreno, Philosophy of the Third Psychiatric Revolution, with Special Emphasis on Group Psychotherapy and Psychodrama, edited by Frieda Fromm-Reichmann and J.L. Moreno, Grune & Stratton, 1956.

want to be—representing the supreme authority of the self-chosen path. The persons are there in space; they may meet for the first time, with all their strengths and weaknesses—human actors seething with spontaneity and zest. It is not *Einfuhlung;* it is *Zweifuhlung* —togetherness, sharing life. It is an intuitive reversal of roles, a realization of the self through the other; it is identity, the rare, unforgotten experience of total reciprocity. The encounter is extemporaneous, unstructured, unplanned, unrehearsed—it occurs on the spur of the moment. It is 'in the moment' and 'in the here,' 'in the now.' It can be thought of as the preamble, the universal frame of all forms of structured meeting, the common matrix of all the psychotherapies, from the total subordination of the patient (as in the hypnotic situation) to the superiority and autonomy of the protagonist (as in psychodrama)."

"Summing up, *Begegnung* is the sum total of interaction, a meeting of two or more persons, not in the dead past or imagined future, but in the here and now, *hic et nunc,* in the fullness of time—the real, concrete and complete situation for experience; it involves physical and psychic contact. It is the convergence of emotional, social and cosmic factors which occur in all age groups, but particularly in adolescence (*Begegnung syndrome*); it is the experience of identity and total reciprocity; but above all, psychodrama is the essence of the encounter."

FORERUNNERS OF ENCOUNTER AND SENSITIVITY GROUPS AND THEIR DEVELOPMENT IN THE USA

Early formulations of the phenomenon of sensitivity and their consequences upon behavior have been published in my European writings.

There are actors who are connected with one another by an invisible correspondence of feelings, who have a sort of heightened sensitivity for their mutual inner processes, one gesture is sufficient and often they do not look at one another, they communicate through a new sense as if by a 'medial understanding.' 6

Some real process in one person's life situation is sensitive and corresponds to some real process in another person's life situation and there are numerous degrees, positive and negative, of these 'interpersonal sensitivities.'7

"The relation between therapist and patient, whether in individual or group psychotherapy, requires telic sensitivity. Telic sensitivity is "trainable." It is tele which establishes natural "correspondence" between therapist and patient. It is an absence of this factor in professional therapeutic relations which is responsible for therapeutic failures; it must be regained in order to make any technology work. Transference of the patient may relate him to a person who is not there, transference of the therapist may relate him to a patient who is not there. The result is that patient and therapist talk past each other, instead of to each other. Similarly, empathy and counterempathy do not add up to tele; they may run parallel, and never mix, that is, never become a telic relationship." 8

In the USA in the thirties and forties, two agencies were engaged in disseminating sensistivity and encounter groups' potentials and in training leaders to conduct them: Sociometric—Psychodramatic Institutes, Beacon and New York, 1937-, and the Bethel Laboratories, Maine, 1946-. In the December, 1969, issue of *The American Journal of Psychiatry*, Vol. 126:6. p. 183, an overview is presented by Gotschalk and

6 See *Das Stegreiftheater*, J.L. Moreno, 1923; translated into *The Theater of Spontaneity*, J.L. Moreno, Beacon House, P. 68, 1947.

7 "Statistics of Social Configurations," *Sociometry*, Volume I, 1937-38.

8 Opus cited.

Pattison,[9] with their assets and liabilities. The authors point out the seniority of the Moreno methods which influenced the Bethel organization:

> The direct development of the training laboratory came from the collaboration of three men: Leland Bradford, Ronald Lippitt and Kenneth Benne. All three had an educational background in psychology, experience in working with community educational projects, and involvement in numerous national projects dealing with major social problems related to human relations. They had been exposed to and influenced by J. L. Moreno's methods of psychodrama and had experimented with various role-playing procedures in community educational projects directed toward effecting social change.

The Bethel leaders published most of their early writings (8-20) between 1938 and 1953 in the publications of the Moreno Institute, *Sociometry, Sociatry* and *Group Psychotherapy,* and were obviously influenced by its teachings. The dependence of the Bethel group upon my work or upon the practices of the Moreno Institute is dramatically espoused and acknowledged in the Foreword to Kenneth Benne's book *Human Relations in Christian Change,* Dryden Press, 1951. As the training in groups and by action method today involves millions of people in the USA and also abroad, and has had extraordinary effects upon the morals, conduct and health of individuals, not only professionals and semi-professionals but also upon laymen, housewives, young adults and teenagers as well as children, the threat of further disintegration of our American culture is alarming, and the time has come not only to evaluate the victims but also the "healers," in this case the leaders behind the Bethel movement and the Moreno Institute groups. If what they preach and practice is of lasting value, they have to be

9 Psychiatric Perspectives on T-Groups and the Laboratory Movement: An Overview, Louis A. Gottschalk, M.D. and E. Mansell Pattison, M.D., *The American Journal of Psychiatry,* 126:6, December 1969, pg. 823-839.

carefully examined before their influence, which is spread to epidemic proportions becomes uncontrollable. The conditions have been observed by numerous enlightened specialists in the field of human relations but the one which is perhaps the 'classic' formulation should be here referred to. It is by Charles Loomis, (21)[10] formerly President of the American Sociological Association, and Zona Loomis, his wife, published in *Sociometry and the Science of Man,* Beacon House, 1956:

> The group being analyzed was one of the six 'Action Groups' or 'A' Groups initiated during the 1950 summer session of the National Training Laboratory for Group Development at Bethel, Maine. Many of the conditions contributing to failure of the action groups during that first trial have been rectified. This and other similar analyses, however, may help to prevent other groups from making the same mistakes. The application of Sociometry as applied in this article and as applied in the National Training Laboratory for Group Development generally will give concrete evidence of the very great contribution of Sociometry and the work of J. L. Moreno, founder of Sociometry, to the field of Group Dynamics. . . .
>
> The central problem of the A Group leaders to be described in this article was that of bringing to the Laboratory training experience in what was called human relations skills in organizational activity. All of the A Group leaders had been chosen because of experiences which seemed to fit them for this task; none foresaw difficulties: yet almost none—certainly least of all the senior author of this article—achieved in any appreciable degree the goal set for A Group leaders. An explanation of why this failure resulted is the purpose of this article. The explanation should also account for such events and conditions as the following which accompanied the failure: All but one of the six A Group leaders were discharged as leaders by their

[10] Sociometry in Community Organization, A Case of Failure in the Achievement of Goals, *Sociometry and the Science of Man,* Charles and Zona Loomis, p. 302.

groups; a considerable number of delegates manifested various symptoms of stress, some so serious as to require medical and psychiatric care; the group described became torn by a rift which as measured by sociometric indices establishes somewhat of a record.

The Moreno Institute branches have also been criticized, f.i., for overexposing their trainees by action methods and stimulating them to violence in its many forms. The time has come therefore to confront the assets and liabilities of both centers in order to establish valid standards of teaching and training. The case of the Bethel groups is perhaps particularly damaging because its trainers apparently do not have the benefit of clinical psychiatric experience thus underplaying the "private" problems of their candidates.

Ex post facto it could be said that paving the way for training and action methods on two separate tracks using different methods has had its advantages. The Bethel people have a larger number of students who come from industrial and government agencies so that underemphasis of private experience is not too noticeable, whereas the Moreno Centers have a larger number from clinical, hospital, educational and mental hygiene establishments.

Trainees from the Bethel Laboratories frequently come to the Moreno Institutes to study with us so that we are able to compare the two models of approach. On the other hand, dozens of our students go to Bethel and report their experiences to us. In the course of the last ten years, from 1960-70, the Bethel group are employing more and more our ideas of approach increasingly using concrete warm-up in the here and now, sociometric methods and roleplaying and we have profited from their industrial counseling studies, so that there is a noticeable rapprochement.

Table of Similarities and Differences
between the Moreno Institute Centers
and the Bethel Laboratories

MORENO INSTITUTE	BETHEL LABORATORIES
1. The setting for training is modeled after life. For instance, the setting is so structured that the trainees can act out and move around as in life itself.	1. The setting itself limits concrete action. It is more like a round-table, set for discussion.
2. Procedure is realistic. It presents as much as possible actual episodes and not constructed ones.	2. Unrealistic.
3. Concretization of events.	3. Tendency towards symbolization and evading actualities.
4. Total involvement.	4. Partial involvement.
5. Risk of overexposure is often threatening.	5. Superficiality and lack of real communication.
6. Risk of traumatizing the participants.	6. Risk of underexposure not leading to real learning.
7. Actual learning versus phantasy learning.	7. Lack of concentration upon real life circumstances of the trainee.
8. Training is adequate to meet the students real life circumstances.	8. The students are not made aware in actu and in situ how the group in which they operate actually functions.
9. The trainee learns how groups actually function thanks to careful sociometric assessment by means of sociograms and role diagrams.	9. There is a split between what they learn in the training group and what they confront in life.
10. Learning in the training groups is continuously related to the situation in the job and life settings.	10. The training groups do not prepare the students for the life situations.
11. Charting of the "sociometric network" of the community of trainees and evaluation of their comparative rankings within it.	11. Knowledge of the "sociometric networks" will prevent therapeutic breakdowns.

THE FORERUNNER OF GROUP
PSYCHOTHERAPY AND PSYCHODRAMA
IN THE VIENNESE GARDENS

Group psychotherapy, psychodrama and sociometry developed between 1908-25 in Vienna and its surroundings. The place of origin were the gardens of Vienna. In addition to the gardens of Vienna the most prominent places where the new experiments were carried out were:

1) Mittendorf, a suburb of Vienna, in a refugee camp of Italian peasants (1915-1916) where I constructed the first sociogram. It portrayed the structure of small groups, the dynamic status and rank of every individual within them.[11]

2) Am Spittelberg, the red light district of Vienna.

3) Bad Voslau where I was between 1918 and 1925 Officer of Health and Director of the Medical Department of the Kammgarnspinnerei, Voslau, a textile factory where 1,000 to 2,000 workers were employed, and,

4) das Stegreiftheater in Vienna, 1922-25, at the Maysedergasse, two blocks from the Viennese Opera.

My most important beginning was however in the gardens of Vienna. After the regular hours in the public schools, the children gathered daily. There classes were held. They consisted of small groups of from fifteen to twenty children, each under a leader chosen by the children themselves. The forming principle of the class was an Impromptu Test which ascertained the creative denominator of the child. Age differences were minimized. Children of four and ten were frequently found in the same group. The general aim of the classes was on one hand to train the whole organism of the child and not merely one of its functions; on the other hand, to lead them into the experience of "wholes." For example, in the botany class, the child was brought into active contact with the thing-in-itself, a direct

11 See my letter An das Osterreichische-ungarische Ministerium des Innern, Wien, I, Am Balhausplatex, 6. II, 1916, contained in *Who Shall Survive?*, 1953.

learned to love the tree before he analyzed it. Our traditional schools reverse this order."

"One of the outstanding events or happenings in the gardens was the choice of parents. Hundreds of children and hundreds of parents gathered to settle their relationships on a more cosmic level than heretofore. This was done by a play in which the children had an opportunity to reject their parents and choose new ones. After the choice process had been carried out, each child returned with their new parents."

"The first time that the parent test was given, however, to the deep satisfaction of their parents, every child had chosen the same parents. But at another period, when another similar opportunity was given, some of the children rejected their own and chose new parents. This produced quite a revolution." All of this has had a parallel in the U.S.A. Recently, McCalls Magazine sent out a questionnaire which children were asked to fill out as to how they feel towards their parents.

Reports of these experiments can be found in my first book, *Einladung zu einer Begegnung*, Anzengruber Verlag, Vienna, 1914, my autobiographic novel,.*Der Konigsroman*, Kiepenheuer Verlag, Berlin, 1923, Chapter, Das Konigreich der Kinder, pg. 21, *Das Stegreiftheater*, Gustav Kiepenheuer Verlag, Verlin, 1923, and in my ten other German publications by the same publisher. Because of the scarcity of my German books in regular libraries the reader may find them in the Library of Congress, Washington, D.C., in the library of Beacon House, Beacon, N.Y. and in the forthcoming Moreneum Library set up in Bad Voslau.

GLOSSARY AND NOTES

The terms "group therapy" and "group psychotherapy" were coined and defined by J.L. Moreno between 1913 (*Group Method*) and 1934 (*Who Shall Survive?*) in his American writings, but he used the phrase "Gruppentherapie" already in

1913, during his Vienese period, as well as synonymous terms describing the processes taking place in groups: Begegnungsgruppe (1914), Arbeitergruppe (1919), Elterngruppe and Kindergruppe (1923).

The term "psychodrama" he coined in 1919 and described in German and in his American publications since 1937. Related terms as "Rollenspieler" appeared in *Das Stegreiftheater,* 1923, as well as "Teilnahme des Publikums," "Theater ohne Zuschauer," "Weihetheater," "Therapeutische Theater," "Mediale Verstandigung," and "Sensitivity Training."

The term "sociometry" he began to use in 1916, the interaction diagram, the forerunner of the sociogram, in 1923.

The term "act out" or "acting out" Moreno coined in 1928 (*Impromptu School,* Plymouth Institute, p. 5, and in *Who Shall Survive?* 1934, p. 325). It is not a Freudian term. Psychoanalytic writers in America have monopolized this English phrase but it is classified by them as pathological behavior; it is noteworthy that in recent years the term acting out is used also by them more and more frequently in the Morenian positive sense and has crept into German psychoanalytic literature in English, without being translated into German.

REFERENCES

1. Moreno, J.L., *Einladung zu Einer Begegnung,*   Anzengruber Verlag, Vienna, 1914.
2. Johnson, Paul, *Psychology of Religion*   (revised and enlarged edition), Abingdon Press, New York, 1945, 1959.
3. Moreno, J.L., *Daimon,*   Anzengruber Verlag, Vienna, 1918-20.
4. Moreno, J.L., *Who Shall Survive?,*   Nervous and Mental Disease Publishing Company, Washington, D.C., 1934, Beacon House Inc., 1953.
5. Moreno, J.L., *Sociometry, A Journal of Interpersonal Relations,* published in 1937.
6. Moreno, J.L., *The Worlds of the Father,*   Anonymously published in

1920, 1922 in German, 1941 by Beacon House Inc., Beacon, N.Y.

7. Moreno, J.L., M.D., Editor, *Group Psychotherapy*, Vol. 21 No. 2-3, p. 93, Beacon House Inc. Publisher.

8. Benne, Kenneth D., and Muntyan, Bodizar, *Human Relations in Curriculum Change*, The Dryden Press, New York, 1951.

9. Bradford, Leland & Sheats, Paul, Complacency shock as a prerequisite to training, *Sociatry*, Vol. II, No. 1-2, 1948.

10. Bradford, Leland P., The use of psychodrama for group consultants, *Sociatry*, Vol. I, No. 2, 1947.

11. Lewin, Kurt and Lippitt, Roland. An experimental approach to the study of autocracy and democracy: a prelim. note, *Sociometry*, Vol. I, No. 2, 1938.

12. Lewin, Kurt, Lippitt, Ronald, and White, Ralph K., Patterns of aggressive behavior in experimentally created social climates. *Journal of Social Psychology*, X, 271-299, May, 1939.

13. Lewin, Kurt, The research center for Group Dynamics at Massachusetts Institute of Technology, *Sociometry*, Vol. VIII, No. 2, 1945.

14. Lippitt, Ronald, An experimental study of authoritarian and democratic group atmospheres, *University of Iowa Studies*, XVI, 43-194, February, 1940.

15. Lippit, Ronald, The psychodrama in leadership training, *Sociometry*, Vol. VI, No. 3, 1943.

16. Lippit, Ronald, Reality practice as educational method, *Sociometry*, Vol. VII, No. 2, 1944.

17 Lippitt, Ronald and Kurt Lewin, 1890-1947, Adventures in the exploration of interdependence, *Sociometry*, Vol. X, No. 1, 1947.

18. Lippitt, Ronald, Bradford, Leland P., & Benne, Kenneth D., Sociodramatic clarification of leader and group roles, *Sociatry*, Vol. I, No. 1, 1947.

19. Lippitt, Ronald, Administrator perception and administrator approval: A Communication problem, *Sociatry*, Vol. I, No. 2, 1947.

20. Lippitt, Rosemary, Popularity among preschool children. *Child Development*, XII, 305-332, December, 1941.

21. Lippitt, Rosemary, Psychodrama in the home, *Sociatry*, Vol. I, No. 2, 1947.

21. SCANDINAVIAN MYTH ABOUT THE PSYCHODRAMA
A Counter-statement to S.R. Slavson's "Preliminary Note"

Joseph Meiers, M.D.

A peculiar myth has been built up around the origin of the psychodrama and, in connection with it, the early formative period of modern group psychotherapy. The October 1955 issue of the *International Journal of Group Psychotherapy* carried a paper which should have destroyed J.L. Moreno's claim to originating the psychodrama. Of course, practically everyone who has witnessed Moreno's performing and enlarging the scope and applicability of the psychodrama through the years, and also everyone who has followed his writings about the practice and theory of psychodrama (from *The Godhead as Comedian* in 1911 and *Das Stegreiftheater* in 1923),[2, 2a] has felt quite confident that J.L. Moreno was thoroughly creditable as the creator of the psychodrama, as a cultural as well as a therapeutic innovation. Not so S. R. Slavson, the author of the aforementioned paper, "A Preliminary Note on the Relation of Psychodrama and Group Psychotherapy." According to Slavson: "The origins of psychodrama date to the early decades of the present century, around 1915, when Dr. Karl Joergensen of Denmark had introduced his *Stegrieftheater* or the *spontaneity theater:* The idea of spontaneity theater was trans-

Reprinted with the permission of the publisher from *Group Psychotherapy*, Vol. X, No. 4 (December, 1957) pp. 349-352.

splanted to the United States by Dr. Jacob L. Moreno, who had conducted such a theater in the early '30's in one of the meeting rooms at Carnegie Hall in New York City."[1]

On what is this "Scandinavian myth" based—so surprisingly novel to all historians of the psychodrama? It deserves careful scrutiny and refutation.* While it appears hard to believe, it still is a fact: it is based on about *five lines*—some of them, evidently, entirely misunderstood by Slavson, and some which were, in parts, also factually incorrect, i.e. inexact, in the original! They are taken from an article by the well known psychologist and author, Dr. Ernest Harms, who in an *Editorial* of his "Nervous Child" (April 1945, pp. 186-95) had written on page 188:[4]

> ... And what has now been imported to America and trade-marked as "Psychodramatics" was actually brought from Denmark to central Europe over a decade ago under the name Stegreif-Buehne. The real originator was a Danish psychiatrist, Joergensen, who as early as 1915 applied what he called "dramatic diagnosis and therapy" with great success.

The following *authentic corrections* were established by my personal correspondence with Dr. Carl Joergensen (M.D., Copenhagen), the innocent "nucleus" of this cloud of errors. Starting with my letter of July 30, 1956, to a leading Danish psychiatrist, Dr. G.K. Stuerup (who transmitted it to Dr. Joergensen whose address was, then, unknown to me), and although four exchanges of letters have taken place, and practically all of his publications have been kindly transmitted to me by Dr. Joergensen: in originals, in reprints, or by titles.

Here follows the decisive statement, concerning his *not* being connected with psychodrama in any way, made by Dr. Carl

* It comes from an otherwise serious writer—not only in his work at the N.Y.C. Jewish Board of Guardians but far beyond—whose standing as author of many books[3] in the field, and as one of the founders of the American Group Psychotherapy Association, as a Consulting Editor of the "International Journal," are too well known to need more than mention.

Joergensen on August 22, 1956. (The language of the original, written by himself in English, is unchanged).**

> Dear Dr. Meiers,
>
> Dr. G. Stuerup has lent me Your letter of July 30th and has asked me to answer it. Born . . . 1888. Neurologist and Psychiatrist. I have known Dr. Ernest Harms very well. He stayed here in Denmark in 1934-1935, before he went to U.S.A. He was a philosopher, with special interest for psychoneuroses, and we had many discussions. He spoke Danish and was full confident*** with my Danish scriptures. I have written but few things in other languages.

(After giving a brief account of his own studies in mental diseases, he tells of breaking with "the pleasure—unpleasure theory," and writing "two small books"—neither bearing either on psychodrama or group psychotherapy.)

> . . . After some years I wrote a critical survey over the medical psychotherapeutics from Janet to J. H. Schultz. This book (1932) was highly appreciated by Dr. Harms . . . *To speak clear: I have never used the psychodrama as such in my therapeutics.* And concerning group therapy as such I have not used it before Dr. Paul Reiter, my chief at that time, in 1949 asked me to make some group therapy."

(There follow 22 lines about his other writings, up to 1953.)

> If you should want further information please write me. You may use this letter as you like it.
>
> Yours very sincerely,
> (Signed) Carl Joergensen

Still puzzled how an error like the above described could have crept into the text of so studious a writer as, for many years, I had known Dr. Harms to be, highly dedicated to exactitude in his papers on medical history, [5,6,7] I wrote Dr. Jorgensen again. In his reply of December 4, 1956—the excerpts of the

---

** The *full* length of this letter exchange, with a clarification of the whole scope of the issues involved, might deserve to be published.

*** Conversant

Danish text of which are given in English below—Dr. Joergensen states:

> Concerning P S Y C H O D R A M A (spaced in typing by Dr. Joergensen himself)—I have dealt already with this question. Dr. Harms' communication about this may be based ("beror") upon a misunderstanding (—"misforstaaelse"). Maybe one can explain this by (the fact) that I had related to him various ("forskellige") dramatic situations which occurred among the patients in the Clinic at Hornbaek, where I was Head physician, 1933-1935.

He added, then, that *his* (Dr. Jorgensen's) "therapeutic method would be called an *ethico-critical analysis* ..."

The preceding little study is but a preliminary, or initial attempt to unravel the 'mystery' of the "Scandinavian" myth about the birth of the psychodrama; a myth, apparently, created by heretofore unnoticed misunderstandings. More might be said about what led to them, about the background of the myth-making. For the start, this may suffice.

REFERENCES

1. Slavson, S. R. A Preliminary Note on the Relation of Psychodrama and Group Psychotherapy—International Journal of Group Psychotherapy, vol. 5, pp. 361-366, October 1955.

2. Moreno, J. L. The Godhead as Comedian (German); No. 11000, in *Corsini-Putzey*, Bibliography of Group Psychotherapy, 1906-1956, published by Beacon House, Beacon, N.Y., 1957.

2a. ——————. Das Stregreiftheater (Impromptu theater); No. 23000, in *Corsini-Putzey*, Bibliography.

3. Slavson, S.R. In *Corsini-Putzey*, Bibliography, pp. 12-62.

4. Harms, Ernest, Group Therapy—Farce, Fashion, or Sociologically Sound?—The Nervous Child, vol. 4, Apr., 1945, pp. 186-195.

5. ——————. The Early Historians of Psychiatry—American Journ. of Psychiatry, vol. 113, February 1957, pp. 749-52.

6. ——————. Historical Considerations in the Science of Psychiatry—Diseases of the Nervous System, vol. 18, October 1957.

7. ——————. Modern Psychiatry—150 Years Ago—Journ. of Ment. Science, vol. 103, No. 433, October 1957.

8. Meiers, J. I. Origins and Development of Group Psychotherapy, A Historial Survey, 1930-45, Psychodrama Monograph, No. 17, 1946. Beacon House, Beacon, N.Y.

9. —————. (In Preparation) Modern Group Psychotherapy, Origins and Motivations, for the forthcoming Handbook on Group Psychotherapy, Basic Books, 1958.

22. PSYCHODRAMA OF SAM SLAVSON

J. L. Moreno, M.D.

I have been asked frequently: "What is the matter with Slavson?" The story goes that he has been one of your early students, that he has borrowed from you terms, ideas, concepts, methods, without any acknowledgment. What is true about it?

Let us look at the record.

Nineteen hundred and thirty-one was the year in which I began to organize group psychotherapy in the U.S.A. At that time I published a magazine, Impromptu, and in the course of the same year, the first edition of my "Application of the Groups Method to Classification" appeared ("Plan for Transforming a Prison into a Socialized Community"). In that book I coined the term "group therapy," discussed the theory underlying it, and gave some illustrations of how it may be applied.

Amongst the many newcomers who attended my open sessions in that year was Sam Slavson. It was one evening in February, 1931. Slavson came for the first time to my impromptu theatre which I conducted in Carnegie Hall. That evening I conducted a psychodrama session there. He was sitting in the first row in a seat to the right of the stage with the late Professor Sam Joseph, then professor of sociology at CCNY. It was customary that every new participant be introduced to me by the person who brought him.

I opened the session and explained the dynamics of group experience and acting out. I asked the members of the audience to volunteer. Slavson volunteered and I presented him with a problem. The situation which I constructed to be portrayed was a matrimonial episode: sitting with his wife in the living room of their home, he, Slavson, played the role of a barber; an auxiliary ego on my staff played the part of his wife. She was a young redhead, two or three inches taller than he, and in the role of a school teacher. After the situation was described they set up a living room and began to act. As customary, the scene was entirely extemporaneous from both sides: it was developed by the protagonists as they felt at the moment.

They began with a quarrel. He stood in the middle of the room, she walked toward him and criticized him violently for being a poor husband, unable to support her, lazy, ineffectual, a sadist, a tyrant. He stood there, stuttered a few words, tried to defend himself, tongue-tied, unable to react adequately. The scene appeared to be extremely real to him, as if every word she spoke rang true.

After the production there was a short discussion, then he came to me and thanked me for the experience. But he wondered how she, the "shrew," knew of his problems. She must have known them because he thought her acting was true to life.

Whenever Slavson talked to me about that meeting later on, he got excited, pointing out that it provoked an anxiety in him which the years have not been able to resolve. But the anxiety proved useful; the psychodramatic situation was a productive stimulus for him, the beginning of finding a real goal for himself. God knows what would have become of Slavson, had he not met me!

Looking back over the years since this episode occurred, I discovered a number of incidents which explain, at least to an extent, why his resentment towards me grew as the years went on and why he was never able to resolve that resentment. In the original scene he was in the role of a barber. The "barber" is in folklore the town physician and psychiatrist of the simple people. Slavson may have felt uncomfortable in this role, that of the unofficial doctor, practicing psychiatry without a license and giving professional advice to people who had medical, psychological or sociological degrees. The barber of former centuries practiced undercover surgery, obstetrics and mental counseling. He often did excellent work but had an inferior status. Looking at the original situation from the vantage point of the present, Slavson's role of the barber on the platform of the stage at Carnegie Hall has many other interesting connotations. His "psychodramatic" wife was a schoolteacher, as such she had a higher social status than he, who was just a barber. She did not show much respect and treated him on the stage as if he would be a low and vulgar character. It is amusing that he, Slavson, remembers this scene to this day, and thinks that it had a traumatic effect on him. But he is obviously not aware *why* he remembers it.

His first encounter with me became a symbol for him, although every time he committed a little crime in relationship to group psychotherapy, a new situation emerged and his original guilt was reinforced. There is a profound logic in this. In the Carnegie Hall scene, he may have wished to be in my place, and for me to be the barber, reversing roles. This was not possible, therefore, as a compensatory device, he tried to reverse the roles in the course of the years by attempts at reducing me and elevating himself.

The following is, of course, a calculation. Slavson had no academic degree, but he wanted to be a doctor, a "Dr." Slavson. He wanted to become a therapist at all costs. He had to be unscrupulous about the means to obtain that glory. He had no degree, but he permitted people to write the title, "Doctor," before his name. It is because he has become a barber that he resents me. It is I who made him act as a barber on the stage. I must have anticipated his future with a keen sense of intuition. He resents me because I made him expose on my stage his deepest complexes, his "barber syndrome." On the Carnegie Hall stage it was merely a projection. It is tragi-comic that as years went by the play became more and more real!

In the beginning, identifying himself with me in the role of a group therapist seemed like an innocent gesture, but the more often he took my role in the course of the years, employing the terms "group psychotherapy" and "group therapy," borrowed from me, organizing a society and publishing a journal of that name like me, the more he felt justified in taking over some of my terminology and my ideas, diluting and modifying them as he saw fit.

23. GROUP PSYCHOTHERAPY AND PSYCHODRAMA
A Footnote to Their History

Anna and Nah Brind

The definitive history of Group Psychotherapy and Psychodrama has not been written yet. It is, however, no great strain on any one's imagination to foresee that the history-to-be-written will try to elucidate the historical sources of Moreno's ample construct, the synchronic milieu, the gradual development of Moreno's own ideas, and the influence they in turn have exercised on contemporaneity and posterity. The history will also contain, to a greater or lesser extent, something of the struggle, despair and triumph woven into the personal, intimate lives of Moreno and his close associates.

The most celebrated couple modern psychotherapy has produced were on one of their many demonstration tours and had made a stop in California.

The Los Angeles audience which participated, Sunday, May 18, 1958, in a workshop headed by J.L. and Zerka Moreno had unexpectedly witnessed the making of a significant footnote to that future history, and this is a frankly non-reportorial account of the memorable incident.

On the surface of things, the all-day meeting, void of tensions and frustrations, was one of the more fruitful psychodrama

Reprinted with the permission of the publishers from *Group Psychotherapy*, Vol. XI, No. 4. (Dec., 1958) pp. 275-277.

workshops, one in which the audience has succeeded in exploiting Moreno's presence to the hilt.

There may have been perhaps, from the beginning, the added—rare—experience of watching teachers practicing their own teachings, as the very first performance of the day involved psychodrama in the family setting of the Morenos themselves.

But in the end the workshop was to offer even more than that.

By a concatenation of circumstances, the family situation chosen to be presented on the psychodrama stage touched upon ultimate human concerns. The theme of the performance was to be the actual acceptance of an intimate group of three— J.L., Zerka, and Jonathan Moreno—of the mutilation of one of its members.

J.L. himself, of course, was fully aware of what the performance was to imply. Indeed, unusually hesitant, he began: "I wonder if Zerka is willing to do it. You see there was recently a very threatening situation in the life of Jonathan. Mrs. Moreno, due to a needed operation, lost her right arm."*

Zerka was willing.

The ensuing performance—Zerka (just discharged from the hospital, one-armed), meeting Jonathan for the first time after the operation—had two clearly discernible levels of significance.

First, there was, to be sure, the business at hand, the necessity to convey to the Los Angeles workshop the efficacy of psychodrama techniques in confronting a most threatening situation.

It was, as it has always been, fascinating to watch Zerka—the most extraordinary Auxiliary Ego psychodrama has produced to-date—warm up to her task, to see her self-training for the job ahead, to observe the seemingly effortless flow of intuition and empathy.

Here is the core line of her brief monologue before meeting

*All quotations are from a tape recording of the session. The few added words, in parentheses, are self-explanatory.

Jonathan.

"I wonder how he is going to act. . . . They tell me he cried last night *because he thought he would see blood. . . .*"

Then assuming the role of the absentee son:

"MOMMY! MOMMY!"

And again, Zerka-Jonathan, thinking aloud:

"I'd better not get close to (mommy) yet. I don't know if she's sore *up there*. I don't know whether I should *touch* her. I don't *see anything up there. . . .* I'll—I'll go over on *this* side." Then, "Well, Mommy, one arm on, one arm off."

As the performance went on, the members of the workshop participants became increasingly aware that they were watching a phenomenon surpassing group techniques, psychodrama, workshop, and all: They were watching sane, mature, creative coping with reality.

The following excerpt from Zerka's post-performance stream-of-thoughts, printedly pale as it is, illustrates the fusion of acceptance and transformation which is—or ought to be—human relation to all reality.

". . . I've discovered it is not as disfiguring as I had thought it would be. . . .

"About the worst response I got (was) from a psychiatrist who took this thing so desperately that—I dropped up at his office one day, and his secretary said, My, how nice you look, and you've got new things on. And I said, No, I haven't got new things on, but I decided to wear all my clothes now; I'm not going to have any 'good' clothes or intermediate clothes; *I'm going to wear them all the time.* And (the psychiatrist) came up with, Please don't talk like that. I began to realize that he was more upset than I was. . . .

"Some people (are) very threatened by this, and other people are very wonderful about it. They say, After all, if you had been in an auto accident and come out the way you have, we would say, How wonderful, she's still here! . . .

"I didn't know there were so many people capable of . . . love and affection and esteem. . . .

". . . Before the operation I always used to project myself into the future as being alone (a widow) . . . and 'singlehandedly' fighting the world, supporting my child, and taking care of myself. And now, oddly enough, since the operation I don't see myself alone any more. I'm more in the cosmos. . . ."

Zerka—the Auxiliary Ego and the person—may have lost her arm, but she has made the most valiant attempt to convert her loss into an exceeding gain.

And Jonathan—and we—have gained with her.

Part V

THERAPEUTICS: SPECIALIZED TECHNIQUES AND TREATMENT

Introduction

Hypnodrama, the first technique presented here, combines the power of psychodrama with the sensitivity of hypnosis. This can be done in a variety of ways, the most common being a hypnodrama in which only the protagonist is under hypnosis. Other methods include having the protagonist and some of the auxiliary egos under hypnosis, having the protagonist, the auxiliary egos and audience members under hypnosis, and finally, having everyone involved, including the director, under hypnosis. Comparatively little has been written about hypnodrama and, like the literature of psychodrama, most of it has been written by Moreno and his followers. Nevertheless, the definitive book on the subject still awaits an author's or editor's undertaking.

In his article, "Hypnodrama, a Synthesis of Hypnosis and Psychodrama," Supple quickly defines the subject matter and describes briefly how Moreno came to invent hypnodrama in 1939. This is then followed by a description of a hypnodrama session directed by Moreno, in which the patient, regressed to the age of two, re-experiences having witnessed a primal scene. The editor of this volume has personally directed about 50 hypnodrama sessions since 1969, besides several hundred psychodrama sessions, and feels the principal reason for an experienced clinician and psychodramatist to employ it is to foster age-regression. Other reasons for employing hypnodrama

283

include helping inhibited protagonists to get in closer touch
with their feelings and to deal with some repressed material
other than through age-regression. It cannot be stated strongly
enough, however, that this is not something for the untrained or
inexperienced to try. Also, it should be noted that psychodrama
in itself is powerful enough to meet most therapeutic requirements.

The second selection, a short paper by Ackerman and
Ackerman entitled, "Emergency Psychodrama for an Acute
Psychosomatic Syndrome," is a protocol of a brief one-session
psychodrama in which a symptom is removed. This is followed
by Corsini's "Immediate Therapy," which also details an
emergency-type psychodrama, while Trautman, also in a short
paper, explores suicide in psychodrama. Trautman's paper is of
especial importance for at one time or another most courageous
and highly skilled psychodrama directors will have occasion to
give the protagonist one or more opportunities to experience
suicidal (and-or homicidal) impulses or wishes. There is very
little to be found on this subject in the literature of
psychodrama. Another approach that places the protagonist in
a fantasy-type situation is described by Sacks in "The
Judgment Technique in Psychodrama." In the situation
described, the protagonist reverses roles with an authority
figure in heaven whose task it is to advise the Deity and to sit in
judgment on who will be admitted to heaven. The protagonist is
given the opportunity to sit in judgment on himself and on
various aspects of his life and relationships which are brought
out by one of the auxiliary egos. He may thus gain some insights into his situation. This is followed by Wolson's article,
"Loss of Impulse Control in Psychodrama," which concerns
itself with hostile and aggressive acts of hospitalized patients in
psychodrama, and how they were handled in three instances.

The final three articles are also short and deal mainly with
various role-training and role-testing aspects of psychodrama. -
The two by Yablonsky, "Future Projection Technique," and

"Preparing Parolees for Essential Roles," show how opportunities to experience some parts of the protagonist's perceptions of the future may be employed through psychodramatic techniques. The last is a sort of syllabus by Otto, "Spontaneity Training with Teachers," and is of more use to those who wish to set up spontaneity training procedures of their own than to those who are primarily students of psychodrama and its techniques. Otto does, however, include some of Moreno's important books as required reading, among which is *Psychodrama, Vol. I* (1964), which contains excellent material on spontaneity tests and training. The testing and training for spontaneity, as presented by Moreno, involves setting up stressful situations in which the individual is called upon to respond quickly and in novel and adequate ways. Training for spontaneity in stressful situations also is involved in the use of psychodrama in police and community relations work, as Hannah B. Weiner explains in the chapter which precedes that by Herb Otto.

24. HYPNODRAMA, A SYNTHESIS OF HYPNOSIS AND PSYCHODRAMA
A Progress Report

Leonard K. Supple, M.D.

Herewith follows a brief description of the origin of the Hypnodramatic Technique. Hypnodrama is a synthesis of psychodrama and hypnosis. The idea of hypnodrama came to Dr. Moreno through an accident. In the summer of 1939 the late Dr. Bruno Solby brought a young woman for treatment. She suffered from paranoid delusions accompanied by nightmares, every night the devil came to visit her. She was unable to get into a psychodramatic re-enactment of the incident. After trying the self-directed technique and methods of mild prompting without results he became highly directive; this put the patient unexpectedly into a hypnotic trance. Dr. Moreno decided to try a psychodrama under these novel circumstances. With the aid of two male auxiliary egos the patient was able to portray two meetings with the devil, one as it had happened the night before, one as she expected it to happen the following night. Apparently hypnosis operated as a "starter" and spurred her spontaneity.

Several years later Dr. Moreno made a number of hypnodramatic experiments in association with James Enneis, the results of which they published in a monograph.[1] Enneis

Reprinted with the permission of the publishers from *Group Psychotherapy*, Vol. XV, No. 1 (March, 1962), pp. 58-62.

[1] Hypnodrama and Psychodrama by J.L. Moreno and James Enneis, Beacon House, Beacon, New York, 1950.

describes the technique as follows:

"In hypnodrama, hypnosis is induced on the stage. Psychodramatic techniques are used to speed the process and to relate it to the patient's everyday experience. The patient is warmed up in a psychodramatic manner to being in his bedroom or some other situation which he associates with sleep. After the setting becomes real to him, the director continues with the usual suggestive technique for the induction of hypnosis. When the patient is hypnotized the procedure continues with the psychodrama, using all its well known techniques."

"The closing of sessions on a high note is a cardinal principle of psychodrama.[2] This applies also in hypnodrama. When the patient has enacted frustrating experiences, it becomes extremely important that he be warmed up to a pleasant situation which he can handle to his satisfaction before he is awakened. If this is not done, anxiety or depression may result. He must be given an opportunity to act a successful if not heroic role, thus allowing the warming-up process to become reoriented."

Since last May we have on various occasions used this combined mode of therapy with different types of patients. It has been quite successful and has allowed the patients to go deeper into their portrayal in the psychodrama while in the hypnotic state than they would without the hypnosis, at least in some cases. In several instances this has been a revelation and in fact, some of the patients who in the usual form of psychodrama did not give their all, once they were in the hypnotic state would eagerly participate in hypnodrama for two hours or more and reveal much deeper levels than in the psychodrama. To explain this more fully, allow me to state that I have seen patients in psychodrama who have revealed themselves on very deep subconscious levels, and in fact, I have seen cataleptic patients respond to the psychodrama where mirror technique, role reversal, auxiliary ego methods and other

[2]*Psychodrama* Vol. I and II, by J.L. Moreno, Beacon House, Beacon, N.Y.

modalities were employed.

Perhaps it would be well if at this juncture I were able to give some details of one particular case in which hypnodrama worked very well. The subject, a young lady, is a teacher in the southwest and holds a Master's degree in Science from a recognized university. Clair came to the Moreno Institute in Beacon to study at a summer seminar held there under the direction of Dr. Moreno. While a group member there, she stated that she herself had problems which had been bothering her for quite a number of years. She had two sessions of psychodrama. I was present at one of these although I did not participate at this particular session. During these sessions, she reenacted certain situations in her past experience at home and elsewhere and was given considerable insight into some of her problems but felt that she had not completely conquered the entire situation. At Dr. Moreno's suggestion, I saw this young lady who had entered into a light hypnotic trance on one previous occasion for her dentist at home. I proceeded to induce a light trance in privacy in this student. The following day, with very little difficulty, I induced her into a medium trance, which I helped her to make much deeper. While in this particular trance, she reacted well to my suggestion that Dr. Moreno would now take over the Psychodrama or Hypnodrama session. Dr. Moreno, together with Mrs. Moreno and others who were present at the teaching seminar then entered into the Hypnodrama and this session continued for approximately 1/2 to 3/4 hours. During this time, I reinforced hypnosis on two or three occasions although I was not certain this was necessary. However, it did quite well. Clair reacted very well and went through several intimate scenes in her past life, especially in childhood without any fear whatsoever of going into the intimacy of these details. At the end of the drama, I awakened her from the hypnotic trance and she stated that she felt well and she was satisfied with what she had presented.

The following day, I was able to induce Clair into a trance by the mere use of one of Dr. Erickson's more streamlined and more dramatic techniques, merely raising her hand in mine and having her look at her hand without knowing it, holding it closer to her face and eyes and as it came closer, she automatically went into a deep trance. With this, I then had her sit down and deepen the trance until it became very deep. I then made the statement that she could if she desired, open her eyes and stay in a state of a very very deep hypnosis and walk around or talk, ask questions, answer questions or whatever else she chose to do but meanwhile staying at all times in this very deep hypnotic trance. On this occasion, Clair remained in a trance for a period of approximately 2 1/2 hours. During this time, she walked about the Psychodrama stage, she literally circled the lowest step on the stage countless times, followed by her auxiliary ego, and she responded beautifully to the suggestions of her auxiliary ego, to those of the Director and the other participants in the session. During this session, she reenacted a scene from her early childhood in which she lay down upon the stage and at the time she lay down was back to about two years of age in her mind, in the hypnotic state. She could see two other participants in the Psychodrama who were taking the roles of her Father and Mother and who were lying upon a mattress which represented a bed upon the stage. She immediately registered all the reactions of horror and fear. She stated that "Daddy is beating Mommy up." It soon developed that what she had seen at this early stage both physically many years ago and also in hypnosis on this occasion was an act of intercourse between her Father and Mother, but at the age when she saw this, she interpreted it as physical abuse of the Mother by the Father. It was interesting that she was able to regress in the hypnotic state on only the third session which I had with her to a state where she could once again visualize this act of aggression as she interpreted it. There is frequently the question raised what regression means in dynamic terms. According to Moreno's hypothesis, regression is a "psychodramatic" regression, not a "physiological" regression. This hypothesis can be empirically tested. This interpretation of regression may not change the therapeutic effect of the re-enactment of past episodes. Later on when she was out of hypnosis, we discussed the matter. She had an entirely different interpretation of what she had seen. She now was able to discuss it at the adult level and understand that what she had seen, was not what she thought she saw when she was two years of age. It is extremely interesting to note that one not versed in hypnosis but versed in Psychodrama can accomplish age regression in a subject who has been put in hypnosis by another individual. Clair discussed many areas of her life, her associations with men, her associations with superiors of the faculty and of her students with complete freedom from embarrassment or difficulty of any kind. She was able to give of her innermost self during this entire period of time and we believe that she did better with this technique than she would have with either Psychodrama or hypnosis alone.

At the end of this session, several of the group who were observing the technique asked me if Clair was still in hypnosis. In order to show them, perhaps one might say "dramatically" the answer to their question, I asked Clair if she was awake or in hypnosis and she said she thought she was awake but she wasn't sure. I therefore asked her if she would not sit down, which she obligingly did. I told her that if she wished to, she could go even deeper into hypnosis by just closing her eyelids. Being a very gracious subject, she closed her eyelids and went into a much deeper trance than she was 2 1/2 hours previously. I then suggested to her that when she awakened from hypnosis, both of her upper extremities would be in a catatonic position and she could not put them down till such as I snapped my fingers. I then aroused her from the hypnotic state and immediately both of her upper extremities went into the catatonic position very comfortably. She sat there and talked to me for a period of about five minutes after which I snapped my fingers and Clair's arms became relaxed and the upper extremities returned to a normal stance.

We do not feel that this is a panacea or cure-all for *every* patient who comes to us for therapy. However, we feel that in some selected cases this can be a very advantageous type of treatment. We feel also that there has not been enough work done in this particular field to fully outline the type of patient who is best treated by this combined technique. Further research should allow us to more accurately determine which type of patient would benefit most by this method.

There are several other cases with which we have worked in this, we believe, new and certainly different technique. We feel that much progress can be made in this direction by a combination of hypnotic and psychodramatic techniques. However, there is much still to be learned and therefore we intend to continue with the research in this field. We feel it is extremely interesting to note that two techniques can be combined so successfully. Dr. Moreno, of course, has done hypnosis in the past but has not specialized in this particular therapy. I have done other things myself but have gone more and more toward the hypnotic technique. It is interesting also to see how easy it is to transfer the patient from the one who induces hypnosis to the one who carries on the Psychodrama. I feel that if the psychodramatist were someone not versed in the hypnotic techniques this could present problems. However, this still remains to be proven. Personally, I believe that by the combination of hypnosis and psychodrama, it may be possible entirely to achieve much more brilliant results. There are certain patients whom I have observed in Psychodrama and Psychotherapy who are somewhat reticent or one might say, bashful in giving their all. They seem to withhold something from the group or from the psychodramatist. In the particular cases which we have studied in the combined form of therapy, this reticence or bashfulness or withholding has been largely overcome. These patients seem to *want* to give all of their innermost and subconscious thoughts for their own benefit and that of the group with whom they are working. Naturally, one can envision the much greater benefits from this type of situation than from one where the patient withholds even a small part of the information which is present in his conscious or subconscious mind. In more recent sessions of hypnodrama, we have observed that the patients have told us that after each session they have been very active at home and have established, in most cases much better rapport with their families or at least several members of each family than had been possible in the past. Since we envisage our program to be one of establishing rapport of the patient with his or her family, we have been encouraged greatly by the reports from the patients. We feel that ours is a teaching situation. In other words, we are teaching the patient to better establish relationships with all members of his or her family and with the others with whom he or she comes in contact. Apparently we are succeeding in this respect.

We hope to publish further reports upon this type of therapy in the near future and to continue our efforts in research in this particular field.

25. EMERGENCY PSYCHODRAMA FOR ACUTE PSYCHOSOMATIC SYNDROME

Max Ackerman, M.D., and Sylvia Ackerman

An emergency psychodrama became necessary when a patient developed a series of psychosomatic symptoms under stress of her conflict. This patient was torn between going on a vacation with her boy friend to Canada or leaving by herself for California without notifying him, in retaliation for what she thought was his lack of interest. Five hours before flight time she became very dizzy, her head pounded, her stomach was tied up in knots, her tongue was thick, and she found thinking difficult.

A one-session psychodrama directed toward her conflict was sufficient to make her symptoms disappear and she was able to join her boy friend on their vacation.

Below is the record of how we utilized psychodrama to remove threatening psychosomatic symptoms in a brief period.

Mary: (*On telephone*) You must help me right away. I am leaving by plane this afternoon on my vacation, but I'm all tied up in knots, my head is pounding, I'm dizzy and my tongue and right arm are numb, and I can hardly talk to you.

Dr.: I can see you about 12 noon. Can you be here at that time?

Mary: I'll be there.

Mary: (*At office*) I was going to California by myself, just to

Reprinted with the permission of the publisher from *Group Psychotherapy,* Vol. XV, No. 1 (March, 1962), pp. 84-88.

get far away from New York and Hal, after I decided I didn't want to go on a vacation with him.

Dr.: Why don't you want to go on a vacation with Hal?

Mary: I lost all zest for going with Hal.

Dr.: Why?

Mary: I guess I am fed up with him.

Dr.: Tell us about it.

Mary: There are so many instances.

Dr.: Tell us about any one which was upsetting to you.

Mary: Well the last incident was a telephone conversation I had with Hal.

Dr.: Show us what happened. Sylvia (*pointing to auxiliary ego*) you be Hal, and Mary you be yourself and enact the conversation as you recall it.

Syl.: (*as Hal*) Hello Mary. How are you?

Mary: (*Looking impatient and annoyed*) Hello.

Hal: What did you decide about our vacation?

Mary: Nothing. I lost interest in it.

Hal: Why? I thought we were going away together.

Mary: I know. But you haven't called me all week, even though I've called your house several times and left messages where I could be reached. (*Pause*) I was looking forward to this vacation all summer and when you didn't even bother to call I forgot about it.

Hal: Well I called now and we can still plan on going away.

Mary: I know, but now I'm not interested. You get so involved with your daughter and her problems that you forget that I exist. She has a husband to worry about her. I'm tired of waiting around until you are ready.

Dr.: Now reverse roles. Mary you be Hal, and Sylvia you be Mary.

Mary: (*as Hal*) Hello Mary. How are you, dear?

Syl: (*as Mary*) All right.

Hal: What shall we do about our vacation?

Mary: (*Aux*) I've lost interest.

Hal: (*Mary*) Why? We can still go.

Mary: (*Aux*) I know, but I'm tired of playing second fiddle to your daughter. I'm tired of competing for your love, time and attention with your grown-up married daughter.

Hal: (*Mary*) Isn't it natural that I have a father's interest in my daughter?

Mary: (*Aux*) It is more than a natural interest. I don't want to come between you and your daughter. But when you are with me I feel your mind is far away thinking of her. When I talk to you I feel I am not reaching you.

Hal: (*Mary*) There you go with your pseudo-psychiatry again, telling me how I think and how I feel.

Mary: (*Aux*) I can't even tell you anything. You just don't understand.

Hal: (*Mary*) You know even if I'm late or if I don't call you right away, I always come anyway. I've gotten into the habit of seeing you.

Mary: (*Aux*) I'll release you from your habit.

Dr.: Mary walk around in a circle and speak of your feelings about Hal. Sylvia you be her double and tell us her thoughts too.

Mary: I feel I have given Hal love, affection and consideration and all I get from him is rejection. When I first met Hal I was impressed by the fact that he was recommended to me by people I thought highly of. I thought he was much more intelligent than I was. I thought I could learn so much from him and was willing to give him everything. But where I thought there was intelligence and strength, I find only weakness.

Double: I consider myself weak, and not too intelligent. I admire people who have a lot of knowledge. I figure by associating with intelligent people, I will learn a lot and in return I am willing to give them love.

Mary: (*Stopping*) Yes that is true. Is it wrong to try to learn from others?

Double: This seems to be following a pattern. Maybe

something is wrong with me. I am so good to others and then I get hurt.

Mary: I admired Emily because she was almost a doctor. I opened up my home to her and offered her everything I had and I did the same with Hal and he disappointed me too. My husband was very intelligent and I gave him everything I had and he, too, hurt me. Maybe I am attracted to the wrong people? Yes. Maybe something is wrong with me. I figured maybe I should go to another state and meet different people.

Double: I would just love to run away—to escape. Sometimes I get so discouraged that I feel I don't want to see anybody or do anything . . . . The trouble is that I can't escape from myself. Maybe I should just lay in bed and die.

Mary: No I don't want to die, but is it wrong to want someone to return the love you give him? When I point out his weaknesses he gets angry.

Double: Maybe I have a cruel streak in me. When I get hurt I strike back. Maybe I threaten him.

Mary: (Laughs)

Dr.: Mary tell us what you think of what has gone on.

Mary: I think my double was very good. At times I actually thought she was me. I hadn't thought of it before, and I never agreed with it, but it may be true that I threaten Hal. Only recently he accused me of acting superior to him and making him feel inferior. I was able to see myself better through Sylvia and I hadn't realized I did some of the things I do. But . . . how did she know these things?

Syl.: You told them to me. I responded to your feeling tones and your clues.

Dr.: Sylvia and I will now constitute a group and will respond to you as a group. Group how do you feel about Mary?

Syl.: I feel that Mary assumes that others are smarter and stronger than she is and therefore associates with those whom she considers smarter and stronger and hopes that some of it will rub off on her.

Mary: What is wrong with trying to learn from others?

Syl.: Nothing, except that you have inordinate expectations from others and too great feelings of your own inadequacy.

Dr.: That is true. I have known Mary for a number of years. I have found her intelligent, sensitive and perceptive. She emphasizes too much the superficial learning and knowledge of others and underestimates her own capacities. She looks for strength in others and then is hurt when she finds weaknesses. She feels Hal has rejected her when he cannot help his personality limitations. Actually no one is rejecting her. She is rejecting herself.

Mary: That may be true, but it still doesn't make me feel better.

Syl.: Do you give love to your son with the expectation that he will give an equal amount back to you?

Mary: Of course not. He is only a little boy.

Syl.: What would happen if you expected your son to bring home a 100 percent paper all the time?

Mary: I would never expect that. That is asking for too much.

Syl.: Exactly.

Dr.: (to Syl.) You be Mary's double now and you think aloud as Mary. Mary you watch carefully and then tell us your reaction.

Double: I am fed up with Hal. I can't compete with his daughter nor do I want to. I want him to love me for myself. I offer him so much and he gives me so little. What am I going to do? He disappoints me so much—yet—I know I would be miserable if I were alone. I can't stand being lonely. It is true that he is never on time and that he constantly keeps me waiting, but at least he comes. Sure he chooses his daughter before me, but he still chooses me. Despite all my criticism, he is good company. If I didn't care for him, why would he upset me so much? Maybe if I accepted him for what he is and not try to make him over, maybe I won't get hurt so readily? I'm trying to change his personality and I'm bound to be disappointed because people don't change so readily. Now that I know his weaknesses, I won't expect too much and will try to enjoy the things we have in common. If that isn't enough to satisfy me, then I can break up the relationship and seek elsewhere.

Dr.: Mary what do you think? Is that how you feel? Could you see yourself a little bit better through your double?

Mary: It is true I have been trying to change him and make him what he is not. It is also true that I was very lonely before and I can't stand being alone.

Dr.: From what I know of you, being alone is the worst thing for you. You get very depressed and you get sick.

Mary: (*Laughing*) You are absolutely right. Now I know that the thought of breaking up with Hal was the reason why my stomach was all tied up in knots and why I felt dizzy and my head pounded and my tongue and arm were numb. I really didn't want to go on my vacation without Hal. I am terribly afraid of being lonely. I now realize that I don't want to give him up and that I need him. (*Laughing again*) I feel amazingly calm now and what's more, nothing is bothering me.

Dr.: I think that the main thing that has been pointed out here is that you are not ready to give up the relationship. In resuming the relationship you will be able to see if there is enough in it to be rewarding. If not, you can gradually build up a readiness to make a change. The other important points were too high expectations from others and not enough attempt to build up your own resources. If you can learn to enjoy a relationship on the basis of what it has to offer, rather than what your idealization of it is, you may be able to minimize tensions and develop more positive qualities to build upon.

SUMMARY

The above session demonstrates that even severe psychosomatic symptoms can be eliminated psychodramatically in a short period of time. Because the symptoms were severe, varying techniques in rapid sequence were used so that the patient was prevented from mobilizing her resistance but was still able to tie up the threads sufficiently to resolve her problem. The patient was being torn by two conflicting emotions on an unconscious level. On the one hand she had a desire to punish Hal by going away without him; and on the other hand she still wanted to be with him. Even though she rationalized that she would have a fine vacation without him, she couldn't carry it out and therefore developed her psychosomatic symptoms. When she gained insight through acting out her problem that she wasn't ready to give him up, she no longer had need for her symptoms.

26. IMMEDIATE THERAPY

Raymond J. Corsini

All schools of therapy of the psyche have reported cures. Those who have investigated the claims of various schools of psychotherapy have come to the conclusion that as far as can be told no very great difference in kind or in quantity of success has been reported by any school of treatment over any other (1). Also, we have learned more recently, it doesn't seem to matter what one says one is doing in therapy, good therapists seem to do more or less the same, no matter what the nature of their theoretical background (2). This is a matter that Dr. Jacob Moreno has stressed again and again. There seems to have arisen a magical semantic misunderstanding so that people who do exactly the same thing nevertheless claim they are doing different things. It is as though we saw a column of men all marching alongside each other in step, and yet each man proclaimed he was going in an independent direction.

The point of these introductory remarks is that it very well may be other matters than methods of treatment, or systematic, theoretical understanding of the nature of character formation and personality change that are behind successful treatment. If I understand the meaning of the early findings of the Chicago experiment on the evaluation of methods of therapy it is that

Reprinted with the permission of the publishers from *Group Psychotherapy*, Vol. IV, No. 4 (March, 1952), pp. 322-330. Paper delivered June 7, 1952 at the Mid-West Section of the American Society for Group Psychotherapy and Psychodrama.

the locus of treatment is not on the method but on the therapist. It was this point that Dr. Thomas Gordon emphasized in his remarks on the theory of psychotherapy.[1]

Now, if for the moment we can accept the fact that we really know nothing about the comparative value of different methods of treatment, let us see what we know about the time-economy of treatment. We shall find—I warn you—that we shall come up with very little that is certain, but even with the prospect of failure we may go on, hoping to find some unexpected crumbs in the empty larder.

Psychoanalysis, we know, is generally considered slow and expensive. The patient lies down, the analyst closes his eyes, and hour after hour in the traditional analysis the patient free-associates, and two, three or more years later the patient is released. I have known several people who have been psychoanalyzed. Perhaps I have met a biased sample, but none of them felt he had finished. One of them had no fewer than four long analyses over a period of several years. Only one of these people did I know before and after. In my opinion he had improved, but unfortunately he felt that he still had a lot to go and was unsatisfied.

I would like to compare the traditional psychoanalysis with psychodrama. While the stereotype of psychoanalysis is the couch, the stereotype of psychodrama is the stage. While the stereotype of the analyst is the grave, pensive Freud, the stereotype of the psychodramatist is the ebullient, dynamic Moreno; while the essence of analysis is deep thought and no action, in psychodrama it appears to be action and emotion. May we not conclude on the basis of all these differences that psychoanalysis is ponderous and slow and that psychodrama is lively and quick. Now, if we go back to a previous statement that I made, namely that all methods of psycho-treatment have

[1] Gordon, Thomas. Some theoretical notions regarding changes during group therapy. *Group Psychotherapy*, 1951, 4 No. 3, 172-178.

shown cures, and that as far as can be told no method is superior to any other in terms of demonstrated quality of treatment, what conclusion do we seem to be coming to? None other than that, if psychodrama as a method of psychic cure is as good as any other, that since it appears to be faster, that at least from an economic point of view it is of greater social value than psychoanalysis.

Let me now return to an earlier point before I really get down to the heart of my argument. You will recall that I claimed that a great many methods of treatment were really the same although the protagonists said they were different, and that I argued that it was then the therapist and not the method that did the trick. Now, what I really meant to say was that all of the individual methods were really the same! Let us see two people in individual therapy, let us listen to them. Who can say whether it is a Freudian, an Adlerian, a Jungian, or a Rogerian analysis? Actually, I suspect that by the time the therapist begins to talk, after listening to his patient, that the therapy has already occurred. The patient listens to some story about the ego, or organic inferiority, or racial unconscious, but by this time he is already cured. I am of course exaggerating this matter for a good reason. The reason is that speaking from an operational point of view psychodrama is actually a completely different kind of therapy from all other purely ratiocinactive methods. Therefore, if in the complete analysis of therapy we wish to correctly evaluate methods, we have to compare methods that are truly different. All individual methods probably have more in common than any group method, since all individual methods are essentially alike. In group therapy alone are enormous real differences possible. Also, of all the group methods that I know of, none approaches psychodrama in terms of the possibilities of affecting the individual. This is the most radical of the methods, and I believe that my own variation of this method is one of the most radical of the variations.

My topic refers to Immediate Therapy. I am concerned with economy. I am now discussing psychodrama, especially with reference to my own experience with this method of treatment in penal institutions, notably San Quentin and the Wisconsin State Prison. The point that I am going to make shortly is that Immediate Therapy can take place—or, that Therapy does not have to be long and drawn out.

I hope that I am touching upon a controversial point. I am sure that many of you, especially those of you who have not had the experience of doing or participating in psychodrama must be convinced that I do not know what I am saying. You are probably thinking: "Does not the speaker know that the formation of neuroses takes years and that the removal of the effects must take months? He is talking about psychotherapy, not surgery."

You will grant me that we still do not know all the answers about psychotherapy. You will at least agree with me that the avalanche of psychic ills that are engulfing us requires us to have tolerance for even crackpot ideas. Therefore, I am going to insist that psychotherapy can learn from surgery. What have the surgeons learned? This—that a quick operation is often best. It reduces the dangers of surgical shock and is best for the patient (3). I am going to argue now that quick psychotherapy is possible and I shall give what I regard to be proof of this, and I shall also give you some hypothetical constructions to account for these ideas.

Let me begin with a simple case having to do with a symptom. Harold in the first session of group therapy informs us that his problem is sleep-talking and sleep-singing. He has not skipped two nights in succession in over twenty years. He tells us that his parents have taken him to dozens of doctors, psychiatrists and psychologists. They have informed him that his sleep-talking behavior can be explained on three bases: (1) he is introverted, keeps things to himself during the day; this dams up his psychic energies which find release at night; (2) he is the victim of a habit, which he contracted in childhood at which time he used sleep-talking to awaken his mother whom he hated; now the sleep-talking is functioning autonomous and persists even though he is away from his mother; (3) there is some vague and unknown brain lesion that affects his sleep.

Harold asks me whether I can do anything for him—can I make him sleep peacefully when a score of others have failed? I tell him that I don't know but I feel hopeful. I ask him to be a member of the group. He stays in the group for a number of weeks and seemingly I pay little attention to him. When I believe he is ready, I ask him to talk. He tells a story that clearly implies that he has hatred for his mother, and he reveals that he has become a criminal mainly to bring shame on his mother. He reveals what I call the Samson complex—Samson killed his enemies by bringing the temple down on the heads of his enemies, but also lost his own life thereby.[2] As he goes on I begin to accept the second theory, namely, that his sleep-talking is now a functionally autonomous act which started as a child as a means of punishing the mother.

We now enact a psychodramatic situation taken from a real incident in his life. We work Harold into a passion of emotion. In one scene he has a make-believe gun in his hand, and he is threatening to kill his mother. He breathes deeply, his nostrils flare, his eyes are open, he calls his cowering mother names as he threatens her. He is deeply moved. I slap my hands twice. I send Harold out of the room, not to appear for a whole week. This is the end of the psychodrama.

Now you can see why I said that my variation of the method of psychodrama is radical. One could add that it is cruel and that it is dangerous. I will only admit the first of the three. I shall argue now that this radical method is neither cruel nor dangerous. One of these charges I can dispel by logic, the other by experience.

2 Corsini, Raymond, Criminal Conversion. J Clin. Psychopath., 1945, 7, 139-146.

Is it cruel for the surgeon to amputate an arm without anesthetics? Not if the surgeon has no anesthetic; not if the surgeon's intention is to help his patient; not if not to operate means death.

But is it not dangerous to do such radical things: to create unbearable anxiety; to work a patient to a point where he cries; to have him suddenly and dramatically discover that he is a weakling; that he hates his father; that he is a homosexual; that he is dependent on his mother? All I can say is that I have seen each of these and many more, and have found absolutely no harmful effects. I have dealt with people diagnosed as psychopathic, psychoneurotic, paranoid, schizophrenic. I have had cases checked before and after by psychiatrists and psychologists, and I have found in no case when the proper precautions were used where any unfortunate result occurred.

Perhaps the structure of this paper is too complex, but I would like to return to Harold for a moment and then I will discuss what I mean when I say "proper precautions."

Harold came back to group therapy the next week. It was quite evident to all that something had happened to Harold. He looked better. He smiled. He spoke in a more confident manner. Finally I asked him. "What were your reactions to the rather unpleasant experience of last week?"

Harold answered: "I see now where I used to hate my mother. I don't any longer. I pity her. And, besides, I don't think I have spoken a word in my sleep all week. And, the strangest thing: Sunday I overslept. I never did that before."

This is already a long paper and I still have much to say and so we will leave Harold in prison, thanking him for merely demonstrating that a single psychodramatic session lasting no more than one-half hour has apparently done what twenty specialists over twenty years were unable to do. Let us go on to the question of the proper procedures for conducting psychodrama, then, I shall postulate some theoretical principles to account for some of the facts of psychodramatic treatment and I shall be done. (4)

The first principle involved in proper treatment is this: In doing psychodrama you are doing individual therapy in a group situation. That means you must create the proper relationship with each individual. He must believe in you and you must want to help him. Unless a common bond of understanding is created, there is no therapy.

The second principle refers to self-direction. The subject must assume ultimate control and responsibility for the therapeutic effort. The therapist works with him, not against him; the therapist treats him but only after continued permission.

The third principle refers to control. The therapist must expend all his energies to achieve a peak of emotional effect, which should be within the subject's limit of tolerance but beyond the threshold of control. It is the therapist's responsibility to refuse to work in group therapy with anyone whose limit of tolerance appears to be low.

These three principles will guarantee a minimum of danger, but there are other reasons why psychodrama is not as dangerous as it looks. First, let me explain to those who do not know what psychodrama really is, and that must take in everyone who has not had experience with it, that psychodrama is not role playing, any more than children playing house is really living in sin. Role-playing, or the acting of a part, is but a device, a phase of the whole treatment, one that takes but a few minutes. Psychodramatic treatment is a fairly extensive procedure having a number of definite stages of which the dramatic action is only one. For the drama to have any therapeutic effect, for it to be more than simple role-playing, it is absolutely necessary for the subject to have been properly prepared, for him to have been matured to the point that he is ready to reveal himself and be ready to be treated. Also, there are steps that follow the treatment that are of some importance.

At this point you may begin to wonder about my insistence on economy. If you will recall that in psychodrama, as I practice it, there is one therapist and fifteen subjects, and that we average two psychodramatic situations per session, you will see the economy.

Also, and this is a point that I would like to emphasize, the process of permitting the patients to become therapists by means of allowing them to be auxiliary egos and discussants has a tremendously powerful social therapeutic effect. They become forced to pay attention to others, to help others, to be concerned with others. This philanthropic effect combined with the therapeutic effect of their own treatment assists them in their resocialization and tears down their narcissistic egoism.

Let me finish this penultimate segment of my talk by saying that the best proof of my contention, as far as I am concerned, is the expression of satisfaction of the treatments from ex-prisoners who have written to me who have told me of the benefit it has had for them. I realize that such proof is weak, but it is the best I can give you at present.

And now, I would like to conclude this presentation by the listing of a number of hypothetical ideas that I have come to accept in reference to group therapy. Many of the ideas come from others. Who they are may now be difficult to discover. But that is of little importance. I submit that these principles that I shall give you are for the most part capable of test; and also I submit that each of them is essential to the rapid ameliorative change of people, which is my definition of therapy.

1. Therapy should, all other factors held constant, be rapid.

The reason for this is that resistances increase as one goes along. Countertransference is undesirable. The patient is backed into a corner, as it were, by an analytic exploration. The more one probes, the more one hurts the patient. Therapeutic shock will be minimized by rapid treatment. A radical method like psychodrama can achieve results quicker than can conservative methods.

2. Tension—the Gestalt analogy.

One of the essential aspects of psychodrama, as I do it, is to create anxiety—and then to refuse to reduce it. The reason for this is that I believe that this experimental (but real) anxiety serves the purpose of reordering the structure of the personality. The individual stumbles out of the therapeutic room in a state of enormous agitation, but this excitement of his emotion has taken place in a neutral field. He cannot displace his anger on anyone except himself and during the process of obtaining emotional homeostasis he gains insight into the causes of his process of self-reconstruction done alone and away from the therapist is, to my mind, the apogee of the therapy.

3. The principle of irradiation.

This next point I believe is the single most important idea that I will present. I have noticed that even though, when one works with psychodrama, one is restricted to a single idea or problem, that the successful solution does not only affect the area of the problem, but also other outlying problem areas. It would seem that therapeutic effects irradiate. It is a good thing that they do, else one would have to spend a great deal of time to clear up innumerable tiny problems. There is a corollary of this principle of irradiation and that is the principle of the ordered hierarchy. It is as though there are levels of problems. The solution of a problem at a certain level of depth, also solves some other problems on that level as well as all other problems below that level. Also, the solution of problems at this level makes it possible to attack problems of a greater depth at a later period.[3]

The function of the therapist includes the ability to see the strategy of defense in depth on the part of the subject and to refuse to be made to skirmish with the simpler problems, but to drive in, select a harder or deeper problem, and dispatch it. The subject himself will mop up these other minor problems. On the

3 Corsini, Raymond, Psychodramatic treatment of a pedophile, *Group Psychotherapy*, 1951, 4, No. 3, 166-171.

next attack the therapist is able to go directly to a deeper level.

4. The principle of release.

I have one other further analogy which will assist in understanding my conceptions of personality and personality change. This is the analogy of the log jam. As logs come down the river they sometimes jam. Because of one or two logs, millions of others are blocked. Loggers solve the problem by blowing up the jam, and this releases all the other logs. In psychotherapy the destruction of a key error also releases many smaller problems. Traditionally, the therapist solves the log jam from the rear, as it were, taking one log away at a time until finally the ultimate cause is found. This takes too much time. It is cheaper to blast your way out!

And now I come to point five, my last theoretical notion. I think that at this point all my positivist operationalist friends will throw up their hands and they will feel that I have sold out to the metaphysicians. I refer to the principle of teleology.

5. Principle of teleology.

I refer you back to my analogy of the log jam. What happened after the jam was blown up? The logs flowed down the stream to the saw-mill. They knew where to go. This is essentially true of subjects who have been subjected to the shock of psychodrama. They are not lost; they know where to go; they know what to do. But the aspect of this that interests me is that the direction of change is always good. They never need guidance. They act better, think better, do better. It is almost as if they had been freed of their chains, and could now do what they had wanted to do for a long time but were unable to do.

It is as though everyone wants to be good, to be healthy, to be normal. Abnormal states are never accepted as normal by those who are afflicted. The idea that the psychotic believes himself normal and all others abnormal is nonsense. Following successful therapy I have invariably seen what can only be regarded as a better, freer, more tolerant, happier, and generally contented state. People see things differently because they are different and, also, they do things differently and they do them better after therapy.

SUMMARY

I don't think I will try to summarize the mass and perhaps the mess of ideas that you have been subjected to. Let me merely emphasize some of the conclusions: therapy must become more economical; rapid, deep, verbal-shock therapy of the group type may be one answer. I believe that psychodrama of the type that I have done may be considered as a possible solution. I believe that the apparent dangers of deep psychodrama are over-stressed and that the therapist capable of producing any change will operate in such a fashion to avoid doing any great harm.

May I finish by indicating that all of my group therapeutic experience has been in prisons and that I do not know whether I am deluded about the whole matter, and if not deluded, I do not know whether similar results can be obtained with other populations. I trust that right or wrong, I may stimulate some others to independent evaluation of some of these ideas.

ADDENDUM

1. A number of questions and comments were raised at the reading of this paper. One question related to my claim that "as far as can be told no very great differences in kind or quality of success has been reported by any school of treatment over any other." For further information on this matter, the reader is referred to the following:

Charen, Sol. Brief methods of psychotherapy—a review. Psychiat. Quart., 1948, 22, 287-301.

Kant, O. Choice of method in psychotherapy. Dis. Nerv. Syst., 194, 5, 324-329.

Katzenelbogen, S. Psychotherapy. Ann. intern. Med., 1944, 21, 412-420.

Knight, Robert P. A critique of the present status of the psychotherapies. Bull. N.Y. acad. Med., 1949, 25, 100-114.

Wilder, J. Facts and figures in psychotherapy, J. Clin. Psychother., 1945, 7, 311-347.

2. A second point that was contested was the statement that "good therapists seem to do more or less the same, no matter what the nature of their theoretic backgrounds." Substantiation of this point is to be found in the following important paper.

Fiedler, Fred E. A comparison of therapeutic relationships in psychoanalytic, non-directive and Adlerian therapy, J. consult. Psychol., 1950, 14, 436-445.

3. The analogy to the importance of speed in surgery was disputed. Of course, not being a surgeon, I should not have accepted one opinion as being accurate. Whether all other factors being constant, surgery should or should not be quick, I do not know. But there can be no question that any therapy that is equally effective as any other method should be preferred if it is more economical.

4. The case of Harold is not presented as a case of "cure." We still do not understand what we mean by this term. Even in the literature of psychoanalysis successful cases are mostly those where the symptoms no longer exist. The important matter in this case is that the symptom was affected spontaneously when no attention was paid to it. From my point of view a "cure" results when the subject goes out of prison and stays out.

27. SUICIDE AS A
PSYCHODRAMATIC ACT

Edgar C. Trautman, M.D.

I am going to describe to you a psychodramatic performance as a form of psychotherapy which is as old as mankind: It is a psychotherapeutic invention of nature itself and it therefore gives natural support to the theory and practice of psychodrama as developed by Dr. Moreno.

What is more of an acting out performance than an act of suicide? What is more dramatic than a suicidal action that is precipitated as a result of an interpersonal conflict or a family argument? And what role playing can be more realistic and more natural than the behavior of husband and wife, or lover and girl friend or mother and daughter, when they fight each other in a heated argument indulging in emotional excitement so completely that even the barrier of the self-preservation instinct goes to pieces?

Not every form of suicide is a dramatic act. The form of suicide I am referring to, is a suicide action committed in an hysterical fit.* This suicidal fit is a performance in which at

Reprinted with the permission of the publishers from *Group Psychotherapy*, Vol. XV, No. 2 (June, 1962), pp. 159-161. Presented at the 21st Annual Meeting of the American Society of Group Psychotherapy and Psychodrama, April 6, 7 and 8, 1962, Hotel Sheraton-Atlantic, New York City.

* See "The Suicidal Fit," Edgar C. Trautman, *Arch. Gener. Psychiatry;* 76-83, July, 1961.

least two actors, a protagonist and an antagonist participate. Both persons, by nature highly emotional and passionate, are very much inclined to uncontrollable and insulting verbal outbursts. The protagonist, long before the critical drama takes place, has been suffering from repressed emotions of distressing nature. In the dramatic act, he reaches an emotional crisis leading to an explosion of such a power that it never could be reproduced on a stage.

In the heating up period of the performance, accumulated resentments of the past, together with insulting remarks during the fight stimulate increasing angry reactions and excitements. When the weaker partner has reached the threshold of tolerance the crisis sets in and the rational self control breaks down. The thinking mind appears paralysed. The patient, for a moment, finds himself out of contact with reality and, like in an orgastic climax, the subsequent actions are carried out automatically and controlled by instinctual forces only.

The patient, like in a panic, would run away from the painful situation to another room, the bedroom or the bathroom where, in a passionate impulse, he grasps a bottle of pills or kitchen chemicals and oblivious of the danger involved, swallows the poison. This acting out often leads to a fatal side effect, which in a scientifically oriented psychotherapy would not be desirable. However, *in the suicidal fit there is no stage director who keeps the acting out within reasonable limits.*

With this act, the drama has reached its climax, and the anticlimax follows immediately. As soon as the pills are down the throat or as soon as the patient has tasted the chemical in his mouth, his excitement has already dissipated, his emotional tension is discharged and his mind is back to reality, and under control again. Now something very interesting happens. The first thing that comes to the patient's mind is the realization of danger, the fear of death. The return of the death fear is almost identical with the return of rationality. It was the temporary loss of the death fear as a part of the eclipse of the mind that made the patient's irrational and suicidal behavior possible. Before the poison takes effect the fear of death dominates the thinking of the patient. Whereas the argument is completely forgotten, the patient now is concerned to find help and protection.

Most of them find help, others die from the effect of the poison. If they survive, can we say that the whole act was a purposeful and staged maneuver to impress or achieve something, as many people believe? The answer is no, because many survive only thanks to the emergency facilities and medical equipment we have ready in the setting of our contemporary civilization. Our civilization, gives us so many tools and means at hand for killing, at the same time is eagerly concerned to rescue us from death, when we are the victims of such inventions. It is the mysterious fear of death that motivates the community to do so much in the interest of suicide preventions.

If a patient dies as a consequence of a suicidal fit, we are confronted with the question, is this a case of intended suicide? Here we have to say: death was not the goal of the patient's action. There was no planning, no preparation for suicide and the thought of death or the struggle with fear of death never entered the mind of the patient. The instinctive urge to escape from an unbearable situation and the discharge of an emotional excitement, that paralyzed the mind, was the real psychodynamics involved. Death is a side effect in such cases. Abreaction is the psycho-biological process of this natural drama. Restoring the emotional equilibrium, essential in rational and balanced behavior, is its goal.

When this emotional balance is restored, a complete change takes place in the patient's attitude and subsequent behavior. The patient now considers his act foolish and regrettable. He is amazed that he could lose his control to such an extent. All patients feel that they were not aware of what they were doing. The patients in the ward of the hospital, are in a surprisingly cheerful mood and they now have a different outlook with regard to the domestic problems that before were the source of the evil. Those who before did not find a way out, now make up their mind to terminate an unhappy situation either by getting a divorce or by giving up the unfaithful boyfriend or by moving out of a broken home and living alone.

The therapeutic effect of the suicidal psychodrama is the balancing of psycho-dynamic forces and the strengthening of the ego and its power to make decisions.

If we compare the psychodrama of suicide with the psychodrama as we apply it in our psychotherapy then we find in principle the same mechanisms at work. A few differences, however, may be pointed out. First in the suicidal fit-drama, we reach complete spontaneity. Second: The role playing does not make use of auxiliary figures. The principles in the setting are the authentic originals. The antagonist and the protagonist, both are partners in the misery of life. They do not play a role. They play themselves. Third: The suicidal fit has a bilateral therapeutic effect. Whereas the suicider is cured by abreaction, the antagonist or, for that matter, the whole family is treated by the shock of being exposed to the fear of death, an experience which is able to break the most stubborn hostility and selfishness that existed before the suicidal act. As a matter of fact, a wave of sympathy and understanding befalls the hearts and minds of those who are involved through guilt feelings. This refers particularly to the culprit who was the participant in the dramatic act itself.

Flowers, candies and other expressions of affection are showered on the survivor who made everybody so happy by not dying. Embraced by her loving husband or shaky boyfriend the heroine sits in her hospital bed, enjoying life like a queen.

A suicide attempt is always a big family affair and a psychodrama with tremendous results.

28. THE JUDGMENT TECHNIQUE IN PSYCHODRAMA

James M. Sacks

Employing specific, structured techniques in psychodrama would seem overly restricting since the director can normally operate better on the basis of general principles, trusting the group process and his own spontaneity to evolve scenes which each individual situation requires. Still, the "behind-the-back,"[1] the "magic shop,[2] the "empty chair"[3] and such bag of technical tricks, if not used in a wooden or mechanical way, are often helpful. They are especially useful with patients who become more inhibited rather than freer when they are required to structure their own scenes. If nothing else, these techniques increase the director's confidence by giving him something to fall back on when his own spontaneity lags. Even psychodrama directors do not have infinite tolerance for ambiguity. With this

Reprinted with the permission of the publisher from *Group Psychotherapy*, Vol. XVIII, Nos. 1-2, (March-June, 1965), pp. 67-72.

1 Introduced by J.L. Moreno as a mirror technique; described by R.J. Corsini, *Group Psychotherapy*, Vol. 6, 1953.

2 See J.L. Moreno, *Psychodrama*, Vol. I, Third Edition, p. X-XI; also Z.T. Moreno, "A Survey of Psychodramatic Techniques," *Group Psychotherapy*, Vol. 12, 1959, p. 13014.

3 Rosemary Lippit. "The Auxiliary Chair," *Group Psychotherapy*, Vol. 11, 1958. J.L. Moreno, *Psychodrama*, Vol. I, First Edition, 1946, p. 3; Third Edition, p. 3.

apology I should like to describe a particular scene which I have found provocative in a large number of groups.

The sense of being judged is often mentioned as an inhibiting feeling even when no actual punishment is expected. For this reason, one of the essential characteristics of nearly all forms of psychotherapy is that they be "non-judgmental." Many patients continue to see themselves in a defendant-judge relationship even when the therapist has been consistently non-evaluative. He remains alert for fantasied signs of acquittal or conviction from the therapist. Rather than rely on the therapist's acceptance alone to overcome the patient's apprehensions, the protagonist in psychodrama is encouraged to explore the judgment situation by role reversal. This can be done by placing him in the role of the judgmental figures in his life or by the use of partially hypothetical situations such as courtroom scenes.[4] The example here is from the powerful symbolism of religion—the tribunal of divine judgment. Most protagonists tend to be diffident at first about role reversal with God and they are therefore permitted to remain nominally in their own role but to act as a sort of advisor to Him in deciding the destiny of the people in his life who make application for entrance to heaven.

The timing of the scene is important since it usually requires considerable warm-up and much knowledge of the protagonist's immediate emotional status. For this reason, it is best used late in the session, often as a climatic scene. Considerable discussion time should be left after such a scene since it frequently mobilizes guilty and depressive emotions which must then be resolved with the help of the group. As will be seen, this scene is especially applicable with protagonists who are suppressing emotion, especially hostility, which the director feels is ready to

[4] Moreno, "Psychodrama and the Psychopathology of Interpersonal Relations," *Sociometry,* Vol. I, 1937, pp. 45-46. "Psychodrama of an Adolescent," *Sociatry,* Vol. II, 1948, p. 7.

be exposed on the psychodrama stage.

The scene may begin as follows: An auxiliary ego is selected to take the role of God. "God" then takes the protagonist to the back of the stage or on to the balcony. He explains to the protagonist that, unfortunately, he has died but that, happily, he has been living in heaven where he will spend eternity. He then explains that the person against whom the latent hostility is directed has just recently died and is now at the door of heaven applying for admission. "God" explains further that he has not yet decided the fate of the applicant but he makes the alternatives clear: heaven, which may be described in terms which the auxiliary feels would be most favorable in the protagonist's values, or hell, which may be described briefly as being filled with the horrors of physical torture, etc. "God" may then ask the protagonist for his advice as to where the applicant should be sent. Even when the protagonist feels conscious hostility to the applicant, he nearly always advises "God" to have the applicant admitted to heaven. Occasionally, the protagonist will hesitate about advising that the applicant should be admitted because he does not want to share his company for eternity. This fear may be explored itself or it may be alleviated simply by telling the protagonist that in the expanse of heaven privacy is available to everyone and that the two of them may live their own versions of paradise without ever seeing each other.

Another auxiliary ego in the form of a soul-hungry Satan waits eagerly on the side of the stage while the auxiliary taking the role of the applicant approaches the bar of justice. "God" now explains that only one impediment stands in the way of allowing the applicant into heaven—he has not repented his sins. He may have stubbornly insisted that he lived a life of perfection or he may have pretended repentance by some insincere confessions but he has shown no evidence of honest acknowledgments of his misdeeds. "God," however, is still willing to be convinced. He agrees to permit the protagonist a given period of time to bring the applicant to repentance and win his admission. The period of time is set at 5 or 10 minutes to give a note of urgency to the protagonist's task but the time limit need not be adhered to if the scene becomes productive. While the protagonist may have been reticent about taking the applicant to task for his faults in a realistic scene, in this situation his guilt feelings become even stronger if he *fails* to confront the applicant effectively with his complaint since he would thus condemn him to damnation.

The protagonist now tries, in one way or another, to convince the applicant that he has been selfish, cruel, neglectful, etc. Whatever he is accused of, the applicant denies and demands proof. He asks when he has ever done such acts and forces the protagonist to leave the level of generality and recount specific instances. The applicant then minimizes and rationalizes these incidents, insisting that they were not really sins at all. The protagonist is thus not only encouraged to recall these significant events but to allow himself to appreciate the full emotional significance of them in his attempts to influence the applicant. If the protagonist wavers in his rhetoric, satan moves closer and pulls on the applicant's arm. The stage which has been in a soft blue light flashes red. From the events which the protagonist uses to confront the applicant, later scenes can be developed.

After the maximum catharsis has been achieved, the applicant breaks down and confesses to the accusations. He may ask for the protagonist's personal forgiveness. Granting this, ususally helps relieve the protagonist of some of the residual guilt which his outburst may have caused. The applicant is always admitted to heaven in the end.

According to the time available, as many of the significant individuals in the protagonist's life as possible apply for admission to heaven. One by one, his parents, his wife, his boss, his children, etc., place themselves under his scrutiny. "God's" final judgment may be delayed until the end and given *en masse.* Just before the judgment, the protagonist may stand above and behind a semi-circle of the people in his life and in a sentence or two summarize to each of them in order how, in his view, they have fallen short. In another variation, despite the seeming illogic of it, just when the protagonist has finished with the last applicant and is fully warmed up to his role of the incisive critic, he is told that he himself has "died again" and is applying for admission under the same conditions. Most protagonists have no difficulty in this separation of the ego and are often able to be quite constructively self-critical.

The subsequent discussion may follow many directions but is usually best heavily weighted with emphatic testimonials from other group members who have had similar emotions. Analytic interpretation by the therapist or by the group members is discouraged until the initial residue of guilt feelings has been dealt with.

The director must make a judgment about the protagonist's readiness to face the material which the technique may expose. The technique is contraindicated when the potential material would be too threatening for the protagonist to integrate. He will either resist totally or will feel increased guilt and anxiety after the session. A second contraindication is the case of individuals with overt paranoid attitudes. Instead of exposing new material, these patients simply use this opportunity to further reinforce their blaming defenses. When the situation inadvertently arises, it can often be turned to advantage by reversing the roles of the protagonist and applicant.

In actual practice, of course, the scene cannot and should not follow this rigid format. One sullen young man, for example, detested his mother so intensely that, when asked where she should be sent, he coldly consigned her to hell. The director then asked him to prove his case to God by extracting a confession from his mother so that he would have a basis for condemning her. The same kind of scene followed, during which the protagonist had an opportunity to examine the nature of his long cherished hostility to his mother. After the cathartic effect of the session, he relented on his decision to damn her and, having worked off his anger verbally for the moment, he lost his sullen look and with a smile decided that he might forgive her as long as he would not have to live with her. Another protagonist insisted that the middle ground of purgatory was the only appropriate place for his sister.

The reaction of religious protagonists to this scene has been interesting. Many of them, especially religious psychotics, who do not easily distinguish reality from the psychodrama fantasy, are deeply offended at the whole idea of such a blasphemous enactment. They may refuse to participate. It rarely helps to interpret this attitude since the religious defense is so strongly rooted in consensual validation. It is best to allow such individuals to remain in the role of observers. Healthier religious people are often excellent protagonists with this technique since the religious content of the scene has deep emotional associations for them. One clergyman learned much about himself from his behavior while indulging himself freely in the ultimate grandiosity of the God-role.

29. LOSS OF IMPULSE CONTROL IN PSYCHODRAMA ON INPATIENT SERVICES

Peter Wolson

Efforts to establish psychodrama on inpatient wards, particularly private ones, often meet with devastating resistance from mental health professionals who view any departure from conventional therapy as potentially dangerous. These practitioners frequently identify the risk of precipitating psychotic decompensations and loss of impulse control as the greatest dangers of psychodrama. They claim that psychodrama, by inducing patients to relive traumatic experiences which they have banished from consciousness for their own self-protection mercilessly breaks down the defenses and leaves the fragile patient flooded and overwhelmed by threatening impulses. This would be regarded as a traumatic experience, rather than a therapeutic one, that is directly in opposition to the conventional approach which makes an explicit effort to protect rather than to break down the defenses of patients by helping them to shore up painful affects by encouraging denial and repression.

Furthermore, traditional practitioners are inclined to view any departure from conventional psychoanalytically-oriented therapy as irresponsible and the innovaters as incompetent heretics, lacking clinical expertise, taking insufficient precautions in their selection procedures, being indifferent to the possible harmful effects of their treatments and letting their patients decompensate without attempting to pick up the pieces. The same criticisms are frequently leveled at other innovative approaches such as Gestalt Therapy, marathon group therapy and sensory-awareness training. Too often these criticisms seem to be based upon a blind adherence to an ideology rather than concrete evidence and actual experience with the treatment approach that is being critisized.

This paper is intended to discuss clinical evidence pertaining to the danger of precipitating mental breakdowns in psychodrama and the management of loss of impulse control in this form of therapy when it is about to, or when it actually occurs.

Fear of inducing psychotic decompensation in fragile patients is perhaps the greatest concern among psychodrama critics. As director, I have never seen a patient decompensate or become psychotic in psychodrama. Moreover, I have observed extremely fragile patients portray "protagonists" with no subsequent exacerbation of their psychopathology. Reports from the attending staff have generally indicated that such patients instead of falling apart have usually become more motivated to confront their problems and socialize with others and that this enhancement of motivation and self-evaluation frequently carries over into individual therapy.

In patient selection for psychodrama, of much greater concern than the diagnosis of "fragility" or "ego-strength" per se is the assessment of ability to attend to and participate meaningfully in psychodrama. Patients excluded from psychodrama on this basis would include those who are so anxious, combative, or out of contact with reality that they cannot participate even as a member of the audience without becoming disruptive. For example, this may pertain to severe chronic schizophrenics who even when heavily tranquilized cannot understand any but the simplest of communications or carry on intelligible conversations, or those who become so overwhelmed in the company of others that they cannot tolerate more than a few minutes of social contact without withdrawing; or severe manic depressive psychotics who in the excited phase of their pathology become narcissistically disruptive and attention getting. One could probably make a long list of so-called "inappropriate" patients since the crucial variable is not so much the specific diagnostic category, although this is partly a factor, as whether the patient can participate as an actor or member of the audience in a beneficial way and without interfering with the procedure.

The most dangerous phenomenon I have observed in psychodrama—which might be superficially construed as an excerbation of psychopathology—is loss of impulse control. In my experience, this has occurred in approximately four out of one hundred and fifty cases which I have treated and in each case the impulse which got out of hand was anger. The uncontrolled expressions of anger were remarkably abrupt, and were managed completely within the psychodrama session. The only psychotic consequence of these episodes was an occasional momentary impairment of reality testing accompanying the discharge of aggression wherein the patient responded as if he were unleashing his hostility against his real-life opponents rather than the auxiliary egos. There was no lingering disruption of reality testing beyond this momentary lapse, nor was there any indication of bizarreness, thought disorder, or psychotic decompensation during or after psychodrama. In fact, such pathognomic transference reactions were apparently managed so as to foster beneficial therapeutic change.

Critics of psychodrama may interpret a momentary loss of reality contact as too much of a danger to risk, but this conclusion would ignore the unusual rarity of this occurrence and the fact that such lapses occur probably with as high if not higher frequency in individual and group thereapy and certainly on inpatient services. Loss of impulse control therefore cannot be uniquely attributed to the effects of psychodrama. Moreover, indicting psychodrama on the basis of risking loss of impulse control completely ignores the therapeutic benefit that frequently takes place when such episodes are handled in the proper way. This point will be illustrated by means of three case studies. The critical issue, however, is whether direct confrontation, and the active inducement of catharsis is theoretically and empirically justifiable in weak patients.

As noted earlier, traditional treatment has emphasized the necessity of conducting supportive psychotherapy with patients possessing fragile ego structures. The traditional approach condemns direct analytic or confrontational therapy as undermining already weakened defenses and inevitibly leading to a worsening of the illness and possibly psychotic decompensation. In recent years these assumptions have been challenged, not only in experimental research, but also in clinical practice. One of the forerunners of this challenge was Dr. John Rosen (1935) who reported remarkable improvement in chronic schizophrenics after exposure to his radical form of uncovering therapy "direct analysis." These same patients had previously been regarded as hopeless for many years. In the following decades, an increasing trend toward direct confrontation has occurred, especially in the newer therapies. Probably the greatest challenge to the traditional model has been Dr. Thomas Stampfl's (1966) "implosive therapy" whose chief purpose is to induce a catharsis, if you will, or as much anxiety as possible and maintain it at its highest level during the course of treatment. Stampfl does this with patients, varying from the most to the lease disturbed as long as anxiety or unrealistic fear is a significant feature of the diagnostic profile.

What makes implosive therapy a significant challenge to the traditional assumptions about supportive therapy is that its aim is to do precisely what the tradational school feared would "blow the patient's mind," that is to have the patient experience imaginally what he would fear the most. When this has occurred, decompensation did not ensue. Stampfl reports instead that his patients generally experienced considerable reduction of anxiety and diminution of their psychological problems. Implosive therapy has allegedly worked well with the most disturbed of patients such as paranoid schizophrenics. Moreover, this approach has been derived from laboratory experimentation with animals and human beings and is based upon learning theory, one of the most empirical and testable of current personality theories.

In contrast, the development of psychodrama was not based upon laboratory experimentation, but upon observations and creative intuition of Dr. J. L. Moreno (1934, 1946) who was partly influenced by classical psychoanalytical theory, which he ultimately rejects. Unlike classical psychoanalysis, psychodrama places a heavy emphasis upon uncovering and confrontation through role playing, in a manner similar to direct analysis and implosive therapy. Both direct analysis and implosive therapy were developed after psychodrama. Since the results of these confrontational uncovering approaches have ostensibly disconfirmed the traditional school's fears about the dangers of extreme directiveness, even in so called "fragile" patients, one must conclude that psychodrama is relatively safe in the hands of a competent practitioner. My experience bears this out in full.

The following three case studies will be used to illustrate this point. My form of psychodrama focuses upon intensive role playing as the primary variable. Such classical Moreno-derived techniques as interpersonal conflicts, scene setting, audience responsivity, spontaneity, doubles and auxiliary egos are employed when deemed necessary or useful following psychodramas. These psychodramas took place in a large community room of a psychiatric training hospital.

Case 1. A 26-year-old white housewife diagnosed as having an acute schizophrenic reaction was in an extremely infantile, regressed state at the time of hospitalization. One of her main problems concerned her inability to control her frustrated dependency strivings and to modulate her subsequent oral rage. The genetic antecedents of this conflict involved her relationship with her mother, a pathologically self-centered woman who provided her with minimal nurturance and angrily demanded the gratification of her own narcissistic appetites. For several weeks the patient was too disturbed to participate meaningfully in psychodrama as a "protagonist," but was able to sit in the audience and comprehend what was happening. As she began to feel stronger and more self-reliant she asked if she could re-enact the conflict she anticipated having with her mother. Lately, she had been preoccupied with the thought of contacting her mother and telling her about her hospitalization, but dreaded the prospect of being rejected. Her scene focused upon a telephone conversation in which she hesitatingly revealed her long-held secret. She imagined that her mother instead of showing appropriate concern about her wellbeing, would angrily accuse her of ruining the family name, of gratifying her own selfish interests by taking a vacation in the hospital and of callously ignoring her mother's needs. The patient attempted to respond by expressing exactly how she felt about being forced into the role of mother's nursemaid and martyring herself to buy her mother's love.

As the scene unfolded, it quickly became apparent that the patient was becoming increasingly angrier. Her tone of voice sounded hostile, her facial expression became threatening and her posture forward and menacing. Suddenly, her anger snowballed and her face reddened. She clenched her fists and couldn't speak. I cut the action, asking how she felt. She was unable to respond verbally, but answered with an expression that conveyed her distress. I told her to do what she thought would help her control her feelings, since she was in the best position at that moment to know what would have that effect. She arose from the chair, her fists still clenched and her arms locked at her sides and walked to a corner of the room fighting down her anger. During this period, the group carried on a highly profitable discussion about how anger affected them, but tactfully left her out. This allowed her the privacy and time to calm down. After a few minutes she regained her composure and returned to the group. She said that she was not aware of how angry she had felt toward her mother and that she thought it was helpful to have let herself get as angry as she did. She realized that she had to come to terms with her hostility before actually speaking to her mother and in the next few weeks worked on this problem in individual therapy.

Although the patient experienced a loss of impulse control, she viewed this as an achievement compared with her many years of emotional suppression. Instead of making her more psychotic, this episode helped her integrate her feelings and thoughts in a way that increased her motivation to work on her problems. Subsequently she was able to call her mother without experiencing the loss of control and impending failure that she feared.

This psychodrama poses the technical problem of how to transform potential loss of impulse control into therapeutic gains. The initial step was to assess which direction the patient could most beneficially proceed. She was obviously terrified of losing further control and it seemed in light of her regressed infantile condition that she could not benefit by additional role-playing, even with strong external guidance from the director. By helping her acquire impulse control immediately through time-out from a threatening situation, she was prevented from coming to associate the experience of anger with overwhelming fear and thereby possibly exacerbating her pathological suppression of affect. This shows the necessity of judging how far each patient can go in psychodrama in helping them to achieve their optimal level of expression. Any less is to fall short of using psychodrama to its full potential, and any more is to risk the possibility of adverse consequences.

Case 2. This example differs from the first in two essential respects. The patient was not as severely disturbed, and the loss of impulse control was more extreme. In this psychodrama, a small, wiry 20-year-old male inpatient asked me to portray his rejecting father. In the conflict situation he was to approach me in my study with a drawing he had made for the purpose of getting my attention and approval. I was to be absorbed in my accounts, too busy to pay attention to him, and to dismiss him with a curt, "Don't bother me!" He was then to leave the room hurt and angry, but saying nothing.

After we enacted this much of the conflict, I instructed him to continue the action as if he had not left the room, and tell me what he would have liked to tell his father. In the replay, he had great difficulty initiating a response, but with prompting from the audience, and help from a patient "double," he said that he wanted some of my time. As the father, I told him that he didn't deserve my time and that any drawing of his was not worth my attention. He had no comeback. Instead, he wrung his hands, breathed deeply and seemed on the verge of hyperventilation. The audience and "double" encouraged him to be more aggressive but he remained immobilized. Half an hour went by with no progress.

In a final effort I decided to provoke him intensely. I felt that he possessed enough ego-strength to risk loss of impulse control, and that without expressing his anger he would leave the psychodrama feeling more worthless than before. To do this I told him exactly what I guessed he would not like his father to say, but what he usually gleaned behind most of his father's messages. "You're a worthless punk," I said, "and nothing you could ever do would please me. You'll never be as industrious and as competent as I am, so bug off." I continued in this way but he remained immobilized. His breathing began to become heavier. I was beginning to think that the psychodrama had failed when suddenly I saw a blur before me and the next moment was shocked to find the patient angrily bowling me out of my chair and swinging away. I wrestled him to the floor and encouraged him to tell me what he was feeling in words, but to no avail. After a few minutes, he calmed down enough for me to escort him out of the room while another staff member conducted what was later described as an extremely valuable - discussion of the group's reaction to this incident and their fears of losing control.

In another part of the ward, the patient flung himself on his bed, sobbing. I told him he did a terrific job in releasing his anger, but that it would be more effective if he would express himself verbally. He perked up quickly and said that he had never been that aggressive before. He really enjoyed it and wanted to do it again. I firmly pointed out that such assaultive aggression would usually get him into trouble, cause him to lose friends and would probably ruin his chances of ever reconciling with his father. He reluctantly agreed. I again urged him to return to psychodrama and express his feelings verbally but he was afraid that he might lose control again. I reassured him that I was prepared for him this time and that he would be flanked by two attendants who would help him control himself. He returned to the meeting room and re-enacted the psychodrama. Although he was again immobilized initially and then almost lost control twice, he restrained himself and was able to release a couple of low-voiced "you son of a bitch," for which he was resoundedly applauded by the audience.

This psychodrama left him feeling a tremendous sense of achievement and made him poignantly aware of his difficulty in expressing anger and his lack of control when he did. It also helped other patients to objectively examine their problems with impulse control.

A couple of problems in this psychodrama warrant re-examination. The first is whether it was necessary to provoke him to the extent that I did, precipitating his loss of impulse control. I made the judgment to do so based upon my impression that if he did not express the anger he was suppressing, he would have felt terrible afterwards having placed his self-esteem and masculine integrity on the chopping block. In contrast to the first case my diagnostic impression led me to believe that loss of impulse control in this patient did not threaten the possibility of overwhelming anxiety or personality disorganization, but had the strong possibility of overcoming tremendous fear of discharging aggression and of subsequent retaliation, a fear which immobilized him in his relationship with his father and others.

A crucial issue was how readily the consequences of the patient's aggression could be dealt with. To answer this question two factors had to be considered: 1) the patient's degree of ego-strength and responsiveness to external feedback when affectually overwhelmed, and 2) the ability of the director, staff and patients to manage his loss of impulse control if it occurred. In my estimation he was strong enough to benefit from correction, particularly if it were forceful enough, and I also felt that loss of impulse control could be effectively managed by the psychodrama group if I provided the proper direction.

Let us return for a moment to the point in the psychodrama when he attacked me. The first task was to stop his aggression and help him gain control. Although wiry he was small enough for me to stop alone. If he had given me too much trouble I would have called for assistance from the attendants or other patients who felt capable of helping. I would have wanted to involve as much of the group as possible to encourage their sense of responsibility for one another. If the patient had been too large to manage constructively, I would have had him punch a pillow or observe his conflict "mirrored" by other members of the group. Once his attack was stopped, it was important to get him to express his anger verbally but this didn't work because he was too emotionally flooded. It was therefore necessary to calm him down sufficiently to benefit from external guidance. It was especially important to tell him that he had not committed a cardinal sin, but had done well in view of his great difficulty in releasing anger, that his combative method of release was unfortunately a maladaptive one and that he must try to express his anger verbally. Getting him to return to the "scene of the crime" and helping him to alter his mode of expression with the aid of two attendants demonstrated to him and the rest of the patients that anger could be controlled and discharged adaptively.

Case 3. Two patients had become engaged in a fist fight a few hours before the psychodrama was to take place. Both men had prominent homosexual tendencies. One was a strong, weatherbeaten, 45-year-old paranoid schizophrenic who would have denied his homosexual inclinations at all costs. He had for some years been helping his mother, a domineering woman, maintain a secluded ranch until he became increasingly troubled by murderous thoughts toward some old neighbors whom he believed were taking advantage of him. The other man was a thin, sinewy picture-framer who had an extensive history of rebelliousness against a commanding, authoritative father. His rebellion took the form of pursuing art and other "unmanly activities" in opposition to his father's supermasculine attitudes. The first fight occurred when the picture-framer, who up until this point had appeared to be cultivating the rancher's friendship, insulted him by characterizing his life as "manure-sweeping." The rancher angrily called the picture framer a "sissy," and the fight was on.

Although the exchange of blows was brief and the injuries minor, the anger between the two continued into the psychodrama session unabated. The rancher was threatening to "kill that sissy", and the picture-framer was dangerously boiling with range. Their anger was too volatile to have them face one another in open confrontation, so I decided to play one of the roles. I chose the rancher to be the protagonist since he seemed more willing to discuss his problems openly in contrast to the picture-framer who held his anger inside brooding around the ward. Another reason was that the rancher's impulse-control seemed more precarious than the picture-framer's, and he may have had greater difficulty assuming a passive role sitting in the audience without becoming combative if the picture-framer as the protagonist had insulted him again. I chose to play the role of the picture-framer in case the situation got out of hand.

In the psychodrama, the rancher explained his side of the conflict—how the picture-framer had demeaned him and how he felt the picture-framer was a "chicken" because he did not assert himself more in group therapy. I tried to explain the picture-framer's side periodically turning to him in the audience and asking for corrections. It soon became evident that a misunderstanding had taken place and that the picture-framer had not consciously intended to insult the rancher, but the picture-framer did not apologize and the rancher was too angry to accept this explanation. As the action continued the rancher's talk became progressively more menacing until he overtly threatened to kill me. His reality-testing had dangerously slipped. I stopped the action and asked if he meant what he said. He ominously added, "You can think of it as you like." I then asked the audience what their reaction was and most of those who spoke mentioned how scared they felt and thought he was being unrealistic. I pointed out that his anger seemed to be getting out of control and he countered with "Well isn't it better to get it off your chest than to hold it back like most of you do in this room? You're all chickens, I'd rather blow it off and make myself feel good than let it tear me to pieces."

"You have a point," I said, "But expressing anger must be within realistic limits. If you go around threatening to kill people or actually killing them you may feel better momentarily but then you'll be punished and hurt in the end. There are ways of expressing anger that don't have to involve killing or beating up people even though that may seem to be the most reasonable way to you now." I then noted how the patient had irrationally transformed the role-playing situation into the real-life situation and how easily his anger reached murderous proportions. The group confronted him with his frightening aggressiveness and he toned down to a manageable level. By the end of psychodrama the picture-framer had apologized and even defended the rancher, saying that he, the picture-framer, was also partly to blame. Although this psychodrama was not conducive to a discussion of the underlying dynamics of the pathological interaction, namely, the homosexual attractions and fears, the picture-framer setting up the rancher as a domineering father-figure and trying to castrate him, the rancher's fluid displacement of aggression and paranoid sensitivity to abuse it, it succeeded in settling a "hot" problem on the ward which may have led to further fighting if it had not been nipped in the bud. The rancher's lapse in reality-testing was handled by firmly confronting him and helping him to reality-test better and his highly upsetting "threat to kill" was managed through audience discussion.

These cases show that potential and actual loss of impulse-control in fragile patients precipitated by intensive confrontation and uncovering can not only occur without harmful effects, but may also provide a ripe opportunity for incisive therapeutic intervention in psychodrama. To maximize the probability of therapeutic results, the director should be acutely attuned to the patient's 1) capacity to tolerate stress and regression; 2) capacity to observe himself with some objectivity when emotionally upset, and 3) capacity to be responsive to external controls and limit-setting techniques. A fourth criterion involves the staff's ability to control the patient against his will.

All of these criteria emphasize ability to regain control of the situation once it has been lost. The first and second criteria mainly imply an assessment of ego-strength that would illuminate whether the patient can regress without becoming so confused as to be incapable of reorganizing and integrating his personality functioning in such a way as to be receptive to therapeutic interventions by the director and the audience. In the case studies these points applied most meaningfully to Cases 1 and 2. In Case 1 the patient was judged to be incapable of tolerating more stress or regression without becoming affectually overwhelmed to a point where she could not reflect objectively upon her experience. She was consequently not confronted further. In Case 2, the patient was thought to be capable of tolerating regression and recovering adaptively, and so he was confronted until he lost control. The third and fourth criteria concerning responsiveness to external controls applied to all the cases, but primarily to Cases 2 and 3. In Case 2, while the patient was not responsive to direction once he lost control, his small stature made him relatively easy to restrain. In Case 3, however, the rancher was too large to restrain physically and his reality contact too poor to risk the ventilation of his murderous impulses onto a pillow without the possibility of dangerous generalization to the auxiliary-ego or his antagonist in the audience. Therefore the action was terminated and a group discussion initiated to help him test reality better.

In order to make such critical judgements the director must employ his diagnostic and therapeutic skills to the fullest. Therefore, the clinical competence of the director is of primary importance in managing loss of impulse control effectively. Moreover, if the patients, nursing staff and doctors are to view psychodrama as a safe procedure, the director must communicate what has transpired in psychodrama to the ward as a whole. I have found it necessary when loss of impulse-control or self-destructive tendencies have been revealed to alert the therapist and attending staff immediately. Without keeping the staff abreast of what has happened, psychodrama can become an isolated, unintegrated aspect of the hospital experience, and the patient may be left with the enormous burden of applying what he has learned to his life affairs without any meaningful carry-over into his individual therapy and other ward activities.

It is like inspiring an illiterate with a desire to read and then providing him with no teachers or other means of fulfilling his ambiton.

Emphasizing precautions, safeguards and effective collaboration with ward personnel is a good way to introduce inpatient psychodrama to therapists who resist the establishment of psychodrama on the basis of their fears of psychotic decompensation and loss of impulse control. It is often valuable to hold a forum among the attending staff where one can openly discuss the type of psychodrama one conducts and the way one treats the loss of impulse control. Exposing one's approach to objective scrutiny and being able to clarify unrealistic beliefs is an excellent way to diminish unwarranted anxiety and apprehension in intelligent therapists. This approach has worked exceedingly well for me in developing successful psychodrama programs on three psychiatric wards in the past two years. One ward was in a private hospital and the other two were in a university training hospital.

REFERENCES

1. Rosen, J. *Direct Analysis*, Grune, New York, 1953.

2. Moreno, J.L. *Who Shall Survive?* Washington, D.C.: Nervous and Mental Health Publishing Co., 1934.

3. Moreno, J.L. *Psychodrama*, Vo. 1, Beacon House, New

4. Stampfl, T.G. Possible use of conditioning therapy with chronic schizophrenia, *V.A. Publication*, Battle Creek, Michigan, 1966.

30. FUTURE-PROJECTION TECHNIQUE

Lewis Yablonsky

This method involves having the subject act out, with the support of auxiliary egos and a group, a meaningful situation in which the subject expects to act in the future. The effectiveness of this procedure depends on the significance and importance of the situation for the subject and the extent to which the auxiliary egos are able to project him into the future. It is also important that the subject *really* is going to participate in the situation in the future at a given time. An intense, effective warm-up is the essence in the application of this method. As many particulars and specifics of the situation as possible should be emphasized in the warm-up.

This method, like other effective psychodramatic approaches, rests on the solid foundation that an individual's thought level can be acted out with the help of a group. The "future" is often most detailed on the thought level. For example, the writer recalls a session using this technique where the subject exclaimed "he didn't say that" about a situation which he had never lived out. This indicated that he was psychodramatically presenting a situation that was not new to him. It had been "acted out" many times on the thought level. However, psychodramatically the action with its many added dimensions

Reprinted with the permission of the publishers from *Group Psychotherapy*, Vol. VII, Nos. 3 and 4 (1954), pp. 303-305.

was more vivid and productive for the subject through the aid of
the method and the group.

EXAMPLE OF APPLICATION OF FUTURE
PROJECTION TECHNIQUE

In the process of a psychodramatic session it was found that
the subject, a young married man, was separated from his wife
after a violent argument which had occurred three months in the
past. The young man was quite anxious about meeting his wife.
As he put it: "7:05 Wednesday, November first she is returning
by plane with my son."

He was warmed up to the situation by first describing the
plane as it came in from where he stood at the airport. He then
soliloquized what he was thinking while waiting with the help of
the "double-technique." It was determined through the
soliloquy that he had not decided whether to act "nice" or
"nasty" toward her and that he was unsure about continuing
the marriage. He also felt that "she has probably poisoned my
son's mind against me" and did not know how the boy would
act toward him.

He then psychodramatically met his wife and child portrayed
by auxiliary egos. The egos fulfilled his precise conception of
how they would act. This was accomplished through having the
subject reverse roles with his "son" and "wife" and act out his
view of what they would do. It was a very smooth production as
the subject had lived through this situation many times on the
"thought level."

With the help of the group and the auxiliaries the subject
then explored many other possibilities, e.g., his wife wanted a
divorce, she was glad to see him and sorry she had left, she was
indifferent, his son ignored him, his son was glad to see him, his
son was full of misconceptions about him, etc.

The subject felt much less tense after the session. As he
expressed it: "I now have a much clearer picture of what I can

expect and I don't feel as worried as I was." He also felt that he had learned a great deal more about how he "really" felt about his wife. After the session he felt that he really loved her and wanted to try to "start all over again," whereas before the session he was unsure on this point.

On talking with the subject after the "real" meeting he remarked that he felt much more sure of himself and was able to communicate this to his wife who was quite tense. He felt that his clarification of the situation produced by the future-projection-technique helped him and his wife get through a most difficult period in their relationship.

SUMMARY AND CONCLUSIONS

1. The future-projection-technique helps the subject to articulate for himself his objectives in the situation. In the same vein it helps him to clarify his role within the situation in relation to others. He may discover that he is anxious about the forthcoming situation because he really loves (or hates) the other, a feeling he had not considered.

2. Many dimensions of the situation will emerge in the psychodrama which the subject never considered on the thought level and might not even emerge when he acts out the situation in life. This helps him to better understand his motivations.

3. The future-projection-technique is a *preparation* for an important life situation which will aid the subject in presenting himself most effectively and honestly while at the same time enabling him to be helpful to the other individual(s) involved. He will know the life situation better as he has "been there" before psychodramatically.

4. A skilled director with the help of auxiliary egos can produce many different angles to a situation which might never come up in the real one but would be useful for the subject to explore. This prepares the subject for many different possible responses.

5. The "group" is invaluable in the future-projection-techniques and can, if properly warmed up, share with the subject similar experiences which they had encountered as an aid to the subject's preparation.

If properly administered the technique can be most useful in a wide range of possible future situations. From one loaded with emotional intensity and anxiety, e.g., a man who has a meeting scheduled with his former wife, to a simpler situation involving a conference with a potential employer. The situation may be within a complex of other related ones, e.g., part of an engaged couple's relationship or a somewhat isolated situation involving meeting a "blind date."

It is important to bear in mind when applying the future-projection-technique, (1) the necessity of producing an intense warm-up and (2) that the psychodramatic action will influence the subject's behavior in the "real-life" situation.[1]

---

[1] For the definition of the future projection technique, see J.L. Moreno, "A Case of Paranoia Treated Through Psychodrama," *Sociometry*, Vol. VII, No. 3, 1944, p. 325.

31. PREPARING PAROLEES FOR ESSENTIAL SOCIAL ROLES

Lewis Yablonsky

Psychodrama can be useful as a method of training for life roles which are *necessary* for an individual as requisites for his participation in community life. One particular area, where it has been found useful, is in preparing parolees and recently released mental patients to participate in necessary roles and life situations. The parolee from a correctional institution must find and maintain a job as a necessary condition of his release, whether he finds it unpleasant or not. The mental patient on release if he is to function must be equipped in some minimal way to operate in everyday situations.

Although their fear and anxiety may be rooted in more complex psychological dynamics, it is still absolutely necessary that these people be prepared to act effectively in key areas of social life. Psychodrama and role playing can often cut through the complexity of the personality problem and help prepare individuals for these situations. Although it is recognized that the subject requires further therapeutic attention, "getting by" vital situations is an important wedge to keep him interacting on the "normal" social scene, where a favorable sociometric position may produce therapeutic results.

† Reprinted with the permission of the publishers from *Group Psychotherapy*, Vol. VIII, No. 1 (April 1955), pp. 38-40.

SUMMARY OF PROCEDURE

1. With the cooperation of the subject select key situations and roles.

2. Project subject into the situations with the aid of auxiliary egos, role reversal, double and other psychodramatic techniques which seem indicated.

3. Follow up with subject on his performance in actual situations.

4. Use psychodramatic procedures to have the subject further explore situations and reinforce his positive actions.

CASE SUMMARIZED

The subject is a 50-year-old parolee recently released from a state prison whom we will call Bill. He has spent more time in correctional institutions than in the open community. His offenses include narcotics addiction, assault and robbery. He came to my attention as a member of a group with whom I was meeting weekly in an effort to help them become better integrated into their jobs and the community. With Bill and the group it was determined that two basic key roles and situations necessary for Bill to maintain were his job and reporting to his parole officer.

Bill role-played a number of situations on his job with members of the group playing auxiliary roles. The major problem in this area for Bill was the big gap between his conception of what was adequate performance on the job and that of his employer. Slowly, Bill began to accept the fact that perhaps many of the gripes he had were not valid. Although he still felt he was right, he agreed that he would have to accept his employer's view of his performance, as the job was a necessary condition for his remaining in the community.

His second major role, that of reporting to his parole officer, was also acted out. After a number of sessions Bill accepted more fully the fact that he had to report or he would be returned to prison.

Role reversal was most effective in this situation. Bill, while playing the role of his parole officer, soliloquized, "This guy needs to report somewhere at least once a week so that he can be reminded that he is on parole and that if he fouls up one more time we're going to lock him up and throw away the key. Maybe I don't really do him any good with his problems, mainly because I'm so busy with other guys, but he has to come in regularly or else." The group at first sided with Bill and his attitude of "why report, it doesn't do me any good"; however, after considerable psychodramatic exploration they reinforced Bill's conclusion that it was essential for him to report to his parole officer.

Although the sessions didn't greatly reorganize Bill's basic personality structure they did help him to accept two essential conditions necessary for his remaining on the job. This enabled him to remain in relationship with a group whose understanding of him and his problems put them in a position to be therapeutic agents. The sessions were instrumental in placing Bill in a favorable sociometric position where it would be possible for day to day *in situ* interaction to produce successful therapeutic results.*

SUMMARY AND CONCLUSIONS

1. There are certain cultural key roles and situations which are difficult. This is especially true of individuals who have been institutionalized.

2. Although it is recognized that preparation for these roles through psychodrama may not significantly shift personality

* J.L. Moreno: *Group Method and Group Psychotherapy* 1931. A report prepared for the *National Committee on Prisons and Prison Labor* as a result of a conference held under the auspices of the American Psychiatric Association Annual Convention, Toronto, 1931.

structure and dynamics, its application can enable the individual to remain in the open community.

3. Functioning in these roles gives the subject an opportunity to receive therapeutic benefits from "normal" interaction conditions.

4. This type of role training has usefulness not only with people who have been institutionalized. It offers a possibility for "cutting through" into new spheres of social relations which had been closed to the individual because of his inability to function adequately in the "key" roles and situations.

32. PSYCHODRAMA IN LAW ENFORCEMENT AND COMMUNITY RELATIONS

Hannah B. Weiner

When one of my students, Rocko Laury, and his best friend, Gregory Foster, were killed by bullets from a speeding car in lower Manhattan while walking their beat, I was overwhelmed with a sense of man's inhumanity to man. Both men had returned from Vietnam safely. Both were men of deep integrity who had become policemen to help other people—while studying for other roles when they retired. Gregory Foster was a student at John Jay College of Criminal Justice. He was black, he was going to be a professional policeman and he was in the B.A. program. Rocko Laury was in the Prelict Program which encouraged police officers to upgrade their educational and sociological skills.

Gregory Foster used to sit in on our classes. Both men were of the New Centurion mold: they believed in the professionalism of police and were eager to discover how to reach the community they were to serve. When they died, the community was shocked, the precinct felt deep remorse, the children lost a friend in the neighborhood and I became determined to work in police training.

When I went to Rocko Laury's funeral, I became fascinated with the display of "role playing" that the police were already involved with, because there were many hippies, cripples, derelicts and peddlers—all distinguishable only by the badges they were wearing taken from their uniforms. I became involved with the community and their quest for justice and protection as I stood in line and heard people discussing the role of "cop"—of policemen . . . such as the patrolman, the enacter of justice, the counselor, the consultant, the implementer, the information giver, the problem solver, the clarifier.

I began to look at society as a radical theater with ill-defined boundaries that extend far—the scenes include demonstrations, murders, riots, religious holidays, political rallies, political conventions, day-to-day living, violence, muggings and hostile confrontations. Some strategies include police and citizens taking both law and justice into their own hands—each with political and private battles. Other strategies see the policeman breathing life into an infant whose mother is screaming "she is dead, she is dead!"; a policeman sitting in his car and being struck by a civilian vehicle driven by a woman screaming "stop him, he raped me," as a man escapes from her car. Another shows a policeman holding his gun at a crowd that is trying to stop him from interrupting a robbery because they feel the man being robbed owed the robber money from a poker game—the policeman doesn't want to shoot, and then he sees a car coming toward him and thinks: "Damn, I'm in trouble."

Another scene is a civilian being knifed and stomped, even though he has turned over his wallet to his attackers; another a lost child in a hostile environment. The policeman is expected to meet all situations in the community spontaneously. The community needs his protection and assistance, but wants to be understood.

Psychodrama as a training model for police and community relations is inclusive and positive. The philosophy of psychodrama considers man dynamically in a process of personal growth in a cosmic universe; through action techniques it increases the development of emerging qualities within the human being that are present all along, but dormant when he plays only one role from his repertoire. The method develops inner and outer resources in a practical framework. Integration and synthesis of strategies develop in existential situations.

Throughout the United States, but particularly in Connecticut and New York, there are sociodramas run with the police and welfare mothers, with people on welfare, with one-room occupancy people, with black/white relations, and with the gilded ghetto. These sessions have developed out of a will to survive and the form comes from the needs and traditions of the community involved and the environment. Enrique Vargas and his Gut Theater and Hazel Bryant and her Afro-American Theater are examples of conserved sociodramas where problems of racism, drug addiction, politics and survival were explored in action, responded to and shared. They involved methods of approaches to reality with the impetus to help individuals know who they are, what their best tools for communicating are, and how they can survive in the community. Weiner, in working with Vargas, conducted follow-up sociodramas in the open community dealing with events and emotions evolving from the theatrical productions.

Role playing has been used on a supervisory level with police recruits, preparing them for the future; with campus police; security, state and local police; with police on the precinct level and with civilian and community relations. The sessions have included theater games, rap sessions, Ariba techniques, systematic de-sensitization, relaxation, primal screaming, non-verbal techniques, spontaneous experiences, structural relations, fantasy play and problem solving, improvizations, case histories and reading. The role playing has ranged from skit completion to role reversal, to an extreme where police wear wigs with longer hair to achieve the effect of being hippies, or have manure and stones thrown at them as might be done in the community. Since both structured roleplaying and spontaneous roleplaying are used in police and community training programs, a presentation of the two techniques follows:

TABLE 1

	STRUCTURED ROLE PLAYING	SPONTANEOUS ROLE PLAYING
Purpose	Teach a skill or some systematic approach in dealing with a particular problem.	Develop a better understanding of the dynamics of interpersonal relations. Develop insight.
Orientation	Skill-centered.	Feeling-centered.
Method	• written skits or cases • fewer trainer interventions • little, if any, role reversal • feedback focuses on skills & techniques.	• cases developed spontaneously with group • frequent trainer interventions • frequent use of role reversal • feedback focuses on human feelings, needs and identifications
Content	Scenes structured and predetermined in content of problem areas to be covered.	Scenes unstructured and spontaneous, not predetermined by trainer but established by group to focus on current needs.

Marlon Brando talks of the role within the role that goes on and on and says everybody acts all the time, thus: "You can't *live* and not act. If you expressed everything you thought, nobody could live with you."* In my mind he talks about the structured role playing we often do. And it is this kind of role playing that permits the policeman to select one role at a time to problem solve. The spontaneous role playing develops an awareness and an intuitive reaction to the situation, which may or may not include acting, but does include correct performance.

In working with police we are working with the total citizen— the pivotal politician, the healer, the social worker, the arrester, and the victim. We are really testing ourselves as social scientists because we are training people to work in the environment of the past, present and future, all at the same time. We are involved in confronting one image against another. In terms of a survival strategy, the policeman must communicate a sense of support and point out to many groups of people, as well as to individuals, that they are not really helpless in a hostile environment. Maybe we have to point that out to policemen also, that they have unique resources and strengths to call upon and that they must be positive forces in the group. In working with community and police, the community develops a common base of experience which is often helpful in getting at feelings quickly and promoting interaction. Social action is a powerful antidote to individual isolation and hopelessness. The policeman and the community must not feel alienated from each other.

At a typical joint meeting called to further mutual understanding between police and community, the police members of the group began by responding to citizen complaints of neglect and disrespect by trying to discredit the complainers, with placating or defensive smiles, or with silence. The Director finally expressed frustration with the frozen situation and the

Life Magazine, March 10, 1972, p. 42.

non-cooperation and lack of social courage of the police. Using the techniques of mirroring and doubling, the group explored possible power and defense motivation and both police and citizens began to relate on a more authentic and equal feeling basis. The appropriateness of various police role styles and self-perceptions as they might contribute to the resultant attitudes in the community was discussed. By lowering anxiety and frustration the situation became more realistic and the police officer's role as a person called upon to handle social and emotional crises became a principal focus of the discussion.

In training the police and/or community, both structured and spontaneous role playing methods were used. Some of the structured role playing involved situation tests, spontaneity tests, the frustration test, skits, theatrical performances (actors from Plays for Living and actors in general), and included the police and training staffs and in some instances citizens.

The spontaneous role playing ranged from dealing with here-and-now situations that were real and symbolized the civilized world, to "way out" experiences—doing publicly that which is considered impossible, so as to get beyond the limitations of the finite society, its ethos and values—to confronting dignity, integrity, crime, and inaction—with imaginative reality. These spontaneous role plays were important in the effort to produce change in the attitudes of the police and the community and to indicate the need for spontaneity and creativity.

Police departments throughout the United States which are using role playing usually have situations revolving around family disputes, procedures including serving sumonses, how to behave in handling prisoners, walking down the street, how human relations are woven into police duty, controlling traffic, aiding the injured, protection on the scene itself, homicide, accident cases, argumentative neighborhoods, molesting a female, fights and riots, shooting situations, departmental procedure application at the site, death notification, gang relations, handling the mentally disturbed, legal obligations, gaining citizen consent, tolerating behavior, "saving face," presentation of self, and handling hostility.

As an example, in one role playing test exercise dealing with language communication, two patrolmen played the roles of (1) an alleged thief who spoke only Spanish and (2) his friend who spoke Spanish and English but would not volunteer that information unless directly asked by the patrolman. Various police officers, playing their own roles, were introduced separately into the scene. Almost all of them failed to ask the friend if he spoke English and instead began raising their voices steadily to repeatedly ask in English questions of the suspect who only spoke Spanish.

Role playing sessions have certain advantages over field training. Mistakes that are made are not irreversible as they might be in the field, and role playing exercises can be much more closely supervised than a field learning experience. The learning content can be more closely determined through careful direction of sessions and selection of topics to be considered.

The methods and techniques of psychodrama and role playing seem to offer the best means available for the development of role taking skills. Role reversal seems particularly suitable in this respect. For example, in one session recruits were instructed to act out a situation in which a patrolman was required to have a group of juveniles move away from a street corner. Recruits played the part of the juveniles and communicated to the class how they were likely to be feeling and how they would respond to different approaches by other officers. When the roles were reversed, it was apparent that the recruits who had played the juvenile roles were much more aware of the other's point of view and could handle the situation more effectively and spontaneously. Some of the other more effective role playing techniques in police training are self-presentation, mirroring, the empty chair, the Magic Shop and the behind-the-back technique.

Overall the response of current police training has been to

foster the growth of a "professional attitude" in police training. By this is meant that a police officer is encouraged to have a better understanding of his own feelings in order to heighten his awareness of the feelings of the public. This outlook contends that an officer who offers respect will acquire respect. The techniques and applications described have been widely and effectively used over a long period of time in individual and group training to help individuals solve day-to-day problems and increase their spontaneity and productivity in recognizing and handling difficult situations. They make possible the re-creation of on-the-job situations which will undoubtedly confront the officer, and enable him to gain skill in handling these situations within the requirements of a democratic society. They facilitate his process of active, involved thinking and his ability to make creative decisions in the domain of social relations. They uncover the horizon of the officer's feelings and concerns and teach him how to accept these and still render a service to the public.

Spontaneous role playing between members of the community and the police does more than establish an empathetic relationship. Through role playing it becomes possible to detach oneself from the realities of the situation on a personal level and to function on a professional level with the correct amount of distance. It is a necessary and important instrument in developing police-community relations and in building healthy police bonds, and a positive vehicle in establishing good relations with the community and within the community.

REFERENCES

1. Bahn, Charles. "Value of the Action Lab in Police Training." *Group Psychotherapy & Psychodrama*, 1972, 25(1 & 2).

2. Bard, M. "Family Disturbance as a Police Function." In S. I. Cohn (Ed.), *Law Enforcement: Science & Technology, Vol II*. Chicago: ITT Research Institute, 1968.

3. Barocas, H. "Psychodrama Techniques in Training Police in Family Crisis Intervention." *Group Psychotherapy & Psychodrama,* 1972, 25.

4. Corsini, Raymond J. "The Method of Psychodrama in Prison." *Group Psychotherapy,* 1951, 3.

5. Deeths, Adele. "Psychodrama Crisis Intervention with Delinquent Male Drug Users." *Group Psychotherapy,* 1970, 23.

6. Enneis, James M. "Establishing a Psychodrama Program." *Group Psychotherapy,* 1952, 5.

7. ————————. "Psychodrama in Police Training at a 12-Year High." *Trends in Training,* 1952, 1 (spring).

8. Greenbaum, C. W. & Zemoch, M. "Role Playing and Change of Attitude Toward the Police After a Campus Riot: Effects of Situational Demand and Justification." *Human Relations,* 1972, 25 (Feb.).

9. Haas, Robert B. Action Counseling and Process Analysis. *Psychodrama Monograph No. 25,* Beacon, N.Y.: Beacon House, Inc., 1948.

10. Haskell, Martin R. "Role Training and Job Placement of Adolescent Delinquents: The Berkshire Farm After-Care Program." *Group Psychotherapy,* 1960, 12.

11. ————————. "Psychodramatic Role Training in Preparation for Release on Parole." *Group Psychotherapy,* 1957, 10.

12. ————————. "Group Psychotherapy and Psychodrama in Prison." *Group Psychotherapy,* 1960, 8.

13. ———————— & Weeks, H. Ashley. "Role Training as Preparation for Release from a Correctional Institution." *Journal of Criminal Law, Criminology & Police Science,* 1960, 5 (Jan.-Feb.).

14. ————————. "An Alternative to More and Larger Prisons: A Role Training Program for Socio Reconnection." *Group Psychotherapy,* 1961, 14.

15. Lassner, R. "Psychodrama in Prison." *Group Psychotherapy,* 1950, 3.

16. McNamara, John H. "Uncertainties in Police Work: The Relevance of Police Recruits, Background and Training." In D. J. Bordua (Ed.), *The Police.* New York: Wiley, 1967.

17. Miller, M.M. "Psychodrama in the Treatment Program of a Juvenile Court." *Journal of Criminal Law & Criminology*, 1960, 50.

18. Moreno, J. L. *Psychodrama, Vol. I.* Beacon, N.Y.: Beacon House, Inc., 1946. Revised 1964.

19. ————. "Psychodrama." Chapter 68 in *American Handbook of Psychiatry, Vol. 2.* New York: Basic Books, 1959.

20. ———— & Whitin, E. S. "Plan and Technique of Developing a Prison into a Socialized Community." New York: National Committee on Prison and Prison Labor, 1932.

21. O'Connell, Walter & Hanson, Philip. "Anxieties of Group Leaders in Police-Community Confrontations." Paper read at the 76th Annual Convention of the American Psychological Association, San Francisco, 1968.

22. Shaw, Malcolm E., Wohlking, Wallace & Weiner, Hannah B. "Increasing Training Effectiveness in Achieving Educational Goals and Targets with Special Reference to the Use of Role Playing." Cornell University, 1967.

23. Solby, B. "Note on Psychodrama in a Reformatory." *Sociometry*, 1939, 2.

24. Weiner, Hannah B. "The Use of Psychodrama in Vocational Counseling." Civic Center Clinic, 1965.

25. ————. "Treating the Alcoholic with Psychodrama." *Group Psychotherapy*, 1968, 18.

26. ————. "A Report on the Use of Psychodrama on a Television Show: 'Alcoholism, Our Great Failure'." *International Journal of Sociometry & Sociatry*, 1966, 5.

27. ————. "Psychodramatic Treatment of the Alcoholic. In Ruth Fox (Ed.), *Alcoholism.* New York: Springer Publishing Co., 1967.

28. ———— & McNamara, John H. "On Both Sides of the Law: An Overview of the Uses of Psychodrama, Roleplaying and Sociodrama." Paper presented at the 81st Annual Convention of the American Psychological Association, Montreal, 1973.

29. ———— & Shapiro, Felix. "The Use of Psychodrama and Videotape in Role Training." Presentation at the New York Medical College, 1969.

30. Yablonsky, Lewis. "Sociopathology of the Violent Gang and Its Treatment. *Progress in Psychotherapy*, 1960, 5.

33. SPONTANEITY TRAINING WITH TEACHERS

Herbert A. Otto

Over a period of eight years spontaneity training with teachers has been conducted at the University of Georgia. These training sessions were a part of a special offering in the area of mental health in education, open to enrollees in the annual summer workshop for school personnel offered by the College of Education. Spontaneity training was also conducted with teachers in off-campus workshops on mental health, and in in-service training sessions for school faculties conducted in Georgia and other states.

Classes or groups in which spontaneity training was undertaken varied in size from twelve to thirty members. Participants were usually seated informally in a circle, and when possible, smoking was permitted. In about 60 percent of the groups school administrators and school social workers as well as teachers were enrollees.

As a general procedure and in order to stimulate interest in spontaneity training, the topic "The Place of Spontaneity in Professional Functioning and Interpersonal Relations" was presented for group discussion. In all instances the group was asked whether discussion of this topic would be of interest and value. Group decision then governed whether the topic was covered. Preceding discussion of the topic the writer took ten

Reprinted with permission of the publishers from *Group Psychotherapy*, Vol. XV, No. 1, (March, 1962) pp. 74-79.

minutes to share his views on the subject. The following major points were made:

A. Educational emphasis and procedures seem to successively "train out" or eliminate spontaneity from the professional and inter-personal functioning of our students. Roughly, the more training, the less spontaneous the individual.

B. Spontaneity and creativity are closely linked. As the wellsprings of spontaneity dry, creativity is all too often similarly effected.

C. The origins of spontaneity training as traceable to Moreno's work in the Stegreif Theatre and his contribution to the development of sociodrama and psychodrama were briefly covered.

D. It was mentioned that various ways and means existed to develop spontaneity and that the group may be interested in considering some forms of what is generally called spontaneity training.

When appropriate during the beginning of the session, two questions would be raised by the writer, who functioned as discussion leader—1. "What keeps us from being spontaneous?" 2. "Why is it especially important for teachers to have spontaneity?"

If the group had been meeting for some time and group members had an opportunity to develop a fairly close relationship, considerable sharing of personal experience would usually take place around question one (above). It was interesting to note that it was the concensus of the majority of groups that spontaneity was equated with the *expression* of emotions and feelings. The expression of feelings or emotions meant to the groups (and seemed to be both consciously and unconsciously equated with) the expression of destructive and violent feelings such as aggression and hostility. In a number of groups this conclusion led participants to explore their feelings toward authority and, in some instances, colleagues. The presence of school administrators was seen as an advantage as it offered teachers an opportunity to hear how it felt to be "on the other side of the fence." Sociodrama could also be used to greater advantage with as much role reversal as possible with teachers and principals.

The majority of these groups were able to work through to a recognition of the fact that the pressure of accumulated and unexpressed hostile feelings tended to impede or make difficult the expression of tender or loving feelings. It was possible for some groups to spontaneously develop the insight that "a rich and varied expressive emotional life is usually a characteristic of a spontaneous and creative person."

The second question "Why is it especially important for teachers to have spontaneity?" helped group members to focus on the role of spontaneity in the professional functioning of the teacher. Most important, an opportunity was presented to examine closely the quality of pupil-teacher relationship within the authoritarian framework and to examine how this is related to the development of spontaneity in students. In a number of instances groups used this part of the discussion to examine their philosophy and functioning as educators. They then began to develop and work out programs and means by which spontaneity (and creativity) could be fostered in students. This topic also offered the discussion leader the opportunity to raise another question—"To help students develop spontaneity, wouldn't it be best to begin with ourselves?"

As a part of the democratic philosophy of group functioning, the discussion group leader asked the group to list on the blackboard methods and means by which spontaneity training could be achieved. When the group had completed the blackboard listing the writer would then add any methods and means which had been omitted. Training methods most often listed were the following:

1. Sociodrama.

2. Free expression of feelings and basic values, beliefs and convictions.

3. Use of finger paints, painting and drawing.

4. "Brain-storming."

5. Use of music.

6. Use of abstract and representative art works.

7. Interpretive dancing.

8. Group story and group drawing.

9. Psychodrama.

Following the blackboard listing, discussion would be utilized to select the various methods and means the group wished to employ in spontaneity training. Similarly, the length of time and number of sessions to be devoted to this type of training were determined.

Methods used in spontaneity training with teachers will be briefly discussed and findings and conclusions presented.

1. *Sociodrama and psychodrama* Sociodrama was used in the majority of groups. Since many teachers were in need of additional information about the origins and educational uses of this method, when possible Moreno's volume *Who Shall Survive?*, *Foundations of Sociometry, Group Psychotherapy and Sociodrama,* Moreno's monograph entitled "The Theatre of Spontaneity" and his related works were assigned readings and recommended for the professional library of participants. Role playing sequences were organized around the following:

a. Vital examples of student spontaneity—both constructive, creative incidents as well as hostile or destructive (pupil toward teacher directed) incidents.

b. Examples of spontaneity observed in the professional functioning of teachers or administrators.

c. Examples of spontaneity observed in a non-professional setting—neighborhood, friendship or family circles.

d. Role reversal situations with all group members acting

the role of students in a "spontaneity centered classroom."

The majority of the group derived considerable satisfaction and enjoyment from the role playing sequences. The role reversal situations and sociodrama dealing with spontaneous teacher-directed pupil hostility were reported to be most profitable. Although role playing practice in spontaneity did not seem to greatly enhance the role players' capacity for spontaneity, participants appeared to develop increased motivation to become spontaneous individuals. One outstanding by-product of role playing was the teachers' increasing familiarity with the technique and the expressed desire to make optimal and creative use of this method on their return to the classroom.

Psychodrama was used on a much smaller scale as the preponderant majority of groups preferred to use sociodrama. Psychodrama was especially effective when teachers volunteered to act out such themes as "An outstanding spontaneous moment during my adolescent years," or "The most outstanding incident of my use of spontaneity with students." Moreno's *Psychodrama*, Vols. I & II were assigned readings and used as a basis for reports or discussion. Shoob's monograph *Psychodrama in the Schools* was also used.

2. *Free expression of feelings, basic values, beliefs and convictions*—Extensive group discussions were held around such questions as "Why are we afraid to express our feelings?" "Why do we often fail to express our basic values and beliefs?" "What does this have to do with spontaneity?" These discussions had as their purpose to help individuals develop increased freedom in the expression of their feelings and convictions—initially within the framework of the group experience and hopefully, later, "on the outside."

This type of discussion not only enabled participants to increasingly express their feelings and beliefs, but also seemed to help them to become more sensitive to the feelings of other group members. To facilitate the expression of feelings, a series of ten minute practice sessions were held around such topics as "How we feel about bosses," "My feelings about nature." This provided an opportunity for expression of feelings by the group as a whole, beginning with hostile feelings and moving toward more "positive" feelings. This experience was reported by group members to have a freeing effect and was believed by some group members to facilitate more spontaneous self-expression.

3. *Use of finger paints, drawings and paintings*— Due to a lack of materials and facilities these methods were used in only a limited number of situations, although they ranked high on the methods list of all groups. Groups using finger paints and "spontaneous drawings" reported that use of these media had a very marked effect in terms of fostering both spontaneity and creativity. Finger painting especially seemed to be a markedly satisfying activity and was noted by group participants as being the highlight of their spontaneity training experience.

4. *Brain Storming*— Brain storming as developed by Alex Osborn and described in his book *Applied Imagination* was used during the majority of the group experiences. Topics for brain storming were suggested by the group. A number of small sub-groups were then formed and these competed with each other in the production of ideas. Group reported this as a very satisfying experience and in many instances group members later reported to the discussion leader that it had started them to do "more free-wheeling thinking" than they had previously done.

5. *Use of music*— Selected passages from symphonic, operatic and jazz sources were used. For example, the "Liebestod" passage from Wagner's Tristan and Isolde was used. Dixieland Jazz selections from George Lewis' "Burgundy Street Blues" and "When the Saints Come Marching In," also proved especially effective. No titles or names of musical selections were announced when excerpts were played. Group participants were asked either to share the feelings, imagery and fantasies they had while the music was playing, or to share

these feelings at the end of the selection. In most groups the use of music elicited spirited participation and sharing of feelings and fantasies.

6. *Interpretive dancing*— Although many groups listed this as a method, no group has attempted to use interpretive dancing. However, in approximately 30% of the groups, group members confided to the discussion leader that they had tried out this method in order to develop spontaneity and with highly satisfactory results. As one teacher put it—"I got up my courage and danced through the woods one Sunday morning and I believe it has helped me more than anything." It is of interest to note that only women teachers had the freedom to use this method.

7. *Use of abstract and representational art works*— Group members were asked to spontaneously share feelings, image and fantasies on viewing selected representational and abstract art works. The use of abstract works of art was especially effective. It was found that a great deal of confusion, anger or frustration seemed to exist in relation to abstract art, per se. *It was easier for most group members to spontaneously express feelings in reference to abstract art than to any other media used.* (The writer found that a similar use was made of abstract art in the leadership training programs of the Christian Faith and Life Community in Austin, Texas, by W. Jack Lewis, Joseph A. Slicker and associates. This group of trainers made very skillful use of a large reproduction of Picasso's abstract work entitled "Guernica," as well as other abstract paintings.)

It was found that on occasion group members would spontaneously paint or draw abstract themes or compositions outside of the group experience and bring them to the group to get their reaction. The groups were invariably supportive of these efforts although the artistic merit of these reproductions might be questioned. The tenor of group feelings was expressed by one member, who remarked "what does it matter whether it's art or not—you have done something spontaneously and enjoyed doing it. You've got something out of it—keep it up!"

The use of abstract art can make a definite contribution to spontaneity training. This is a relatively unexplored and challenging medium and additional experimental work is much needed.

8. Group story and group drawing—"Group story" was effectively used as an "ice breaker" during the intial meetings. The procedure was to begin a story with a starting sentence, such as "Once upon a time a teacher had a class of happy, bright youngsters eager to learn and grow," or "A teacher felt sad and depressed at the end of a long hard day with 38 pupils." Each group member in turn would then rapidly add a sentence to the growing story until everyone had contributed.

When group drawing was used, a drawing would be started on one side of along blackboard or a piece of paper, when these were available. Group members then participated in the conclusion of the drawing. This enabled 8-12 people to work simultaneously, with the majority making an attempt to relate their section both to their neighbors' effort and the whole emerging drawing. As a result, considerable spontaneous interaction took place and individual (as well as group) creativity was fostered.

The group story was especially effective as a source of humor and occasioned much laughter, which seemed to weld the group closer together. In addition, many insights and increasing understandings of group members was provided by use of both of these methods.

It is hoped that the discussion spontaneity training with teachers will serve as a stimulus for further efforts in this area with the teaching profession. In view of their key position in relation to the character and personality development of the coming generation, *the teacher, perhaps more than any other professional person, needs to be a spontaneous, creative and emotionally mature individual.*

Part VI
THEORY: COMPARISONS

Introduction

After one has examined a theorist and practitioner such as Moreno from a variety of viewpoints that include his personal and professional development, his scientific and therapeutic creations, and the contributions of his followers, there yet remains another important means to better understand the man and his works. This is to be found in the comparison of the man and his accomplishments to others who have been similarly acclaimed for their achievements. Unfortunately, there is a paucity of well done articles that compare Moreno to other leaders in the social and behavioral sciences, but the best of these have been chosen for inclusion here. Since the other theorists dealt with are Freud, Rogers, John Rosen, Erving Goffman, and the religious philosopher Martin Buber, and very brief presentations of C.G. Jung and Gordon Allport, the approach to understanding Moreno through comparisons is at this writing much too sketchy and disconnected to be conclusive. All that can be expected in this part of the volume is that some additional insights into Moreno and his system are to be gained. Many other important theorists, such as Adler, Sullivan, Horney, Lewin, Gardner Murphy, George Kelly, and Henry A. Murray, to name a few, would have to be included for any fully developed study of Moreno by means of comparisons to be academically acceptable. Such an encompassing work still remains to be written.

The opening article, "Freud, Rogers, and Moreno, an Inquiry into the Possible Relationship between Manifest Personality, Theory, and Methods of Some Eminent Psychotherapists," has as its major purpose the delineation of the relationship between what is known of the personality of each of the three therapists and their form of psychotherapy, as seen by Corsini in 1956. Corsini knew Freud through his works and through the efforts of Freud's biographers, and he knew Rogers and Moreno personally and had expressed warm feelings toward each. Thus, he is ideally suited for undertaking the comparative study of these three therapeutic giants. Corsini sees Freud as a pedant and scientist, Rogers as a gentle and warm man, and Moreno as a dynamic man of action. Although he acknowledges that all are men of brilliance and achievement, Corsini pictures them respectively as the intellectual, the emotional, and the actional. In regard to the last, Corsini writes: "Moreno, as we have stated, is a dynamo of action, always on the go, full of plots, plans and procedures [and] it is not to be wondered then that psychodrama takes place out in the open, on a stage in front of all humanity, that the therapeutic behavior consists of action — that intellectualizations and expressions of feelings are subordinated to outright spontaneous behavior." Corsini further notes that "how one does therapy should be a function of the type of person one is," and concludes with the argument that theory and method need not be united, a significant point.

The second article, by Simon, compares psychodrama and Moreno with direct analysis and John Rosen in the treatment of severe schizophrenics. Both Moreno and Rosen successfully refute Freud's claim that psychotics are incapable of undergoing a transference neurosis, and each in his way utilizes the material of this refutation in his therapeutic endeavors, although Moreno, as has been stated in several other places in this volume, incorporates the transference phenomenon into his concept of tele, and it is the tele that is important in Morenean therapy. Where the auxiliary egos in psychodrama, taking their cues from the director and from the protagonist, enter into the delusional world of the psychotic, Rosen himself does this as therapist. He portrays the important "other" in the patient's private world as he seeks to evoke a transference. Although Simon mentions several other points for comparing and contrasting the two, perhaps the most interesting lies in that Rosen also works before an audience. However, where in psychodrama the audience is an integral part of the totality and is both target for therapy and a support to the protagonist, in direct analysis, according to Simon, the audience is there, but it does not affect therapy.

Moreno and Erving Goffman have much in common in their employment of the dramatic, but, again as with Rosen, they differ in their major philosophical orientations and in the way they give structure and life to these orientations. As Gosnell points out in his article, "Some Similarities and Dissimilarities between the Psychodramaturgical Approaches of J.L. Moreno and Erving Goffman," Goffman describes dramaturgical aspects of life and focuses on ways in which a definition of a situation may be *maintained,* while Moreno applies the dramaturgical principles in psychodrama and seeks ways in which a situation's definition may be *changed;* Goffman concentrates on "conserved" behavior and Moreno calls for spontaneity in behavior. Other points of similarity and contrast are developed by Gosnell, who documents each point with quotations from important works of each theorist: Moreno's *Psychodrama, Vol. I,* and Goffman's *The Presentation of Self in Everyday Life.*

In Haskell's article, "Socioanalysis and Psychoanalysis," there is again a comparison with the Freudian and neo-Freudian systems, but this is presented almost in passing toward the end of the article. Haskell spends the better part of the article outlining the Morenean system from a socioanalytic viewpoint, and this includes the following components: (1) an image of man, (2) theory of spontaneity, (3) theory of sociometry, (4) methodology of psychodrama, and (5) socioanalytic therapy, "which seeks to promote functioning in society." In "Moreno and Mowrer, or the New Group Therapy," Wolfe, a student of Dr. Lewis Yablonsky at San Fernando Valley State College at Northridge, California, compares Moreno with a leading learning theorist and finds a contrast between the action of Moreno and the calls for confession of Mowrer.

The final two articles, "The Tragic Origins and Counter-tragic Evolution of Psychodrama," by the late Anna B. Brind and her husband Nah Brind, and Johnson's "Interpersonal Psychology of Religion," tend to fit more comfortably into a category of the humanities than into a category of either the social or behavioral sciences; yet, in the fact that these articles also compare and contrast, their inclusion here is considered appropriate. The Brinds, using examples from Shakespeare and the French neo-classicists, seek to show Moreno's interaction with tragic theater, together with "Moreno's ingenious dethronement of Tragedy, with his extraordinary transmutation of litero-esthetic theater into therapeutic psychodrama." Moreno managed to accomplish this transmutation, the Brinds conclude, by means of the technique of role reversal. They state: "Through role reversal Moreno offered his protagonists what no drama could ever do. He offered his protagonists the means and the opportunities to meet their adversaries in an experimental, experiential, controlled, and entirely new form of co-action. . ."

Role reversal, as has already been mentioned in a number of the articles included in this volume, has several dimensions, and one of which is the experiencing of the important "other" in a psychodrama. Thus, in the Johnson article, the comparison of Moreno and Buber brings to mind the suitability of bringing Moreno's role reversal and his concept of tele to stand alongside Buber's I-Thou relationship. The obvious contrast which many might make is that Moreno's concepts relate to man in a therapeutic situation while Buber's relate to man and the deity, but here again one should beware of underestimating Moreno, whose view has always been cosmic. Moreno, too, sees man in terms of the godhead, a view that has been examined earlier in Part III of this volume. Suffice it to say that it is entirely possible that Moreno may have more in common with the religious philosopher Buber than with most of the psychotherapists he has been compared with.

34. FREUD, ROGERS, AND MORENO
An Inquiry into the Possible Relationship between Manifest Personality, Theory and Method of Some Eminent Psychotherapists

Raymond J. Corsini

Why are there so many schools of psychotherapy? Why do methods vary so much? How do people come to select particular procedures for their own therapy or as their method of practice? How is it that intelligent and sincere people exposed to various theories and procedures reject some and accept others? What are the basic determiners of choice in this area?

Without doubt, proponents of various systems would give "intellectual" answers: would attempt to show the validity of their theoretical constructs, the logic of intervening variables; point out clinical successes; and may even attempt, when pertinent, to present nomothetic evidence based on approved hypothetico-deductive investigations using objective criteria. However, the naive investigator of systems would still be puzzled since various proponents would give, in essence, the same arguments for different systems.

There can be quite a different kind of explanation for this

Reprinted with the permission of the publishers from *Group Psychotherapy,* Vol. IX, No. 4 (December, 1956), pp. 274-281.

human phenomenon, the subject of this inquiry, namely "emotional." As used here, this term differentiates from "logical." Personal, private, emotional or feeling determiners may precede and determine action, while logical, intellectual, or unemotional reasons may be post hoc rationalizations.

There is one outstanding study in this genre which may be cited, although it is in another area. Pastore[1] was interested in why eminent scientists took either side of the nature-nurture controversy. He hypothesized that the side they took could be explained by political liberalism or conservatism, with the liberals being on the side of nurture and the conservatives on the side of nature. He did find evidence to support his views: hereditarians were conservative, environmentalists were liberal; the former believing in eugenics, the latter in euthenics. In short, how these scientists came to side themselves on this perennially unsettled topic appeared to be a function of social-political opinions, which presumably came first—and which presumably themselves were a function of what is generally called "personality."

The protopostulate of this essay is that selection or adherence or "discovery" of a theory and method of psychotherapy is not fortuitous in terms of personality, but rather that they are a function of the self. That is to say, what a person believes and does in this area can, by and large, be understood in terms of his personality.

SOME PRELIMINARY IDEAS

This complex and sensitive question is complicated by the vagueness and indefiniteness of the terms "schools of psychotherapy" and "personality." Below, an explicit denotation of the precise way these terms are used will ensure

[1] Pastore, N. The Nature-nurture Controversy, New York: King's Crown, 1949.

some degree of control and restriction in the manipulation of the concepts.

Personality

Personality may be conceived of in three general ways: (a) real, true, basic, essential, (b) phenomenological, (c) manifest. These will be now defined and an explanation will be given why the third definition is used in this paper.

Real personality. What a real personality is remains a philosophical question, unanswerable by science. People are readily deluded about themselves; this is a common experience for those who do psychotherapy. The purpose of psychology as a personalistic science is to attain understanding of final and fundamental reality of self, but it can be said that no method of analysis or of testing has yet been claimed to attain this end. We may say that "real" personality is a metaphysical issue, and not currently scientifically meaningful.

Phenomenological personality. Is personality what a person thinks he is? Surely, no matter what the opinions of others may be, one can argue that an individual operates in terms of his conception of self, and that he sees things and behaves in accordance to self-perceptions. However, to depend on phenomenological impressions to define personality has many hazards in terms of reality. The paranoid's system of perception may be readily established, but can one say that it is operationally or reality valid?

Preston[2] and associates argue that personality may be considered an impression. A's personality is what B sees it to be. A's personality does not reside in the realm of reality, nor in the area of self-perception, but rather in the minds of others. Therefore A has many selves as observers. If we take this view,

[2] Preston, M.G., Peltz, W.L., Mudd, E.T., and Frosher, H.B. Impressions of Personality as a Function of Marital Conflict. J. Abnorm, Soc. Psychol., 1952, 47, 116-336.

we can argue that the personality of any person is the consensus of observers.

To handle the problem to be set up, we shall use the concept of *manifest personality,* that is the impression of the personality of several people as obtained by the writer. If these impressions accord with those of the reader, we may say that consensual validity exists, but if there is difference it will be unknown which of the several views is closer to the metaphysical conception of true personality or the phenomenological impressions of the individuals involved. In short, no claim is made that these impressions are valid; they are merely the writer's opinions.

Schools of Psychotherapy

No one, to the writer's knowledge, has established any classification of schools of psychotherapy. Nevertheless, it appears intuitively valid that some schools have much in common with others. Adler's and Horney's version of psychoanalysis appears to have many points in common; McCann's Round Table Psychotherapy resembles in some respects Bion's Leaderless Psychotherapy; Klapman's Textbook mediated therapy has some resemblance to Low's Will therapy, etc. However, what is needed is some over-all general classification scheme to subdivide the therapies. If this system can also be used to classify individuals, then one can handle the main issue of this paper—the comparison of theories and methods to personalities.

Corsini and Rosenberg[3] located a total of 166 different mechanisms of group psychotherapy, which after a kind of semantic factor analysis were classified into three groups: *Intellectual,* or dynamics that stressed understanding, logic,

3 Corsini, R.J., & Rosenberg, B. Mechanics of Group Psychotherapy, Processes and Mechanisms. J. Abnorm. Soc. Psychol., 1955, 51, 406-411.

explanation, learning—in short mechanisms which depended on cognitive process; *Emotional*, that is to say dynamics that depended on feeling processes, acceptance, transference, and the like; and *Actional*, or therapeutic processes that were characterized by behavior or physical expression.

This trichotomy appears to reflect three maxims found in philosophy and religion: *Know thyself* (intellectual), *Love thy neighbor* (emotional); and *Do good works* (actional).

It appears to the writer that the psychoanalysis of Sigmund Freud with its emphasis on understanding the individual is an example of a psychotherapy that relies heavily on *intellectual* elements. The *client-centered psychotherapy* of Carl Rogers with its core insistences on the importance of the acceptance of feelings is a school which depends considerably on the *effect* of the *emotions*. The *Psychodrama* of J. L. Moreno with its emphasis on action is a psychotherapy based essentially on the importance of spontaneous *behavior*.

STATEMENT OF THE PROBLEM

The major purpose of this paper is to illustrate the relationship of "personality" to "psychotherapy." Personality is viewed from the point of reference of the writer, i.e., the manifest personality of various therapists. Both personality and psychotherapy are to be classified in terms of Intellectual, Emotional and Actional factors.

The specific hypothesis is that there is a direct relationship between the "personality" of eminent therapists and the procedures and theories they employ. More specifically, it will be argued that Freud was manifestly an intellectual individual; Rogers an emotional person; and Moreno a man of action.

However, one additional problem arises: each of these three men were initiators in this field, who had the daring to break away from tradition. Are there commonalities in their manifest personalities which explains their leadership behavior?

With some comprehension of the superficiality and naivete of this approach, as a first approximation to an interesting and perhaps important problem, let us try to determine what these men have in common which made them initiators, how they differ, and what made them go in different directions.

MANIFEST PERSONALITIES

Freud's manifest-to-me personality comes from secondary sources: his own writings, and those of his various biographers, all of which appear to have the virtue of consistency. Freud appears to be almost the stereotype of the pedant: a precise, meticulous, compulsive student of minutia: patient, untiring and logical. Clues are picked up and welded into an inductively built system of great logical coherence. While he may have been personally warm and kind, he gives nevertheless an impression of courtliness, distance, even coldness. He was in the tradition of Wundt, Kant, Ebbinghaus—the gentleman German scientist.

Rogers, known to the writer as a member of his doctoral committee and psychotherapist, is regarded by all known to the writer as a person whose manifest personality qualities are those of consideration, gentleness, confidence in others, warmth, modesty, and acceptance. He is quiet, friendly, maintains a high regard for others, is sympathetic and empathic.

Moreno is known personally to the writer by interviews, participation on committees, correspondence, etc., and certainly gives a major manifest impression of dynamic action. He is the almost pure type of *l'homme social*, gathering groups around him, continually on the go, moving rapidly and excitedly— sometimes giving the impression of a person suffering from mania.

Commonalities

Above we have attempted, in terms of the system, to portray Freud as essentially an intellectual, Rogers as a feeling person, and Moreno as a man of physical action. However, to complete the portraits, it is necessary to stress the commonalities of these men to understand their strivings in this field.

Intellectual. It can hardly be doubted these men each have a superior level of what the psychometrists call "G" or general intelligence. However, it is how the intelligence is used that is of interest to us. We may label it *cleverness.*

Intellectual. Freud was a genius at exposition. He was able to present evidence in such a manner that cynics and skeptics of psychoanalysis were readily convinced. Freud had a knack of permitting the reader to come to his own conclusions, which were really those of Freud. He could well have been a supreme pleader at law or an advertising genius.

Rogers' intelligence is seen in his artful capacity to avoid controversy, to use words with extreme precision and delicacy. It is perhaps no accident that Rogers is a student of semantics. The terms "non-directive" and "client-centered" have a built-in appeal, with their sly dig at other procedures which become by implication "directive" and "therapist-centered."

Moreno perhaps manifests his cleverness best in his capacity to manipulate people; to organize movements, to be able to feel the pulse of a movement and to know when to initiate steps.

Emotional. The common aspect of these three people in this area is courage. Each of these men have faced hostility and have not run away from it.

Freud, a product of a puritanical era, investigated sex, even in the face of opposition of his early collaborator, Breuer. In the face of followers who opposed him, he showed an intransigent attitude, when a little diplomacy might have kept the group together. He held tenaciously to his ideas and discussed unpopular issues. He attacked religion and he even argued that physicians did not make good psychotherapists—a point which we must return to—, but of the most pertinency is that Freud was no Freudian, since he continually changed his ideas, having no respect for doctrinaire philosophies.

Rogers' courage is also seen in many respects. As a psychologist venturing into areas that physicians had staked out for themselves, he suffered from almost united disapproval of medical groups. It is stated that he spoke before assemblies of people he knew would attack him. He maintains a kind of gentle stubbornness, rarely attacking people, as Moreno is wont to do, but defending his opinions as Voltaire is said to have stated, to the very end.

Moreno's courage is seen in many respects. It is found in his capacity to pioneer: starting societies and journals. It is seen in his writings, which are sometimes more candid than anything found in Rousseau or Koestler. He calls himself a genius, declares this is one reason why he may never be elected president of the American Psychiatric Association, boldly considering his ideas of an importance equal to those of Jesus, Buddha, and Socrates, *and* claiming to have written bibles.

Actional. If in the intellectual sphere, cleverness characterizes these men, and if courage characterizes them in the area of the emotions, then it is work that unites them in the area of action. Each of these men shows a prodigious capacity for labor.

Freud's heavy writing and analytic schedule is well known. In his later years, wracked with cancer-pain he stubbornly continued his work.

Rogers has produced a large number of books and articles, maintains a normal teaching schedule, a strong lecture program, and nevertheless keeps a normal 18-hour-a-week therapy schedule. In addition, he directs the equivalent of a small institution and as a professor is loaded with all kinds of committee meetings. Nevertheless, Rogers is a person who is known always to be available.

Moreno's wife once stated "he does the work of six"; he is the author of more than a dozen books, the editor of two journals, the superintendent of an institution, the director of a teacher institution. He still maintains a heavy patient load, lectures and demonstrates in Europe and the United States, and is an indefatigable writer of letters, of which the present writer has more than one hundred. One who is dealing with Moreno may expect to be called on the telephone any hour of the day or night.

Above, what has been done is to attempt to explain the eminence of these individuals by claiming they are alike in that they are clever, are courageous and work hard. Let us now attempt to see why they have gone in such different directions in their systems of psychotherapy.

PERSONALITY AND PSYCHOTHERAPY

We have already stated that Freud was a reserved person who operated in a cautious and logical manner. In his method of psychotherapy, the patient was made to lie on his back so that neither could see the other. He had a horror of personal relationships with his patients: transference was given the label of "neurosis" and acting out was called "regression." Actually, Freud was not a psychotherapist: he was a scientist. In stating that physicians were not equipped to be psychoanalysts he was most probably projecting, realizing his own deficiencies as a therapist.

It seems evident that the method he used was entirely consistent with his manifest personality. It is of interest to note that Freud was aware of his peculiar method and argued that other people, differently constituted, would probably do best to operate differently, but nonetheless he was able to pass his own neurosis on to a generation of psychotherapists, who dutifully - put their patients on their backs, and called transference a neurosis.

If Rogers is manifestly a kind, gentle, unobtrusive person, then we must expect that his method of psychotherapy should mirror him. In the client-centered therapy, the therapist tries to get into his patient's frame of reference, to understand the other, to appreciate, value and accept the other. He avoids interpretation and advice, and argues that every person has a potentiality for good adjustment. In short, his system of behavior is entirely consistent with his manifest personality.

Moreno, as we have stated, is a dynamo of action, always on the go, full of plots, plans and procedures. It is not to be wondered then that psychodrama takes place out in the open, on a stage in front of all humanity, that the therapeutic behavior consists of action—that intellectualizations and expressions of feelings are subordinated to outright spontaneous behavior.

DISCUSSION

The argument is that eminence in this field is a function of cleverness, courage and capacity to work. It is also argued that a psychotherapy that bases itself on intellectual elements was begun by a man of intellect; a system based on feelings and acceptance was initiated by a gentle and friendly person; and that a system based on spontaneous behavior was started by a man who himself demonstrates a capacity for immediate action. The conclusions would appear to be that in order to understand why these and possibly other methods of psychotherapy came to be, we have to understand their initators. We may say that schools of psychotherapy, just as institutions, are the shadow of a man.

However, what has gone above may appear to have little meaning in terms of its implications for other therapists. The writer would suggest that a very important generalization derives from the above: the proper method of psychotherapy for any person must be an extension of his own personality. For a therapist of Moreno's disposition to attempt to become a psychoanalyst is ridiculous; for a person like Freud in nature to attempt psychodrama would be a tragedy; for a person who is like Rogers in his temperament to try to be an analyst or a psychodramatist is foolish. How one does psychotherapy should be a function of the type of person one is.

The practice of psychotherapy must be divorced from the theory of psychotherapy. The first refers to *how* one operates and the latter to *what* one believes. The relationship between theory and practice is not unvarying. One can be an analyst and not have his patients lie down; one can accept Rogers' phenomenological theory of psychotherapy and do psychodrama; one can accept Moreno's sociometric theory and be non-directive. There has arisen a horrendous myth that a theory and a method are united. In short, how one does psychotherapy should be consistent and natural for the therapist; what theory the psychotherapist assumes has little or nothing to do with how he operates.

It appears that although these three men were alike in that they were intelligent, were courageous and worked hard, nevertheless they had distinctly different personalities, and intuitively realizing that the method they should use should be a reflection of their essential selves, and found procedures entirely consonant with their personalities.

We may learn from these men several lessons: the manner in which psychotherapy is to be practiced for maximum advantage should be a reflection of the therapist's personality; and that theories of psychotherapy are not welded to procedures. Various proponents of a particular theory may nonetheless operate quite differently.

35. PSYCHOTHERAPY TECHNIQUES AND PROBLEMS WITH SEVERE SCHIZOPHRENICS
Psychodrama versus Direct Analysis

Robert J. Simon

It is an almost indisputable fact that most psychiatrists and orthodox psychoanalysts have enjoyed small success in therapeutic sessions with hospitalized patients. This brief paper will speculate about the underlying reasons for this failure. More important will be the presentation of contrasting techniques employed by Dr. Moreno and others in their treatment of schizophrenics. Pharmacology and physical-therapy appear to have provided better results than the psychotherapy sessions, but even these methods have had their limitations.

As a young man, working in the psychiatric ward of an Army Hospital in the capacity of the psychiatric attendant, this author frequently observed the interaction, or more accurately, lack of it, between the psychiatrists and the patients. My own tasks, beyond the supervision of the psychotic patients, was to observe and report any unusual behavior. The psychiatrist would either impassively listen to the patient's delusions or hallucinations or, more frequently, attempt to convince the schizophrenic of the distortions and inaccuracies of the perceptions he was presenting. Most patients were emotionally indifferent to the prospect of the therapeutic session which was in marked contrast to the extreme negative and fearful emotional response exhibited when electric shock therapy was

Reprinted with the permission of the publishers from *International Journal of Sociometry and Sociatry,* Vol. IV, Nos. 3 and 4 (September-December, 1964) pp. 83-87.

scheduled.

The Freudian-oriented psychiatrist views schizophrenic psychoses as a narcissistic withdrawal and regression associated with ego weakness. More drastic than the regression is the theoretical assertion that there is a destruction of the capacity for transference. Without this ability to project, many analysts insist that successful therapy with psychotic patients is impossible. The psychiatrist merely makes a diagnosis of the type of psychotic reaction involved, decides upon a course of treatment which is usually a course of shock or drug therapy and then meets with the patient in order to check upon the progress being made. In classical terms this is all that can be accomplished by the therapist since the nature of the psychotic illness precludes successful therapy.

This author vividly recalls the long and frustrating hours spent with paranoid schizophrenics attempting to persuade them that their particular delusion or hallucination was a faulty interpretation of reality. Logic, disputation and patience were of no avail. Particularly frustrating was the fact that the patient was often able to deal with reality situations very well, exclusive of his particular delusional or hallucinatory system. The constant aim was to apprise the patient of his perceptual error. Never once was the acceptance of the patient's world discussed or attempted. One catatonic, who had after months of silence evolved paranoid symptoms, related to the author how he had heard all attempts to communicate, but just had decided not to respond. Attempts to cajole, reason and even provoke were received only by silence. The attitude that the patient must be made to see his error in interpretation of the world was paramount, and never was the acceptance by the staff of the reality construct of the patient's world discussed. If psychosis is viewed as the extreme adjustment to life's threatening situations, then before the patient will return to reality the threats it imposes must be reduced. As a first step towards making the world less fearful and threatening, the patient's world must be accepted and the patient shown love necessary for his sustenance. The therapist can no longer represent the impersonal or rejecting authority figure.

Certainly any psychotic, in his withdrawal from reality, has suffered severe ego impairment which is illustrated by frequent expressions of unreality, depersonalization and loss of identity. Moreno discusses the need to aid the ego by the introduction of the trained auxiliary ego or egos. With the more deeply disturbed and long term psychotics the task confronting the auxiliary egos requires more support than the auxiliary egos can provide. An auxiliary world has to be provided. Thus, instead of understanding the patient on the level of his overt behavior as interpreted through analysis of the unconscious and dreams, Dr. Moreno proceeds beyond this by actually entering the world of the psychotic. The auxiliary egos now fill roles which coincide with the patient's needs. The commitment is complete and the auxiliary ego talks the patient's language, bizarre as it might be, and joins him in the unique universe which the psychotic has constructed. In this construct the patient is viewed as a poet who is possessed by creations of his own fantasy. These creations of a psychotic are entered in order to be an integral part of the patient's mental confusion and to learn the grammar of his logic. Having accomplished this, it is easy for the auxiliary ego to produce a role at will which will duplicate the compulsive role played by the patient.

Moreno appears to be making the point that if the patient will not voluntarily return to the threatening reality situation, then it is advisable to join him in his fantasy world, until such time as he is able to return. While this seems to be a logical assumption and a unique innovation, this author is troubled by one aspect of it. In dealing with the paranoid who is beset by false perceptual interpretations of reality, will not the acceptance of the delusional and hallucinatory content serve as a reinforcement of these false perceptions? While entering the psychotic's world will often allow for spontaniety on his part, which is the working level of treatment, reinforcement of his psychotic world on a conditioning level might impede the return to reality.

Moreno agrees with the orthodox Freudian psychiatrists who claim that the psychotic is basically incapable of transference, but this does not preclude success with the patient. True transference relationships with the therapist and aids are not affected, but numerous and well developed tele relations are. Real feelings regarding colors, food, and clothes were noted among psychotic patients. There was tele for individual attendants, but only in certain roles and positions which were part of the patient's private world, of his reality.

To this author, Moreno's concept of loving and accepting the psychotic patient as he is, provides a key to what is lacking in the traditional psychiatric approach. Feeling unloved, threatened, rejected and hated and being unable to provide defenses short of a flight from reality are certainly significant in the psychotic's dilemma. The unloving authority figure of the psychiatrist certainly cannot be viewed in a positive therapeutic sense. To accept this frightened, rejected person and provide him with love must precede any attempts to return him to reality. Here again is the problem of accepting the patient's delusional world as part of the acceptance of the entire person. It would appear that a fine delineation would have to be constructed which would provide an atmosphere of acceptance without reinforcing the fantasy aspects of the illness.

John Rosen, in the early 1950's, developed a technique for the treatment of psychotics which is called "Direct Psychoanalysis." Rosen has made the claim that all 37 psychotic patients had recovered and that only six had suffered subsequent relapses. This is the most sweeping claim of success with psychotics known. Essentially the doctor is a Freudian. The Freudian view that psychosis is a regression to the pregenital stage of psychosexual development is implicit. Freudian theory that the super ego is formed at five is modified by Rosen to occur during the first year of life. According to Rosen, the key to all psychoses is the "perversion of the maternal environment." To a culture-and-personality-student this appears to be a gross oversimplification of an extremely complex interaction of factors which are responsible for the development of the psychotic. Rosen employs retrospective logic when he claims that the first few years of life which were unobserved by the psychiatrist are always responsible for current psychotic conditions. If this Freudian concept is accepted as a universal, then it follows that child psychiatrists can without error predict the future mental health of all children, based upon their observations of them during the first few years of life.

Rosen's treatment of psychotics involves finding in the expressions of the patient the motif of his behavior. The patient is then addressed by the doctor who employs the same language as the patient. The psychiatrist avoids the use of technical terminology. The main aim of the therapist is to act as a foster parent in order to compensate for the patient's "bad" mother. The psychiatrist accepts the neo-infantile psychotic as one would a new infant. The "new" infant must be brought up again with new love and discipline given and received. In order to effect this rebirth, an apartment is set up containing three or four assistants whose job it is to protect and care for the patient at all times.

The therapy sessions between the patient and the doctor are conducted before an audience which can number 100. Rosen claims that the audience does not affect the therapy. Why an audience is present if it does not affect the therapy is not explained by Rosen. Gestures, bodily movements, facial expressions and conversation are initiated by either analyst or patient. The stated aim of the therapy is to weaken the "bad" influence of the mother and introduce the therapist's own "good" influence. *The setting of the therapy and the action method employed bears a striking resemblance to the*

Psychodrama method introduced by Moreno.

Rosen contends, in contradiction to Freud and Moreno, that transference does exist among psychotics. It is the tendency to find the mother you know in persons not your mother. The problem is to focus this overabundance of transference upon the patient instead of allowing it to be diffused. If the psychiatrist pretends to be the maternal, omnipotent figure, then the transference can be accomplished. In the transference interpretation Rosen contends that it is essential to have the patient realize that the analyst understands him. This appears more important to this writer than the more theroetical concepts Rosen presents.

In this paper the attempt has been made to show that the classical Freudian therapist has, by default, been strikingly unsuccessful with extreme psychotic patients. They reason that without transference therapy is impossible, and since psychotics are devoid of it success is precluded. This negative attitude colors the relationship between patient and analyst, and prevents any real attempt to empathize with or accept the patient. Since the psychotic patient is in desperate need of acceptance and love the therapist fails to provide the necessary sustenance. Dr. Moreno has accepted and provided love for the psychotic patient and if this is not enough, the patient's distorted world is entered and shared. This represents a great conceptual step forward because no longer is the emphasis on persuading the patient that his interpretations of reality are false. Instead, these interpretations are shared by the therapist in an attempt to better effect a cure. Rosen's methods show that innovations are possible and needed. Certainly it is admitted, aside from Rosen's claim of 100 per cent recovery, that no one has completely uncovered the therapeutic key to unlock the door which locks the psychotic in his world of distorted reality.

There are several important similarities between the methods employed by Rosen in his Direct Analysis and Moreno's earlier Psychodrama methodology. Like Moreno, Rosen has the psychotic patient living in a separate house staffed by three or four assistants, who live on the premises like members of a foster family. These assistants are selected for their responsibility and responsiveness. Dr. Rosen suggests that students and former mental patients are the best qualified assistants. The assistants are charged with caring for and protecting the patient. The concept of the assistants appears to be an imitation of Dr. Moreno's professionally trained auxiliary egos. In Psychodrama the auxiliary ego has a double function. Outside of the theater when the auxiliary ego spends time with the patient, his function is to be an interpreter between the patient and the people of the real world. Since the psychotic has gross distortions in many of his imaginary roles, the auxiliary ego acts as a valuable aid to the patient in the direction of his own fragmented aspirations. Both the assistant and the auxiliary ego are aiding and protecting the patient. However, the auxiliary ego serves as a substitute for the auxiliary egos of the patient's real life, and provides a bridge between the rejecting outside world and the psychotic. The assistant is more a custodian while the auxiliary ego is a therapeutic adjunct.

At the treatment sessions in direct analysis the assistants are usually required to be present, but they remain in the background without actively participating in the therapy. An audience of fifty to one-hundred students and observers may be present, but Dr. Rosen contends that the attention of the patient is never focused on anyone but the therapist. In Moreno's Psychodramatic theater the auxiliary ego becomes the ideal extension of the patient's ego in his effort to establish a self-sufficient psychotic world. Here, once again, the shell of Moreno's method seems to be employed by Rosen, but the essential function and purpose of the trained auxiliary ego has been deleted in the transition.

36. SOME SIMILARITIES AND DISSIMILARITIES BETWEEN THE PSYCHODRAMATURGICAL APPROACHES OF J. L. MORENO* AND ERVING GOFFMANN**

Douglas Gosnell

I

Shortly after a first exposure to a live psychodrama, I recalled that Erving Goffman, in his MacIver Award-winning book, *The Presentation of Self in Everyday Life,* [1] employed the language and structure of the theatrical performance as a vehicle for his description of social interaction in ordinary life. This recollection, coupled with my impression of the psychodrama session as an everyday identity-stripping process, raised the question as to the degree of overlap or convergence, if any, between the everyday world of Erving Goffman and the psychodramatic world of J. L. Moreno.

In *Presentation,* there is only one specific reference to psychodrama. After stating that "ordinary social intercourse is itself put together as a scene is put together," and that "Scripts

Reprinted with the permission of the publishers from *International Journal of Sociometry and Sociatry*, Vol. IV, Nos. 3 and 4 (September-December, 1964), pp. 94-106.

* J.L. Moreno, Psychodrama, First Volume (New York: Beacon House, 1946).

** Erving Goffman, The Presentation of Self in Every-day Life (Garden City, New York: Doubleday & Company, Inc. 1959).

[1] The MacIver Award is granted annually to the author of a publication which "contributed in an outstanding degree to the progress of sociology during the two preceding years" prior to the award.

even in the hands of unpracticed players can come to life because life itself is a dramatically enacted thing," Goffman observes:[2]

> The recent use of "psychodrama" as a therapeutic technique illustrates a further point in this regard. In these psychiatrically staged scenes patients not only act out parts with some effectiveness, but employ no script in doing so. Their own past is available to them in a form which allows them to stage a recapitulation of it. Apparently a part once played honestly and in earnest leaves the performed in a position to contrive a showing of it later. Further, the parts that significant others played to him in the past also seem to be available, allowing him to switch from being the person that he was to being the persons that others were for him. This capacity to switch enacted roles when obliged to do so could have been predicted; everyone apparently can do it. For in learning to perform our parts in real life we guide our own productions by not too consciously maintaining an incipient familiarity with the routine of those to whom we will address ourselves. And when we come to be able properly to manage a real routine we are able to do this in part because of "anticipatory socialization," having already been schooled in the reality that is just coming to be real for us. (72)

This passage suggests some possible points of convergence between everyday performances and psychodrama performances. And, indeed, it is possible to illustrate, by the method of parallel quotations, several apparent similarities between the dramaturgical approaches of Goffman and Moreno. Before undertaking this task, however, I would like to make explicit what appears to me to be some fundamental *dissimilarities* between the theretical, descriptive framework of *Presentation* and the applied, therapeutic method of the Psychodrama.

2 All Goffman quotes in this paper are taken from *The Presentation of Self in Everyday Life; op. cit.*, and all Moreno quotes are taken from *Psychodrama, op. cit.* Following each quotation is the number of the page upon which the quotation will be found.

II

Goffman has committed himself in *Presentation* to explaining virtually all human behavior in terms of interpersonal communication and social interaction patterns. For Goffman, everyday life is a series of performances:

> The implication here is that an honest, sincere, serious performance is less firmly connected with the solid world than one might at first assume . . . ordinary social intercourse is itself put together as a scene is put together, by the exchange of dramatically inflated actions, counter-actions, and terminating replies. Scripts even in the hands of unpracticed players can come to life because life itself is a dramatically enacted thing. All the world is not, of course, a stage, but the crucial ways in which it isn't are not easy to specify. (71-2)

Goffman is thus primarily interested in the "structure of social encounters—the structure of those entities in social life that come into being whenever persons enter one another's physical presence." (254) But what holds everyday performances together, what integrates them? Goffman's answer is the desire on the part of the performers to maintain "a single definition of the situation, this definition having to be expressed, and this expression maintained in the face of a multitude of potential disruptions." (254) Thus, according to Goffman, the "presentation of self in everyday life" involves the attempt of the performers to project and *maintain a single definition of the situation;* it is this characteristic of social intercourse which suggests that the presentation of self in everyday life may be viewed as a kind of psychodrama-in-reverse:

> The expressive coherence that is required in performances points out a crucial discrepancy between our all-too-human selves and our socialized selves. As human beings we are presumably creatures of variable impulse with moods and energies that change from one moment to the next. As characters put on for an audience, however, we must not be subject to ups and downs. . . .

> A certain bureaucratization of the spirit is expected so that we can be relied upon to give a perfectly homogeneous performance at every appointed time. As Santayana suggests, the socialization process not only transfigures, it fixes. . . . (56)

In the psychodramatic theatre, the objectives are strikingly different:

> The ideal is to be free from restraint; from a predetermined place and a predetermined creative product. Both delimit the full, unrestrained emergence of spontaneity. In the legitimate theatre neither the moment nor the place is free. Both are predetermined in content and form—the written play and the rehearsed production determine the moment and make it unfree. . . . In the therapeutic theatre, the supreme form of the theatre, space as well as moment are original. (26)

Psychodrama, as a therapeutic method, has the task of creating a situation which is "as life-like as life but more abundant in possibilities, more flexible. . . ." (152) The objective of treatment for both the individual and the audience is to bring about catharsis—somatic, mental, individual, and group— through spontaneous dramatic action. Far from having as its purpose the maintenance of a single definition of a situation, the goal of psychodramatic therapy is to change the definition of a situation,

> . . . to "deconserve" the learner from time to time, to purge him, so to speak, from emotional and social cliches and to restore in him a condition which would make him fresh and free to participate in the realities of the moment with the greatest possible perspicacity: (151)

Goffman's symbolic interactionist-dramaturgical orientation has led him to eschew explanations and theories of human behavior which assign a significant role to intra-psychic factors such as instinctual urges or, as in the case of psychodrama, to spontaneity states. For Goffman, the self is an outcome of a performance—"a *product* of a scene that comes off, and . . . not a *cause* of it." (252) What, then, does Goffman see as the essence of the "individual as character performed"?

He has a capacity to learn, this being exercised in the task of training for a part. He is given to having fantasies and dreams, some that pleasurably unfold a triumphant performance, others full of anxiety and dread that nervously deal with vital discreditings in a public front region. He often manifests a gregarious desire for teammates and audiences, a tactful considerateness for their concerns; and he has a capacity for deeply felt shame, leading him to minimize the chances he takes of exposure.

These attributes of the individual *qua* performer are not merely a depicted effect of particular performances; they are psychobiological in nature, and yet they seem to arise out of intimate interaction with the contingencies of stage performances. (253-4)

Moreno also sees the self as emerging from the social roles which one plays,[3] but beyond this he has developed concepts of spontaneity, catharsis, creativity, tele, warming-up processes, and action-concepts which suggest a basically different conception of man and the forces that motivate him than that presented in Goffman's work. Here, for example, is Moreno's conceptualization of a "meeting":

"Meeting" means more than a vague inter-personal relation. . . . It means that two or more persons meet, but not only to face one another but to live and experience each other, as actors each in his own right, not like "professional" meeting (a case worker or a physician or a participant observer and their subjects), but a meeting of two people. In a meeting the two persons are there in space, with all their strengths and all their weaknesses, two human actors seething with spontaneity, only partly conscious of their mutual aims. . . . (251)

Indeed, it appears that it was Moreno's recognition of the dramatic aspects of everyday "meetings" that produced the idea of the psychodrama:

Looking backward it is now clear that from the idea of the meeting, the conflict between author and reader, reader and

[3] See the quotations in Section III of this paper which outline Moreno's position with respect to this point.

listener, husband and wife, each in his "role," it was only a short step from putting them on a stage on which they can battle their relationship out, unhindered by the threats and anxieties of their real life situation. This is how the idea of the psychodrama was born. (252)

In summary:

Goffman *describes* the dramaturgical elements of everyday life; Moreno *applies* dramaturgical principles in the psychodrama theatre.

Goffman focuses on ways in which a definition of a situation may be *maintained;* Moreno focuses on ways in which a definition of a situation may be changed.

Goffman concentrates on *"conserved"* behavior; Moreno concentrates on *"spontaneous"* behavior.

Goffman is concerned with the elements of *social control;* Moreno is concerned with the elements of *social liberation.*

Goffman takes the role, primarily, of *scientist-*observer; Moreno takes the role, primarily, of *scientist-actor.*

It is perhaps this last distinction which helps best to account for the fundamental dissimilarities between the conceptualizations of Goffman and Moreno.

III

Despite the basically different orientations of Moreno and Goffman, however, they are in agreement on many of the *elements,* and *contingencies* of dramaturgical action. The following quotations, then, suggest several areas in which Moreno's "psychodrama" and Goffman's "presentation" appear to converge, or are similar.

Both Goffman and Moreno appreciate the reality of the non-verbal level of communication:

Goffman

The expressiveness of the individual (and therefore his capacity to give impressions) appears to involve two radically different kinds of sign activity: the expression that he *gives,* and the expression that he *gives off.* The first involves verbal symbols or their substitutes which he uses admittedly and solely to convey the information that he and the others are known to attach to these symbols. This is communication in the traditional and narrow sense. The second involves a wide range of action that others can treat as symptomatic of the actor, the expectation being that the action was performed for reasons other than the information conveyed in this way. (2)

Moreno

One of the persistent problems of the actor-in-making in the traditional theatre lay in attaining coordination of body and word utterance and of eliminating those personal and idiosyncratic gestures which had nothing to do with the role.... But the old theatre failed to recognize that an organic and unalterable relation existed between the oral and mimetic utterance. Both in the old and in the Impromptu Theatre there is need for such training as will establish a persistent integration and a rich variety of bodily vocabulary. And this statement suggests that such a wealth of expressive facility is a desideratum no less in life at large than in the theatric reflection of it. (43)

... we recognized that non-semantic feeling complexes can be trained and that the exercise had an excellent therapeutic effect... .. Rather than psychotherapy it was *body therapy.* (217)

Both Goffman and Moreno appreciate the fact that much of social interaction is hidden:

Goffman

Many crucial facts lie beyond the time and place of interaction or lie concealed within it. For example, the "true" or "real" attitudes, beliefs, and emotions of the individual can be ascertained only indirectly, through his avowals or through what appears to be involuntary expressive behavior. (2)

Moreno

The problem of technique is to enable the auxiliary ego to overcome the inherent tragedy of our inter-personal world. Yet the insight which one person has about what goes on in the other person's mind is at best sketchy. We live simultaneously in different worlds which communicate only at times, and even then incompletely. The psyche is not transparent. *The full psychodrama of our interrelations does not emerge; it is buried in and between us.* (Italics in original, 190.)

Both Goffman and Moreno appreciate the collective aspects of role playing:

Goffman
Sometimes he will intentionally and consciously express himself in a particular way, but chiefly because the tradition of his group or social status require this kind of expression and not because of any particular response (other than vague acceptance or approval) that is likely to be evoked . . . by the expression. (6)

When an actor takes on an established social role, usually he finds that a particular front has already been established for it. (27)

Moreno
Every role is therefore a fusion of private and collective elements. Every role has two sides, a private and a collective side. (351)

Among the most significant phenomena which recur in practically every psychodramatic session are cultural conserves and cultural stereotypes. The participants fall irresistibly into them, spontaneously as if by tacit understanding. (246-7)

Both Goffman and Moreno see the "self" as arising from the role one plays and the setting in which the role is played, rather than vice-versa:

Goffman
The general notion that we make a presentation of ourselves to others is hardly novel; what ought to be stressed in conclusion is that the very structure of self can be seen in terms of how we

arrange for such performances in our Anglo-American society. (252)

... this self itself does not derive from its possessor, but from the whole scene of his action, being generated by that attribute of local events which renders them interpretable by witnesses. A correctly staged and performed scene leads the audience to impute a self to a performed character, but this imputation—this self—is a *product* of a scene that comes off, and is not the *cause* of it. (252)

In analyzing the self then we are drawn from its possessor, from the person who will profit or lose most by it, for he and his body merely provide a peg on which something will be hung for a time. (253)

Moreno

The resistance against psychodrama . . . arises because private problems are treated in public, private psychological properties, experiences of the most intimate kind which have always been considered as the last anchorage of the individual identity, are urged to be relinquished to the group. The individual is urged to face the truth that these experiences are not really "his," but public psychological property. (10-11)

Role playing is prior to the emergence of the self, but the self may emerge from the roles. (157)

The tangible aspects of what is known as "ego" are the roles in which he operates. . . . We consider roles and relationships between roles the most significant development within any specific culture. (161)

Role can be defined also as an assumed character or function within social realty. . . . Role can be defined as the actual and tangible forms which the self takes. (153)

Both Goffman and Moreno appreciate the importance of the "setting" in conducting performances:

Goffman

It is often felt that control of the setting is an advantage during interaction. In a narrow sense, this control allows a team to introduce strategic devices for determining the information the audience is able to require. (93)

. . . when a performance is given it is usually given in a highly bounded region, to which boundaries with respect to time are often added. The impression and understanding fostered by the performance will tend to saturate the region and time span, so that any individual located in this space-time manifold will be in a position to observe the performance and be guided by the definition of the situation which the performance fosters. (106)

Moreno

The therapeutic theatre is a stage setting so constructed that people can live through and project in an experimental situation, their own problems and actual lives, unhindered by the frozen patterns of daily living or the boundaries and resistance of ordinary existence. (328)

Both Goffman and Moreno appreciate the role of the "director" in guiding performances:

Goffman

When one examines a team-performance, one often finds that someone is given the right to direct and control the progress of the dramatic action. . . . Sometimes the individual who dominates the show in this way and is, in a sense, the director of it, plays an actual part in the performance he directs. (97)

In many performances two important functions must be fulfilled, and if the team has a director he will often be given the special duty of fulfilling these functions.

First, the director may be given the special duty of bringing back into line any member of the team whose performance becomes unsuitable. Soothing and sanctioning are the corrective processes ordinarily involved. . . . Secondly, the director may be given the special duty of allocating the parts in the performance and the personal front that is employed in each part. . . . (98-9)

. . . if the audience appreciates that the performance has a director, they are likely to hold him more responsible than other performers for the success of the performance. (99)

Moreno

The psychodramatic director has three functions: (a) he is a producer, (b) chief therapist, and (c) social analyst.

As a producer he is an engineer of coordination and production. . . . As a therapeutic agent, the last responsibility for the therapeutic value of the total production rests upon his shoulders. . . . As a social analyst he uses the auxiliary egos as extensions of himself to draw information from the subjects on the stage to test them, and to carry influence to them. (252)

. . . the psychodramatic director . . . must also be keenly aware of the abilities and limitations of the staff-members who are to function with or for the subject as auxiliary egos upon the stage. (260)

regardless, indeed, of whether or not [the director] does so subject himself [to analysis by the group of people who compose the psychodramatic audience at any given time]—he is nevertheless continuously exposed to observation and analysis by this group. (253)

Both Goffman and Moreno appreciate the importance of team members in staging a performance:

Goffman

It may even be said that if our special interest is the study of impression management, of the contingencies which arise in fostering an impression, and of the techniques for meeting these

contingencies, then the team and the team-performance may well
be the best units to take as the fundamental point of reference.
(80)

Moreno
The auxiliary ego has three functions: (a) the function of actor,
portraying roles required by the subject's world, (b) the function
of guidance, a therapeutic agent, (c) the function of social investigator. (259)

Both Goffman and Moreno appreciate the interaction of
audience and performers:

Goffman
. . . when we study concrete social establishments we often find
that there will be a significant sense in which all the remaining
participants, in their several performances of response to the
team-show put on before them, will themselves constitute a
team. Since each team will be playing through its routine for the
other, one may speak of dramatic interaction, not dramatic
action, and we can see this interaction not as a medley of as
many voice as there are participants but rather as a kind of
dialogue and interplay between two teams. . . . (91)

. . . it will sometimes be convenient to call one team the performers and to call the other team the audience or the observers. .
. . (92)

Moreno
The audience has two functions: (a) in relation to the subject and
the proceedings on the stage (production centered); (b) in
relation to itself (audience centered).

a) In relation to the subject it is the representation of
the world. . . .

b) In a psychodramatic session the audience is always the
patient, or at least, a learner. It may be unconscious of this
situation, as when witnessing a legitimate drama or a motion

picture or it may be made systematically conscious of it as in the theatre for the psychodrama. (261-2)

Both Goffman and Moreno appreciate that performances may be "disrupted":

Goffman

One over-all objective of any team is to sustain the definition of the situation that its performance fosters. This will involve the over-communication of some facts and the under-communication of others. Given the fragility and the required expressive coherence of reality that is dramatized by a performance, there are usually facts which, if attention is drawn to them during the performance, would discredit, disrupt, or make useless the impression that the performannce fosters. These facts may be said to provide "destructive information." A basic problem for many performances, then, is that of information control; the audience must not acquire destructive information about the situation that is being defined for them. (141)

Moreno

My first clinical observation of role dynamics was provoked by the conflict in which a legitimate actor finds himself when taking a part on the stage. An actor, when taking the part of Hamlet, has to suppress and reduce himself as a private person out of official existence, but the degree to which a given role can replace or fulfill the space of the private person of the actor is chronically incomplete. Behind the mask of Hamlet lurks the actor's private personality. I have often called this the *primary role-person conflict....* This conflict often produces serious disturbances in the private person of the actor, in the role production and in the relationship between the two. (153)

Both Goffman and Moreno appreciate that when audiences are enabled to see "behind" a performance, a learning experience may take place:

Goffman

In spite of the fact that performers and audience employ all of these techniques of impression management, and many others as well, we know, of course, that incidents do occur and that audiences are inadvertently given glimpses behind the scenes of a performance. When such an incident occurs, the members of an audience sometimes learn an important lesson, more important to them than the aggressive pleasure they can obtain by discovering someone's dark, entrusted, inside, or strategic secrets. The members of the audience may discover a fundamental democracy that is well hidden. Whether the character that is being presented is sober or carefree, of high station or low, the individual who performs the character will be seen for what he largely is, a solitary player involved in a harried concern for his production. Behind many masks and many characters, each performer tends to wear a single look, a naked unsocialized look, a look of concentration, a look of one who is privately engaged in a difficult, treacherous task. (235)

Moreno
The audience attending a conventional drama and the audience attending a psychodrama have different attitudes. The audience attending a conventional drama, although it faces a human drama for the first time, is aware that it is up to every particle a created conserve. . . . On the other hand, an audience attending a psychodrama has to develop a different attitude if it is to find any enjoyment at all. . . . What they experience is more painful, more lifelike, more like themselves, harder to accept because it is not always a flight from the present, but a deep penetration into its very essence, not only in content, but also in form and process. (pp. 389-90)

Psychodrama is here a counterpart of nudism. (187)

Both Goffman and Moreno appreciate the utility of the dramaturgical approach in dealing with either the description or the treatment of the problems of everyday life:

Goffman
To summarize, then, I assume that when an individual appears before others he will have many motives for trying to control the

impression they receive of the situation. This report is concerned with some of the common techniques that persons employ to sustain such impressions and with some of the common contingencies associated with the employment of these techniques. The specific content of any activity presented by the individual participant, or the role it plays in the interdependent activities of an ongoing social system, will not be at issue; I shall be concerned only with the person's dramaturgical problems of presenting the activity before others. The issues dealt with by stagecraft and stage management are sometimes trivial but they are quite general; they seem to occur everywhere in social life; providing a clear-cut dimension for formal sociological analysis. (15)

Moreno

The subject in the therapeutic theatre is placed at a distance from his daily life and milieu—a position which he rarely is able to achieve under everyday circumstances. The theatre is an objective setting in which the subject can act out his problems or difficulties relatively free of the anxieties and pressures of the outside world. In order to accomplish this, the total situation of the subject in the outside world has to be duplicated, on a spontaneous level, in the experimental setting of the theatre and—even more than this—the hidden roles and invisible interhuman relations he may have experienced have to find a visible expression. This means that certain functions—a stage, lights, a recording system, auxiliary egos, and a director—have to be introduced. (328)

The quotations here presented by no means exhaust the comparisons which might be made between the Goffman and the Moreno applications of dramaturgical principles to their respective areas of interest. Nor do these quotations by themselves provide a comprehensive picture of the *Presentation* or Psychodrama frameworks in all of their ramifications. Moreover, it must be recognized that removing quotations from their overall context, however carefully, may often change the intended meaning of the quotation. Nevertheless, even while recognizing the drawbacks of the parallel quotation method, it would appear demonstrated that a substantial portion of the Goffman scheme is either explicit or implicit in psychodrama theory and method. Inasmuch as Goffman's analysis may be applied to the description of *any* social establishment, a certain degree of implicitness is probably to be expected; for example, we could say that Goffman's framework is "implicit" in the organization of a football team, as well as in psychodrama. But beyond this necessary degree of implicitness, it seems to me that Moreno, in developing and describing his psychodrama theory and techniques has systematically taken into account most of the elements of dramaturgical interaction to which Goffman has called attention. On the other hand, Goffman has offered a more concise, explicit, and systematic presentation of these elements than is to be found in Moreno's work, and in addition, of course, Goffman has contributed many insights into the dramaturgical organization of everyday life.

IV

Perhaps the Goffman and Psychodrama approaches can most fruitfully converge in the area of the experimental study of the elements of everyday social interaction to which Goffman calls attention. Goffman, himself, has suggested that it might be best to start with the study of smaller social establishments or with particular statuses and "document comparisons and changes in a modest way by means of the case history methods." (245) But it would appear that the psychodrama stage offers greater potential than natural life for systematically studying interactions of various types, under controlled conditions. As Moreno has observed:

> The therapeutic theatre . . . is a place in which, through psychodramatic means, all situations and roles which the world produces or may produce are enacted. (182)

Indeed, the very interaction that occurs between the protagonist, the auxiliary egos, the director, and the audience at a psychodrama session should provide a fruitful testing ground for the Goffman theoretical framework and for the development of new insights and hypotheses into the nature of human cooperation and communication.

Of particular value in systematically exploring social interaction under controlled conditions may be psychodramatic techniques such as the mirror technique, the projection technique of role-reversal, the symbolic distance technique, the substitute role technique, the double ego technique, the technique of alternating role-acting, and the auxiliary world technique. Not the least of the advantages of using the psychodrama stage for the study of everyday social processes is the ability of the experimenter to hold certain variables constant. In fact, Moreno already has shown how this may be done in his development of the Spontaneity Test. (123 ff.) The controlled setting of the psychodrama performance further lends itself to an intimate study of audience-performer interaction, and, indirectly, to the processes of social control. In short, whatever the differences and similarities of the Moreno and Goffman approaches, the techniques of the psychodrama would appear to have considerable utility for the experimental investigation of the social processes of everyday life.

37. SOCIOANALYSIS AND PSYCHOANALYSIS

Martin R. Haskell

At the twenty-first annual meeting of the American Society of Group Psychotherapy and Psychodrama, held in New York City in 1962, Dr. Moreno suggested that those who based their therapeutic approach on sociometric theory, whether engaged in group psychotherapy, individual therapy or psychodrama apply the term "socioanalysis" to describe their work. He expressed the view that it was essential to reach a consensus around a single term which would be clearly differentiated from psychoanalysis. The term "socioanalysis" seemed most appropriate to him because it had always been his position that in psychotherapy we must deal with the socius, the whole man in interaction with others. It is not a segment of an individual that is involved in any action. Since the entire individual must be involved, no reduction to simpler elements of abstraction can prove adequate. The purpose of this paper is to present a discussion of the theoretical basis of socioanalysis and its application to psychotherapy.

The Moreno system, upon which socioanalysis is based, consists of: (1) an image of man; (2) a theory of spontaneity; (3)

Presidential address delivered at the 21st Annual Meeting, American Society of Group Psychotherapy and Psychodrama, April 6-8, 1962, Hotel Sheraton-Atlantic, New York, N.Y. Reprinted with the permission of the publishers from *Group Psychotherapy*, Vol. XV, No. 2 (June, 1962) pp. 105-113.

a theory of sociometry; (4) the methodology of Psychodrama; and (5) Socioanalytic Psychotherapy. Moreno and others have published hundreds of books and articles in these areas. In this discussion an attempt will be made to extract from this enormous literature some aspects which have a direct relevance to socioanalysis as psychotherapy.

1. *The Moreno Image of Man*-To Moreno man is a creative being. Creation is a continuous process in which man, in interaction with other men, is constantly participating in the creation of the world. The universe is a creation in continuous development with every new individual born having a part to play in the creation of the world to come. The world which a man finds at birth is a world which billions of his fellow beings have aided in creating. Man is not seen as opposed to society nor is society seen as hostile to man. On the contrary, man is a willing and active participant sharing in the creation. (9)

2. *Theory of Spontaneity*-The Moreno theory of Spontaneity is the core of his theory of action. Spontaneity he defines as the variable degree of adequate response to a situation with a variable degree of novelty. Of itself, novelty of behavior is not the measure of spontaneity. Novelty must be qualified by adequacy in a situation. The individual must bring into the situation a knowledge of the roles appropriate to that situation and the limits of permissable deviation. (8) Sociologists and Social Psychologists will recognize that Mead (6) and Cooley (2) have formulated postulates explaining the way in which an individual learns to take the role of other and thereby internalizes the culture. But Moreno insists that before the individual learns to take a role he must play the role. He sees man as the role player who, after acquiring the cultural conserve, acts, improvises, exercises spontaneity and creates. It is important to remember, however, that unless the individual is familiar with the cultural conserve, unless he knows the limitations placed by society on performance in a role, his spontaneity may be pathological. The range of responses may

be characterized as follows: (a) A new novel response occurring without adequacy. This may result in undisciplined or pathological spontaneity. (b) An adequate response occurring without significant characteristics of novelty and creativity. This may evidence tendencies toward rigid conformity. (c) An adequate response occurring with characteristics of novelty and creativity. Such a response is evidence of healthy spontaneity.

Warner summarizes the relationship between spontaneity and creativity in his review of "Who Shall Survive?" (12) Spontaneity, he points out, is a concept of organization, that which the actor in interaction participates in reality producing. Alternatives are conflict, evasion, rigidity, or isolation, each of which disrupts the free flow of interaction. The result for the individual and the group is pathological. For the individual it is the pathological phenomenon of ill health. For the actor, action is a learning process. In a series of stages, social perception is sharpened and motive pattern is continuously shaped. When the actor brings to any situation his initial perceptions and motives and gears into the responses perceptions and motives of others there occurs the development of perception and motive patterns of each which is functional to the intergration of personality. To act out one's perceptions and motives under these conditions is reality producing as well as reality testing. Order depends upon change and not to change is disorder producing. The individual does not internalize the cultural patterns in a fixed way. He encounters them in his own variable perceptions and in the forms presented to him by the group. He acts upon them. The way he plays each role is unique. At every stage there is reformulation and fresh construction. The product is a creation. Creativity is the quality of the action that is thus "reality producing." Creativity is a property of the act itself. Spontaneity is related to the readiness for the act.

The implications for therapy are clear. To counter the negative categories of anxiety, fear and defense, Moreno proposes a positive category, spontaneity. Frustration, projection, substitution and sublimation are negative categories and presuppose a positive category, creativity. All men are endowed with spontaneity and creativity although there may be considerable individual differences in degree of endowment. They exist sui generis. They are not identical with intelligence or memory. They are not derived from conditioned reflexes nor are they reducible to instinctive sexual responses. Therapeutic goals would therefore center around the development of spontaneity and creativity, with the qualification that spontaneity in roles be developed along with or subsequent to the development of adequacy. An auxiliary goal would therefore be to develop adequacy of response where this is lacking. Role Training, for example, could be used to familiarize the individual with the cultural and social conserve at the same time facilitating the development of spontaneity that is potentially creative. (3) (5)

3. *Moreno's Sociometric Theory*-As a technique for measurement of social configurations sociometry is so well established in social psychology and sociology that many social scientists and psychotherapists lose sight of the theoretical framework in which Moreno developed it. Sociometric theory puts a strong emphasis upon group dynamics and group action as well as upon measurement and evaluation. There are three concepts essential to an understanding of sociometric theory. Familiarity with these concepts will make clear the relevance of sociometry to socioanalytic therapy. They are; the social atom, sociometric choice, and tele.

The social atom is the nucleus of all individuals toward whom a person is significantly related and who, at the same time, are related to him. The relationship may be emotional, social or cultural. The social atom, then, may be represented as the sum of interpersonal structures resulting from choices and rejections centered about a given individual. The social atom is seen as dynamic. Changes are in process with or without the active intervention of the individual. The individual, however, may initiate changes in his social atom by modifying his behavior or by withdrawing from some groups and-or affiliating with others. Socioanalytic therapy may be directed at obtaining a modification of the social atom of the individual.

Sociometric choice provides us with an instrument for determining the social atom of the individual. All interpersonal actions are conceptualized as mutual interplays of total readiness of individuals. Since they overtly manifest themselves as emotional tensions of attractions and repulsions, we may chart the volume and direction of the actors' tendencies to move toward or away from one another. To chart these choices, we may employ formal methods; sociometric tests and sociograms, or we may note them informally. Every individual is simultaneously the focus of numerous attractions and repulsions, and the focus of numerous roles which are related to the roles of other individuals. These roles are in various stages of development and the tangible aspects of what is known as "ego" or "self" are the roles in which the person operates. Thus, every person is positively or negatively related to an indefinite number of others who in turn may be related to him, positively or negatively. The image the individual develops of himself is developed while he is performing in the various roles and informally preparing his own sociogram. Mead and Cooley came to similar conclusions with respect to the development of the self. Moreno, however, has more clearly related the development of self to the specific roles in which the individual plays and he has, furthermore, established a methodology for producing changes in the "self." (11)

The third key concept is, "Tele." Tele represents insight into and appreciation of feeling for the actual makeup of the other person. It is not merely empathy, the ability to take the role of another in a given situation. It is the ability to assume the feelings of the other to every situation, including the situation involving the self. Tele is responsible for increased mutuality of choices and increased rates of interaction. Neither transference nor empathy can explain the emergent cohesion of a social configuration. Tele can. At the outset of psychotherapy we usually find Tele present to some extent. Increases in Tele are noted as the sessions go on and the patient improves. The development of increased Tele is a goal of socioanalysis and should be of all sound psychotherapy.

Sociometric theory is based, then, on the idea that we never deal with an individual in isolation but with the individual in relationships. The individual appears to seek persistently for regard, esteem and affection towards himself as a person. When this seeking meets with reciprocation he shows himself able to relate well to others and to their goals in common group oriented settings. When, however, he is blocked from fulfillment on a person-to-person level his pattern in group oriented settings is unfulfilling in fundamental satisfactions. It has been demonstrated that fulfillment in less intimate groups (work groups, and school groups), may produce changes in patterns of behavior in our most intimate groups (family). Changes in sociometric position are important criteria of success in therapy. If the individual rises sociometrically, that is, if he is chosen more often in any of his groups, his self image improves and he moves toward recovery. (4) (8)

4. *Psychodrama and Role Playing Methods in Socioanalysis*-The work of Moreno in Psychodrama is too well known and too voluminous to be dealt with adequately in this paper. Psychodrama is an action method as is role playing. Both begin with a warming up process in which the spontaneity of the participants seeks expression. After a warming up period we have what Moreno calls the "Begegnung" or encounter. In the encounter there is an intuitive reversal of roles, a realization of self through the other, reciprocity. The encounter is extemporaneous, unstructured, unplanned and unrehearsed. It is in the here and now and in the becoming. To Moreno, it, rather than psychoanalytic transference is the real basis of the psychotherapeutic process. We then have the action, in which

the director, his instruments and staff assist the actor to proceed to the terminus of the act. Actors act out fully what they bring to and find in a situation. They do not repress or evade the commitments to interaction. It is in the interaction that the actors find out what the interpersonal reality is. The act is an emergent. It is always a new thing depending on what *A* brings to it and how *A* and *B* affect one another in interpersonal relations. The individual brings to the act a cultural conserve, the base of the culture, the stabilized role structure. The contact is invaluable. The emphasis is on how the actors construct their roles in the course of the action itself. If the Psychodrama occurs in a group setting there is then group participation. Each member of the group may identify with any portion of the action presented or any role enacted.

The role of the director in a Psychodrama may be relatively passive or active. He may be non-didactic, serving merely as a catalyst, or he may be didactic if his clinical judgment so dictates. In every case, however, he must respect the integrity of the patient. Psychodrama is socioanalytic because it begins the analysis of an act with a person in a role and develops and expands it in the course of interaction involving the full range of the individual's roles. Any therapy is socioanalytic to the degree in which it gives the patient research status and to the degree in which it is able to measure his activities. Psychodrama seeks to increase spontaneity, tele, creativity, and sociometric status in the therapeutic group and in the social atom of the individual.

To summarize, in Psychodrama and Role Playing, interpersonal action is dealt with as an emergent. Psychodrama and Role Playing replicate, as nearly as possible, interaction, and are thus suitable for the analysis of interaction. Roles and relationships between roles are the most significant elements of every culture. The tangible aspect of what is known as ego or self are the roles in which the self operates. Role Training may be considered as an experimental procedure, a method of learning to perform roles more adequately. In Psychodrama as well as in Role Training, the irreducible character of the data sets its own limits. We can observe data or manipulate them for any therapeutic purpose; goal achieving, efficiency, play or learning. (7) (10)

5. *Socioanalytic Psychotherapy-* Socioanalytic methods, whether applied to individual or group therapy seek to promote functioning in society. As has been previously noted, Moreno totally rejects the assumption that there is a basic conflict between the individual and society or groups. In socioanalytic group psychotherapy each man is a therapeutic agent for the other. The individual is never isolated from the reality of the group. As in Psychodrama, acting-out is a precise point of diagnosis and of treatment. The distinction is merely one of degree. Socioanalytic Group Psychotherapy is conducted more on a verbal level than is Psychodramatic Group Therapy and more emphasis is placed on the structure and function of the synthetic group, the therapeutic group. In both methods the actor and the act are studied through the matrix of a group.

Socioanalytic Psychotherapy may begin with a dyadic relationship including only the therapist and the patient. This form of therapy is usually referred to as individual psychotherapy. In this form socioanalysis focuses on the social atom of the individual, his sociometric positions in the various groups in which he functions or is required to function and his aspirations. Historical regression is not undertaken unless the patient indicates a conscious awareness of the relationship between his position in past groups and his sociometric status in present groups. The socioanalytic therapist does not employ suggestibility in an effort to historically regress to an original trauma. The emphasis of socioanalytic individual psychotherapy is on preparing the individual to function adequately—first in a therapeutic group and finally in the social groups of his society.

Socioanalytic Group Psychotherapy begins with the interaction of members and the participation and guidance of a director. If free spontaneous interaction is permitted, a new operational frame of reference develops from which one can look at the successive stages of a synthetic group.

a. The first concern is immediate behavior. A sociogram, whether arrived at by formal or informal means, reveals subgroups and isolates.

b. The common interactional matrix which the individuals share, with its changing constellation and cohesiveness is expressed in multiple emotional tensions.

c. The longer a synthetic group endures, the more it begins to resemble a natural group and to develop and share an unconscious life, from which members draw strength, knowledge and security.

d. The role reversal of every member with every other member. The more different and especially distant the members are, the more urgent it is that they reverse roles with each other in the course of mutual therapy. It is the final touch, giving unity, identity and universality to the group.

Self awareness and self evaluation are products of social interaction, therefore, as a man rises in sociometric status his self image improves. This begins in the synthetic group and carries over to other groups, from the less intimate to the most intimate.

6. *Socioanalysis and Psychoanalysis* -It should be apparent from the foregoing that socioanalysis and psychoanalysis have basic theoretical and methodological differences. The Moreno image of man, the creator in interaction, differs significantly from Freud's image of man. Freud saw life as a struggle between man and society. The Intrapsychic struggle between Id, Ego and Superego as the basis of psychoanalytic theory differes radically from the 'Spontaneity-Creativity theory of Moreno. Psychoanalysis has no quantitative measure of progress. Socioanalysis rests on sociometry as a method of quantifying change. Finally, the methodology of psychoanalysis, which is based on transference and free

association, employing historical regression to an original trauma, differs completely from Psychodrama and Socioanalytic Psychotherapy which deal with the here and now and the emergent.

Adler rejected the Freudian image of man and recognized the social aspects of man's existence. The three life problems he considered most significant were related to functioning in occupational, family and social roles. Although Adler viewed the person as a striving member of a larger group and inquired into social factors he did not develop a methodology for the analysis of social relationships. His followers still pursue a historical approach exploring early recollections and childhood trauma. (1) Horney, Fromm, Sullivan and other Neo-Freudians considered by Ansbacher to be Neo-Adlerian have introduced modifications to Psychoanalysis. In varying degrees they recognize the social nature of man and accept adequacy in social functioning as a therapeutic goal. They have failed to develop a Socioanalytic methodology, employ methods that are largely verbal, and center their therapies around historical regression.

Freud belonged to nineteenth century Europe. His psychoanalytic theory was based on observations of emotionally disturbed persons socialized in a patriarchal family. The principal group, frequently the only group which influenced the socialization of the nineteenth century child, was the family. It was not unusual for trauma experienced in such a family constellation to have lasting repercussions. Freud confirmed his theoretical framework by observations made on products of this family system.

Moreno, although born in Europe, was involved in considerable research in the United States during the 1930s and subsequent to that time. His theoretical position was either formulated or reformulated as a result of this research. The society he observed was characterized by multi-group membership, a relatively democratic family structure, and increasing peer group influence on socialization. The all powerful patriarch who headed the Viennese family of the nineteenth century was not present. Trauma experienced in the twentieth century American family may be counteracted by satisfying relationships in school groups, play groups, athletic groups and all sorts of other peer groups which influence socialization. Furthermore, trauma experienced as a result of rejection in any of a number of such groups may seriously disturb an individual whose early family life was ideal. Status in all sorts of groups became important in this sort of society. Analysis of status and patterns of choice and rejection in such groups is therefore of great import. The Psychoanalysis of Freud is based upon nineteenth century and early twentieth century Europe characterized by the patriarchal family and the lack of multi-group membership. The Socioanalysis of Moreno is based upon and is applicable to an industrial and urban civilization characterized by multi-group membership and peer group influences on socialization. The Socioanalysis of Moreno belongs to the twentieth century, the here and now.

REFERENCES

1. Ansbacher, H.L., and Ansbacher, Rowena R. (Eds.), *The Individual Psychology of Alfred Adler*, New York: Basic Books, 1956.

2. Cooley, Charles H., *Human Nature and the Social Order*, New York: Scribner's, 1922.

3. Haskell, Martin R., Role Training and Job Placement of Adolescent Delinquents: The Berkshire Farm After-Care Program, *Group Psychotherapy*, September 1959.

4. Haskell, Martin R., Toward a Reference Group Theory of Juvenile Delinquency, *Social Problems*, Winter, 1961.

5. Haskell, Martin R., and Weeks, H. Ashley, Role Training as Preparation for Release from a Correctional Institution. *The Journal of Criminal Law, Criminology and Police Science*, January 1960.

6. Mead, George H., *Mind, Self and Society*, University of Chicago Press, 1934.

7. Moreno, J.L., *Psychodrama Vol. I, 1946 and Psychodrama Vol. II 1958*, Beacon House, Beacon, N.Y.

8. Moreno, J.L. (Ed.), *The Sociometry Reader*, Glencoe, Illinois: The Free Press, 1960.

9. Moreno, J.L., *Who Shall Survive?*, 1953, Beacon House, Beacon, N.Y.

10. Moreno, J.L., and Jennings, Helen H., *Spontaneity Training*, Psychodrama Monograph No. 4, Beacon House, 1944.

11. Moreno, J.L., The Role Concept, A Bridge Between Psychiatry and Sociology. *American Journal of Psychiatry*, Vol. 117, December 1961.

12. Warner, Wellman J., Sociology and Psychiatry, Review of *Who Shall Survive?* by J.L. Moreno. *British Journal of Sociology*, Vol. V., No. 3, September 1954.

38. MORENO AND MOWRER,
OR THE NEW GROUP THERAPY

Lawrence A. Wolfe

What is the "new group therapy"? Hobart Mowrer has recently completed a book called *The New Group Therapy*.[1] In this paper the author attempts to answer this question. If the reader becomes somewhat disheartened by the answer, he is not alone.

Mowrer's New Group Therapy is compared with Moreno's Psychodrama. This comparison is not exhaustive in relationship to either the comparison or the individual theories. The scope of this paper is circumscribed by the limited knowledge of the author.

Psychodrama is not completely presented in this paper. It has been assumed that the reader is familiar with psychodrama.

In essence, the new group therapy "consists of anything which anyone can do to help persuade an estranged, 'neurotic' person (1) to voluntarily confess his mistakes, so that conscience does not have to force the truth out of him 'symptomatically' and (2) to enter into a life of willing sacrifice, instead of the involuntary suffering and sacrifice which neurosis involves."

Reprinted with the permission of the original publishers from *Group Psychotherapy*, Vol. XVIII, No. 3, (September, 1965) pp. 171-176.

[1] Mowrer, O. Hobart. *The New Group Therapy*. New York: D. Van Nostrand, 1964.

Such a macroscopic view is not very enlightening. Let us take a closer look. What does Mowrer mean by it "consists of anything which anyone can do"? This statement is so non-specific that it is almost meaningless. However, Mowrer has few suggestions to implement this procedure. One way is by "example and testimony of other erstwhile sufferers, who have themselves made the 'detour' and found wholeness and strength."

At first glance, this may seem similar to one of the methods in psychodrama. However, from Mowrer's description it does not sound very spontaneous. The erstwhile sufferers, one by one, get up to tell their story. This is artificial, and might be called role taking as defined by Moreno, i.e., the taking of a finished, fully established role which does not permit the individual any variation, any degree of freedom. One could picture these "sufferers" getting up at each new meeting they go to, and telling the same story.

This method may be used in psychodrama, but it will develop spontaneously from the group interaction. It will not be artificially induced.

Another procedure to enhance this new group therapy is for the "therapist" to meet privately with a person and listen to their problem. After discussing the problem, the therapist would suggest the person confess to the group.

In Moreno's terminology, this is a method of "warm-up." In psychodrama, the warm-up is not only helpful, but it is essential. One may question the use of such "private" warm-ups. A psychodrama with only two people is not unheard of but, when they take place, they are not used as a preliminary warm-up to another session. They are important in and of themselves. Such a dyad psychodrama is a "real" psychodrama, not a preliminary.

Another means of promoting the neurotic person to talk about his "sins" is for the therapist to share his emotion. To quote Mowrer:

It has been my recurrent observation that neurotic persons, in general, are much more reluctant to talk about themselves—and their sins—if the therapist himself preserves a highly impersonal, detached, and 'professional' pose than they are if, at appropriate points, the therapist takes the lead in sharing his deepest and most painful personal experiences with the patient, rather than expecting the revelatory transaction to be all in one direction.

In other words, "the chief therapist becomes part of the group." But, this last small quote is taken from Moreno's book, which was written way before Mowrer's "recurrent observations." This two-way empathy is one of the cardinal principles of psychodrama. This principle goes back to the sociometric system, which is the foundation of psychodrama, and the rule of "co-action." The distinction between doctor and patient was broken a long time ago by Moreno.

It is slowly becoming evident that Mowrer's "new" therapy is not so new. Conspicuously absent from Mowrer's book is any reference to Moreno's works. More will be said about this later.

Mowrer points out that one needs courage to make self-disclosures. And the best way to get courage is to have faith. The best way to get that faith and courage is to "hear the testimony of others who have themselves made this journey and are willing to 'stay with' the neophyte while he does so."

Moreno describes a similar process:

. . . in a psychodrama or sociodrama when we instruct a participant, individual, or group, to act out problems we plead with them to expose themselves unselfishly; in other words, these are ethical prescriptions: (1) give truth and receive truth, (2) give love to the group and it will return love to you, and (3) give spontaneity and spontaneity will return.

Once again we will go back to the definition of the new group therapy. Mowrer says it consists of anything which anyone can do, etc. One cannot be sure that Mowrer really means "anyone." Mowrer points out that professional leadership is dimly viewed. If this is true, how does Mowrer, a professional, lead these groups? This seems somewhat contradictory.

On the other hand, in psychodrama, the position of the leader on direction is more lucid. He has three functions: producer, counselor, and analyst. It is not within the scope of this paper to elaborate the functions of a director. Suffice it to say that he must be well trained and extremely flexible. But he is not alone in his responsibilities, for the group shares them with him.

Mowrer speaks of the "estranged neurotic" individual. He views neurotic difficulties as commonly having their roots in unresolved personal guilt, rather than in the unfortunate or traumatic things that happen to us. He goes on to say . . . "guilt which forms the core of neurosis will be admitted involuntarily symptomatically, if it has not previously been revealed to at least a few other persons and atoned for, in a conscious and deliberate way."

Now we begin to see some of the underlying assumptions of Mowrer's therapy. A neurotic is a person who has "sinned," i.e., who has broken the mores of society (or perhaps more accurately, who has broken the mores of Mowrer). But, according to Mowrer, not all mistakes or "sins" lead to neurotic difficulties. Some people "get caught," and some voluntarily confess and "take the consequences." And others just don't have enough conscience to be bothered. But persons of good character who are neither fortunate enough to be caught nor wise enough to confess, develop an increasing disposition, as time goes on, to experience the emotions and display the actions which we call "symptoms."

Here we see the essence of Mowrer's New Group Therapy. If a person voluntarily confesses his mistakes or sins, and enters into a life of willing sacrifice, he is "suddenly" healthy. To quote Mowrer: . . . "those persons who are able to benefit from it do so in an unusually rapid way."

How is it that the neurotic is able to become healthy so fast? Mowrer postulates that the critical element in "mental health" is the degree of openness and communion which a person has with his fellow men. It follows from this premise that the more open an individual is the more healthy he would be. To be more specific, Mowrer "assumes that there is no magic[2] at all in admitting 'who we are' to one person unless we (1) progressively extend our openness to significant others in our lives (2) take active steps to change our behavior and rectify past injustices and (3) becoming willing to use our new openness and strength in a helping relationship with others."

To illuminate the process even more, Mowrer brings in the idea of a balance sheet. Thus, if we perform a good deed we advertise it, display it—and thus collect and enjoy the credit. "But when we do something cheap and mean, we carefully hide it and deny it, with the result that the 'credit'[3] for acts of this kind remain with us and 'accumulate.' A person who follows such a life style is chronically bankrupt in the moral and spiritual sense." Following from this, Mowrer guides neurotic individuals into a "twofold strategy which involves (a) confession of past misdeeds and (b) concealment of present and future 'good works.'"

Mowrer fails to see any contradiction in this last statement. If one conceals things, then one is being less open and if one is less open, it should necessarily follow that one is less healthy.

This type of therapy is rather limited in its application. As Mowrer explains, there are persons who can talk freely and there are those who will not do so under any circumstances. He goes on to say "that it is the group which is in between these two which can often be quickly and deeply reached by this approach." What about the others?

Compare this with psychodrama which includes all of this, but leaves out the "magic" and balance sheet. Psychodrama is not limited to the intermediate group. It is not always necessary to be the subject in a psychodrama to benefit from it. The whole group becomes involved in the psychodrama. One can become

[2] Mowrer even seems to be saying it is magic.
[3] It seems 'liability' would be a better word.

involved without verbal participation. One becomes engrossed both physically and vicariously. It is not necessary to "sin" in order to profit from psychodrama.

Let us examine the concept of "sin" in greater depth. The following quote is helpful in understanding the meaning of sin:

> Conscience is a product of community life and experience, and is designed to keep the individual in community, i.e., "good." Sin, in its most broadly defensible definition, is a rupture of this relationship, and there is, by the very nature of the case, no private solution possible for the personal "condition" thus created.

This is a fairly objective definition of sin. However, Mowrer does not leave it this way. He points out that in a democratic society, the danger is that we will be too self-indulgent, too laissez faire, too tolerant, and not enough disposed toward planful renunciation, and a disciplined way of life. This applies especially to the sexual area.

Mowrer gives an example of how the release of sexual taboos creates a problem. He cites an "experiment" which had taken place in Russia. "Divorce, which had previously been difficult to obtain in Russia, became extremely easy; a postal card notifying the other partner that the relationship was ended would suffice. Incest, bigamy, and adultry were dropped from the list of official crimes and abortion was explicitly permitted by the decree of November 20, 1920." He goes on to say: "Short of sanctioning homosexuality and the other perversions, the government had gone as far as it could, it would seem, in guaranteeing complete sexual liberty."

What were the results? "Dissolution of family ties, especially of the parent-child relations, threatened to produce a wholesale dissolution of community ties, with rapidly increasing juvenile delinquency as the main symptom."

Mowrer presents this example to show us the importance of maintaining high sexual morals. We will not argue with this allegation. However, we will take issue with this example as proof of his statement. Mowrer points out that the reason the government "decreed" this change was because Engel had suggested it. The failure of the experiment would not come as a surprise to students of Moreno. These changes did not develop spontaneously from the group or population, but were "forced" on them by the government. There was no warm-up to the change. The idea of the change came from one man, and the results therefore, depend in part how adequately he was able to gauge the sociodyamic forces operating in the population. Perhaps he was a "stale" leader.

Mowrer indicates the strength that neurotics possess. "If the 'hysteric' has sinned and deceived he also has the decency (ultimately) to punish himself in attempted atonement." He goes on to say, "What we see as 'illness' (depression, anxiety, panic) is thus, in reality, a manifestation of underlying 'health' and characterological 'strength.'" Mowrer goes on to talk about neurotics in such glowing terms that one might feel "ill" because one is not neurotic.

By now it should be apparent that the "new group therapy" is really not very new, nor is it very comprehensive in scope. Individuals that can profit from this type of therapy are rather limited. 'the new group therapy is limited to verbal communication. Psychodrama has no such limit. "According to psychodramatic theory, a considerable part of the psyche is not language-ridden, it is not infiltrated by the ordinary, significant language symbols. Therefore, bodily contact with subjects, if it can be established, touch, caress, embrace, handshake, sharing in silent activities, are an important preliminary to psychodramatic work itself."

The stage or living space is multi-dimensional and extremely flexible. Where reality is often narrow and restraining, the psychodramatic stage is not. Here the person can deal with fantasy, delusions, or hallucinations. In this "surplus" reality, one can try new ways of behaving. Such flexibility is lacking in Mowrer's therapy.

Thus, we see that psychodrama is so much more comprehensive and flexible than Mowrer's new group therapy. The techniques which Mowrer presents are already presented and more fully developed by Moreno. The methods, techniques, and principles behind psychodrama are much more developed than Mowrer's new group therapy.

Mowrer could have saved many "recurrent observations" and much time if he had read Moreno first.

REFERENCES

Moreno, J.L. *Who Shall Survive?* New York: Beacon House, 1953.

Mowrer, O.H., *Some constructive features of the concept of sin.* J. Couns. Pschy. (7) 1960, 185-188.

Mowrer, O.H., *The new group therapy.* New York: D. Van Nostrand, 1964.

Yablonsky, L., & Enneis, J.M., *Psychodrama theory and practice.* Progress in Psychotherapy, 1956, 149-161.

39. THE TRAGIC ORIGINS AND COUNTERTRAGIC EVOLUTION OF PSYCHODRAMA

Anna B. Brind and Nah Brind

Psychodrama had many roots to grow by and from: The stirring undercurrents of Bergsonian thought and early existentialism at the turn of the century, the turbulent, Marx-marked years immediately following World War I, J. L. Moreno's personal make-up, his dream of being God the Brother rather than God the Father, his embryonic social action as pioneer sociometrist, his psychiatrist training, and his theatrical experience, to name but the biographically most discernible tributaries.

This paper is primarily concerned with the last name source of origin, partly in order to avoid dispersion of attention and partly because the authors consider the theatrical experience to have been the most decisively formative matrix of Moreno's early conceptualizations.

Indeed, it seems at times, perhaps erroneously, that Moreno's basic tenets may be deducted directly and unitracedly from his congenial and fruitful contact with the theater and the drama.

We have touched upon this subject in a brief paper published in a quarterly International Journal of Sociometry and Sociatry, v. III, No. 1-2, 1963, and recapitulate here only in passing that the psychodramatic principles of Action, Collectivity, Spon-

Reprinted with the permission of the publishers from *Group Psychotherapy,* Vol. XIX, Nos. 1 and 2 (1966), pp. 94-106.

taneity, and, to be sure, the psychodramatic stage itself are close linear descendants of Moreno's Theater of Improvisations, or, better yet, of his Theater of Selfenactment.

This curtailment of subject matter leaves this paper dealing 'only' with Moreno's ingenious dethronement of Tragedy, with his extraordinary transmutation of litero-esthetic theater into therapeutic psychodrama.

LITERARY DRAMA

Conflict Resolution is the subject of all dramatic literature. The Action which drama portrays is not just any kind of action. It is the action of combat, of belligerent collision. Drama always presents someone's struggle against somebody or something.

While drama's fighting protagonist has always been man, either in his natural semblance or in various symbolic disguises, both his antagonist and the locus luctationis have been less strictly defined.

In the first great concentration of dramatic creativity of our Western civilization, the Classic tragedy, the deadly bout had been between man and the super-power of a god, or between man and the inexorable march of some mysterious destiny.

By the very nature of this contest, its arena was outside man, somewhere between him and his external adversary. Very vaguely visualized, the field of battle of the Greek tragedy was the entirety of life, the cosmos, the great unknown.

Man himself was seen as essentially unbroken, as an indivisibly whole entity. A great deal of the cathartic experience induced by tragedy consisted exactly in the spectator's exhilirating and prideful identification with the protagonist's unyielding assertion of his monolithic immutability, even in defeat—particularly in his hour of final defeat. Man could be crushed, but he could not be made to give in, to compromise his identity at the will of whatever power in heaven or on earth.

The theater of the Renaissance, despite some surface appearances, was not a simple reiteration or emulation of the Greek achievement. In its culminating summit, that is, in Shakespeare, a major substantial metamorphosis of the total dramatic concept had been accomplished.

With Shakespeare, man became, for the first time in the history of literary drama, his own antagonist, and the jousting arena was consequently located within man himself.

When King Lear ragingly suffers the consequences of his decisions, it is a wise Lear flagellating his own blind and foolish self. When Macbeth hears the otherwise inaudible voices crying out: "Macbeth does murder sleep! Macbeth shall sleep no more!"—something within his own self has obviously destroyed his one-goal, one-character integrity. As a matter of fact, Lady Macbeth makes it explicit as she asks him: "Who was it that thus cried: Why do you unbend your noble strength to think so brainsickly of things?" (Note: Her words appropriately sound like a diagnosis of hallucinatory paranoia rather than a literary, or rhetorical, or wifely question!)

And Hamlet, the fascinating, psychologically precocious prince, one of Shakespeare's greatest discoveries and the perennial prototype of man against himself, actually raises the ultimate question whether man can go on at all with this forever bifurcating innermost core of his.

Indeed, Shakespeare's prodigious fecundity, his obsessive and unequaled spawning of more and more idiosyncratically nuanced characters, including fools, buffoons, madmen, and simulators of mental derangement, his passim outcropping and truly tragic thought flashes (like Gloster's, Though the wisdom of nature can reason it thus and thus, yet nature finds itself scourged by sequent events . . .) permit the assumption that mankind's greatest tragedian—if he was indeed a single person—had an intuitive inkling of man's psychic fragmentation way beyond the innocuous schizoid vacillation between two alternatives, and that Shakespeare kept mustering his creative power out of sheer despair over the horror of his vision.

We are not enough well-read to know whether this absolutely new and mind-shattering dramatic concept of man battling against all the himselves within has ever been duly emphasized in the Shakespeare literature. We do believe, though, that the extremely well-read and multi-interested Freud was not entirely aware of Shakespeare's upsetting innovation when he (Freud) projected into pre-Shakesperean Oedipus a Shakespearean, imminent fissure.

On the other hand, Shakespeare was, of course, utterly pre-Freudian. Libidinally naive, he apparently held the somber view that man indiscriminately slaughtered his father, occasionally his mother, or both, murdered his older and younger brother, killed himself, his father-in-law and his second cousin thrice removed, wiped out male and female, relative and non-kin, with sex thrown in and without the sweet motivation of sex, while ungratifiably and desperately craving all along for some uncluttered identity, for any kind of certain and definite oneness.

A brief look at what has immediately preceded and what followed Shakespeare may help us appreciate the more this aspect of Shakespeare's multifaceted genius.

The medieval theater also dealt with fragmented man. The arena of struggle was also within man's own self. But the embattled forces were not really part of him. The fight was between God and Satan for the possession of man's soul. Man, the ought-to-be interested onlooker, was the prize object of the confrontation, not one of the duelists.

In a sense, this dramatic concept was actually a regression from the antique one. In the medieval drama man's role was 'degraded' to some sort of spectatorial side-taking, to a choice of alliance with—or betting on—one or the other side, preferably that of the ultimate winner-to-be, God.

After Shakespeare, the magnificently eloquent French 'pseudo-classic' tragedy (Corneille's Racine's . . .) became a mere formalized paradigmatization of Shakespeare's revolutionary intuition. Man's auto-antagonism was reduced to a clear-cut, static, palpable, rational, and overexpressed conflict between two well-defined, equally valid, equally approved of, ardors, like Duty and Passion, for instance, or any two equally comprehensible loyalties.

It became the task of the literary world after the French Revolution to complete the work of Greece and Shakespeare and to give definite form to man's third conflictual situation, to the clash of arms between the individual (fighting for his freedom) and a (freedom-restraining) group, or to man as representative of one group ideology (say, progress) and the representative(s) of another ideology (say, reaction).

By the nature of its fight-content, this third dramatic concept is only indirectly, or tangentially, or secondarily, psychological. Its central trait is moral indignation, socially significant insurgence. It shifts the emphasis from existence to history, from individual to spokesman, from apocalyptic tragedy to contingency-close drama.

But be it as it may, all three known forms of dramatic presentation of life are built around, and based on, irreconcilable conflict, whether it is the struggle of the individual against the universe, or that of the individual against himself, or lastly, that between individual and society.

Outside the literary world there were close to, or within, the span of J. L. Moreno's formative years two spiritual currents which stood up against man's self-subjection to unabridgeable antagonism. One was the freshly—particularly, through Schopenhauer—re-infused Buddhism with its total abnegation of all, intrinsically Armageddonan, existence, and the other was the Tolstoian-Ghandian non-resistance to belligerent force.

On the other hand, there were two potent extra-literary corroborations of · ruthless dramamachy. There was, first, Marxism, pitting socio-economic antithesis against unyielding thesis, and, second, Freud's budding insight into the fatally hopeless fight between culture and instinctual drive.

PSYCHODRAMA

Not even J. L. Moreno himself can possibly re-live and re-tell the slow, gradual, and imperceptible process of his metabasic growth.

One has to look very closely at Moreno's formulations and reformulations of his ideas, concepts and techniques to grasp fully the essence of the questions that were plaguing him and the nature of the answers he was groping for.

On the surface, Moreno's first theatrical innovations might have appeared rather formal, or even faddish. All the world was looking for theatrical novelties in those hectic days and years after World War I. And half the half-baked geniuses mounted Commedia-del-Arte-like theaters of improvisations, discarded written-out stage plays, and tore down barriers dividing actors and audience.

But Moreno went just one portentous step further. He made his protagonists discard also the fixed theatrical characters firmly established in the world literature. (Ingenue, Raisonneur, Noble Father, Harlequin, etc.)

Moreno's protagonists played themselves, and the amazing, instantaneous, psychotherapeutic effect of their doing so burst open the merely theatrical, or literary, or esthetic frame of values.

As the protagonists enacted themselves, improvising as they went along, they were actually discarding also their own past and present, fixed, characters. They were in a sense creating themselves anew with the assistance of the audience, getting insight into their acts and the motivations behind them, seeing alternatives, choosing, making decisions, and, above all, learning and changing with each ensuing performance.

Coming at a time when the decibal-gaining—though

otherwise contending—psychological trends were proclaiming the dogma that man's basic character formation, be it psycho-sexually fixed or a gelled style of life, was rather completed at the age of about five, Moreno's concept of the potentiality of ongoing change and metamorphic growth was looked upon askance, if paid attention to at all.

It still is. Moreno's hardest job is still persuading his learned opponents that given the universal force of spontaneity—and given the proper setting and involvement (Warming Up)—man can and will go on creatively enacting himself, that, he can and will constantly evolve his inexhaustible potential.

The preponderant part of all his theoretical work has been consecrated by Moreno to the elaboration of the concept of spontaneity (as process) in contrast to the rigidity, 'fixity,' and dead weight of product (Conserve), and to the constant refinement of the devices of spontaneity training.

But Moreno achieved with his little Stegreiftheater much more than creative energization of drama and actors through spontaneity. He has paved his own way to a higher form of conflict resolution, way beyond that which drama could ever offer.

Moreno's voluminous writings contain almost no theoretical analysis of literary drama, beyond the above mentioned, repeated statements of drama as cultural conserve.

We must then take the liberty of using one of psychodrama's own devices, assume for a brief moment the role of Moreno the theoretician, and take a closer look at drama with our-his eyes.

Drama, one of man's most brilliant achievements, reflects a form of conflict resolution which is a complex absurdity.

Fight to the bitter end, struggle aiming at annihilation, rigid unyielding combat between man and his alter ego(s), between man and group, or even the impossible unquestioning and total submission of man to inscrutable God (the religious variation of Classic tragedy)—all this is a biological absurdity.

It represents an evolutionary unprecedented specio-suicidal abnormality.

Tragic conflict resolution is also a telelogical absurdity. It leads to a dead-end, or, worse yet, nowhere. There are no victors in drama on either side. There is no triumph over a dead adversary. By removing, by wiping out the defeated antagonist, or even by subduing him and rendering him impotent, the victor removes the only being he wanted to triumph over, the only one worth triumphing over. That is, perhaps, why fighters, victors, supermen, have to go on fighting and conquering for ever and ever. They keep chasing a goal which their very attainment keeps destroying. No triumphant synthesis can possibly be ever achieved when the antithesis annihilates the thesis, be it on the intra-individual, inter-individual, or individuo-universe level.

Then there is a semantic absurdity. Drama's action is no action at all. It is counter action, it is re-action. It is essentially sterile. Whatever little it achieves, it does so at an exhorbitant price and at a loss of the victor's own energy and essence in the process. Counter action is deranged dialectics, whether it is the terror-dialectics plying between God and man, or between man and his neurotic selves, or between social classes.

Lastly, there is the minor esthetic absurdity of raging and ranting carnage, the nauseating sight of corpses on the stages of all ages, both theatrical and historical.

In brief, drama mirrors a worse-than-primordial, sub-animal response to a non-primordial, human situation.

And now let us return to J.L. Moreno. Lo and behold, one of the central devices, if not THE central device he had introduced was most brilliantly fashioned to overcome the fundamental flaw of all drama, as though the above presented absurdity of drama's conflict resolution had been thought of and formulated not by us but by Moreno himself.

This extraordinary concept-device which transforms literary drama into psychodrama, this surpassing innovation, has been Moreno's Role Reversal.

Through role reversal Moreno offered his protagonists what no drama could ever do. He offered his protagonists the means and the opportunities to meet their adversaries in an experimental, experienced, controlled, and entirely new form of co-action. Role reversal offered both protagonist and antagonist the chance of dramatic learning, of mutual triumph, without tragic dead-end outcome. Role Reversal has creatively, that is, truly dialectically, overcome mostly sterile and always lethal counter-action.

CONCLUDING WORDS

The subject of Spontaneity and Role Reversal, as well as Moreno's aspiration to enlarge small group therapeutic achievement to global endeavors are too vast and too important to be glossed over in this scope-limited paper. They deserve special treatment, which, we hope, will be forthcoming in the near future.

But we should not conclude this rather introductory discussion of Moreno's accomplishments without placing it in the proper perspective of place and time.

The time of this writing is late summer of 1964. The world commemorates almost on this very day two world-wide tragic events: The conflagrations of World War I and II. Viet Nam, Cyprus, the Congo—are more or less in flames. In many other spots the fire is being barely contained. By sheer historical coincidence, this is also the quadricentennial year of the most encompassing tragedian of all times, William Shakespeare.

But the most menacing of all non-wars, the Cold War, is cooling off. Indeed, we also commemorate right now the first anniversary of the first nuclear agreement and hear the public and solemn promise of the three great signatory powers, Britain, Soviet Russia, and the United Nations, to strive for a settling of their differences through peaceful negotiations.

The portentous term Coexistence is uttered, or hopefully muttered, everywhere. Coexistence means a livable-with degree of tolerance. It means avoidance of tragic, that is, all-destructive collision, involving in its unspeakable havoc victor, victim, and spectator. It means, at its best, parallel existence, non-collision. It does not necessarily imply pervasive and creative co-action yet.

And again, by a historical coincidence we need not be pompous about, the occasion and place of this brief discussion is the First International Congress of Psychodrama convening in Paris these days of August-September of this same year, 1964.

Suffice it to say that this congress is to-date the crowning glory of J. L. Moreno's life-long labor of furthering mutually creative human communality.

40. INTERPERSONAL PSYCHOLOGY OF RELIGION
Moreno and Buber

Paul E. Johnson

How do psychologists understand religious behavior? To reduce the welter of theories into a square of opposition, we may note four contemporary points of view in dialectic relation to each other.

FOUR PSYCHOLOGIES

First, there is the conflictual theory which sees man as a profoundly complex personality, who is caught in the distress of internal contradictions, struggling desperately to resolve conflicts and come to a reconciling position of productive maturity. This is the view of Freud (7) and he offers psychoanalysis as a therapy to unify the unconscious conflicts and painful fragmentation of life. He looks on religion as an obsessional neurosis seeking to relieve inner anxiety and guilt of the family romance (Oedipus) through reconciliation with a father symbol. The depth of the conflict is affirmed by Boisen (3), and the cure he finds is a religious conversion whereby a person becomes responsibly related to larger loyalties.

Second, there is the collective theory which also rises from conflicts, yet sees them as complemental tendencies capable of mutual support when integrated into larger wholeness. This is the view of Jung (9) in his psychology of the collective unconscious. To him the religious thrust is an overpowering invasion of psychic energy from the collective unconscious, whose mysterious meaning is to be discovered in archetypes or universal symbols, appearing in many cultures as racial memories to inform and guide the individual as he wrestles with his destiny to fulfill the hidden potentialities of his being.

Third, there is the personalistic theory which is dubious of all collectivisms that submerge the uniqueness of the individual, and of all instinctual or segmental views that would reduce him by causal determinism to a lesser creature of the past. This is the protest of Allport (1,2), who holds that the direction of the growing person is forward, and his business is to overcome the blocks which arrest his becoming, thus to move into effective maturity by new motives to replace former ones. The religious sentiment may be instrumental to effective maturing by outreaching neurotic aggressions in response to an all-embracing system of values. Mature religious behavior follows conscious intention to worthy goals by orientation to the future.

Fourth, there is interpersonal theory which finds the distinctive nature of man in his encounter with other persons. This is what personalistic psychology overlooks in its effort to explicate the uniqueness of the individual. It is what collectivism loses in the mass which submerges the individuality recaptured and enriched by the relation of person to person. It is what conflictual psychoanalysis misses in viewing man "from the bottom up," as a product of infantile and primitive wants. It is what interpersonal dialogue addresses as I confronting Thou in the decisive relation of the present moment.

THE INTERPERSONAL THEORY
OF MORENO

The interpersonal theory is a vigorous counterthrust to each of the three theories, redirecting and extending dynamic principles inherent in them. A frontiersman who contributed to the development of interpersonal psychology is Jacob Levy Moreno (1892-   ). He was born in Bucharest, Rumania, the first of six children, three boys and three girls. His father, a merchant, and his mother, a housewife, were Sephardi, or Spanish Jews, and his mother tongues were Spanish and Rumanian. At the age of four he went to Bible school and began to read the Bible in Hebrew. When he was six, his family moved to Vienna, and there he learned German and attended public school and the university, where he pursued studies in philosophy, theology, and mathematics before turning to medicine and completing the doctor's degree in 1917. While a medical student he was a research assistant of the Psychiatric Clinic at the University of Vienna, and in the year 1911 he met Freud and attended one of his lectures. But the analytic reductionism of Freud left him cold, for he was already moving in another direction.

Moreno recognized the deep conflicts of life, but to him they demand a creative solution in religious dimensions. He was not satisfied with the religious institutions which were preoccupied in conserving the traditions of the past but was more impressed by the dramatic dialogue of Jesus and Socrates. His idea of God was of the Creator on the first day of creation, acting spontaneously to bring into being a new world. And spontaneity became to him the basic principle motivating behavior in creative action. With this as the revolutionary principle to change life from confining rigidity to creativity, he saw the need of a new religious movement employing the new discoveries of science.

In the spring of 1914 Moreno published in Vienna the first of a series of poetic writings entitled *Einladung zu einer Begegnung [Invitation to an Encounter],* which is evidently *the first literary definition of encounter,* the concept which has become central in the existentialist movement. To describe the encounter, he portrays two persons exchanging eyes to comprehend and know each other:

A meeting of two: eye to eye, face to face.

And when you are near I will tear your eyes out and place them instead of mine, and you will tear my eyes out and will place them instead of yours, then I will look at you with your eyes and you will look at me with mine (11).

The literary magazine *Daimon,* of which he was the editor, carried in the February issue, 1918, a dramatic dialogue by Moreno entitled "Einladung Zuener Begegnung: Die Gottheit als Autor" (Invitation to an Encounter: The Godhead as Author"). In this article (page 6) appears the term "interpersonal communication" ("zwischenmenschlicken Verkehr"). The term "interpersonal relations," which Robert Macdougall (10) used in 1912, came to prominence in his book *Who Shall Survive* (1934) (14) and in the journal he founded in 1937, *Sociometry: A Journal of Interpersonal Relations.* During the years 1918-20 Martin Buber was a contributing editor of *Daimon,* and his articles appeared side by side with Moreno's, prophetic of the role each would have in the history of interpersonal theory. The I-Thou concept of God was the keystone of the interpersonal arch as documented in their publications of 1920-23. *Das Testamentes des Vaters,* 1920 *[The Words of the Father]* (13), contains dialogues of direct address in the form of Ich und Du. Buber's *Ich und Du* (1923) (4) is the definitive statement of the I-Thou relationship.

Moreno is best known for his pioneer work in sociometry, psychodrama, and group therapy (1911). What is not so well known and yet is clearly stated in his writings is that the basic motivation for all of his work is religious. "The theory of interpersonal relations is born of religion." Sociometry (the psychological and experimental measurement of interpersonal relations) he began first with a community of displaced persons at Mittendorf near Vienna, 1915-17. The classic study he conducted at the Hudson (New York) Training School for Girls,

1932-36, during which the essential concepts and procedures of this science were developed (14). Here the sociometric test invited the girls to decide with whom they would and would not like to live, and the psychological currents were shown in sociograms. In this way the emotional dynamics of group life were revealed and therapy for personal needs was provided.

Psychodrama had its beginning in Vienna with the Theater of Spontaneity (12), which Moreno first conducted in 1921. He found the legitimate theater stifled by the practice giving the actor lines to memorize written by another, to portray a character which he was not, on a shrouded stage with the audience in darkness. He invented the open stage in the center of the room with access from the audience all around. His theater invited actors and audience to portray their own dramatic situations from the here and now, and to speak impromptu, without written lines, in response to one another. He perceived this as a kind of dramatic religion, a theater to call forth the spontaneously creative self and learn with God what it means to be a creator. This became the therapeutic theater to heal the distresses and conflicts of the inner life by allowing the patient to act them out in the face-to-face encounter of psychodrama. This method has been widely used in schools, churches, and hospitals to provide catharsis, role learning, and the working through of individual and social dilemmas.

THE INTERPERSONAL THEORY
OF BUBER

The interpersonal theory of man has come to further development in the work of Martin Buber (1878-   ). While Moreno has been at work with interpersonal relations in psychiatry and the social sciences, Buber has been pioneering a philosophical anthropology of I and Thou. He was born in Vienna, fourteen years before Moreno, in the year 1878, of a famous Galician Rabbinical family. His early youth was spent in Lemberg, steeped in great Hebrew traditions in which piety and culture flowered in the spirit of the Enlightenment. During his student years at the universities of Vienna, Berlin, Leipzig, and Zurich he devoted himself to philosophy, literature, and art among the great thinkers of that day. His early scholarship illuminated the Chassidic movement of ethical mysticism within the human community, and his dialogic view of man makes him, now at Hebrew University in Israel, one of the prophetic voices of our time.

His most influential book is a slender volume of poetic beauty published as *Ich und Du* in 1923 and translated as *I and Thou* in 1937. (4) Later writings on this theme were published as *Between Man and Man* (5). We have noted that Moreno and Buber were associated in the literary journal *Daimon* and that both were concerned with the encounter of person with person. How much they may have influenced each other is not altogether clear, but they moved in a common stream of fertile significance, the inter-personal theory of man and God. Buber does acknowledge a germinal idea which Feuerbach gave in his *Principles of the Philosophy of the Future* in 1843:

> The individual man for himself does not have man's being in himself, either as a moral being or as thinking being. Man's being is contained only in community, in the unity of man with man—a unity which rests, however, only on the reality of the difference between I and Thou (6).

Buber sees that man is incomplete as the single one; he is not himself in isolation. Neither does he find his fulfillment in the crowd by submerging himself in the collective mass. Real life is in meeting, lived in the relation between man and man. This meeting is the life of dialogue in which one person addresses another, turns to him to make him present and perceive what life means to him. As we communicate person with person, my whole being says something to you, and your whole being speaks something that enters my life.

In this dialogic relation the person whom I encounter is not the object of my experience; he is the subject who addresses me as subject. There are two primary words, each indicating a relation. If I say the primary word I-it, I am defining a relation to a thing, and my attitude is that of separation from an object. The I of such a connection has no present, only the past in which things are classified. The living experience of the present arises when I confront Thou in this moment. The real, filled present occurs in meeting in which there is living and mutual relationship. The primary word I-It can never be spoken with my whole being. But when Thou is spoken, the speaker takes his stand in relation. I became a person through my relation to Thou.

Man does not become a whole self alone or in reference to objects, but only in relation to another self. The whole self is a unity of opposition, in which tension and conflict arise from the essential duality of personal existence. This Buber calls the inborn Thou, which from birth will always be over against my singleness. To enter into a relation is to accept this tension of duality as essential to my being and to live the life of confrontation. So ultimate is the meaning of relationship that Buber finds in every relation the eternal Thou revealed. Not by turning away from human persons do we meet God, but God meets us in all of our interpersonal relationships. "In each Thou we address the eternal Thou."

God is not one object to be inferred from another as philosophers do by abstract reasoning, for this reduces Thou to It like any other thing. "God is the being that is directly, most nearly, and lastingly over against us, that may properly be only addressed not expressed." God in the direct relation of encounter is not an idea in the abstract sense of logical argument, induced or deduced from some other givens. Rather He meets us as Thou in the present moment of living relationship. He is not to be proved or disproved but known in the dialogue of personal relationship. Religious experience for Buber is at once psychological in the intimate sense of meeting and theological in the affirmation of ultimate Being so revealed.

Though not himself a psychologist, Buber contributes significantly to the psychology of religion in submitting data and description of the religious life which psychologists will seek to understand. He further sharpens our focus upon the nature of man and offers a frame of reference for contemporary study that gives meaning and dignity to the human encounter.

CONCLUSION

It is evident that every theory of man emerges from a philosophy whether latent or manifest. For theory is constructed of principles which assume universality in one way or another. Psychological research will continue to gather significant data by ingenious methods to fill in needed details and at times to upset established theories. But data are only a collection of meaningless items in a heap of confusion until viewed in the clarifying and integrating perspective of a theory. Facts and theories are not interchangeable parts from mechanical assembly lines. They are the tools fashioned by a purposive intention to wrestle with elusive unknowns and hold a steady course to a goal we may decide to seek. Interpersonal psychology offers a fruitful set of hypotheses to explore, if we seek to comprehend both the depth and the breadth of religious experience. This I have undertaken to do in the revised edition of my *Psychology of Religion* (8), from which this article is an excerpt.

REFERENCES

1. Allport, Gordon W.: Becoming: Basic Considerations for a Psychology of Personality. New Haven, Yale University Press, 1955.

2. ————: The Individual and His Religion: A Psychological Interpretation. New York, The Macmillan Company, 1950.

3. Boisen, Anton: Explorations of the Inner World. New York, Harper & Brothers, 1935, 1952.

4. Buber, Martin: I and Thou. New York, Charles Scribner's Sons, 1937.

5. ————: Between Man and Man. New York, The Macmillan Company, 1948.

6. Feuerbach, Ludwig A.: Principles of the Philosophy of the Future. 1843.

7. Freud, Sigmund: The Illusion of Religion. London, Hobart Press, 1928.

8. Johnson, Paul E.: Psychology of Religion. New York: Abingdon Press, 1945; 1959.

9. Jung, Carl G.: Psychology and Religion: West and East. New York, Pantheon Books, Inc. 1958.

10. MacDougall: "The Social Basis of Individuality," American Journal of Sociology, Vol. XVIII (July, 1912), 1-20.

11. Moreno, J.L.: Einladung Zu einer Begegnung. Vienna, R. Thimmas Erbe, 1914.

12. — — — — — — —: The Theatre of Spontaneity. New York, Beacon House, 1947.

13. — — — — — — —: The Psychodrama of God. New York, Beacon House, 1947.

14. — — — — — — —: Who Shall Survive? New York, Beacon House, 1953.

Part VII
CONCLUSION:
COMMENTS AND FORECASTS

Introduction

The concluding articles attempt to evaluate psychodrama in terms of its ability to meet individual and societal needs. The first of the articles raises the issue of dangers possible in psychodrama when it is directed by poorly prepared individuals, but its major purpose is to show psychodrama's potential for bringing therapy to large groups. This same potential, and its possible fulfillment in the near future, is the main point of the final article, which seeks to make an assessment of Moreno and his works.

The paper, "Audience in Action Trhough Simulated Psychodrama," is an assessment of the impact psychodrama can have on large audiences, and introduces the idea of "simulated psychodrama" (which Moreno invented some 30 years ago). The principal purpose of the paper is to introduce psychodrama as an answer to a need for therapy by many people for whom it might not otherwise be available. The paper also describes a safety factor (simulated psychodrama) which might prevent any harmful effects that could be brought about either by unskilled directors or by persons uneducated in personality theory, psychopathology, or insensitive to their own unconscious needs and the needs of others.

One of the authorities cited in the first paper maintains that man's defense mechanisms tend to protect him from bringing forth material he is not ready to deal with in a psychodrama session. The editor feels that someone skilled in psychodramatic techniques can break down an individual's defenses and cause him to release feelings and impulses that the subject cannot handle. This can occur if the director approaches a session without any awareness of his own needs and without the

455

humility to realize how little he knows in spite of his experience and education.

41. AUDIENCE IN ACTION THROUGH SIMULATED PSYCHODRAMA

Ira A. Greenberg

THE NEED

Every human being has emotional problems of one sort or another. Most people are able to function effectively in spite of their problems, but many are so handicapped by them that they fall far short of fulfilling their potential and can become burdens or a cause of discomfort to those with whom they associate.

All of us, including the most psychologically "healthy," might benefit at times from some form of psychotherapy. However, due to prohibitive costs or a shortage of qualified personnel, therapy is not available to those who need it. This shortage of psychotherapists is expected to continue because no matter how quickly graduate and medical schools enlarge and accelerate their programs, the supply inevitably will be far below the demands of a population that is daily increasing at both ends of the age-continuum and of a society that is daily growing more and more complex.

This article is drawn from a 61-page term paper written in the Spring of 1964 as part of the requirements for a course in counseling and psychotherapy taught by Dr. Robert Allen Keith, professor of psychology at Claremont Graduate School, Claremont, Calif. A section of this paper was published under the title, "Audience in Action Through Psychodrama" (*Group Psychotherapy,* Vol. XVIII, No. 2-3 (June-September, 1964), pp. 104-122).

Another factor that keeps a prospective patient from a counselor or therapist is that a person in need of help often has little conscious awareness of his need. Even if he suspects that his pattern of living is not all that it might be, the partial awareness of the underlying causes and effects of his problems may be too threatening for him to face, much less than to take positive action toward remedying them.

Most large institutions have counseling or psychotherapeutic facilities available to the groups they serve, and most cities have established and support some form of mental health clinic, public welfare agency and/or family service bureau. Many of these facilities are staffed by qualified psychotherapists, while, more often than not, many are staffed by persons whose training in personality theory and therapy techniques falls short of the minimum set by professional groups. As a result, these facilities offer surface or situational counseling that in many instances is inadequate for the needs of an individual. Even at the best staffed centers, particularly those at university facilities, a client's needs tend to exceed the time available to satisfy them.

The dilemma that thus results from an increasing need for qualified counselors and psychotherapists on the one hand and the unlikelihood that the need will be met in the near future on the other seems to preclude a satisfactory solution to the problem. And as long as a solution is sought through the "ideal" method of making available the services of a skilled counselor or psychotherapist to individuals and small groups the problem will remain unsolved.

In seeking a practical solution that will fulfill the pssychotherapeutic needs of society in general and the college campus specifically, any answer should try to resolve (1) the need for psychotherapy by many individuals; (2) the inability of many individuals to obtain psychotherapy because of its high cost; (3) an inability of many individuals to obtain psychotherapy because they cannot accept the fact that they need help; (4) a shortage of qualified psychotherapists.

AN ANSWER

Psychodrama is one psychotherapeutic technique that can answer this complex problem. It would not be the psychodrama usually employed by J.L. Moreno because in this application the emphasis would be reversed. As it is usually employed, psychodrama consists of a patient acting out various aspects of his problem on a stage, assisted by several actor therapists. Both patient and assistants are directed by the chief psychotherapist, and appear before an audience of patients or individuals not undergoing therapy.

It is part of Moreno's theory that all who participate in the psychodrama profit by the experience: the patient, the audience, the psychotherapist and his assistants, all receive of the   action on the stage. Moreno discovered the therapeutic effect of psychodrama on an audience in 1921, several years after psychodrama itself was born.[1] Thus, from its early period, psychodrama was both stage-oriented and audience-oriented, and although emphasis is usually on a patient acting out a part of his problem, the therapeutic effect of this enactment on the audience is never overlooked.

Therefore, it appears that the psychodrama technique, with various modifications and safeguards, might prove to be the answer to each of the four parts of the overall problem that concerns making psychotherapy available to more people. Psychodrama is a process that can make its effect upon large audiences, so that each member can serve not only as his own therapist, but individually and collectively as a therapist to other audience members. One of Moreno's disciples, Enneis, writing about the effect of psychodrama on audience-patients at St. Elizabeths Hospital, Washington, D.C., notes:

> It is the purpose . . . to create a climate in which there can be a maximum of catharsis, or relearning and insight gained, to

[1] J.L. Moreno, Psychodrama, Vol. I (3rd ed.) (Beacon, N.Y.: Beacon House, Inc., 1964), pp. 1-5.

stimulate therapeutic potentials within the group, and to make each patient something of a therapist in his relationship to other patients. Personality growth is facilitated through the closure of tension systems, development of insights, and the expansion of concept of self.[2]

The importance of a skilled psychodramatic director and the need for his having a strong background in psychological theory and therapy techniques is extremely important. Because the persons he treats on stage and in the audience have problems that range from situational difficulties in everyday life to psychosés that require a patient's confinement in a mental institution he must have sufficient background to recognize and handle these problems as they arise. Because psychodrama is a means of bringing psychotherapy to those people for whom it might not otherwise be available, the question remains as to what causes the therapeutic effect on the audience and how it is brought about. The "what," is the technique of *acting out*, by means of which Moreno ". . launched a technological revolution in psychotherapy."[3] Thus, according to Smith, "by isolating, clarifying, and utilizing the most plaguing problem, the problem of acting out, he has contributed perhaps the most original and profound change in the theory and technique of psychotherapy since its incipience."[4] Stated another way, Hass and Moreno claim that "one of Moreno's greatest therapeutic achievements has been to break the deadlock of the traditional secretive interview situation and to open the counseling session to a selected group of participant actors and participant observers

---

[2] James M. Enneis, "The Dynamics of Group Action Processes in Therapy," *Group Psychotherapy* 1951, 4, 17-22; in *Psychological Abstracts*, Vol. 26 (Lancaster, Pa.: American Psychological Association, 1952), No. 4030.

[3] W. Lynn Smith, "Discussion," in J.L. Moreno, *Psychodrama, II* (Beacon, N.Y.: Beacon House, 1959), 107.

[4] *Ibid.*

who may take part in and actually facilitate the therapy."[5] The question of "How" is explained, in part, through the concept of *catharsis*. In this regard, Klapman states:

> Dr. J. L. Moreno, who introduced the dramatic technic [sic] into therapy, conceives it to encompass all or most of the values of psychotherapy. It is, in his opinion, the psychiatric interview equivalent, with the additional advantage that all the others, cast and audience, also participate. It is, too, a lecture on a carefully chosen topic, a discussion, a catharsis, an analysis of acted-out events as the audience is allowed to discuss the dramatic action presented, and lastly, it is re-education.[6]

In other words, the acting-out effects catharsis, both in the patient and the participant observers, while insight or re-education occurs as a result of discussion afterward.

APPLICATIONS

The application of psychodrama and its techniques seems to be as limitless as the variety of situations in which people interrelate with each other. These techniques can be effortlessly shifted from one situation to another as circumstances, customs, and degrees of affinity require. Aside from their use in psychotherapy, psychodramatic techniques have been used in industrial and sales training programs; in community, race, and labor-management relations (often in the forms of sociodramas and sociograms, as described in Moreno's *Who Shall Survive?*); in educational indsitutions as teaching devices; in prisons and in playgrounds, and in personnel offices as a method to help screen applicants for a variety of positions. The list of uses for

[5] Robert Bartlett Haas and J.L. Moreno, "Psychodrama as a Projective Technique," Chapter 23 of Harold H. Anderson and Gladys L. Anderson, *An Introduction to Projective Techniques* (Englewood Cliffs, N.J.: Prentice-Hall, Inc. 1961), p. 672.

[6] J.W. Klapman, *Group Psychotherapy: Theory and Practice*, 2nd ed. (New York: Grune & Stratton, 1959), p. 144.

psychodrama and its techniques can be as long as one's active imagination will make it, and the literature is filled with many and varied examples of its utilization. One area where psychodramatic and role-playing techniques have been advantageously employed is that of education, but even here the applications might be considered infinitesimal when compared to the potential for these techniques as classroom tools.

Torrance finds a similarity between the basic philosophies of collegiate student personnel work and those of psychodrama, sociodrama, and sociometry in that "both are interested in the 'whole' individuals and not in just one narrow segment of their development /and/ that both are interested in the welfare of whole institutions, not just in this and that individual or this and that group."[7] Torrance lists[8] the following services which educational leaders consider essential to a collegiate student personnel program and which he says offer "considerable opportunity" for the application of psychodramatic techniques, i.e., diagnosis and counseling, orientation, precollege counseling remedial assistance, supervision of student activities, supervision of living, job placement, and coordination of religious activities. In regard to the problems of the paraphernalia of psychodrama, Torrance presents several suggestions to show how these difficulties could be overcome. He outlines his case by recommending that psychodrama be added to the resources of a college counseling center:

> The chief difficulties ordinarily presenting themselves in the college guidance clinic are provisions for "auxiliary egos" and space. Secretaries, student assistants, psychometrists and other staff members can be trained as "auxiliary egos," and a directory of idle classrooms in the buildings may provide the space. The usual counselor's office is ill-suited to action counseling, except

7 Paul Torrance, "Psychodramatic Methods in the College," Chapter 22 of *Psychodrama and Sociodrama in American Education*, Robert B. Haas (ed.) (Beacon, N.Y.: Beacon House, 1949), p. 180.

8 *Ibid.*

in an extremely limited fashion. The desired solution would be the construction of a small theater as a part of the physical setup of the college guidance center. It could then be used for action counseling and testing, seminars, and as a laboratory for action research.[9]

Moreno avidly supports the idea of bringing psychodrama to the campus and sees it as a means of helping man solve current and future problems. "The establishment of psychodramatic units within educational institutions is not only feasible but imperative at this moment," he writes. "The world-wide crisis in which the entire nation is enmeshed affects the younger generation more gravely than any other part of the nation." [10] In a later passage, he adds, "Learning by doing has been replaced or perhaps better said remodeled, with learning by spontaneity training and psychodramatic procedure, in which therapy and doing go hand in hand, one being an intrinsic part of the other."[11]

There is little to be said against the important contribution psychodrama and its techniques can make to many fields, particularly that of education and particularly a college and university setting. Aside from its uses in teaching and psychotherapy, there is much reason to believe that it also could implement each of the collegiate student personnel functions listed by Torrance. Nevertheless, a cloud of doubt, or at least of questioning, hovers in the mind's eye of this writer in regard the use of classical psychodrama as a tool in action counseling. The question concerns the possibility of dangers—or at least disadvantages—in the widespread and conceivably un-controlled use of this dynamic procedure by counselors whose training, experience, and personality might be insufficient for the multiple demands of this intense emotion-filled psychotherapeutic process.

9 *Ibid.*

10 Moreno, *Psychodrama, Vol. I op. cit.*, p. 145.

11 *Ibid.*, p. 152.

DANGERS & DISADVANTAGES

Classical psychodrama, according to its theoretical and functional concepts, is a dynamic process that often probes into the patient's hidden motivations and conflicts. It brings forth, through sudden spontaneous actions and outpourings, the material of unresolved difficulties that can be threatening to a dangerous degree. One of the purposes of psychodrama is to expose the sore spots in the patient's psyche so that he may be helped in healing them. Therefore, the presence of the psychiatrist at a psychodramatic session involves far more than directing a situation to achieve an emotional interaction in and among the protagonist, auxiliary egos, and audience. The primary purpose of his presence is to protect the patient, to know when to explore into the depths of the patient's unconscious and when to postpone such actions. His knowledge of personality dynamics, his background of training, and his experience as a therapist must be such that he is able to determine instantly, as Moreno states,[12] when to "leave many territories of his subjects' personalities unexpressed and unexplored if their energies are not, at the time, equal to the strain.'

Thus, despite its minor place in Moreno's theory, the existence of unconscious sources of conflict in a patient[13] and the dangers that are inherent in their ill-timed exposure demand that the capabilities of the director in bringing about therapeutic actions and in knowing when to interrupt stage activity in order to prevent the patient from revealing certain aspects of his difficulties to the audience—and to himself are of utmost importance.

The effect of the dangers involved in classical psychodrama is directly related to some of the disadvantages that would accompany any attempt to substitute this technique for in-

12 *Ibid.*, p. 330.
13 *Ibid.*, pp. 152-330.

dividual and small group therapy. As we noted earlier, the availability of highly trained and experienced psychotherapists is insufficient to meet the tremendous need that would arise if classical psychodrama were employed by institutions and communities which sought to bring to their populations a form of therapy that can affect large audiences.

Another disadvantage that can be cited is the use of classical psychodrama before large groups also involves a personnel shortage. Even if the availability of qualified therapists was adequate, a certain type of therapist-personality is essential to the creating of a successful psychodramatic session. It must be a personality capable of creating situations of a high emotional pitch so that the session is able to effect a cathartic impact on, or bring insight to, each individual in a large group. The requirement here is for a personality of an extremely extraverted type, a personality that flourishes in the often boisterous "give-and-take" interactions between the director and the group that is necessary to warm up for the psychodramatic enactment. The shortage of this type of personality among psychotherapists may be extreme. Because of the rigorous intellectual training involved in the developing of psychotherapists, the field is likely to attract many introverted individuals and introvert-extravert personality types who may have a natural love for learning, research, and involvement in ideas. Another possible explanation for this shortage is that many successful psychotherapists of the introvert or introvert-extrovert type have proven themselves to be highly effective in treating individuals or small groups, and so one might conclude that these restrained personality types are better suited to the intimate interpersonal relations of an office consulting room or small gathering.

Whatever the reasons, the dangers and disadvantages that would accompany any attempt to enlarge the practice of classical psychodrama and increase the size of the audiences would tend to outweigh the many benefits that can be found in this therapeutic process. The dangers and disadvantages that an introverted or untrained director could produce might prove to make the implementation of this procedure on a large-scale basis a formidable and possibly fruitless task—a task which institutional and community leaders might justifiably find questionable and which audience members might respond to with doubt or with boredom. In either, the effectiveness of such a program would be negative, both for this particular procedure and for the general practice of psychotherapy.

Moreno's View of the Problem

Although Moreno hints at the possible dangers involved in a psychodramatic production by an ill-informed, untrained, or inept director throughout his multitude of books and articles, no specific statement of warning as such has been obtained from his works. The assumption to be made from his writings is that Moreno takes for granted that only the most qualified psychotherapists would undertake the director's role in a psychodramatic production. A warning, boldly stated, might thus be considered unnecessary. And, as classical psychodrama is practiced at present, the director is generally a skilled therapist, and a specific warning of danger is therefore point-less. Yet, a warning as such would be extremely necessary if the practice of psychodrama became so widespread that the appointment or the self-appointment of directors would be difficult to control.

Despite the lack of a formal warning, Moreno is cognizant of possible dangers involved in psychodrama, and hints of warnings are included in his writings. In one example, he notes that the patient "may be harmed rather than helped,"[14] when discussing the failure of an auxiliary ego to adequately portray the role of a person the patient may need to interact with on the

---

[14] Moreno, *Psychodrama, Vol. I, Ibid.,* p. XIX.

stage. Another typical example of a warning by Moreno follows:

> By far the most conspicuous marriage conflict brought to the attention of the psychodramatic consultant is the triangle, or better, the psychological triangle of husband, wife, and a third party; man or woman. This situation is so delicate and can bring so much misery and bitterness that the slightest tactlessness in the course of action or during the analysis of the action may produce a deadlock. The director must take great care to make no suggestion as to what course of action might be preferable. The therapeutic theatre is not a court, the auxiliary egos who may be present are no jury, and the director is not a judge. Moreover, the therapeutic theatre is not a hospital where the subjects come to show their wounds and have them healed by skilled professionals. The initiative, the spontaneity, the decisions must all arise within the subjects themselves.[15]

The warning cited is concerned primarily with a surface situation. Although it may have deep psychological implications, it is treated on the psychodramatic stage in terms of the problems presented and which in the instance of the marriage triangle is both situational and emotional. It is incumbent upon the director not only to be aware of the deeper implications of the problem, but, on the basis of his knowledge and training, to be able to guide the problem towards some temporary solution or "holding action" if continued treatment is indicated. If it is possible he should help those involved in the triangle resolve the situation through their interaction on the stage. In this type of triangle situation, and in many other situations, it is also incumbent upon the director that he be ready to manipulate the stage situation, either to help bring forth or to forestall the eruption of unconscious material.

Thus, the director in a classical psychodramatic session must not only be an expert on every aspect of the procedure but he must be in complete control of it to avoid its dangers.

15 *Ibid.*, p. 330.

Bordin's Warnings

While psychodrama depends heavily on direction by the chief therapist, there is much in the patient's acting-out process that may be considered non-directional or client-centered. The patient usually designates the characters who will appear in his personal drama and then often has the option of selecting the actors who will portray these characters. The patient also informs the auxiliary egos how the characters he has designated have behaved toward him in the past and how he expects them to behave in the drama about to be enacted. Under a capable director's hands, these actors may not always portray their roles in the manner indicated by the protagonist but may react and interact thereby challenging the protagonist. The results of this sort of direction are often therapeutically effective. Nevertheless, there is much that can be ambiguous for the patient as the psychodrama progresses.

Ambiguity, or what Dr. Edward S. Bordin refers to as the *ambiguity dimension* can be a highly effective technique in psychotherapy. Bordin describes the concept as being such that "when the stimulus configuration to which we are exposed is incomplete and vague, in that no clear-cut response is predetermined, we say that the stimulus configuration is ambiguous,"[16] He adds that the "demand character" varies from one patient to another and that "the degree of ambiguity that exists in therapeutic interpersonal relationships is controlled by the thrapist."[17]

Bordin warns of dangers inherent in the ambiguity dimension and urges it to be used with extreme caution during the psychotherapeutic session. Bordin makes this warning in terms of its use in an one-to-one therapist-client relationship, but it seems just as appropriate to an inadequately trained or inex-

[16] Edward S. Bordin, *Psychological Counseling* (N.Y.: Appleton-Century-Crofts, Inc., 1955) p. 138.
[17] *Ibid.*

perienced psychotherapist directing a psychodramatic session, whether or not there is ambiguity involved in the stage enactment. Bordin writes:

> It is our conviction that ambiguity is a powerful tool in therapeutic relationships. To the degree to which this conviction is a valid one, its use without adequate training, without a sufficiently deep knowledge of human behavior and personality, is irresponsibly playing with other people's lives. To do this is equivalent to prescribing powerful antibiotic drugs without knowledge of the conditions under which they will be harmful or helpful.
>
> This is no imaginary danger. It has been attested too many times by our experience with relatively untrained counselors who have attempted to be "nondirective" with their clients. On such occasions, the effort to be nondirective often results in a counselor's being relatively ambiguous. We have seen the inexperienced counselor becoming involved in a very intense relationship in which the client exhibits feelings with which neither he nor the counselor is prepared to cope, and the result may be considerable emotional disturbance, sometimes even actual psychotic breaks.
>
> We assert, therefore, that relatively untrained personnel workers, such as teachers, counselors, financial aid advisors, and so on, should establish definite limitations on the amount of ambiguity which they permit to arise in their advising relationships. Under these circumstances it is potentially much less harmful and much more appropriate to encourage rational, factual discussions of problems and decisions that must be faced, in the form that these are brought to the counselor, than to set as the goal of counseling the relatively free exploration of feelings, motivations, and emotions.[18]

McNassor's Suggestions

Another educator and psychologist, Dr. Donald McNassor, though not disagreeing with Bordin's warning as it applies to an individual counseling relationship, takes a somewhat different

[18] *Ibid.*, pp. 150-151.

view of the ambiguity dimension as it relates to the psychodramatic situation. McNassor, who himself has conducted psychodramatic sessions, suggests[19] that it is hardly likely that an inexperienced director will bring forth during a single session material too threatening for a protagonist to be able to handle. The human organism, McNassor feels, has too many built-in defense mechanisms to make it likely that a protagonist will suffer permanent harm from what emerges in one psychodramatic enactment. The worst that might be expected at the hands of an untrained therapist and inexperienced director, according to McNassor, is that the protagonist would suffer some embarrassment, which can hardly be considered dangerous.

McNassor agrees that material too threatening for a protagonist to cope with might emerge after he had undergone several psychodramatic sessions under the direction of an untrained therapist. But he precludes the probability that repressed material will break through a protagonist's well fortified defenses in a single session. At the same time, it appears very possible, that a highly skilled psychodramatic director could in one session induce a strongly charged emotional situation. Such a situation could release unconscious fear and hate, terrifying the actor and leaving him with a rservoir of guilt the director had not bargained for.

However, whether the protagonist in a psychodramatic session is endangered or merely embarrassed by what occurs, he has nevertheless been placed in a situation where his person has been violated as a result of an irresponsible undertaking by the director's incompetence. The problem at hand, therefore, is to seek a means of utilizing psychodrama so that it may be employed in many places for mass psychotherapy, in spite of the shortage of qualified therapists. One method of accomplishing

19 The statements were made during a discussion of psychodrama on April 28, 1964, at Claremont Graduate School, Claremont, Calif.

this might be through the use of partially trained (sub-doctoral) therapists as psychodrama directors, but the risk of the protagonist's being endangered or embarrassed must be removed.

REDIRECTION TO REMOVE RISK

The surest and most obvious way to remove the risk of danger or embarrassment to a patient is to remove the patient from the protagonist role in the psychodrama. This is not to suggest that the protagonist role itself be eliminated, but merely that the person portraying the protagonist role be called upon the play the part without himself being a subject for psychotherapy. In other words, the therapy would be directed specifically at the audience, and the protagonist would serve simply as one of the several instruments used to bring about this therapy.

Actors and Improvisation.

Every institution and community will have among its members certain individuals possessing some degree of acting ability. These persons can be trained to employ their talents as protagonists and auxiliary egos in a production of what may be referred to as "simulated psychodrama," since without a patient the production would be merely an imitation of psychodramatic therapy. In a college or university setting, a counselor planning to put on a series of simulated psychodrama productions could draw upon the drama department for acting talent.

Should these actors be unavilable when the psychodramatic director needs them the required actors could be volunteers from among the general student body. Locating and training of actors for simulated psychodramatic presentations would probably be the least of the counselor's difficulties, since, as has been proved often in the past, talent will be found wherever it is sought, whether it be at military installations, prisons, old-age homes, and even in mental institutions.

After having obtained his actors and actresses, the director should be able to train them for spontaneity in simulated psychodrama through the practice of improvisation as it was developed by Stanislavski and modified by Moreno. The actors would be taught to perform both as patient-protagonists and as auxiliary egos, with the emphasis in training placed on developing spontaneous creativity and the manifestation of various aspects of emotional problems and situational and relational difficulties.

In preparing for a simulated psychodramatic production, the director would choose from a "repertoire" of common problems the one he intends to deal with at the forthcoming session. He would then select the actors and actresses he wishes to use as "patients," describe to them the problem they are to assume they have and give them an opportunity to think about the character each will create (but not permit them to discuss their ideas with their fellow actors). He will then either discuss the problem with each individually, or, if he has sufficient confidence in himself as a director and in his actors as protagonists, he will let them present their problems as they see them and as they pretend to experience them before an audience during the warm up.

The production itself would be conducted like a classical psychodramatic session: the director would interview the protagonist during the warm up and would permit the protagonist to set up the scene and designate the auxiliary egos he would want to appear in it, and instruct them in the roles they are to play and the manner in which they are to portray them, just as an actual patient would in a psychodrama.

The principal advantage to be found in a partially trained and/or inexperienced therapist's use of actors instead of patients is that he is not working with actual problems, so far as the actors are concerned, but simply with people portraying problems that need have no real connection with them. Therefore, no matter how many mistakes the director makes, there is little likelihood of the actors' being harmed. Should they be embarrassed by what comes out during the session—even if it is of a personal nature—it is not the actors themselves who will be embarrassed (although they may feel this at the time), but the characters they are portraying.

Another advantage the unskilled director will find in using actors as protagonists is less mental and emotional demand on him during the warming up process. The actors would know what is expected of them, and they would be much more reliable in carrying out the process than a patient who may be under a considerable emotional strain because he is not sure what is expected of him or whether or not he wants to go through with it. Thus, in the actual psychodramatic situation, the challenge to the director is far greater than it would be in a simulated situation.

One more advantage in the simulated situation to the untrained director is that, although he must still control everything that occurs on the stage, he can concentrate less on the stage than if there were an actual patient present. He therefore can give more of his attention to the audience, which in this instance is the real and only patient.

Audience and Involvement

Large audiences may be expected at sufficiently publicized simulated psychodramatic sessions for a number of reasons, chief among which are (1) a realized need for psychotherapy which otherwise might be unavailable, (2) an unrealized need for psychotherapy but an awareness that something could be wrong somewhere, as might be indicated by such things as loneliness, fatigue, free-floating anxiety, nightmares, and inability to concentrate on studies, among others, (3) an intellectual curiosity, and (4) a desire to be entertained. Each of these reasons should be considered valid, as far as the audience members and the director are concerned, but it is the director's purpose to make his production so exciting that all in the audience would want to return for the next session. In this way is he able to reach everyone in the audience and provide some degree of therapy for all—even for the curious and the entertainment seekers.

Just as the warm up is important to the audience in classical psychodrama, it should be considered important in simulated psychodrama, for in this instance the only purpose for the production is to reach the audience so effectively that it becomes completely involved with what is taking place on the stage. The warm-up also makes the audience interact with the actors and the director and thereby receives the combined therapeutic benefits that are intrinsic to spontaneity, tele, and catharsis. What actually is involved in the rationale of simulated psychodrama is the Aristotelean concept of catharsis but one that is additionally stimulated by the excitement that is a part of psychodrama. (The principal difference between catharsis as Aristotle saw it and catharsis that is effected by classical and simulated psychodrama is that in the former the stage action was predetermined and studied, while in the latter two instances it is spontaneous.)

Accompanying the excitement of psychodrama, which should be credited initially with "bringing in" the majority of the audience, is the discussion that follows each stage enactment. It should prove beneficial both to the bolder members who voice their opinions, criticize the actors, and question the director (and audience analysts) and to the more timid, who simply listen, absorb, and passively interact. Among the questions voiced invariably will be many that have little to do with what has been portrayed on the stage but which are important in the questioner's emotional problems. Besides answering these questions as best he can during the excitement of the moment, the director should always take the opportunity to inform the audience of available psychotherapeutic services. For example, many college students are unaware of counseling center facilities, or may have ill-founded ideas about them and an announcement of the time of the next session, the possible formation of actual psychodramatic groups (providing a qualified director is available), and whatever other information he might have for the audience, might prove profitable.

From a community mental health point of view, simulated psychodrama may prove to be an important solution to a serious problem. Because of its entertainment qualities—like court trials of sensational cases, it can be more exciting than the legitimate theater or motion picture films—it has the capacity to attract large audiences. Through the announcements, much useful information about therapy and therapeutic facilities may be disseminated. Through the enactments, catharsis may be experienced. And through the discussions, important insights may be gained.

Simulated psychodrama seems to have two important advantages over traditional group therapy. The first, of course, is that it can reach more people, since there is no restriction on the audience size for the former, while for the latter, the size must be limited to a comparative few in order for it to be effective. The second advantage is that many people who require psychotherapy but are incapable of facing up to the fact might attend a simulated psychodrama session whereas they would probably not attend a group therapy session. The reasoning behind this assumption is that no commitment is required by a person attending an event as part of a large audience, but in signing up for or attending a traditional group therapy session he is admitting to himself and to others that he needs help. Many emotionally disturbed people are incapable of making this admission and must therefore be "eased" into a therapy situation, possibly through simulated psychodrama.

Moreno and Innovation

The idea of simulated psychodrama came to this writer during the summer of 1963 while listening to a lecture[20] on sociometry and psychodrama, but this does not mark the beginnings of the technique that has been termed simulated psychodrama. Just as he is the father of psychodrama and sociometry, so is Moreno also the creator of simulated psychodrama. Moreno designates this as *psychodrama: Non-confessional type* or *indirect* type. This form is simply an innovation of classical psychodrama, which Moreno also refers to as *psychodrama: Confessional type*, or *direct*. Both the direct, or confessional type, and the indirect, or non-confessional type, of psychodrama are oriented primarily toward group psychotherapy, although in psychodrama: confessional type an individual patient is treated on the stage. The only difference between direct and classical psychodrama is that in the former the patient is selected specifically from a therapy-seeking audience, while in the latter the patient is sometimes brought to the stage after having consulted with the therapist privately one or more times.

However, it is the more pronounced innovation from classical psychodrama that is of particular interest to this study. Moreno explains it as follows:

> ... Here the actions on the stage are produced, instead of by actual subjects, by a staff of auxiliary egos. The members of the audience are permitted to discuss the proceedings as if they would have no bearing on their own. This form of psychodrama is the indirect or the *Non-confessional type*.   Non-confessional psychodrama is characterized by the following three steps: the interview of every subject who is to participate in a session—the careful analysis of these materials—and the classification of every subject according to his dominant mental syndrome or problem. On the basis of these classifications the group for every session is organized so that they may attain the greatest possible

20 Delivered by the late Dr. F. Theodore Perkins, professor of psychology, Claremont Graduate School.

benefit from the treatment. For instance, certain types of alcoholics may be put into one group, certain types of matrimonial problems into another group, etc.

The non-confessional group approach in the psychodrama appears to be of particular value in minor maladjustments, incipient neuroses and simple interpersonal conflicts. In such cases the mirroring of typical situations on the stage similar to the spectators' own stimulate attempts at autonomous objectification of their actual problem when left to their own resources. In more serious cases, however, this approach is but a prelude to the direct quasi-confessional form of treatment which culminates in the direct presentation of problems on the stage.[21]

Thus, the main difference between the indirect and the simulated psychodrama is that in the former the audience is a selected group of patients having a common problem, while in the latter the audience consists of a large gathering, the members of which are in attendance for a number of diverse reasons. They may have a variety of problems that tend to cluster around certain types of difficulties, depending on the type of population from which the audience was drawn (*i.e.,* college, prison, community). The principal point of similarity, and one that marks the two types of psychodrama as almost identical, is the fact that the actors in each case are not patients. They are instead participants who are portraying particular types of roles primarily for the purpose of providing therapy for the audience.

REFERENCES

1. Anastasi, Anne. *Psychological Testing.* New York: The Macmillan Company. 1961.

2. Bordin, Edward S. *Psychological Counseling.* New York: Appleton-Century-Crofts, Inc. 1955.

[21] Moreno, *Psychodrama, Vol. I,* op. cit., pp. 324-325.

3. Bromberg, Walter. *The Mind of Man: A History of Psychotherapy and Psychoanalysis.* New York: Harper Colophon Books. 1963.

4. Clark, Barrett H. *European Theories of the Drama.* New York: Crown Publishers, Inc., 1957.

5. Drever, James. *A Dictionary of Psychology.* Baltimore: Penguin Books, 1961.

6. *Encyclopaedia Britannica,* 14th ed. Chicago: Encyclopaedia Britannica, Inc. 1957.

7. Enneis, James M. "The Dynamics of Group Action Processes in Therapy," *Group Psychotherapy.* 1951 4, 17-22.

8. Haas, Robert Bartlett, and Moreno, J. L., "Psychodrama as a Projective Technique." Chapter 23 in Anderson, Harold H., and Anderson, Gladys L. *An Introduction to Projective Techniques.* Englewood Cliffs, N.J.: Prentice Hall, Inc. 1961.

9. Hall, Calvin S., and Lindzey, Gardner. *Theories of Personality.* New York: John Wiley & Sons, Inc., 1961.

10. Johnson, V. Abstract of "The Function of an Audience Analyst in Psychodrama," by Gerard Schauer. *Psychological Abstracts.* Vol. 26. Lancaster, Pa.: The American Psychological Association. 1952. No. 7040.

11. Klapman, J.W. *Group Psychotherapy: Theory and Practice.* New York: Grune & Stratton, 1959.

12. Moreno, J.L. *Psychodrama, Vol. I.* Beacon, N.Y.: Beacon House, Inc. 1964. (First published in 1946.)

13. — — — — — —. *Psychodrama, Vol. II.* Beacon, N.Y.: Beacon House, 1959.

14. — — — — — —. "Psychodrama and Group Psychotherapy." Read at American Psychiatric Association meeting, May 30, 1946, Chicago.

15. — — — — — —. *Who Shall Survive?* Washington, D.C.: Nervous and Mental Disease Publishing Co. 1934.

16. — — — — — —. Moreno, Zerka T. & Jonathan. *The First Psychodramatic Family.* Beacon, N.Y.: Beacon House, Inc. 1964.

17. Torrance, E. Paul. "Psychodramatic Methods in the College." Chapter 22 of *Psychodrama and Sociodrama in American Education,* by Paul Bartlett Haas. Beacon, N.Y.: Beacon House, Inc. 1949.

18. Walker, Nigel. *A Short History of Psychotherapy in Theory and Practice.* New York: The Noonday Press. 1960.

42. MORENO'S PSYCHOTHERAPEUTIC SYSTEM
An Evaluation

Ira A. Greenberg

Moreno, the man and the legend, as well as his theories and his techniques of therapy, have all been examined in careful detail throughout this volume, and the point has now been reached for some sort of an evaluation of the totality of his contributions. If one were to confine himself to examining and evaluating the many techniques that have emerged from Moreno's ever fertile mind, there would be no question as to the mark he has made in the history of the social and behavioral science.

For Freud, the approach to the study and treatment of man was singular in its one-to-one application, was lengthy in its duration, and was pointed in its penetration of defenses to get at repressed fears and traumas. For Jung, the approach to the study and treatment of man was a duality, with both the patient and the analyst probing the former's individual unconscious by means of mutual free-association as the two journeyed through the Stygian waters of the collective unconscious, encountering the many primordial archetypes along the way and learning to make their peace with these ordinarily frightening entities. It goes without saying that the successful outcome of Freudian psychoanalysis or Jungian analysis would be seen in an individual who is mature, responsible, and capable of enjoying his work and his relations with others and who generally is or can be successful at most of the things he undertakes. In short, one might expect that the result of successful Freudian or Jungian psychotherapy—after many years of one-to-one involvement between the patient and the analyst would be an individual who is "free from his anxieties, unconstrained in his thinking, uninhibited in his actions—in short, a spontaneous being . . . one who is in complete control of himself and his environment." These words were taken from the early part of my long term paper, which immediately precedes this concluding article, and the words were found originally under the heading, "Spontaneity," in that category of the paper that deals with the theatrical concepts of psychodrama.* The words I quoted were (in the term paper from which they were taken) in reference to a spontaneity-filled individual living life fully in a society of such individuals, which Moreno saw in 1934 or earlier as being the next stage in man's evolutionary development, and stated that man would achieve this next stage by means of spontaneity. (Moreno, 1934, pp. 366-367.)

MORENO AND THE MASS MEDIA

"A truly therapeutic procedure cannot have less an objective than the whole of mankind," declared Moreno in the opening sentence of *Who Shall Survive?* (153, p. 3), his most widely acclaimed work. The statement has a grand and exciting ring to it, and the sincerity of its challenge can neither be denied nor questioned. Although Moreno is more than simply a psychiatrist—just as were Freud and Jung, who, like Moreno, also were philosophers and scientists—the physician that is within Moreno wants to heal. But that he would have all of mankind as his patient is very much in the Morenean tradition. Both Freud and Jung, as well as many of the other outstanding theorists in the areas of personality and psychotherapy, might see all of mankind as suffering from various types of neuroses

Greenberg. I.A. "Audience in Action through Psychodrama." *Group Psychotherapy,* XVIII, Nos. 2 & 3 (1964), pp. 104-122.

and psychoses, and each saw his own therapeutic system as having the answers to man's unconscious conflictual needs. But neither saw in his own system the means of treating all of mankind. At best, it might be said that successful Freudian or Jungian treatment of the world's leaders could serve as an indirect and perhaps highly effective way of treating mankind, but nowhere is there mention of treating mankind directly in both its individual and collective selves. This is not to say that the possibilities do not exist at some future time for many men—perhaps millions—to undergo successful Freudian or Jungian type psychotherapies and become "happy" inhabitants in the Brave New World of some tomorrow. But the possibilities do not exist today. For Moreno, however, if he and his challenge that "a truly therapeutic procedure cannot have less an objective than the whole of mankind" are to be taken seriously in any evaluation to determine greatness, then the possibilities for the treatment of millions *must* exist today.

When Moreno first issued his declaration of therapy in 1934, the only means available to possibly bring this about were the radio, which lacked visual communication, and motion pictures, wonderful cultural conserves which, however, lacked a sense of immediacy, or, as Moreno would put it, an involvement with the moment. Television at that time was an actuality only to science fiction writers and merely a dream to scientists and engineers. Had television not been invented and marketed when it was, the radio and the motion picture might have sufficed, but the results would not have been as effective as Moreno could have desired and the administrative problems involved in making filmed psychodramas available to large audiences would have been many. Nevertheless, Moreno was working towards this end (Moreno, 1942) and had already produced some filmed psychodramas when television was made available, first to Americans shortly after World War II, and later to peoples in other countries. Today, there are few places in the world where there are no television sets, and the possibility of bringing therapeutic procedures to all of mankind is perhaps only a few years away.

The potential for putting the full impact of televised psychodrama before the public already is great and has been for a number of years but the fulfillment of this potential is nowhere near being realized. There have been a few televised psychodramas for the general public on the East and West Coasts, and a number of closed-circuit televised psychodrama programs presented as parts of ongoing psychotherapy procedures, particularly at mental hospitals. At Camarillo State Hospital, located some 40 miles northwest of Los Angeles, televised psychodrama has been in use for most of the time since Moreno introduced it at that hospital in May of 1964 when he and Zerka T. Moreno put on a one-day lecture-demonstration there. Subsequently, E.J. Vogeler, Jr., MD., then an assistant superintendent in one of the adult psychiatric divisions, began conducting televised psychodrama, which he continued for some three years until he became medical program director of the Adolescent Treatment Center there. At about this time, in early 1968, he was succeeded by the present writer who continued the presentation of weekly televised psychodrama over the hospital's closed-circuit television system. When Division III (one of the three psychiatric divisions containing about 300 adult mentally ill patients in three male and three female wards) organized an intensive Coordinated Group Psychotherapy Program in September of 1969, and which in 1971 became the hospital's Intensive Psychiatric Intervention Program, this writer's weekly televised psychodrama presentation was included as an important part of the coordinated therapy program with patients referred to it from the various wards in the division and program. George M. Plagens, M.D.,* medical program director in charge of the division and later in charge of the IPI Program for acute patients, and the man responsible for the ongoing intensive group therapy program, strongly com-

* Dr. Plagens retired at the end of July, 1972, and has been succeeded by Clementine J. Paolone, M.D. Shortly afterward, the I.P.I. split in two; Program Directors in 1973-74 are William Punmont, M.D., and Robert B. Voelker, M.D.

mended the psychodrama presentations because of the manner in which it can reach patients, through the ward television sets, who might not at the time be ready to participate in any of the more than 20 therapy groups in the division and program. "It reaches those who are otherwise unreachable," he said, "and sometimes it serves to spark something within them that might get them more involved with other patients and nursing personnel on their wards. This can be the first step on their road to recovery. We want to get our patients out of the hospital; that's why we're here, to help them get well."

Helping people to get well or helping large numbers of fairly well functioning people function even more effectively is one of the things psychodrama should be able to accomplish, and it should be able to accomplish this with many millions in the population in a comparatively short period of time. There are a multitude of individual and group problems throughout the nation and the world that might find their solutions in psychodramatic or sociodramatic encounters. Presented by means of network television, the encounters could bring millions of diverse peoples together though involvement in the psychodramatic or sociodramatic situations enacted before the television cameras. Such at least is seen as the answer by one commentator in a recently published article. William Greaves, an independent film and television producer, writing in the Sunday television section of The New York Times Magazine (Aug. 9, 1970), states as follows:

America is caught in the grip of myriad neurotic and psychotic trends. Call these trends racism, sexism, chauvinism, militariam, sadism, what you will. The fact remains that it is virtually impossible to develop the necessary number of psychiatrists, psychologists, analysts, therapist, and the like to cope with America's emotionally disturbed population. The concept of television group encounter, patterned after the inter-personal encounters which take place at such organizations as the Moreno Institute, headed by Dr. J.L. Moreno, the pioneer of psychodrama, offer a stop-gap mechanism to arrest the deteriorating social diseases which are presently eating away at American society. Using the techniques of 20th century communications, we are now in a position to put the rednecks of Alabama in a direct encounter with the Black militants of Harlem, either on public or closed-circuit television. This is but one way to help America achieve mental health. Spending money on escapist crash programs in outer space will not solve the problem. Of course, the big question is, can this kind of programing surface from the present flood of video trivia, or will it have to wait upon the courage of some forward thinking programers in 1994?

CONCLUSION

Moreno, as a personality theorist, must be considered as merely one among many, all of whom have made substantial contributions to psychology, and where he fits in a study of leading theorists, such as that found in Bischof's *Interpreting Personality Theories* (1964, 1970), would depend as much upon the assesser's own personality, his graduate training, and his own predilections as upon anything else. Whether the comparison is that involving Freud, Jung, and Moreno or that of Moreno and the 18 other theorists in the revised edition of Bischof's book (1970), the assessment depends as much upon the assessor as upon the theory itself. Actually, of the 19 theorists Bischof studied, Moreno is among the dozen for whom an individual chapter is devoted. The others are Freud, Murray, Jung, Adler, Horney, Allport, Rogers, Murphy, Sheldon, Cattell, and Eysenck. Those for whom Bischof devoted only parts of chapters are Lewin, Mowrer, Maslow, Kelly, Eriksen, Sullivan, and Fromm. This reflects to some extent the fact that Bischof views Moreno as one of the major personality theorists. Bischof, in his introduction to the chapter on Moreno, states the following:

Although Moreno eulogized Freud on the occasion of the hundredth anniversary of Freud's birth in 1956, he felt that his own techniques were far more advanced than Freud's because at last they freed the therapist from the couch and the chair. Through the spontaneity of psychodrama both the client and the therapist could actively participate in lifelike situations that really changed human behavior *in situ*. Also Moreno felt that the heavy emphasis which Freud placed upon the unconscious states of man was in error. Moreno preferred to regard the formulations of spontaneity-creativity as the root-form of all behavior—indeed of the entire behavior of the universe itself. "Spontaneity-creativity is *the* problem of psychology." In comparing his theory with the theories of the big three—Freud, Jung, and Adler—Moreno found his system superior. He rejected Freud's repetition compulsion principle on the grounds that man does not continue slavishly to repeat infantile behavior but always builds his roles on the success or failure of past roles. He felt the "big three" neither had a theoretical foundation based on a logical approach nor, in their clinical methods, went much beyond the understanding of the one person being analyzed, whereas Moreno's own treatment of interpersonal groups was wider and included total understanding of human behavior. Moreno felt that it is far more efficient to deal with groups in sociodrama situations than to spend time in the one-to-one relationship that individual psychotherapy demands. Moreno was a precursor to Lewin in regard to the positional diagrams which Lewin so brilliantly espoused. As far back as 1916 Moreno used diagrams to indicate the space and movements between the psychodrama actors, much in the same way that Lewin was to adopt them in 1936. Moreno published these diagrams in his first book on the theater for spontaneity (*Stegreiftheater*) in Berlin, Germany, in 1923. (1970, p. 237.)

Although there is some question as to where Moreno belongs in relation to other personality theorists, the fact that he *does* belong is not open to question. Using the example of the Olympian-type feast as a point of illustration, Moreno could justifiably expect to find himself half-way down the long banquet table, as far from the giants at the head as from the lesser theorists at the end. This, however, merely takes into consideration Moreno's theories as compared with those of other leading theorists. Still, should one evaluate Moreno in terms of the therapeutic application of his theories, then the situation changes to something entirely different.

It then becomes incumbent upon the would-be evaluator to consider the application of Moreno's therapeutic procedures not merely in terms of producing psychodramas and sociodramas. before gatherings of people but in terms of producing them in behalf of multitudes. For any true assessment of Moreno's work must be done in terms of his own challenge. Thus, Moreno's therapeutic system must be looked at with a hard eye, and it must be evaluated in terms of the most stringent criteria, particularly since it was he himself who threw down the challenge that "a truly therapeutic procedure cannot have less an objective than the whole of mankind." And it is at this point that one can come to grips with the principal criterion in any evaluation of Moreno's system, for society has now reached a level of development where it is technically feasible—perhaps easy—to utilize the media of mass communications to bring Moreno's brand of therapy to all of mankind, no matter where in the world man might be found. It is here, in the grandiosity of his declaration, that Moreno's system must be evaluated, and it is here that it can be found to emerge triumphant.

Therefore, if Moreno were to find his proper place at the long banquet table of the Great Ones, he would most naturally stride to the head of the table, where he would find Freud and Jung sitting in the grandeur of their beings and in the glory of their contributions. And it could come as no surprise that Moreno, being Moreno, might wonder about this and then demand to know what the hell these other two guys were doing there in his place of honor.

AUTHOR INDEX*

Editor's note: The page numbers listed under the "Author Index" refer to persons, when cited in the text. The page numbers listed under the "Subject Index" refer to the same persons' writings or ideas.

SUBJECT INDEX

Abreaction 317-318

Acting out 207, 247, 263, 315-316, 383, 409, 415, 420, 460-461

Action 114, 131, 164-165, 304, 350-351, 370, 372, 380-381, 391, 399, 419-420, 433-434, 463
co-action 441-442

Actor, *see also* Auxiliary Ego
theatrical 249, 256, 407, 438
therapist 327, 415, 459, 470-473, 476

Adler, Alfred 11, 249-250, 305, 378, 422, 484-485

Allport, Gordon 369, 444

Ambiguity dimension 468-470

American Society of Group Psychotherapy and Psychodrama 211

Antagonist 23, 106, 316

Anxiety 328-329, 334, 339

Aristotle 12, 18, 157-158, 177-178, 188, 191-192, 474

Audience 14, 18, 20, 25-26, 53, 58, 188, 190, 283, 326-327, 332-333, 336-338, 391, 393, 403-408, 410, 438, 459-460, 464-466, 471-477

Audience sharing 15, 19-20, 337, 475

Auxiliary ego 13, 17-18, 20-22, 24-25, 49, 114, 122, 191, 274, 283-284, 287-288, 290, 310, 318, 321, 329, 338, 342-343, 370, 389, 405-406, 409-410, 462, 466-468, 471-472

Auxiliary world 95, 389, 411

Axiological scale 159

Beacon-on-the-Hudson, *also* Beacon Hill, Beacon House, Beacon, N.Y. 8, 35, 189, 210, 219-220, 227-233, 240, 262

Behavioral Studies Institute XIV

Behaviorism 102, 203, 247

Behind-the-Back 23, 63-64, 97, 319, 355

Benne, Kenneth 257

Bergner, Elizabeth 42

Bergson, Henri 73-74, 159-160, 433

Berne, Eric 8

494